THE FARMINGTON TRUST is administered by a council, the chairman of which is A.D.C. Peterson, M.A., O.B.E., Director of the Department of Education at Oxford University, with the assistance of an academic steering committee. The Research Unit is the chief concern of the Trust, and was set up in October 1965 to conduct research on the topic of moral education. It consists, at the time of writing, of a director and two research fellows – John Wilson (philosophy), Norman Williams (psychology), and Dr Barry Sugarman (sociology) – with secretarial and other assistance. The work is expected to continue for at least ten years. The Unit is situated at No. 4, Park Town, Oxford. This is the first publication of the Trust.

John Wilson was born in 1928 and read classics and philosophy at New College, Oxford. From 1954 to 1961 he taught those subjects at the King's School, Canterbury, where he was housemaster and Second Master. He held the post of Professor of Religious Knowledge at Trinity College, Toronto, from 1961 to 1962 and in 1963 he went to the University of Sussex as a lecturer in philosophy, becoming a university proctor in 1964. His publications include works on moral philosophy, the philosophy of religion, and education (see bibliography for titles).

Norman Williams was born in 1930, and studied psychology and education at Durham University. He spent seven years teaching, first in a secondary modern school and later (for five years) in a school for maladjusted children. Before joining the Farmington Trust Research Unit he was, from 1961 to 1964, a lecturer in educational psychology at Victoria University, Wellington, New Zealand.

Barry Sugarman was born in 1939, and studied sociology at the University of Exeter from 1957 to 1960. He then went to the U.S.A. for post-graduate work, spending two years at Southern Illinois University and three at Princeton. For his doctoral thesis he returned to London to study the behaviour of teenagers at school, and completed the thesis in the U.S.A. in 1965.

INTRODUCTION TO
MORAL EDUCATION

JOHN WILSON
NORMAN WILLIAMS
BARRY SUGARMAN

PENGUIN BOOKS

Penguin Books Ltd, Harmondsworth, Middlesex, England
Penguin Books Inc., 3300 Clipper Mill Road, Baltimore, Md 21211, U.S.A.
Penguin Books Australia Ltd, Ringwood, Victoria, Australia

—

First published 1967
Copyright © The Farmington Trust, 1967

—

Made and printed in Great Britain by
C. Nicholls & Company Ltd
Set in Monotype Plantin

CONTENTS

Part I

WHAT IS MORAL EDUCATION?
(J.B.W.)

Part III

WHAT CAN WE DO ABOUT MORAL EDUCATION?
(J.B.W.)

PREFACE

THE trouble with 'moral education' as a topic is that almost everybody is interested in it. This includes those whose interests are primarily academic or scholarly, as well as those who have to deal with urgent practical problems. Of course it is impossible to satisfy all these interests in one book. It would have been easier (at least by comparison) to write either something on more strictly 'academic' lines, or something more 'popular' and 'practical'.

Neither of these, however, would meet what I take to be the most urgent and important demand. Within a few months after this Research Unit began its work (October 1965), it became abundantly clear that concern with moral education was very widespread, that this concern was largely incoherent and disorganized, and that our first task was to try to make sense of the topic for other people as well as for ourselves. It seemed that almost everybody suffered from some confusion. Teachers, academics, educational authorities and others might have some particular practical or theoretical understanding which was relevent to moral education: but nobody had really made sense of it *as a topic*, however much progress may have been made in particular disciplines or in the classroom. This book tries to meet that demand.

Part II of the book is largely based on psychological and sociological material submitted by my colleagues in the Unit; and indeed the whole book is much more the result of our joint discussions than of any one person. It was thought desirable that I should be responsible for welding all the material into a single book: but Mr Williams and Dr Sugarman are generally responsible for Part II (A) and II (B) respectively, although they cannot be held strictly to account for the way the material is presented.*

I should like to thank the Chairman and Council of the Farmington Trust (see flyleaf) for making the book possible, and the members of the Steering Committee for their most valuable comments and criticism. We are also grateful to many other critics, too numerous to mention, for their advice.

J.B.W.
Oxford, 1967.

* Responsibility for the various parts of the book is indicated by initials in the Contents pages, and in the text.

GENERAL INTRODUCTION

'MORAL EDUCATION' is a name for nothing clear. Yet morality and education are two things which everybody has, or has undergone, and about which most people hold strong views of their own. This makes it more, rather than less, difficult to write about them: it is not like writing a book about Sanskrit or Polish foreign policy in the sixteenth century – subjects about which most people do not have prejudiced views because they do not have views at all. Chiefly for this reason, it would not be much use writing a very short or simple introduction to 'moral education'. There are a great many muddles to be cleared up, and prejudices to be removed, before we can get a clear view of the subject at all. (By a 'clear view' I do not mean a final, definitive pronouncement which will solve all the problems: that we shall never get. I mean a view sufficiently clear to enable research workers, education authorities, teachers and others – both in this country and elsewhere* – to develop the

* Members (or students) of some societies, very different from this one, may think that much of our argument will not apply to them. But before dismissing it as irrelevant, they should consider the following:
(i) Their social situation may become like ours. The rapid spread of industrialization, improved communications and various other factors are likely to face these societies with problems essentially similar to those which we are now facing.
(ii) The *concept* of moral education developed in this book is, no doubt, the product of a particular kind of society which might roughly be described as 'liberal' or 'pluralistic'. But it is not intended to *apply* only to that kind of society. If the way we have developed it is right, then as a concept – as an ideal, if you like – it is right for all: even though different societies may have to take different measures to realize this ideal.
(iii) We shall not argue for this concept on the grounds that it fits 'the British way of life', 'a liberal philosophy', 'western democracy', 'a mobile society', 'the twentieth-century world', or for any such culture-bound reasons. We shall argue for it simply on the grounds that it is *reasonable*. Whatever the merits of our particular arguments, anyone who dismisses the concept as being partisan, or designed to meet a particular social situation which may not arise elsewhere, will have missed the point.

topic of moral education, and to work out practical methods, in a coherent and rational way.)

Before turning to the first chapter, therefore, it will be worth while to approach our topic obliquely. In this Introduction I want to discuss four things: (A) the peculiar importance of moral education at the present time; (B) some doctrinaire reactions to the phrase 'moral education'; (C) where we should look for a new starting-point; and (D) the way in which the topic should be tackled, which will also give the reader some idea of the plan and arrangement of this book.

A. WHY MORAL EDUCATION IS IMPORTANT NOW

It is worth remembering that moral education, in various forms and under various titles, has been a matter of perennial concern. In western society, Socrates was perhaps the first to question the concept philosophically, by asking whether virtue could be taught and, if so, how: but all cultures and societies that we know of have at least paid lip-service to the notion that education should do more than teach social skills, increase factual knowledge, or improve intellectual ability. Many have tried to build methods of doing this into their educational system: and some may even have succeeded. Under such headings as 'bringing up children in the fear of the Lord', 'the education of a gentleman', 'educating the whole man', 'character-training' and many others,[1] various ideals and values have been held up by churches, states, political parties or social classes as the proper content of moral education.

A great deal of what is said and written today about moral education consists of a more or less incoherent acceptance of, or reaction against, one or more of these traditional notions. In this society, reactions tend to be stronger than acceptances, because authority seems to have broken down, or to be breaking down, in so many areas.[2] Defenders of traditional values, such as committed Christians or those who control and support the public boarding schools, usually speak and write with none of the self-confidence (amounting sometimes to arrogance) which characterized their pronouncements in the past: they woo their readers rather than laying down the law, and admit to as much doubt as certainty. On the other hand, any challenge to tradi-

---

On this see Chapter 1: Chapter 4, pp. 212–17: and Chapter 7, pp. 313–31.

tional values is so fashionable as no longer even to seem rebellious and exciting. Those who are mature enough to tolerate doubt, and whose identity is not bound up either with a compulsion to defend traditional values or a compulsion to attack them, are unheard: partly because they do not know what to say, and partly because anything that can usefully be said at this stage needs more patience and sustained attention than most of us can manage.

I stress the intellectual incoherence in this situation, if only because it is too easy simply to point to brute social phenomena which seem to us chaotic or unsatisfactory. It is one thing to lament or feel anxious about crime, juvenile delinquency, neurosis, war, social inertia, lack of idealism, and so forth, and another to admit to being intellectually muddled. The former can easily be overemphasized; the extent to which young people or our whole society, are – by any standards – less 'moral', or well-behaved, or law-abiding, or 'Christian' than they used to be is a matter of dispute.[3] Certainly in some areas and by some standards we might seem to have improved: consider the treatment of factory workers, our attitude towards cruelty, and the whole apparatus and moral implications of the welfare state, as contrasted with the position a hundred years ago. But it is rather at the conceptual level, at least initially, that our problem lies. The rejection of authority is evidenced, more obviously than by any 'immoral' behaviour, by the apparent increase in non-authoritarian ways of thinking.

Amongst these one might count the rise of humanism, existentialism, modern analytic philosophy, psychoanalysis, and the social sciences: and perhaps the increased popularity of a scientific or quasi-scientific approach to life in general. But at least as important for our purposes are the constant references in educational literature (usually of a rather woolly kind) to the importance of teaching children to be 'responsible', to 'think for themselves' and 'adopt a critical attitude': references to 'mental health', 'maturity', 'adjustment', 'the whole man', 'self-development', and so forth. All this, and many other things, testify to a vast but confused desire to substitute *something* for the vanished or vanishing authority, in that field of education and social life that might be called 'moral'. The whole difficulty is that we are not at all clear about *what* to substitute. It is not surprising that quite a few people, perhaps particularly the young, sometimes seem to go overboard into a kind of anti-rationalism which, though logically incoherent, has to be taken seriously as a phenomenon. For it testifies to the immense difficulty of filling in the authority-gap, and to our failure to do so hitherto.

The breakdown in authority presents a serious problem for society in general: that is, for each and every one of us. But the position is worse for those who occupy the traditional and accepted places of political and moral authority in society – governments, the monarchy, members of Parliament, the established church, and those bodies or individuals whose unique influence on or connection with the political authorities may qualify them for some such term as the 'establishment'. The reason why they are on the spot is obvious enough. 'The state' (to use a convenient term) has governed, in almost all societies in the past and in most present societies, on the basis of a commonly-accepted and shared morality, often backed by a religion or near-religion (such as Communism). It has been enabled to do this more easily, in that the distinction between rulers and ruled was sharper than it is now becoming in the mobile liberal societies of the western world. The submerged mass of the people might erupt, as in the French or Russian revolutions, if too economically or politically under-privileged: but for the most part they accepted the traditional moral or religious myth. Those states which have come to profess liberal ideals have kept going partly because these conditions still applied until fairly recently. There was, one might say, a traditional acceptance of or agreement about certain moral or religious standards: certain things were 'done' or 'not done': on the whole the rulers were trusted to maintain this tradition, and indeed they were often admired or emulated: and the mass of people lacked the education, opportunity, energy, ability or economic resources – and perhaps also the will – to make any effective intellectual challenge.

Much of this is still true today: but over the past few decades the increase in welfare, prosperity and education have radically altered the position. For the first time states are beginning to face the joint facts (a) that their societies are committed to such liberal notions as freedom, equality and social welfare for all, and (b) that they have not been planned in the past on any such basis. States show some awareness of this in the economic field: they are aware, for instance, that things like housing, road-using, health and so forth must be organized for their entire populations and not just for a particular social class. But in the fields of social legislation, morality and religion (and consequently in the field of education so far as it is concerned with these) the state shows very little awareness of the change. In Britain it is still possible to hear Government committees, or *The Times*, or the officials of the established church, talking about 'common standards', 'what all decent Englishmen believe', 'the opinion of all responsible people', and so forth. We find it hard to realize that there has grown up, not only a new generation, but a vast new social class, of people who may (for all we know) fundamentally disagree with much that is regarded as essential in our moral and religious traditions: just as they may have a totally new concept of music, or dancing, or sex, or the significance of work or money. Moreover, any state which purports to run its society on liberal lines must inevitably lack the confidence to give clear moral judgments about these new ideas: for it cannot consistently pose as the representative of God, as guardian of proven moral values, or as any kind of father-figure.

State authorities have for the most part been concerned with such material issues as economics, defence and enforcement of the law: and it is therefore not surprising that they regard it as outside their province to make any coherent intellectual attempt to meet this situation.[4] This is perhaps particularly true in countries where liberalism has been combined with an empirical approach to government, and where it is consequently felt that if you go in for such things as moral education, you are bound to end up as authoritarian and totalitarian, along the lines of Plato's *Republic* or Stalinist Russia. Such an attitude reflects the doctrinaire reaction: 'Either you indoctrinate people, or else you leave them alone and do nothing: the former is illiberal, so we must choose the latter'.[5] This policy is plainly misguided: not only because it is based on a false dichotomy, but because it may be self-defeating. What the state takes as its real concerns all depend on people. You cannot defend a country if people do not think it worth defending, or are pacifists. You cannot implement a policy of hard work for a higher standard of living if people no longer believe in the merits of hard work, and do not earnestly desire a higher standard of living. You cannot enforce the law if people do not approve of it, or regard the police as enemies.

The observation that we are 'living on capital', therefore, which is often quoted with reference to morality and religion, has a far wider relevance. In the past states could take certain values and psychological dispositions for granted, and on the basis of these make plans for economy and welfare. But now no such assumptions can easily be made. Although we cannot assess just how different these values and dispositions are in our society, it would be rash to underestimate the degree to which, in principle, the break-down of traditional values requires a totally new approach. Whereas in the past most people had a set of reasons for their behaviour which were based on traditional acceptance, these reasons no longer operate. It may be true that different reasons will automatically fill the gap to produce the same behaviour: but it may not be true. Thus, a person might have worked 'because one ought not to be idle', or kept the law 'because one ought to keep the law', or stayed with his wife and children 'because Christians ought not to divorce'. A new set of reasons – 'because I enjoy working', 'because the law is sensible', 'because I've learned to get on with my wife' – *may* exist as adequate substitutes: but it is highly unlikely, since the new set of reasons (not being derived directly from authority) will require more thinking out, more education, and more general understanding. And there is little evidence to show that we have produced contexts in which such thought, education and understanding may flourish.

Further, there is an important sense in which a liberal society has a harder job than an authoritarian one. In politics, there is a simplicity about a dictatorship which is lacking to a democracy. If you go in for a master-slave system, you need only a few orders and a whip: if you go in for freedom, you need all sorts of complicated mechanisms and contexts of communication – availability of information, voting, debates, rules of procedure and so forth. In the same way, moral education requires more attention in liberal societies. Indeed, as I shall try to show, the concepts of morality and education themselves imply some kind of liberal theory, which is to be contrasted with the mere conditioning of behaviour: and any genuine form of moral education will therefore require more thought and planning than a comparatively simple programme of brain-washing or indoctrination. But in practice we do rather less deliberate moral education in any form than we used to. Lacking the confidence in the old moral and religious values, the teaching or indoctrination of which was a major feature in past educational programmes, many states have taken the line of least resistance and simply dropped the whole notion. This may partly be because of the conceptual difficulties involved (though states are not usually much influenced by conceptual difficulties): but probably it is chiefly because less people are offended if a neutral or isolationist policy is adopted. (Compare the unconscious argument: 'We can't force a particular brand of religion on children whose parents don't want it, so we will confine ourselves to the neutral teaching of some inoffensive aspect of religion – Biblical knowledge or comparative religion. This isn't actually teaching *religion*, but never mind'.)[6]

As I have suggested, this inactivity on the part of the state may be tantamount to suicide. For there are many situations in which all states need to make some kind of appeal to their societies: an appeal for more work, or for national unity in time of crisis or war, or for more money from taxation, or for more respect for the law, or whatever. If this appeal is not to be made on the basis of some accepted first-order morality, it must be made on the basis of democratic agreement. In other words, if we can no longer rely on a kind of half-asleep acceptance of traditional values, we must rely on a set of rules to which individuals in our society consciously and willingly subscribe. But this involves an enormous effort in communication: we need to know what people think, what they are prepared to contract for, what changes they want made, and so forth. Most states do not seem particularly concerned to find out these things. Yet if they cannot establish some such basis, they have the worst of both worlds: no indoctrinated values, and no conscious agreement. It is as if their citizens had suddenly stopped being children who could be ordered about, but were not yet being treated as adults who made contracts with each other to keep certain rules. Indeed, it is not accidental that we find problems connected with the teenage group particularly worrying in our society; there is a close analogy between the state and its citizens on the one hand, and parents and teenagers on the other. And just as parents are beginning to feel that they can no longer give orders to teenagers as to children, but that they have not succeeded in retaining their respect as adults and equals, so states may come to realize that their paternalistic powers have vanished, and have not been replaced with powers granted to them by freely contracting adult citizens: so that a kind of crypto-anarchy exists, in which it is not worth anyone's while to start a revolution, but not worth anyone's while to support the state either – a situation less dramatic than revolution, but probably no less dangerous.

Moreover, the break-down in authority has produced a lack of leadership which is very hard for ordinary people to tolerate. We neither can nor should revert to an authoritarian élite: but we do desperately need a new set of standards which will define for us a class of people whom we can admire, and whose skills we can whole-heartedly attempt to emulate. It is perhaps dangerous to call them 'moral experts', and it would certainly be premature to envisage an élite class of 'the morally educated'. Yet, inevitably and rightly, we are driven somewhat in this direction. It is vitally important, not only for education, but also for the future of our society in general, that the supposed expertise of past authority-figures, such as the priest or the political leader, should be replaced by the public acceptance of more rationally-defensible expertises. These must stand on firm philosophical foundations, and must be able to be tested or measured adequately. Not until this immensely difficult task has been accomplished will we acquire the confidence which comes from united understanding and acceptance.

*

In view of all these points, states can no longer afford to behave amateurishly. It is now recognized that the findings of natural science not only may but must be brought into the political arena. In due course it will no doubt be understood that what philosophers and social scientists have to say – or, in some matters, have in fact been saying for some time – is also vital to the state, and need not be confined to academic circles.[7] Whether this will happen in time to prevent a dramatic breakdown is an interesting question: it has certainly not happened in time to prevent a great deal of inefficiency, financial loss, and suffering.

I suppose it is characteristic of certain types of societies that the people with the most practical power (I do not talk of influence) in some particular field – e.g. (in education) the Minister, the key civil servants, the directors of local authorities and so forth – should be administrators rather than 'thinkers'. This is an invidious-sounding distinction: but contrast a possible situation in which experts in economics or education transmute what the nation wants or needs into a general policy, and then hire practical politicians to execute it, with the existing situation in which practical politicians do their own transmutation of the nation's needs, and then hire (or don't hire) experts to help them execute the already transmuted policy. To put it another way: experts are needed at the 'transmutation' level, not just to help carry out approved ends.[8]

This point should not be confused with the question of how much central control should be exercised, as against local independence. It may well be that, in this country, some important features of education are (or have in the past been) saved by the remarkable independence possessed by schools, universities, local authorities and so forth: and this may be because their decisions are based on thought and experience which is more genuinely connected with *education* (as opposed to, say, the needs of a modern technology) than those of people at a higher political level. But because of this same independence, it may well happen that changes which are both urgent and plainly desirable get blocked. Governments and other high-level authorities may fail, that is, by inaction as well as action. The point here is that whoever has the power, however centralized or decentralized it should be, need not necessarily be trained or expert in *administration*. Not that 'administration' is a dirty word, although some young people tend to act as if this were so: of course it is an expertise in its own right, and a very difficult and important one. Nevertheless, making a coherent policy out of something like education is far too serious a matter to be left to administrators.

I cannot here pursue the very difficult question of how these relevant expertises can be integrated with the political authorities: one can only note the strength of the British tradition of amateur empiricism, and suggest that any efforts that may have been made to incorporate expert critics into areas of decision-making seem to have been somewhat less than strenuous. Most of these critics earn a moderate but pleasant living on the touch-line, talking to each other while the game goes on elsewhere. This makes many of the critics either into irresponsible and alienated satirists, or dwellers in ivory towers: and it makes the state look more and more like a well-produced piece of machinery, tolerably efficient in certain contexts, but unable to cope with some modern conditions. We must just hope that there is still some life in it, however much it creaks: or else that it is flexible enough to change.

B. Some Doctrinaire Reactions

The reactions of various people to the phrase 'moral education', and to the setting-up of a research team with these terms of reference,[9] would make a separate study in itself. It is a truism that strong images and feelings are evoked by the names of actual or possible areas of study, such as 'psychoanalysis', 'spiritualism', 'philosophy', 'religion' and many others. This applies especially to areas which (whether with wisdom or un-wisdom) have been newly demarcated. Because of the strength of these images and feelings, these areas are not often rationally considered and assessed. The degree of rationality does not appear to correlate to any great extent with the intelligence of the assessor, his (or her) social or academic position, education or sophistication.[10] I shall here present a number of these doctrinaire attitudes or reactions in schematic form.

These attitudes can be grouped into four pairs:

(a) The two most common may be labelled 'indoctrinatory' and 'isolationist'. It is characteristic of both attitudes that the person takes the phrase 'moral education' to imply the training of children to think and act in accordance with some first-order norm. This norm may be the views of a church or religious sect, the law of the land, the ideals of some non-religious group, organization or writer, the accepted public standards of con-temporary society, or some fairly nebulous notion of 'what all societies have always practised' or 'what all decent people think'. Members of the 'indoctrinatory' group accept this view, and are often eager that more efficient methods of training children in this way should be found: perhaps because certain social phenomena – delinquency, drug-taking, etc. – seem urgently to demand a solution. Members of the 'isolationist' group reject 'moral education' chiefly *because* it seems to them to imply this view, and to involve indoctrination and other sus-pect or illegitimate modes of training for conformity. They react with hostility to any attempt to formalize 'moral education', identifying such attempts as authoritarian, interfering, or at least over-inquisitive – perhaps as naive also. They tend to minimize, and disclaim responsibility for or involvement with, the social phenomena that strike the former group so forcibly.

I categorize these attitudes as doctrinaire because there is a viable concept of 'moral education' that does not involve training in accordance with a first-order norm.[11] Such a concept is not without its difficulties, but it is not likely to be reached unless (a) we are impressed with the logical and practical dangers of mere conformity, which the 'indoctrinatory' group is not, and (b) we are sufficiently moved by social chaos and personal misery to search for some adequate remedy, which the second group is not.

(b) Operating in very much the same dimension are the 'activ-ist' and 'academic' attitudes. 'Activists', who tend to be as unworried by the dangers of conformism as are members of the 'indoctrinatory' group, are those who wish to buy, or sell, some immediate *practical* programme. To them the notion of the philosophical direction of a research unit which is supposed to have practical results does not wholly commend itself. They are not impressed by the conceptual difficulties of the research task: perhaps one ought to define one's terms, they may think, but that is soon settled, and then we can start doing something practical. These people may be administrators, practising teachers, suffering parents, or overworked probation officers. 'Academics' – and this class does in fact include many people in academic posts of high status – tend to react against the idea of 'education' (and perhaps *a fortiori* 'moral education') as a sensible subject for research, or even as a subject at all. This is sometimes argued on the various grounds (a) that it is a mixture of different disciplines, (b) that the logical foundations of such a 'subject' are unclear, so that there is too much room for 'waffle' or 'bogus' talk, (c) that 'educationalists' are an unimpressive bunch. The criteria of what counts as a 'sensible subject' that actually weigh with such people seem sometimes to connect with how long-established a 'subject' is, and whether it is socially or academically accepted, rather than with how (logically) well-established it is and whether it is (rationally) acceptable. There is also a good deal of conceptual muddle involving such terms as 'subject' and 'discipline', and about the whole question of the justification of 'subjects', which I cannot attempt to resolve here.[12]

The 'activist' attitude would not be doctrinaire, if it were not clear that problems of methodology, and some general philosophical problems, are central to the whole notion of 'moral education'. This I shall show later. The 'academic' attitude would not be doctrinaire if it consisted only of a recommendation to be cautious, especially when engaged in new areas of study. But in practice the propositions in (a), (b) and (c) above (if these propositions are true) ought to serve, not as reasons for steering clear of such new enterprises, but as reasons for devoting more effort, attention and constructive criticism to their proper organization. Both attitudes, I think, share a feature common to many prejudices: a tendency to minimize the need and importance of communication, particularly in fields where academic and practical interests interconnect.

(c) Another pair of attitudes also displays similarities to the first two. We may label them 'intuitive' and 'psychometric'. Members of the 'intuitive' group tend to think that they know, either which people are the most 'morally educated', and/or what processes make them so. Perhaps they think that it is all a matter of love, or an open-air life, or being psychoanalysed, or doing good to others. This seems to them so obvious that they suppose that a research unit could start on this basis, rather than further back. On this view, our job should be to spread the light (rather than measure it). The 'psychometric' group tends to suppose that one should be interested only in what is measurable: that one should find an operational definition of 'moral education' as quickly as possible, and take it from there: that it is no good messing about with intangibles: that we need 'solid results'.

Here again these attitudes are only doctrinaire because they are distorted versions of quite reasonable points. We must eventually define 'moral education' in operational terms, so that our results can be as objective as possible: but an operational definition requires a good deal of preliminary thought, if it is not to be arbitrary and hence to measure nothing interesting. Equally, intuitions and insights are valuable as subject-matter, as a quarry for potential hypotheses: but they are not valid just because they strike one forcibly. In this case also neither side is sufficiently impressed with the conceptual difficulties attaching to 'moral education', and the need for a good deal of hard thinking before we can use either intuitions or measurement.[13]

(d) Finally, a pair of much more general attitudes, which nevertheless also closely connect with those already listed: the 'tough-minded' and 'tender-minded'. Faced with phenomena like juvenile crime, vandalism, or even the normal naughtiness of children, most of us react in one of two fairly distinct ways. Either we feel anger, and instinctively advocate some 'tough' policy (re-introduction of the birch, more discipline, severer punishments, stricter rules): or else we feel guilt, and advocate a 'tender' policy (more child-care, psychotherapy, loving teachers, all-delinquents-are-really-just-sociologically-sick-it's-our-fault-and-not-theirs). We ought to admit to feeling the pull of both these attitudes, which only become doctrinaire if we deny one or the other of them. Their co-existence is a good witness of the kind of problem we face. We all know quite well that children and young people need both discipline and love, both firmness and kindness. But we are not clear about how these fit together, or about what justification we should use for employing 'tough' or 'tender' policies on different occasions. The contemporary break-down in authority has produced a striking increase in guilt-inspired reactions, naturally most common among those whose general attitude may be called 'liberal', 'left-wing', or 'progressive'; but though these are perhaps the more vocal, it is doubtful whether they are in the majority.[14]

The crisis of confidence which the conflict between these two attitudes has produced is indeed a sign of malaise; and it might possibly be argued that almost any policy adopted, would be a better basis for moral education than the prevailing uncertainty. But apart from the impossibility of putting the clock back, the tension is a hopeful sign. If we can stand it, we may be able to win through to an understanding at once more firm and more broadly-based than our present ideas.

C. A New Starting-point

I now want to give a brief preview of the sort of way in which we are going to try, in this book, to fight clear of some of these doctrinaire attitudes. The best way of starting is to describe, as well as I can, one general reaction to the prevailing state of confusion and uncertainty, of which the particular attitudes mentioned above are only facets. What happens is surely something like this: For some people, the old values, faiths, creeds and so on begin to lose their force. Of course many other people are still solidly attached to them: and other people (a certain type of extreme atheist, for instance) maintain a kind of identity by a continued passionate opposition to them: but many of us feel lost. Indeed we may feel robbed, as if somebody had taken away the props which sustained our values. So we seek to replace them. We seeks a new basis for our morality, a new ground on which to build, perhaps a new authority to accept, admire and obey. Even if we do not seek a new basis for ourselves (because we feel reasonably satisfied with what we have already), we may wonder what basis to offer our children. So far, so good.

But the only kind of 'basis' for morality of which most of us have had any experience has been an authoritarian basis. We have accepted (if only half-heartedly) some particular creed or set of values without asking too many questions: or, if we have asked questions, we have not been clear about how they should be answered. Now that the old basis has let us down, we naturally look for a new basis *of the same logical type*. An extreme form of this is the type of person who starts by accepting some very clearly-defined authority (perhaps the Roman Catholic Church), finds it unsatisfactory, and then switches to another authority (perhaps the Communist Party). He has acquired a 'new basis' for his morality, but it isn't *really* new: he has just changed one authority for another. The new authority may *happen* to be a better one (or a worse): but unless he is in some position to judge whether it is better, unless he knows *how* to make this sort of judgement, he cannot know whether he is any better off.

Moreover, unless we are able to judge intelligently between one basis and another, we cannot know whether this change of authority will be more than a short-term solution to the practical problem. If one basis or authority can be rejected and hence result in break-down, chaos, uncertainty, etc., then so can another. We may give our children a 'new basis' by devising a new moral code (drawn from whatever source), but will this do the job better than the old one? Is it likely to last? *Ought* it to last? It may seem immediately attractive, and be easily available, but what are its real merits? If the next generation of adolescents is going to challenge it, have we an answer? If we just want *any* 'new basis' to adopt, any authority to follow, then we can find one for ourselves tomorrow without any trouble at all. But if we want to find the right basis, or at least a more reasonable basis, then we shall have to think about it: we shall have to try to answer the general question 'How are we to judge between one basis and another?'

Now as soon as we take this question seriously, we begin to see that it isn't the 'new basis' itself which is going to be ultimately authoritative, but the *criteria by which we judge*. As soon as we get into the position of questioning authorities, of asking for a 'new basis' – and as soon as we begin questioning we can't get out of this position, whether we like it or not – then in a sense these authorities are no longer ultimate. We are no longer searching only for a leader, a hero, a clear and simple moral code to put all our trust in: we are searching for general principles which will enable us to assess and perhaps choose between leaders and codes. Hence it is really *these principles* (whatever they may be) which we are going to put our money on. It will be these principles which, if we can get clear about them, may form a genuinely 'new basis'. But it is now fairly obvious that these principles will not themselves be moral principles or codes: they will be principles *by which one judges between* various moral codes or authorities.

This is why we shall have no hope of success if we continue to search for a 'new basis' in the old way. We might be tempted, for instance, to look for 'the best features of the different religious and moral codes', or to look for 'what most people have always thought about morals', or 'what the great moral and religious writers have said'. But we immediately meet with the following difficulties:

(a) How do we know who *are* the 'great' moral and religious writers? Do we include Marx and Freud, or just Jesus and the Buddha? How about St Augustine, Bertrand Russell, Nietzsche, D. H. Lawrence? We can just pick and choose to suit our own taste, but this is to do no more than sell our own values under the aegis of respectable names. Moreover, some writers and thinkers considered now as 'great' have not always been so, and may cease to be so in a short time. Some of those we now admire we may laugh at tomorrow, and *vice versa*. And even if we could justify a 'short list' of great moralists, we should still not know how to select what was best in their work, unless we already had criteria by which to judge this.

(b) How do we know 'what most people always thought about morals'? Either we would really have to mean *most people*; and then we might get some very surprising results, since we should have to include the many generations of cave-men and other primitives that existed before the dawn of history (and this hardly seems a sensible policy, apart from the difficulties of discovering the facts): or else we are going to pick and choose, counting in some people and excluding others, in which case we are thrown back to the difficulty in (a) above.

(c) Even if we were quite sure that everyone in the world believed in some moral principle, this would not at all show that the principle was right. (Consider the time when everyone believed that the earth was flat). Correctness in morality is not a matter of what is commonly accepted. (For most of human history people – even the 'greatest' – seem to have approved of slavery, the subjection of women, and the persecution of those of different religions or races. This hardly gives one faith in the reliability of a 'commonly-accepted morality').

Now (as I shall say later in the book) this does not at all mean that it is a waste of time to look at the moral views of other people, both past and present; or that we should not try to get our own morality as correct as possible; or that we may not be able to prove (in some sense of the word) that some moral views are right and others wrong. But to start here would be to start at the wrong end. For we cannot do any of these things until we know *how to settle* such matters. We should be like children trying to play a game without knowing what the rules were: indeed, this is perhaps a fair description of the position children and adolescents (and we ourselves) are now in. What we need first to agree about is not some specific authority or set of values, but about the rules or principles by which we are to judge.

Our concern with moral *education* – rather than just with our own morality – reinforces this point. For if we are educating our children, we are setting out to give them some idea about *how to do* morality (to put it crudely): and obviously we shall not succeed until we ourselves are clear about this. We may feel – perhaps quite wrongly – that we know 'the right answers' for ourselves: but there is more to education than just handing out right answers. It is one thing to work out our own moral values, for ourselves and perhaps for our society as well: and it is quite another thing to say that these alone will form an acceptable basis for moral *education*. Of course the two interconnect. But the view which may be expressed as 'First we find out the right answers, and then we tell them to children, and that's moral education' is plainly inadequate.

Much of the book will consist of an exposition of this point and connected points: but perhaps a parallel will make it clearer for the time being. Suppose we were in the Middle Ages, and tried to find a 'basis for scientific education' by combining those beliefs which were generally accepted. We might say 'Well, at least we all agree that the earth's round, that there are unicorns, that the sun goes round the earth, etc., so let's call that science and teach people to believe it, and then they'll be educated in science'. The point here is not (or not only) that some of these beliefs are mistaken. It is rather that 'educating people scientifically' is not simply to make them repeat certain scientific truths, but to get clear about what scientific method is and to *teach them how to do science well*. It is to get clear about what counts as success in science, and give them the skills to be successful: to show them that it involves, for instance, close and patient observation, accuracy, testing by experiment, and so forth. So too, with history, literary criticism, and any other field of human activity. Educating people in these activities is not to extract 'right answers' from them, but to teach them what counts as 'a good reason' in history, literary criticism etc., and how to think and act in accordance with these reasons. Hence any 'basis for moral education' should consist of imparting those skills which are necessary to make good or reasonable moral decisions and to act on them. We are not primarily out to impart any specific *content*, but to give other people facility in a *method*. This is what eventually happened with science, and this is why science and education in science eventually prospered: and this is what must happen to morality. Such an approach does not deny that we have moral knowledge now, any more than we would deny that the Middle Ages had scientific knowledge: but it does involve trying first to reach agreement about the second-order principles governing morality, rather than about what should be the (first-order) content of particular moral beliefs.

Now of course this is very difficult: but I think that the study of the principles governing morality (which we can call 'moral philosophy' if we like) is sufficiently far advanced to make it worth while trying to bring it to bear on education. Indeed, whilst of course there are many important disputes amongst moral philosophers and many objections that might be made to any statement of such principles, I do not think that the main difficulties in forming a reasonable conceptual framework for moral education are primarily intellectual or academic at all. To put it in a grotesquely extreme way, we all really know how to do morals – if we think about it, are prepared to be honest, and are willing not to 'run wild' or play some other game instead. It isn't that the rules of the game are wholly obscure: it's mostly that we just don't attend to them. What was crucial to the development of science at the time of Galileo was not so much whether people believed that the earth moved or not: it was whether people were willing to use their eyes, their telescopes and their mathematics in an honest effort to find out the facts. This sort of move requires a psychological readjustment, of which a clear and precise account of scientific method is (in a sense) only a subsequent symptom. In the same way, much of what passes as 'theories about morality', 'moral beliefs', or even 'moral behaviour' today may in fact be nothing of the kind: it may rather represent the twistings and turnings of people who are trying to do morality but aren't quite sure how – or even of people who aren't really trying.

If we are to approach moral education properly, therefore, we must not remain too firmly wedded to our own particular moral codes and beliefs: initially, at least, we must be willing to start from scratch. It is very tempting to say things like 'Well, everyone agrees about so-and-so at least' or 'There isn't much dispute about such-and-such, anyway'; and of course nobody would want to throw away commonly-held beliefs without the most careful and painstaking examination. But we have to remember that this *may* be like saying 'Everybody accepts X and Y as scientifically true', in a society whose 'science' was merely astrology and superstition. And we can't tell without going into the whole question of what the subject – whether it's morality or science or anything else – actually *is*.

The point can be put another way. Different societies at different times might have called certain people 'moral', 'virtuous', 'good' or even 'morally educated'. The ancient Spartans would have chosen some people for this description, the ancient Athenians others: in the Middle Ages, the Renaissance, Victorian England and Nazi Germany others again would have been selected. Now it is one thing to say whom we (or some other society) would describe in this way: *but quite another thing to say whether this description is accurate*. We may *think* we know who these people are: but unless we are clear about what it *means* to talk of somebody being 'good' or 'moral' or 'morally educated', we can't be sure that we do know. For instance, is a 'good' man simply somebody who (as it were) goes through the right motions, performing 'good actions' and never doing anything wrong? Or do his motives also matter, and the reasons for which he does what he does? Are the people we want to 'morally educate' just the rule-breakers, the delinquents, and the people who get into trouble? Or are we out to catch the insensitive, the Pharisees, those who sin by omission rather than commission, the slobs, the fanatics, and others as well?

Of course deciding these questions is only half the battle. Once we are clearer about what it means to talk about a 'morally educated' person, about what moral education *is*, we still want to know how to do it effectively. We want to know what preconditions are necessary – what sort of general upbringing children must have, what kind of rules and frameworks they need, what arrangements to make in our schools, and so forth. This naturally leads us to consider the question of how moral education should be studied, and to say something about the general plan and intentions of this book.

D. THE STUDY OF MORAL EDUCATION

THE PLAN OF THE BOOK

Both as a research subject and as a practical undertaking, moral education must rely very largely upon the application of different disciplines: and the importance of good communications can hardly be over-emphasized. In this Unit we have tried to do our best in facing the implications of having workers trained in philosophy, psychology and sociology living and working in the same building and on the same project. The generosity and good sense of the Trust produced this framework, which we suspect to be essential to any such enterprise.[15] But the importance of communication must not be used as an excuse for giving conferences, working groups, committees, research units, etc., some such title as 'moral education' to play with, and failing to support this with an adequate methodology. This is to do little more than provide the members of such groups with the opportunity to propound their own faiths, creeds, moral beliefs, views of life, prejudices or insights: and though this may sometimes be interesting, it is not clear that anything very concrete is achieved. Titles like 'moral education', and indeed 'education' in general, will not be titles of coherent and respectable subjects until they are broken down in practice into a number of disciplines. Theoretically it is not too hard to see how this can happen: how the disciplines of philosophy, psychology, sociology and others can be deployed to answer certain questions in the field of education. But in practice this is hard to do, and there is a temptation to water down these disciplines rather than to deploy them.

Worse still, the methodology can be neglected altogether in a natural but misguided desire to obtain some kind of 'answer' without having to work for it. There is still a strong tradition of wanting to be *told*, preferably by people who have the aura of wisdom, or some other charismatic quality. They may be 'great names' who have made some sort of impact on the public mind, 'well-known educationalists', or 'philosophers'; they may hold some important position in church or state, or perhaps even hit the headlines as pop singers or television personalities. This temptation has to be resisted: many people are famous but wrong. (Many are famous precisely because they have cashed in on the temptation.)[16] This is not at all to say that the academic experts – the philosophers, psychologists, etc. – are always right, or that we should spend *all* our time working terribly hard to understand what they are talking about. But it is to say that we should at least recognize that there are these disciplines: that we should acknowledge them, not as new substitutes for the charismatic sage who will do our work for us, but as honest attempts to tackle particular kinds of problems systematically: and that, whether we are running a ten-year research project or a two-day conference, we can do something better than just talk vaguely about 'morality' or 'education'.[17]

This means that we must try, in this book, to present a convincing picture of how the topic should be understood: and this in turn makes it inevitable that we should go into some conceptual and other problems at some length. In effect, I shall be trying to apply what I take to be the findings of research workers in various fields (particularly in philosophy) to this topic. Of course these findings may be disputed, and may themselves not be definitive or 'proved'. But unless somebody succeeds in communicating at least the most important points, I do not think that moral education, either as a theoretical study or a practical movement, will ever get off the ground.[18]

In Part I, I shall try to outline the concept of moral education, and to deal with some of the conceptual confusion which exists in the minds of both practical workers and research workers on this topic. The selection of material in Part II is governed by two considerations:

(a) The way in which we have outlined the concept in Part I. A great deal of work in the psychological and sociological fields has been done which is of great interest and importance in itself, and which may even have gone under (I would say, masqueraded under) some such titles as 'moral education', but which nevertheless is not directly relevant to the notion of moral education as we conceive it.

(b) The practical possibilities for schools and other institutions. As an operational rather than a purely academic research team, we have to keep an eye on what is being or could be done in this field: and here again, a good deal of empirical material, interesting and important in itself, is not immediately relevant.

For these two reasons, the material in Part II must not be regarded either as a purely academic study in psychology and sociology, or as a compendious account of all the work in these fields that might be thought relevant to the topic.[19] We have rather been concerned to extract from these fields such material as we take to be relevant to our particular concern, bearing the two criteria (a) and (b) above very much in mind. In the same way, Part I is not intended as a philosophical essay about the nature of morality or education. Like the book as a whole, its object is primarily to reorientate and clarify the thinking of those many people in schools, training colleges, and elsewhere who are concerned with the subject.

This seems to me a very necessary task; and I have throughout been guided by the kinds of questions raised, and interests expressed, by various teachers and other educators at conferences, discussions and elsewhere. On the whole these questions and interests have not varied very greatly; and they form a fairly consistent set of demands, which I feel reasonably confident about having identified correctly, and which I shall try to meet in this book. From the viewpoint of those who are very well-read in one or other of the relevant disciplines, much of what follows may appear 'thin' or oversimplified: though I would hope that they too might find that some useful and important points emerge in our attempt to bring the disciplines to bear on a common subject. For there is a gulf between the different disciplines, as well as between the disciplines and the practical workers.

If this book helps to bridge either of these gulfs, it will have achieved its main purpose. That part of our future work which might, by contrast, be more precisely described as 'research' will, of course, be governed by considerations of a more strictly academic nature. The design of tests and particular research projects is a highly specialized matter. But without giving the topic the kind of coherence we have tried to give it here, we cannot proceed with any confidence to this stage. This point applies, I believe, not just to our own unit, but to any research on a topic of similar vagueness. One can hardly fail to be impressed by the extent to which, in such undertakings, something may easily go wrong *in the first stage*, so that the resulting researches – although perhaps interesting in themselves – may have no relation to our original interests. At this first stage, unfortunately, no particular discipline (except perhaps philosophy) is more valid than any other: it is a matter of hammering out the topic into some kind of adequate shape. This is what we have tried to do.

The reader will not, of course, expect to find very many practical and detailed recommendations about moral education after so short a period of research on our part. These will follow later. But he may still feel disappointed, particularly if he is someone who in the meantime is faced with urgent practical problems involving school discipline, delinquency, teenagers and so forth. We would ask him to entertain the possibility that our book may be helpful in the following way also: that precisely by clarifying some of the important issues, and removing some of the muddles, fallacies and false steps that bedevil this subject, it may give his own practical experience, local knowledge, and personal insight an opportunity to work more freely and effectively on the problems he faces. Just this should perhaps be the objective of a great deal of research: not to give the practical worker a detailed set of instructions of the 'Join-A-to-B-holding-C-between-the-index-finger-and-thumb' type, but to give him a set of concepts, categories and lines of approach which he alone can know best how to apply to his particular task. This seems to me particularly true of our present subject.

Because the topic is so vast and so amorphous, I cannot begin to do justice to all the questions which we need to raise. Many of these questions are ones which the Unit will have to try to answer with more precision, and in more detail, later on. Meanwhile, the reader must forgive me for a piece of writing which is bound to seem inconclusive and unscholarly – though I am not sure whether the criteria normally governing 'scholarship', as I understand the word, are really appropriate to the sort of thing we are trying to do.[20] I should also warn him that the style of the book, though I hope it is clear, is discursive rather than neatly-tabulated. But this too is intentional: in order to grasp the general picture properly, it is absolutely necessary to work through a number of basic points in detail and from different angles. The working through is everything: there are no quick answers. 'Moral education', as we began by saying, is as yet a name for nothing clear: and there is no short cut to clarity.

J.B.W.

Notes to General Introduction

1. 'Human relations', 'learning to live', 'citizenship', 'ethics', 'social responsibility', 'religious instruction' – these are just a few of the various titles, no clearer in meaning than 'moral education', under which this concern sometimes expresses itself today.

2. One might prefer to say that people are accepting *different* authorities, or different *sorts* of authorities, or that there is a *wider variety* of authorities available: it isn't necessary to analyse these different theses here.

3. Partly a conceptual dispute, because we have first to decide what to mean by 'well-behaved', 'Christian', etc. This isn't easy.

4. Of course this is sweeping; but I still find it a little surprising that the original existence of a project like our own depended on the initiative and generosity of a private patron, rather than on any awareness (or at least any action) on the part of the state. Perhaps the state believes (or hopes) that it is the business of universities. How far this belief/hope is justified is another matter.

5. See pp. 20–21.

6. See pp. 176–83.

7. See M. Argyle *Psychology and Social Problems* (Methuen), Chapter 16: also Note A of the present work.

8. Of course we have first to find out which ends *are* approved by the electorate, i.e. what the people want. This is not the job of economic or similar 'experts': it is supposed to be the job of politicians, but it's not clear that they do it properly. One could imagine a kind of 'public opinion' experts who did it better. A good deal more radical and careful thinking needs to be done here.

9. See flyleaf.

10. We hope to undertake some empirical investigations later, which will enable us to speak more accurately on this point.

11. See Chapter 2.

12. But see pp. 185–6 (note 8).

13. See pp. 203–17.

14. There is also a sense in which a reaction of anger is more natural and spontaneous, even though it may be less sophisticated.

15. See Note A (pp. 441–6).

16. 'The masses of the people prefer the ruler to the suppliant and are filled with a stronger sense of mental security by a teaching that brooks no rival than by teaching which offers them a liberal choice.

They have very little idea of how to make such a choice and thus are prone to feel that they have been abandoned. Whereas they feel very little shame at being terrorized intellectually and are scarcely conscious of the fact that their freedom as human beings is impudently abused ...' A. Hitler, *Mein Kampf*, p. 47, quoted by Alan Bullock in *Hitler*, p. 44 (Penguin Books).

17. Better too, one hopes, than the current vogue for finding 'common ground', or administering a tepid mixture of 'shared humanist values' and 'those parts of the Christian ethic which are acceptable to all of us'. These watered-down, less overtly authoritarian approaches look more like political compromises than genuine attempts to tackle the problem. Problems of religious education are bedevilled by a similar vogue: 'modern', 'progressive' or 'liberal' educators try to sell some inoffensive 'common ground' religion, which omits spiky doctrines (perhaps about original sin, or hell, or the virgin birth), and includes only what is publicly acceptable. See pp. 176–83.

18. Of course many other writers have succeeded in doing this. In reference to Part I, I would like to mention three in particular: Professors R. M. Hare, R. S. Peters, and A. C. MacIntyre (for their writings, see section A of the Bibliography). Most of the important points in the first part of this book have been made by them elsewhere – not that they would necessarily agree with the way I have handled them. But despite all that they and others have done, it still seems that the points are not properly grasped by teachers, educators and other interested members of the public. And since I don't think that much can be done until they are grasped, I hope I may be forgiven for repeating them here.

19. Readers who are familiar with these fields will notice that various topics which are usually discussed at some length either do not appear or are only briefly touched on. For instance, most textbooks on sociology devote a great deal of space to making the point that in different societies different customs, norms and values govern the lives of their members. Of course this topic may be highly relevant to particular research projects, but (as the reader will see) it does not fit in very well with criteria (a) and (b) above, which must govern a book of this kind: and in general the topic of 'moral education' is substantially different from the history, or psychology, or sociology of morals (though of course they are connected). See also the introduction to Part II (pp. 223–6).

20. There are a good many myths which dominate our judgement not only of books, but also of 'academic' and 'practical' approaches

to existing problems in general. Most of the myths are due to quite simple psychological deficiencies, and I have said something about the more obviously doctrinaire or monolithic views in Part III, pp. 426–7 and pp. 434–9; but it would take a whole book to explicate the topic fully.

PART I

WHAT IS MORAL EDUCATION?

INTRODUCTION

THIS Research Unit was not committed to any particular interpretation of 'moral education': still less was it committed to any
particular religious (or anti-religious) sect, or any specific set of
moral values or patterns of moral behaviour. Consequently we
have had to work out our own interpretation of moral education:
we have not been able to assume that being 'morally educated'
means behaving like a good Christian, or an emancipated artist,
or a decent member of the British middle classes, or anything at
all. We have not been able to take our own moral values, or those
of our Trust, as the right ones, and then get on with the job of
finding out how to make children and teenagers believe in those
values and live up to them.

Had we in fact done anything of the kind, we should have
made two very bad mistakes which would have vitiated most of
our work. In some of the research already done on this subject,
or tangentially connected with it, many workers seem to have
failed to cope adequately with the problem of definition, because
of the temptation to make one of two errors. To quote examples
would be long-winded and might be unduly polemic, but they
amount to:

(a) Failure to realize the difficulties that attach to the justification of any set of moral values, and to the whole notion of imposing one's specific moral or religious views on other people.
Thus if this Unit had taken a certain set of moral values for
granted, and shown the most efficient way in which children
could be made to believe them, not only might many people disagree with these values and so refuse to teach them, but even
those who agreed and taught them would not (we shall try to
show) have really been 'morally educating' the children. They
would have told them about what *this Unit thinks* is morally
right, but this is not *moral* education at all. Information about the
value-judgements of the Unit would be neither interesting nor
profitable, since we do not set up as expert moralists: indeed, it
is not at all clear in what sense there can be such things as 'expert moralists'.[1] They might also have indoctrinated[2] their

children with our moral values; but this too (apart from being, in our view, unjustifiable) would not be moral *education*. This we shall also try to show.

(b) The second error is to assume that definitions can be arbitrary. Before inflicting a certain amount of conceptual analysis on the reader, we must make it plain that without both a *clear* and an *adequate* interpretation of 'moral education', a good deal of research and practical work in this field is likely to miss the point. It is easy to produce a clear definition: we could say, for instance, that 'morally educated' people are simply those who do not come before the juvenile courts, or who win medals for bravery: but to make it adequate as well as clear calls for a lot of hard work. It is here that some philosophizing is essential: for there is no way of getting an adequate definition except by examining the use and meanings of words, and the ways in which those uses and meanings are interconnected. Words are governed by rules, of which we are often unaware. Because they are governed by rules, we can speak of an 'adequate' interpretation of the phrase 'moral education' and because we are often unaware of them, we need to do some philosophy. How we use the phrase is not wholly a matter for decision, much less for arbitrary decision. Of course it would be nice to be able to frame one's own definition, particularly since an adequate definition may be difficult to cash out in terms of empirical tests: but it would be cheating. In the same way, we could easily enough run a research project on 'Marital Happiness', and check up on how often married couples kissed each other or called each other 'darling'. The only trouble is that this would not tell us much about marital happiness.

It is worth noting that the second error really includes the first. If we are right in what we have already implied, and will go on to say, about not imposing one's values on others, or about indoctrination and conditioning being different from education, we shall not be right because of some superior moral insight, or because it is fashionable to be liberal, or because we have had much practical experience in this field. Our thesis will depend on whether we can so direct the reader's attention to the use of logic and language that he will come to see the relevant points for himself.

One can readily understand why many people lack the patience or the inclination to work out adequate definitions. The research worker, for instance, who is anxious to prove *something* at least, cannot wait while we argue about words like 'love' or 'democracy' or 'morality'. He wants an operational definition as soon as possible: and preferably one which will enable him to observe behaviour experimentally. The snag with this is not only that we cannot be sure that what he is doing research on is really at all related to what we usually mean by 'love', 'democracy' or 'morality': that is perhaps inevitable, and the research may be valuable just the same. It is rather that, as we shall see,[3] any research which covers the field of human action, in the full sense of the phrase, will miss the point if it is restricted to observation of physical movements. Unfortunately, many interesting research topics involve human action and intention and hence fall into this category. This is a difficulty which some empirical psychologists and sociologists have perhaps not fully faced.

One can also sympathize with those who feel that this sort of linguistic analysis is unnecessary – a form of academic quibbling or logic-chopping. Perhaps they feel that we already know well enough what we mean by X, or Y, or Z. In a sense this is true: that is, we usually employ the words correctly enough when we talk. But in another sense it is false: that is, we are not conscious of the rules governing their use.[4] Because of this, we are liable to make mistakes and get into muddles. 'Are all criminals really insane?' 'Can we help indoctrinating children?', 'Is there an absolute right and wrong?', 'Can you prove that there is a God?' – all these questions include words which we normally use quite correctly: yet they all betoken our ignorance of the rules. For the questions are only answerable by a closer look at what we mean by 'criminals', 'insane', 'indoctrinate', 'right', 'prove', 'God' and so on. They are not questions of fact, but conceptual questions. And if anybody doubts whether conceptual questions have more than academic importance, let him consider whether 'academic' would be the *mot juste* for a situation in which a man was forcibly committed to an asylum, or sentenced to death, because of one particular and questionable interpretation of a word like 'sane'.

We are faced, therefore, with the very difficult task of trying to make some sort of conceptual sense of the notion of 'moral education'. The difficulty is increased by the joint facts (a) that this is not the place to attempt a very scholarly account which might be of interest only to professional philosophers, (b) nevertheless it is essential that the ordinary reader should grasp the conceptual considerations which lie behind our general approach, if the approach as a whole is to make sense to him. Arguments about moral philosophy are endless, and we cannot of course hope that this account will settle anything definitively. But we owe it to the reader to give as full an account as possible, if only because a very brief account would not paint an honest picture of the way in which this Unit is starting off – whether the way be right or wrong. So I hope that readers of various kinds will forgive the slightly uneasy compromise which is bound to result from a task of this sort: indeed, from any task which consists in trying to bring a particular academic discipline to bear on what is ultimately a practical subject.

Notes to Introduction

1. See pp. 168–76.
2. In this Part of the book I use words like 'indoctrinate', 'condition', and others in a very general way, which does not accord with the more specific meanings attached to them by psychologists. See p. 176.
3. See pp. 52–5.
4. This is perhaps one of the most important, and certainly one of the most difficult, points to get across. It's really this: People may *say* that they mean something by a word, *but they may be wrong*. For instance, someone might say 'Well, what *I* mean by "moral" is such-and-such' (having feelings of guilt, being law-abiding, or whatever), as if that settled the question for him, and as if any attempt to show him that he was wrong was just bullying him into accepting someone else's definition. But if in fact he doesn't normally use the word 'moral' in this way, then he doesn't mean what he says he means by it. Thus if he would in fact describe some situations as 'moral' even if a man didn't feel guilty or didn't abide by the law, then he hasn't given a correct account of the rules by which he actually uses the word. Words can of course be used in different senses, but for a word to have any sense at all it must be used in accordance with a set of rules governing its use, and not just arbitrarily. Meaning depends on following these rules, and we can always be mistaken about what rules we are actually following: hence we can always be mistaken about what we mean.

CHAPTER I

MORALITY AND FREEDOM

WE might begin by asking 'What is "moral education"?' and a quick answer to this question might be 'Getting children to behave morally'. I want to show here in what respects this answer is inadequate, and indeed dangerously misleading; and then to sketch the outlines of a more satisfactory picture of moral education.

The words 'moral', 'morality' and 'morally' are used in all sorts of ways, and we need not get involved in too lengthy a dispute about their various senses. It is sufficient for our purposes in this chapter to draw a general distinction between two types of use:

A. 'Moral' (as contrasted with 'immoral'), is often used as a term of approval.

B. 'Moral' is used as a descriptive term, to classify a particular kind of action or belief. Its opposite here is simply 'not moral' or 'non-moral' (as when we say, 'It's not a moral issue, it's simply a matter of taste').

But this descriptive or classificatory sense can be based on different criteria and hence mean different things:

(i) It can be used in a 'sociological' sense. Sociologists and historians commonly talk about 'the morality' of a particular society or social group, about what counted as 'moral' or 'immoral' behaviour in ancient Sparta or during the Victorian age in England. Here we refer to a particular code, or set of *mores*. When we use these words with reference to our own society we often bring in sense A. above, with its overtones of praise or blame: we say 'that's a most immoral thing to do', meaning that it is against the current moral code, and probably also implying our condemnation of the action.

(ii) It can be used to mark out a particular kind of human thought and action, not on the basis of what the *mores* of a particular society are, but on some other basis. Thus when we say 'The ancient Hebrews thought that whether or not you ate certain kinds of food was a moral issue, but I don't think it is', or

'What sort of clothes you wear isn't really a moral issue, it's a matter of taste', we are obviously not thinking just of what the *mores* of a particular society are. We seem rather to be making some kind of logical or conceptual classification of the area of morality, quite apart from what anyone *regards* (rightly or wrongly) as that area.

Quite a lot of this book will be devoted to elucidating the notion of 'moral' in sense B. (ii) above. In order to do this, it will be convenient to start from a naïve picture of 'moral education' which is cast in terms of getting people to 'behave morally' in sense B. (i) above. Let us see whether we want to make people 'behave morally' in this sense:[1] that is, whether we want to make them act in accordance with the rules current in our society, or in accordance with some other specific set of rules. To many people this may seem not only an attractive but even an adequate programme. It appears at least to have the merit of simplicity. We know which actions count as 'moral' and 'immoral', i.e. which actions keep the rules and which break the rules: all we have to do is to find out how to make people perform actions of the first type and avoid actions of the second type. We might formulate this programme by saying that we want people to tell the truth, keep promises, respect other people's property, refrain from murder, and so on. What are the difficulties with this programme?

A. INTENTIONS AND REASONS

The essential point to understand here is that such concepts as 'telling the truth', 'keeping a promise', 'stealing', 'being kind', etc. *involve more than just a set of noises or physical movements*. They involve also the notions of *intention*, of *understanding*, and *knowing what you are doing*. The general importance of these can be grasped most quickly if we ask ourselves why animals, or machines, or infants cannot tell the truth, or keep promises, or steal, or be kind or cruel. A parrot might say 'It's a fine day' when it was a fine day, or when it wasn't: but it would not be telling the truth or lying. You could build a robot to say 'I promise to be here when you come back', and it might be there when you came back: but it would not have made or kept a promise. If

I put sixpence in a ticket machine, and it doesn't give me a ticket but just takes the money, I couldn't say it had *stolen* it, except as a sort of joke. It is significant that the joke would really consist of regarding the machine as if it were a person, as if there were a little man inside.

People can do these things because they know what they are doing. They don't just go through the motions: they *act intentionally*. Similarly, they don't just make noises that happen to be words: they *speak meaningfully*. Moral words are all tied down, in varying degrees, to the notion of intention. You can't murder somebody by mistake, because 'murder' means 'intending to kill'. You can't lie by mistake, because in order to lie you've got to know that you're lying. You can't make a promise entirely by accident, because 'making a promise' entails committing yourself, usually by some form of words (like 'I promise') uttered in a context which you know is regarded as morally binding: if a foreigner said 'I promise', thinking that it meant 'I hope', he might be very stupid or negligent, but he wouldn't have made a promise.

Another way of putting this is in terms of free will. Suppose somebody throws me forcibly against another person, so that my body hits that person and kills him. I have not murdered him, since what happened was not the result of any free choice of mine. Indeed, it would be rather misleading to say 'I killed him', at least without further explanation, since even the word 'kill' often implies that I did something intentionally, whereas in this case I have, in a sense, done nothing at all: I have merely had my body used as an instrument. We could imagine a series of cases, in which varying degrees of kinds of pressure were put upon me: physical force, hypnotic commands, threats, and so forth. In all these cases, my responsibility is diminished,[2] because I am acting to some extent under duress. The point here is that my *moral* responsibility is diminished, because my responsibility for *what happens* is diminished; what happens is not something that *I* (freely) *do*.

It can be seen from this that if a person is to act morally, he must know what he is doing, and must do it freely – that is, it must really be *he* who does it, and not some form of duress or compulsion that makes him do it. One difficulty with a programme of 'making people behave morally', even in the primitive sense of 'keeping the rules of society', is now apparent. For even in this sense there is a conflict between the idea of *making* or *forcing* (in a very strong sense) somebody to do something, and his doing it *freely* or *intentionally*:[3] and if intentionality is required for moral action, then we cannot make people act morally. For instance, we could in principle devise a machine which paralysed a person's arm if he tried to touch anything that belonged to someone else, or tried to assault someone else: and we might be tempted to say that we had 'made him refrain' from stealing or from assault. But this would only be true in a very weak sense. It is true that he doesn't take the property, but not true that he (deliberately or intentionally) refrains from taking it: he just doesn't take it – he can't take it.

What we can do, if we want, is to make people go through certain motions, or sets of physical movements, which might *look like* cases of people acting morally. The object of this might be to keep them out of trouble, or to stop them being a nuisance. If I condition a child, by giving it electric shocks, so that it can never shout loudly or bump into other people, then one might be tempted to talk of the child as 'well-behaved'. The same result could be achieved by putting a silencer over its mouth and tying it in a straitjacket. Certainly it is 'well-behaved' in a sense: but in another sense it is not *behaving* or *acting* at all:[3] it has no choice. Later[4] we will go into the question of whether this kind of conditioning is legitimate: here I want to make the point that it will not do as an account of 'moral education'.

'Raw' feelings

If the notion of a moral action demands more than a set of physical movements, so too does it demand more than a set of feelings. Thus moral virtues like 'kindness' or 'honesty' are not reducible to a collection of consistent impulses or psychological promptings. Somebody who is kind to animals is not *simply* somebody who feels impelled to feed cats, angry when horses are ill-treated, or guilty at having to leave his dog in a dog's home. These 'raw' feelings and impulses may *motivate* kind actions, but they are not the whole story. The impulse to feed animals may result in over-feeding them, so that they become ill or die. Here we feel inclined to say that this is not kindness but cruelty. What we should say is that it is neither. A raw feeling which leads to an action, may – accidentally, as it were – result in behaviour which we might call 'kind' (just as an electric shock might result in a chess-player making 'the right' move): but kindness is not just the feeling-plus-action. Kindness is an intentional or voluntary disposition: a person who is kind to animals is disposed to act in the animals' interests, and he will follow or check his impulses to feed animals according to those interests.

Similarly, a man may have raw feelings of guilt on certain occasions, e.g. when confronted by customs officers. Sometimes these may correlate with his 'immoral' behaviour, if for instance he is actually smuggling something: but at other times they may not – some people feel guilty even if they aren't smuggling anything at all. To *feel* guilty in itself is no indication of honesty or dishonesty. Morality begins only when the man *thinks* that he ought or ought not to smuggle. He might arrive at either of these beliefs partly as a result of his feeling guilty, but he might also arrive at them as a result of other considerations (such as whether he is damaging the country's economy, whether it will involve him in lying, and so on). He behaves honestly if he is following some rule or acting on some belief, not if he is merely impelled by a feeling of guilt.[5]

Reasons and Causes

The notion of acting intentionally or freely, whether in the moral field or elsewhere, is connected logically with other equally important notions. One way of noticing this is to see that we may ask for two quite different kinds of explanation for somebody's behaviour, using two different senses of the word 'Why', as follows:

(a) We may be asking for a scientific cause, or for some general law of nature of which this particular occurrence is an instance. Thus we can ask 'Why did Newton's apple fall downwards?', and give some such answer as 'Whenever there is mass, there is gravitational attraction'; and we can ask 'Why did he fall over the cliff?', and answer 'He was pushed hard enough to carry him over the edge'. The 'Why?' here means simply 'As a result of what cause?'

(b) We may be asking for his rational justification. 'Why did you build a castle?', 'To protect my king'; or 'Why did you suddenly put on the brakes?', 'In order to avoid a smash'. The 'why' here means something like 'For what purpose?', or 'With what aim or intention?', or 'For what reasons?'

'Why', 'because', 'for the reason that' and other words and phrases are ambiguous between these two senses: and in fact, when we ask questions beginning 'Why ... ?', we often get the kind of answer which we did not expect (assuming we were clear about what sort of answer we *did* expect, which is not always the case). Thus we might ask 'Why did you go to church?', and he might reply by giving some sort of justification 'In order to worship God, in whom I believe for the following reasons ...'. But he might reply to the first sense of 'Why?', treating himself not as a human being with intentions, but as a sort of psychological case – almost as a physical object: 'Oh, I expect I was indoctrinated with religion by my nanny', or 'Well, upper-middle class people in this area always do go to church', or even 'Her father made me go, he had a shotgun stuck in my back'. Similarly we might ask 'Why did you brake the car?', expect him to say 'In order to avoid a smash', but actually get the answer 'I didn't intend to, I suddenly got cramp and my foot shot out onto the brake pedal'.

It is plain from these examples that 'Why?'-questions about human action normally expect an answer of the second type: that is, some explanation or justification in terms of the agent's intentions, aims, purposes or reasons. All intentional action can be explained in this way: part of what we mean by an intentional action is, precisely, that this sort of 'Why?'-question can be applied to it.[6] Thus if we asked somebody why he cheated at a game, or told a lie, or broke a promise, we would expect him to say something like 'In order to win the prize', or 'I wanted the other person to think I was a hero', or 'Because keeping the promise would have meant leaving my old mother to die alone'. If it turned out that he could not (sincerely) quote a reason if asked, we would suspect that he had no reason or intention at all; and we would have to stop thinking that he had, in fact, cheated or lied or broken a promise: for all these are, as we have seen,[7] tied to the notion of intention.

Acting for a reason

It is roughly on these grounds that moral action is tied to the notion of rationality. But we must be careful to understand what is meant by 'rationality' here. Take again the case of the person who brakes his car to avoid a smash. This is a rational action, and the man 'has a reason' for doing it. But it need not be the case that he acted deliberately, in the sense of making a conscious choice, or going through any process of ratiocination: he need not be *thinking about* what he is doing. In a sense, one might say that he did it out of habit: just as he habitually turns on the ignition before pressing the self-starter.[8] Nor is it the case that his action has got to be a good or sensible one. A motorist might apply the brakes when his car skids, though in fact it might be better if he did not brake, but straightened the wheels instead. But this would still be, in one sense, a rational action: that is, he would have braked *in order to* stop the car skidding. He would have been following a rule ('when skids, then brake'), even though it would have been a wrong rule.

If people are to act morally at all, therefore, they must act for a reason in this sense: they must not be, so to speak, just pushed around by causes. There is thus a vital distinction between feelings of guilt, repulsion, aversion, taboo, etc. (or strong desires, passions, and impulses) which make people avoid or seek out certain things, and people acting voluntarily, intentionally, and for a reason.[9] If I ask somebody 'Why don't you eat human flesh?' and he says 'I just can't swallow it, my revulsion is so great', he has given me a causal answer, and has said nothing about having moral reasons or any sort of justification. If, on the other hand, he says, 'Well, I could eat it, but I think it is wrong to do so, because . . .' then he has given me a rational justification (whether a good or a bad justification does not matter here).

Rational actions, we might say, are those for which the agent is responsible. They are attempts which *we* make (not physical movements forced on us) to meet a particular situation in the

Not "morality"?

external world: the situation of an imminent crash, or of pieces placed on a chess-board, or of people living in a particular relationship or in society at large. Rationality is the characteristically human way of dealing with the world. Consequently we can be had up, so to speak, for dealing with it well or badly. If we are not acting rationally (in this narrow sense), we cannot be had up at all: for it is not *we* who are responsible. We can neither get good marks for good moral behaviour, or bad marks for bad behaviour.

Rationalization

If an action is to fall within the moral sphere, therefore, it must be rational: and this implies that it must be done for a reason (not just as a result of a cause).[10] But this means more than that the agent must in principle be able to say why he did it. It means that the reason must also be causally operative: it must not be a rationalization. Thus a man might never eat human beings, be able to give excellent reasons why eating them was wrong, and think that these reasons were what influenced his behaviour: yet it might still be true that what really stopped him eating people was some unconscious feeling of guilt or taboo. We could indeed say in one sense that what he did, considered by itself, was rational: that is, that reasons could be given for it. But in a more important sense *he* would not be acting rationally.

It is likely that a great deal of our behaviour is rationalized rather than rational, in this sense. To take another example, it may be that there are good biological reasons for not committing incest: but it is not at all clear that these reasons are *our* reasons, except in the sense that we can quote them. One could test this by supposing a situation where it was rationally desirable to mate with one's close relations (perhaps we are the last survivors of the human race), and seeing whether this change in the facts would actually produce a change of behaviour – for if our anti-incest behaviour was rationally motivated, then we would be flexible enough to alter it. In the same way there are pacifists who never fight because, in effect, they are not psychologically capable of killing (perhaps they have a deep unconscious dread of shedding blood, or something), and pacifists who never figh because they believe (rightly or wrongly) that no situation could arise in which killing would be justified. Both may give the same account of why they act as they do, but the former would be rationalizing: whereas the latter, if presented with a situation in which killing was justified, would be prepared to kill.[11]

The degree to which an action or a belief are rational is connected with how far they are really *our own*: that is, how far they are the result of our facing facts and responding freely, rather than compulsively, to them. Insofar as our actions approximate to mere reactions or reflex movements, and our beliefs to sets of words which are merely parrotted or accepted solely on authority, to that extent we fall away from acting and thinking as moral agents.[12]

Morality without intentions?

Perhaps this will suffice at least to raise some general doubts about the sort of programme I have been criticizing. But let us now examine more closely the respects in which a minimal sense of 'acting morally' falls short of what I take to be a more normal or at least a fuller sense: and see also why these deficiences are important.

What have we lost if we use a weaker sense of 'acting morally'? We could certainly condition people so that they did not steal, did not lie, did not break promises, etc.: but only in the sense that ticket-machines do not steal, cameras do not lie, and planets do not break promises. They do not do these things, not because they are 'morally educated', but because these things belong to a category which does not apply to ticket-machines and other physical objects. Pigs can't fly: but this is not the sense of 'can't' to which I am pointing. The sense is that in which pigs can't be fish, or in which justice can't weigh a ton. In the same way, we could not wholly condition people to 'refrain from stealing' or to 'keep a promise': because, to the extent to which we have conditioned them, they would have lost the power of choice and, we might say, to that extent ceased to be people. They couldn't steal *or* refrain from stealing: the category just wouldn't apply to them.

We may still say, if we like, that such people would 'act

morally' or 'behave morally'. We could say that pigs 'behave morally' (unless they are wild boars and kill people, in which case one might say they were 'behaving immorally'): but all we would mean by this is that they were 'doing' things which happened to be against the moral rules of our society. But the whole notion of knowing rules and following rules is obviously intended to apply to creatures who act intentionally – that is, to men with some freedom of choice: and words like 'act', 'behave', and all moral words are at home in this context, and appear grotesque out of it. Non-intentional creatures can, by accident or conditioning, in a sense 'act' *in accordance with* the rules set up by intentional creatures: but they cannot *follow* such rules, since 'follow' normally implies intention. Parrots 'talk', but they don't deliberately follow the rules of language.

Let us consider a chess game. We can see why it is that people who were conditioned, rather than *taught*, to make certain moves in certain situations could only be said to be 'playing chess' in an unusually weak sense: the sense in which a robot might be programmed to play chess, or a trained seal might play a tune on a xylophone. 'But what is wrong with this?' we might say. 'If we can be conditioned to play chess, in whatever sense you like, so well that we always win, wouldn't this be very useful? Does it matter if we're not "really" playing?' There are, after all, plenty of situations where we do not want to have scope for different intentions or free choice. If I am a parachute jumper in a war, it might be much better for me to be trained or conditioned so that I could not help jumping on the word of command, rather than be allowed or encouraged to jump deliberately. In the same way, so long as what I do in the moral field (in however weak a sense of 'do') is good, in that it will keep me happy, not give trouble to others, etc., does it matter whether I do it intentionally or as a result of conditioning?

Some objections

Now there are all sorts of considerations that may make us hesitate before accepting this, and it is important to distinguish them.

(a) First, we might have some practical doubts about the

efficacy and wisdom of such a process. These would perhaps take
three forms:

(i)[13] Would the process be delicate or flexible enough to cover the
moral contingencies that the individual meets with? We
should have to 'programme' the person very subtly in order
to allow for the many exceptions: 'Do not steal – except in
wartime from the enemy, or to get a first-aid kit in an emer-
gency, or perhaps if your little children are starving': 'Do not
physically restrain people – except when they are about to
fall under buses, or go mad and brandish axes, or . . .' and so
forth.

(ii)[13] Would the process be reversible? For certain conditioned
behaviour originally thought good might, as a result of
individual reflection or social changes, come to seem undesirable: and then we would want the conditioning altered or reversed.

(iii) Would we lose more than we gained by the process? Thus
we can prevent people from stealing by paralysing their limbs,
but we also thereby prevent them from moving. We would, no
doubt, prevent outbursts of aggression by constant sedation:
but we should also thereby diminish energy, enthusiasm and
so forth. This is a familiar worry to those that use brain surgery and other non-rational methods to cope with mental illness, and we do well to bear it in mind.

(b) Other doubts would arise if the conditioning were to be
done against the will, or without the consent, of the person concerned. Thus if I volunteer to be a parachute jumper, knowing
that this will involve my being conditioned to jump on the word
of command, or if I go to a hypnotist in order to be conditioned
against smoking, this might be acceptable: but if I am conditioned against my will, as happened to people in Huxley's *Brave
New World* or Orwell's *1984*, we might have objections to make.

(c) Another set of doubts may arise once we realize how far we
have strayed from our normal conception of morality: not only,
as we have hitherto argued, in that we shall be producing people
who cannot in a full sense act morally (refrain from stealing, tell
the truth, etc.), for that has been admitted: but in that there can
now be no question of people acting from the right sort of
motives, or on the right *principles*, for the right reasons, or with

the right *ideals* or *sentiments*. For all these words are essentially
connected with freedom and intention. Duty, love, moral obligations, unselfishness, noble principles, high ideals – all these become meaningless: even words standing for specific moral
virtues – courage, honesty, temperance, chastity, and so on – lose
their sense. For these all involve a disposition to act deliberately
in certain ways. Machines, animals and conditioned people cannot be honest or dishonest, chaste or unchaste.

(d) The people we condition could not themselves use moral
language in its normal sense. For such language is essentially
connected with choice and commitment. Thus to describe certain actions as 'good' in the moral sense involves committing
oneself to a rule, just as acting involves following a rule. To say
that one ought to do something, in the moral sense, or that it is
right to do it implies that one can do it: that one is free to do it or
not to do it. A person who had no powers of moral choice would
have no use for a language which made moral discriminations:
any more than a person who had been conditioned to make certain moves in chess, without the least understanding of what the
game was about, would have any use for phrases like 'a skilful
move', or 'a well-planned defence'.

(e) We might also have doubts about how far this programme
could be carried. This sort of conditioning only seems to have
point for beings who, when they are not so conditioned, act
freely and purposely in order to achieve their own ends. The
point of conditioning a paratrooper to jump on the word of command is so that *somebody* at least can achieve the end of fighting
the enemy effectively. The 'somebody' may be the general
rather than the paratrooper: the paratrooper may be conditioned
against his will, in which case our doubts in (b) above would
recur. Similarly I may programme a computer so that it wins a
game of chess for me (or would we more naturally say that *I* had
won it?). But if somebody at least was not acting freely and intentionally in these situations, there would be no point at all in
the conditioning: it would serve no purpose. Conditioning is thus
a tool which you can use: but its point depends on there being a
free 'you' to use it, to gain some advantage by it.

B. What Kind of Reasons?

So far we have tried to elucidate one basic difficulty with the apparently simple programme we have been criticizing, the programme which interprets 'moral education' as 'getting people to behave morally'. Because the notions of intention and rationality are so closely linked with the notions of human action and behaviour, we can see that there is more to the word 'acting', in the phrase 'acting morally', than met the eye. I want now to turn to another basic difficulty, of a different kind. This may be obscurely hinted at by saying that we have to be sure, not only that a person is *acting* morally, but that he is acting *morally*; and I shall now try to clarify this hint.

The reader who has followed us so far may still be inclined to say something like this: 'I understand that action involves intention, and I grant that if we are to talk of people acting morally they must be acting for a reason, neither just "going through the motions" nor just rationalizing. I also grant that merely to condition people's behaviour, even though it may often be useful, cannot be the whole of moral education, and that there are many serious objections to it. But then, I never intended to bring up children in the sort of way you have been criticizing, as if they were pigs or machines, merely by conditioning. Indeed, I want them to act intentionally and act for reasons. But so long as they do this, it doesn't seem to me to matter what *sorts* of reasons or intentions they have. Thus so long as they don't steal, I don't care whether they do it "because they fear God", "because they do what their mother tells them", "because it's against the law" or for any other reason – just so long as they deliberately refrain from it, I shall call them "morally educated". Is there anything wrong with this?'

It is not so much wrong as inadequate. Consider the parallel case of a person playing chess. Suppose first that his intentions and choices do not enter into the matter at all – for instance, that somebody grasps his hand and forces him to move certain pieces, or that he is just responding to hypnotic commands. He can hardly be said to be playing chess at all: for it is not really *he* who is making the moves. Now suppose that he makes all his moves intentionally and for reasons, but for reasons which have no real connexion with the purpose or state of the game: for instance, he might try to keep the arrangement of his pieces always symmetrical, or make moves his father used to make just because he admired his father as a person. In what sense can he be said to be 'playing chess'?

There is certainly an obvious sense in which he is doing so: that is, he is keeping the rules of chess and making his moves intentionally. But we might be tempted to say that what he is really doing is to make up pretty patterns of symmetrical pieces on the board, or to go through ritual moves in honour of his admired father. If he had no thought for the actual chess-situation before him, we could not speak of him as 'building up an attack', or 'threatening his opponent's bishop', or 'strengthening his defence': for all these phrases normally imply that he is acting intelligently – that he is deliberately following certain rules and principles of the chess-strategy, rather than just moving his pieces in a way that happens accidentally to accord with such rules and principles. For the same reasons, we could not *praise* or *blame* him as a chessplayer, since all the words and phrases we would use to praise or blame him ('making full use of his queen', 'keeping his king out of trouble', 'being careless about his pawns', etc.) imply that he is acting with an eye on the real situation – that he is 'chess-orientated', so to speak.

A casual external observer might say that he was playing chess: and within limits this would be correct. But a more serious observer, who put himself in the place of the agent, might prefer to say that he was *using* the game of chess to do something different: perhaps to make patterns or carry out rituals. Such a player might not understand what chess is about at all – what the purpose of a chess-game is, or how to play it well. In the same way, a person might be said to 'act morally', in the sense that his actions were deliberate and intentional, and accorded with recognized moral rules, even though his reasons for acting might have nothing to do with the real moral situations. But this sense reminds us of the 'sociological' sense of 'morality' which we noticed at the beginning of this chapter: and there is something missing if we adhere wholly to this sense. What is missing may perhaps be put by saying that he is not necessarily acting *as a moral being*.

The implications of this notion of a 'moral being' – what we could describe as a 'morally educated' person – can be brought out by considering two remarks of Aristotle. He says: 'Actions, to be sure, are *called* just and temperate when they are such as a just or temperate man would do. But the doer is just or temperate not because he does such things but when he does them in the way of just and temperate persons':[14] and earlier, using a parallel: 'It is possible to spell a word right by accident or because somebody tips you the answer. But you will be a scholar only if your spelling is done as a scholar does it, that is thanks to the scholarship in your own mind'.[15] The point here is that, if we are interested in the man himself, and not just in his overt behaviour, we have to take into account the nature of his motives, reasons or intentions, and not just what he (overtly) does.

Thus, suppose a person refuses a drink before driving simply because he is frightened that the police will catch and convict him: then it would be wrong to describe him as a temperate *man*. It would even be misleading to say that he was 'acting temperately'. From the external observer's point of view this might be accurate enough: but we feel tempted to say something like 'He isn't *really* being temperate, he's just trying to avoid being convicted by the police'. Again, if a person distributes sweets to children in a fair and equitable manner, we can no doubt say that he is 'acting justly': but if we learn that his only reason for doing this is that he is frightened of what the childrens' parents will say if he doesn't do it, then we should say that he is not acting out of a belief in justice, but out of fear: and certainly that he is not necessarily a just *man*.

The case is even stronger when we talk of people acting 'kindly', 'unselfishly', 'sympathetically' or 'courageously'. Here we seem to be even more interested in the man's *motives* or *reasons* for action. We say things like 'He wasn't really being unselfish, he had an ulterior motive' or 'What he did only seemed to be brave, actually he didn't realize the danger'. As Aristotle says, we can of course *call* what these people do 'a kind action', 'a brave action', etc. But the connexion between action and intention is so close that this can often be more misleading than accurate. We can say 'This is the sort of thing a kind, brave, etc. person would do'. But in so far as we are interested in the man himself, or his motives, then we have to go further than the overt behaviour. It is not enough to know that he is behaving intentionally (rather than just 'going through the motions' as a result of conditioning): we have to know what *sort* of intentions he has.

Any serious concern with moral education must surely take motives and reasons into account. Whether or not we can say that a person is 'acting morally' if his motives and reasons are of the wrong kind[16] is, indeed, a more open question, which we shall consider briefly in the next chapter. We shall have to allow room for saying that a person's actions and beliefs can be genuinely moral but also misguided, mistaken, and (in certain senses) irrational. It would be too high-handed to say that if a man does not have the right moral beliefs, then he does not have moral beliefs at all. All I hope to have shown here is that the 'internal' point of view, where we try to find out what a person intends and what he is trying to do, what his reasons and motives are, is as important for moral education as any knowledge of his external behaviour.

C. DISPOSITIONS AND FEELINGS

The present objection, then, to that interpretation of 'getting people to act morally' which entails simply that people intentionally follow the moral code or *mores* of their society (or any other *mores*) is that it is inadequate for the notion of moral education. Until we know what morality is about, we cannot be sure than any particular *mores* enshrine *moral* rules, or that any particular individual is following them *as* moral rules. Hence we are driven to the notion of the individual as a moral being: that is, as somebody who partakes of a particular activity involving a particular kind of thought and action – somebody, we might say, who partakes in a particular form of life. We are driven most obviously in this direction by the case just mentioned, which indicates that the *kinds* of reasons a person has are important if we are to say that he is acting morally, as opposed to just acting intentionally in what is socially accepted as a moral area. But I think we should want to go further still. We should want to assess people, not only by the kinds of reasons that motivate them, but by their general attitudes, feelings and dispositions: that is, not only by what they *do* (even if we include the reasons they have for doing it), but also by what they *feel*.

This may also be illustrated from what Aristotle says: 'But virtuous actions are not done in a virtuous – a just or temperate – way merely because *they* have the appropriate quality. The *doer* must be in a certain frame of mind when he does them. Three conditions are involved. (1) The agent must act in full consciousness of what he is doing. (2) He must "will" his action, and will it for its own sake. (3) The act must proceed from a fixed and unchangeable disposition.'[17] Later he adds 'By "dispositions" I mean states of mind in virtue of which we are well or ill disposed in respect of the feelings concerned'.[18] This is to say that, if we are interested in a truly 'morally educated' man, we need to look not only at (1) whether what he does is done freely, 'in full consciousness'; nor only at (2) whether he has the right sort of reasons: that is, whether he chooses to do what he does 'for its own sake' (rather than out of fear, or merely in obedience to authority); but also (3) whether he has the right sort of disposition, the right state of mind.

There are many very important cases of people being morally inadequate, or wicked, or having a bad character, which we should most naturally describe in terms of his disposition or 'state of mind', rather than in other terms. Consider a mother who is cruel or indifferent to her children, without actually beating or starving them. We might find it comparatively hard to pin down specifically immoral pieces of behaviour, but we might nevertheless want to say 'She doesn't love them': and we might well feel strongly about this, and consider that it does great harm to the children. Now no doubt her lack of love will be evinced in some form of behaviour: she will do things, or fail to do things, that she would not do or fail to do if she loved the children. But in criticizing her we would not be criticizing her *solely*, nor perhaps even chiefly, for what she *did*. We should criticize what she felt (or did not feel), and this would certainly be moral criticism in some sense of the word.[19] We all know parents who, in a fairly obvious sense, 'do all the right things' for their children, but nevertheless bring them up badly because they fail to show affection in various ways, some of which may be in practice undetectable. What is basically wrong is that they are not disposed in the right way towards their children: and to improve them, we would first have to change that disposition. It might, in this and other similar cases, be comparatively useless to lay down rules of behaviour for the parents to follow: it may be impossible to put on the necessary display of affection unless they genuinely loved them.

In the next chapter we shall see that the notion of morality, as it affects moral education, includes much more than adherence to particular *mores*. Thus, as we may guess, it includes the notion of relating to other people as to equals, and knowing what their interests are, as well as acting in accordance with those interests. It also includes the notion of managing one's own desires and feelings in the right way, even if the interest of others is not obviously involved: this would apply to such cases as choosing whom to marry, what job to do, whether to take drugs or whether to engage in 'perverse' sexual behaviour. Both of these notions go beyond conformity to *mores*, and both lead us to stress the importance of feeling and attitude.[20]

The tradition of western moral philosophy, from Aristotle to the present day, by laying stress on the question 'What shall I *do*?' as the central (generalized) question with which morality is concerned, has tended to mask the importance of attitude as against action. At the risk of grossly over-simplifying, therefore, we may conclude by some brief remarks tending to the opposite extreme. These may at least serve to redress a balance which, I believe, badly needs to be redressed if we are to have an adequate picture of what 'moral education' is really about.

Suppose I collect paintings, and want to collect good ones. Suppose that my only reason for buying some and rejecting others is that I follow the judgement of some art critic. In such a case we can say, first, that what I am doing may be perfectly rational, if my object is simply to possess good paintings, and if the critic is a good critic: and secondly, that I can make aesthetic judgements about the paintings on a rational basis – I can say This is a good painting, because Sir Kenneth Clark says so'. Now, what is missing in this situation? Nothing is missing in the field of what I overtly *do* or choose to do: I might buy, sell, take care of, give advice about and otherwise *act* in relation to pictures in just the same way as a person who appreciated pictures for their own sake and whose actions were determined by his own appreciation. What is missing is that I do not *feel* anything about the pictures aesthetically. I do not see them as works of art: I see them only as means to an end, the end of possessing good pictures.

This situation by itself will not teach me aesthetics, or make me 'aesthetically educated'. It may nevertheless be a very good basis for such education, by providing me with the preconditions: that is, I may say 'I want to appreciate good pictures, so I will start by buying those which Sir Kenneth Clark recommends, and then I will look at them very hard and see if I can see something in them'. But the essentially aesthetic part of this consists in my own reactions to the pictures. The fact that, when I come to have appropriate reactions of my own, I may then be able to make correct choices without using the authority of the critic, is purely incidental: though it may of course be very useful if the critic is ill, or if I come up against a situation where the critic's authority is not to be trusted.

This is, so to speak, like the chess-game where the man is told what moves to make, only more so. In fact we might construct a rough scale of different activities, as follows:

(a) There are some situations in which we are anxious to get something done, and do not much mind how it gets done. A schoolboy who has to write 1,000 lines is quite willing to use a line-writing machine (if there is such a thing), or to get someone else to write them for him, so long as the lines are written in time. Similarly a sick man seeks only to be cured: he does not care if he swallows pills, or is injected by a doctor, or has to do exercises every morning so long as he achieves his goal – in fact, the less trouble he has to take the better.

(b) In other situations the ostensible object of the activity may not be its only point. Thus the object of the game of chess is to mate the opponent's king: and a man might play with this object in view. But he would not like another person to tell him all his moves: for apart from wanting to win, he also wants the pleasure and interest of working the situations out for himself. Similarly a boy who wants to understand and enjoy mathematics will not want his father to do *all* his homework for him.

(c) In other situations again we may indulge in an activity for its own sake. I may enjoy music or paintings, or the company of another person. Here it is nonsensical to say that somebody else could do these things *for* me, though of course someone else could do them *instead* of me: these are not things I simply want to get done and over with, but things I want to do. Thus an art critic can tell me what pictures to buy, or buy them for me: but he cannot (logically) appreciate them for me or enjoy them for me.

Now in so far as morality is a matter of following rules, or adopting means designed to achieve a particular end, it is like (a) above. We can imagine a person whose ends or purposes in life were fairly clearly defined, and who could be taught to follow rules designed to achieve them, without his being in any sense *inside* the moral situations. He might accept the rules on authority, or condition himself to keep them. This could equally well be true of a group. Suppose a group had the ends of wanting to perform certain tasks efficiently, keep property intact, and live as long as possible. Then in principle the group could hire experts to tell them what rules they should follow to achieve these ends. The experts might say, for instance, that one form of social organization would enable them to perform tasks more efficiently: that there had to be rules about theft and murder backed up by certain kinds of sanctions, and so forth. Then the group could be conditioned or brainwashed in such a way that its members would always keep these rules. Why does the group need 'moral education' in a fuller sense?

The proper answer to this is now reasonably plain. An essential part of morality is about our ends, about what we consider valuable in itself, about what we choose for its own sake. There are two sorts of tools we can use as means to achieve these ends: tools that help us to discover what means will, as a matter of fact, achieve them – the advice of friends, the factual knowledge of experts, our own knowledge of the world, and so on: and tools that help us actually to *adopt* the means – the exhortation of friends, some process of conditioning or indoctrination, or our own will-power. But there is an important sense in which these tools, though of the utmost importance, are not central to

morality. Suppose two men who might have the same attitude
to other people, or the same moral values or ends: suppose A
commands the knowledge of a body of factual experts, and has
some machine which immediately overcomes any obstacles there
may be to his translating his values into action (it conditions
him on the spot, or nags at him until he does what he thinks
right – a sort of super-conscience): suppose B has neither of
these advantages. As regards their *particular* actions and choices,
A will cut a much better figure than B: for B will both be ignorant of the right means to adopt, and less capable of adopting
them. Yet there is surely an important sense in which A is not *a
better man* than B. A might have these advantages only because
he can afford them: B might be just as aware of their importance,
and try just as hard as A, but simply lack the means – perhaps
in the literal sense that he cannot afford A's experts and technological assistance.

Of course we must not overstate this point. First, we must
remember that many cases of factual ignorance or compulsion
may be at least partly the fault of the person concerned: he may
simply not have *tried* to find out, or to do the action. Secondly, it
is always difficult to distinguish ignorance of the facts from
refusal to face them, and compulsion from inconsistency of moral
principle. Thirdly, since we do not in fact possess the factual
expertise and the conscience-machines we might wish, it is
everyone's duty to inform themselves of facts relevant to moral
decisions, and to develop their will-power. For these reasons I
am far from regarding factual knowledge and will-power as
irrelevant to the notion of moral education: indeed, they are
essential to it. But they are not the whole of it: and in one sense
they are not *central* to it in the way that moral attitudes, principles and intentions are central.

In this respect morality is like aesthetics, as illustrated by the
example of collecting paintings. The adoption of means to ends,
such as the avoidance of conflict with our neighbours, or keeping ourselves out of trouble, could be in principle achieved by
conditioning methods, which are adjuncts to morality rather than
its core. What is peculiar to morality is our understanding of and
relationship with other people, rather than our overt actions
considered in themselves; just as what is peculiar to aesthetics is

our appreciation of pictures, and not the specific act of buying certain pictures. Morality is about what we ought to desire for its own sake, and not essentially about what we ought to do in order to achieve what we desire: and teaching the former is logically different from teaching the latter. The former is concerned with the appreciation of situations, with our feelings and emotional reactions to them, just as aesthetics is concerned with our reactions to pictures and other art forms. No question of *choosing what to do* arises until we have a reasonably clear set of desires and reactions: and by the time this stage is reached, an expert can in principle choose for us. The process of 'choosing what to do' in morality, like the process of choosing what picture to buy in aesthetics, can in a loose sense be said to include an examination of our own feelings and desires: but the essential part of the process is not choice but this examination itself. Hence the essence of moral education is not the inculcation of right choices, but the improvement and clarification of feeling: or, more precisely, it aims at the former, via the latter.

In the same way, the real point of a moral argument or a moral dilemma is not to examine facts and logic. (Here too we could in principle envisage a computing machine checking our logic, and telling us appropriate means to ends.) The point is rather that by such internal or external dialogues we give ourselves the chance to react psychologically to the facts in a more efficient, or more discriminating, or more honest way. We remind ourselves of what we already, in a sense, know: we use our imaginations: we consider what would happen if we did this or that: we try to perceive our own feelings or those of other people. All this is much more like what goes on in a psychoanalytic session than what goes on in a straightforward factual argument. If we miss this point we are likely to wonder, as some philosophers have done, how there can be such things as moral arguments, as opposed to fact-and-logic arguments, at all. Thus the peculiar function of morality, to put it sententiously, is to bring us into a right relationship with other people: and this is something which cannot be done by conditioning alone. To say this is simply to spell out in a little more detail what many great moral teachers have said about the importance of inner attitudes.

Another way of putting this general point is as follows:

There is one sphere of decision and action in which we normally consider ourselves bound by a specific set of rules. We know we are supposed to keep promises, tell the truth, and repay debts. These are the rules current in our social group, and there is an obvious sense (see p. 44) in which we are acting 'immorally' if we break them. But equally there is another sphere, in which we cannot prevent questions arising (i) about when we (as individuals) ought to make exceptions to these rules (e.g. perhaps when we make very silly promises, or when madmen with axes ask us where their victims are and we ought to lie): (ii) about what rules ought to be current in our group, what expectations we ought to have of each other, what exceptions we (jointly) are going to allow, and so forth: and (iii) what sort of individuals we ought, ideally, to be. What I have tried to argue is that, even if the various narrow pictures of 'moral education' which I have been criticizing will fit the first of these spheres – and the fit is not very good – it cannot fit the second. For the second sphere requires that we should be able, so to speak, to *get outside* the rules, to inspect their point and purpose, and make decisions about them which must of necessity be based on something other than the rules themselves: that is, on the wants, wills, feelings or interests of other people.

*

If the above is read as a general account of morality, it must of course seem both one-sided and imprecise. One-sided, because my chief purpose has been the negative one of showing the inadequacy of one very common account of moral education: and imprecise, because I have done no more than hint vaguely at a more positive account. (Thus to say that morality is essentially a matter of 'right relationships' is either just a truism, leaving us wholly in the dark about what relationships *are* right: or else misleading, in so far as some very important moral concepts do not seem to be connected with 'right relationships' in any precise sense. The notion of justice or fairness, for instance, seems often to conflict in practice with such 'inner attitudes' as benevolence, charity, or the desire for other people's happiness.) But we shall have occasion in the next chapter to examine rather more closely what it is to have a moral principle, and whether there are any general standards which we use for assessing such principles. In this chapter I hope to have shown only in what respects any authoritarian account of moral education must fail, as must any sociological or psychological account which does not do justice to the free and rational nature of moral thought and action.

To summarize briefly: The concept of moral education demands more than just a set of overt (perhaps conditioned) movements. It demands more than intentional behaviour, since we are interested in a person having the right sort of intentions, reasons and motives. It demands more even than this, since we are interested in a person's disposition or state of mind, from which his reasons and motives – and hence ultimately his behaviour – will flow.

Same as question of "Which rules are in fact ultimate?"

Notes to Chapter 1

1. It is perhaps worth mentioning that the Oxford English Dictionary (like most others) makes little or no mention of this sense of 'moral', but seems to fall in with the wider sense which we shall investigate in this book: 'Of or pertaining to character or disposition; of or pertaining to the distinction between right and wrong, or good and evil, in relation to action, volitions or character; ethical'. The tendency of many people, even in the face of the linguistic evidence, to cling uniquely to the 'sociological' or some other sense is interesting in itself, though I should not like to draw any psychological conclusions from it. But no wonder we don't know what to do about moral education, if we don't even know what we mean by 'moral'.

2. It is diminished in different degrees by different cases, of course. Physical force abolishes it completely, because it is no longer my action: threats and other forms of duress only diminish it.

3. Here and elsewhere I have deliberately oversimplified the issues, in an endeavour to make the main point as forcibly as possible. It would be more correct to say that words like 'behaving', 'acting', 'doing' (and other verbs with a more specific meaning) are sometimes used in contexts which imply the notion of intentionality, and sometimes not. (One does not require an excuse for talking of 'animal behaviour', or for saying that someone did something (or acted) unintentionally.) Again, if a man (for instance) threatens me with a gun, it is perfectly correct to say that he can 'make me do something', that I choose to do it, and do it intentionally. All I intend to exclude here are those cases which would cut out intention and freedom altogether.

4. See pp. 53–5.

5. In this section I have been, inevitably, far too brief in criticizing those interpretations of 'moral' which are framed in terms of overt behaviour ('going through the motions') and 'raw' feelings. Perhaps the most important general point is that these interpretations are often intended or taken as *definitions*, answering the question 'What do we usually mean by "moral"?': but they are better understood as *descriptions*, pointing to certain psychological or sociological facts which may often pertain in those situations which we call 'moral'. For example, it may be tempting to define 'moral' as 'the sort of thing you feel guilty about'. This won't do, because you can feel guilty about situations which you know aren't moral, and conversely you can fail to feel guilty about situations which you know are moral. If, in-

stead of offering a definition, we say 'In such-and-such societies or for such-and-such people moral situations (otherwise defined) are commonly (or even always) accompanied by guilt-feelings', then this may be perfectly acceptable: but acceptable as a psychological fact *about* morality, not as a definition *of* it.

6. G.E.M. Anscombe, *Intention*, p. 84 *et seq*.

7. See pp. 45-7.

8. See R.S. Peters, *Reason and Habit*, in Scheffler's collection (bibliography).

9. Actually, words like 'aversion', 'attitude', 'prejudice' and many others are conceptually tied to rationality in a way of which psychologists sometimes seem unaware (e.g. in attitude-testing). So the above is over-simplified: but I hope the main point is clear.

10. Cases of negligence or 'sins of omission' may raise special difficulties here: for certainly moral blame attaches to these, yet at first sight they may not seem to be 'actions done for a reason' – indeed, don't we blame people precisely for *not* acting? Against this, however, one could argue that either (i) the person was under compulsion at the time, in which case we would not blame him for failing to act, or (ii) the person was not under compulsion, in which case he would be acting for a reason: we can blame him, indeed, but only because he was acting for a reason and could have acted otherwise.

It is misleading to say simply that we blame people for not acting. We blame such a man not just because he does A, nor just because he does not do B, but because he does A *rather than* B. It's not simply that Nero fiddled (there's nothing wrong with fiddling), nor simply that he did not help to stop the fire in Rome (he might not have been free to do so), but that he fiddled rather than helping to stop the fire. And this may mean either that he was aware of the situation but didn't care, or that he wasn't aware but could have been – that he failed to make himself aware. How far one can reasonably demand that people should make themselves aware of things seems a very open question (see p. 120, note 16).

11. The last example shows that the concept of rationality applies to beliefs as well as to actions. A moral belief, like any other belief, must be held *for a reason*: otherwise it is not a belief, but merely a form of words which a person utters: just as an action must be done for a reason, if it is not to be merely a set of physical movements. If we asked somebody 'Why do you believe so-and-so?' and he said 'For absolutely no reason at all', we would be thoroughly mystified. Moreover, there is a close connexion between the content of a belief and its reasons. Suppose that a person said 'Birth control is wrong', and gave as his sole reason that his church said so: suppose that the church

changes its mind, so that he then goes around saying 'Birth control is right'. How misleading is it to say that he believes that birth control is wrong, and then that it is right? We might feel tempted to say that what he really believes is that whatever his church says is right. (He might not even know what 'birth control' *meant*.)

There is also a problem about where the giving of reasons for beliefs comes to an end: if a reason can be demanded for *any* belief, we are involved in an infinite regress.

12. See A. C. MacIntyre's 'Determinism' (*Mind*, January 1957).

13. These two doubts must surely seem particularly significant in a very fluid and mobile society like our own, where individuals need a morality that can handle rapid changes. In both of them we see the temptation of an authoritarian system, whereby the individual just does what the authority tells him: for the authority can tell him, if the system of communication is good enough, when to make exceptions in the standardized code, and can also reverse the whole code if it wishes.

14. *Nichomachean Ethics*, II, 4 (J. A. K. Thomson's translation, Penguin Classics) p. 62.

15. *ibid:* p. 61.

16. Whatever the 'wrong kind' may be. Thus Jesus is reported as having offended against certain recognized *mores*, by plucking ears of corn and healing on the Sabbath. One might say that he was 'acting morally' in a fuller sense than the Pharisees were: not because Jesus was right and the Pharisees were wrong, but because Jesus' reasons and motives were more appropriate to morality than those of the Pharisees. Again, consider the case of Huckleberry Finn helping a negro slave to escape. Here the established 'moral code' was (we now think) bad. We would regard Huck as more 'morally educated' than somebody who just followed this code and handed the slave over to the authorities: again, as with Jesus and the Pharisees, not so much because what Huck did was right, but because he made an effort to decide whether the accepted *mores* were right or wrong – because he made a moral effort and a moral choice, using the right kind of feelings and reasons. This is not to say that the Pharisees and the slave-owners didn't have moral beliefs in some sense. But see Chapter 2, pp. 78–83.

17. op. cit., p. 61.

18. op. cit., pp. 62–3.

19. That is, it would be a criticism of her character. Whether or not she could be blamed, or could help feeling as she did, is another matter. See also Bernard Williams' *Morality and the Emotions* (Bedford College, University of London, 1965).

20. It may even be argued that a truly 'morally educated' person must find *pleasure* in having the right moral dispositions and feelings. Aristotle says (perhaps rather too strongly): 'A man is temperate who abstaining from bodily pleasures finds this abstinence pleasant; if he finds it irksome, he is intemperate' (*op. cit.* Chapter 3).

CHAPTER 2

MORALITY AND REASON

A. The Problem

In the last few decades many philosophers, both those of the British empirical tradition, and of the continental tradition followed by the existentialists, have been concerned in different ways to stress the autonomy of value. The philosophical issues involved go right back to Plato, and what the moderns have said has been repeated recently and often, in many various forms. So it ought by now to be familiar to all literate people:[1] but as experience persuades me that it is not, a very brief (and hence inevitably misleading) summary must first be given.

Facts and Values

There is commonly supposed to be a crucially important difference between judgements of fact and judgements of value, which runs as follows: A matter of fact, of observation, of experience, of description, of what is, is one thing: a matter of value, of morality, of idealism, of what is right or what ought to be, is another. No amount of facts can prove by strictly logical entailment, that something is valuable, good, right or to be chosen: words of value ('ought', 'good', 'right', etc.) are in a quite different logical category from the purely descriptive words ('red', 'square', etc.) which we use to formulate our factual observations. Hence, since (to put it crudely) values are not facts, neither religion, nor any philosophical system, nor our own consciences, nor the expertise of the psychologist, nor any other alleged authority, can make our moral choices for us. It is only we ourselves who can decide what is right and wrong, though we may use these and other authorities as useful guides. We have to make our own moral choices. This is supposed to be a necessary truth of logic.

Of course these points are controversial. I have stated them very briefly, and a fuller discussion would involve a much more detailed explication of what the points actually are, and how far they may be admitted. But even those philosophers most concerned to oppose them have hardly maintained that all, or even most, moral questions can be settled in the same sort of way, or as easily, as we settle factual questions. At any rate it has become clear that some moral questions are problematic in a way in which at least some factual questions are not – that there are difficulties of principle about how to answer them. It would be a very bold philosopher who maintained that we could, in some comparatively uncomplicated sense, *know* what was morally right and wrong in all important cases: and that, in consequence, a research unit of this kind should begin by simply finding this out and holding it up for all the world to see.

On the other hand, it does not follow from these points that our moral values and beliefs are 'arbitrary', or 'a matter of taste', or 'irrational', in the sense that one reason for a moral belief is as good as another. It is possible to represent the fact-value distinction neither as purely 'linguistic', nor as implying that there is no question of knowledge, evidence or rationality in the moral field, but rather as pointing to the consequences of recognizing the difference between morality and other spheres of human activity and discourse. Valuing, choosing, commending, etc. are certainly different from stating, describing, or noting facts. But they are not arbitrary activities: they have their own criteria of success. Consequently we are bound to direct our attention towards sketching those rules, principles or standards in virtue of which we can say that one moral belief is better than another. The words which we should most naturally use, in making this sort of judgement, would include 'reasonable', 'rational', 'unprejudiced', 'sensible', 'wise' and 'sane'. In this chapter I shall in fact make most use of the word 'rational', and attempt to outline the senses in which we can say that one moral belief is more rational than another, or that one person is more rational than another in the sphere of morality. My purpose in doing this should be plain. For although we cannot hope to establish a full set of immediate, first-order moral values, we may be able to establish a set of second-order principles or norms, by reference to which we can assess the merits of a moral belief or believer, and hence be able to describe one person as more 'morally educated' than another. These then become the new first order

People, not only beliefs, can be called rational

From the point of view of the moral educator, it is natural to begin by trying to consider what we mean when we call *people*, rather than *beliefs*, rational or irrational. When we describe somebody as 'irrational', 'unreasonable', 'intolerant', 'prejudiced', 'insane', etc. we do not (or should not) refer primarily to the truth or falsehood of his beliefs. A man may hold beliefs which are perfectly correct in an unreasonable, intolerant, prejudiced or insane *manner* – and, of course, vice versa. We are talking about the *way in which* or the *reasons for which* he comes to believe, and continues to believe, rather than *what* he believes. A 'reasonable' man is not essentially a man who believes x y and z, but a man who is prepared to listen to argument, attend to the facts, to logic, to the meanings of words, and so on. We tend to assume that certain beliefs, being so obviously false, could only be held by somebody who was unreasonable or prejudiced or insane: for instance, it seems to most of us that anyone who thought the earth was flat, or that all those of Aryan blood were superior to all non-Aryans, must have failed to attend to the evidence. But we must not be tempted to suppose that it is the belief itself which justifies our charge of unreasonableness. Plenty of inventors and scientists have been thought unreasonable or insane because their views did not find favour at the time: and afterwards they were found to be correct. It is the sort of reasons a man has for his beliefs which count.

To put this another way: We can distinguish the merits of a person when playing a particular role from the correctness or incorrectness of his beliefs. For instance, we can talk about a 'good scientist', meaning (roughly) a person who observes the physical world closely and patiently, who frames hypotheses intelligently and submits them to experimental tests, and who is prepared to abide by the relevant evidence. More obscurely, but still intelligibly, a 'good literary critic' is someone who is widely and deeply read in literature, is well-versed in certain studies which are relevant to literature (perhaps the history of the period, or the life of the author), shows an acute perception of human nature and the literary forms which portray it, and so forth. We can categorize individuals – schoolboys, for instance –

as 'good at' these activities without necessarily maintaining that their scientific or literary opinions are, in any particular case, correct. We mean rather that they are good at following certain rules of procedure, or principles of thought, which are relevant to their fields of study; in much the same way as somebody can be a good bridge-player without necessarily making all his contracts, or a good barrister without winning all his cases.

Rules of Procedure

What is it, then, to be 'good' at morality? I am suggesting that we ought not to try to answer this question by saying 'Holding the right moral views'. If we say this, we shall find ourselves asking next 'But what *are* the right moral views?'; and to this question we may fail to find an answer. We may fail for two reasons: first, because we may be in doubt about the sense, if any, in which we can talk at all about the 'right' moral views, since morality seems to be in some degree a matter of choice: and second, because we still might not know which actual views were right, even if we knew what we meant by calling a view 'right' – we might, for instance, not have enough factual information to decide between conflicting views. We should rather ask 'What are the rules of procedure, or the canons of relevance, which we actually use to assess the merits of a moral view?', or 'What sort of demands do we make on a person who puts forward a moral view, when we want him to justify it?' I don't think it should worry us too much to realize that, even if and when we have established the rules of procedure for morality, we still cannot in a strict sense *prove* this or that specific moral view to be 'right' beyond any possible doubt.

After all, we are in a not very dissimilar position as regards scientific views. We have a fairly good idea of what rules and criteria govern the activity of science, and how scientific arguments and justifications are supposed to work. But this does not mean that we never hold mistaken scientific beliefs, however careful we try to be in attending to the rules and criteria – we may have overlooked some vital fact, or our instruments may not be good enough to collect all the evidence we need. Nor does it mean that our scientific beliefs can be shown to follow logically

from certain pieces of evidence – that they are *necessarily* true.
A person can, without actual contradiction, accept all the evidence normally taken[2] to show that the earth is round, and still maintain that it is flat: it would be irrational of him to do so, because he would not be abiding by the rules of procedure which govern scientific activity, but it would not be nonsensical – any more than it would be nonsensical of him to hold a particular moral view, whatever the facts might be. Yet we can still talk about 'proof', 'knowledge', and 'certainty' in science as in logic or mathematics. And so we can in morals. These words will relate to different rules of procedure according to the activity. Different activities have different standards, but this does not mean that one is inferior to another: they are just different.

With some of the rules of procedure in morality we are perfectly familiar, because they are rules which enter into other activities besides morality. Briefly they are:

(a) That we should stick to the laws of logic:
(b) That we should use language correctly:
(c) That we should attend to the facts.

Many examples have been given of these kinds of rationality: they may be found elsewhere, and I will not repeat them here.[3] We all know that if, during a moral argument, a person contradicts himself, or disregards some fact which is relevant to his opinion, or plays fast and loose with the meanings of words, he is behaving irrationally. This may seem somewhat dogmatic, but we shall have more to say about it later.[4]

B. Other People's Interests

These particular rules of procedure, however, are not peculiar to morality, even though they enter into it. In our search for other rules of procedure, it seems most profitable to begin by one account of a certain type of thinking which has a right be be called 'moral', and which can be defined *formally* rather than in terms of *content*. These formal criteria may not be sufficient to give us everything we need for the concept of a 'morally educated' person, but they will at least serve to distinguish some kinds of moral thought and action from non-moral thought and action, without forcing us to assign a particular content to morality. The close analysis of moral language on which this account rests, and which is required to elucidate these criteria, has been done elsewhere, and I need not repeat it here at length.

We may summarize the criteria which a man's opinions must satisfy if they are to count as moral opinions, under five headings: (1) They must be autonomous (freely held). (2) They must be rational.[5] These two criteria we have discussed already. (3) They must be impartial as between persons. (4) They must be prescriptive. One might very roughly express the last two criteria as follows: if someone expresses a moral opinion ('It is wrong to steal', 'It is a good thing to keep one's promises', or whatever), then (i) he is laying down a principle of behaviour, not just for one particular person or occasion, but for all people on all similar occasions[6] (ii) he commits himself to acting on that principle (though of course he may sometimes lack the means or the willpower so to act); that is, a moral opinion does not just make an *observation* about what is good or bad, but (if sincerely held) *prescribes* for the person, or commits him to, a certain type of behaviour. (5) They must be overriding: that is, they must take precedence over his other opinions.[7]

There are a number of questions which may be raised about this account;[8] but the most important for our present argument is the notion of the impartiality of moral judgements ((3) above). The account suggests that, in making moral judgements, we consider other people as being on an equal footing with ourselves: what goes for us, goes for them too, and vice versa. Without this, it is suggested, the whole business of morality and interpersonal rules could not get started. Moreover, if a man's moral opinions have to *prescribe* conduct for others as well as for himself ((4) above), the implication is that he regards them as equals: one might think that he could not advance these opinions with any show of reason, or with much chance of success, unless he so regarded them. But what is it to accept other people as equals? Do we have to accept *all* other people as equals? Or only some? Or only to accept that our moral judgements apply in principle to other people – that is, that they would apply if other people were in the same position as ourselves, which perhaps in fact they are not? Or is it rather that the onus lies on us to show that they are not – to point out relevant differences between their

case and ours? And anyway, whatever is demanded by the notion
of equality or impartiality, are there any reasons for accepting
this notion?

Despite these philosophical difficulties, many of us (at least in
this society) would perhaps accept some such notion without
serious hesitation. Partly for this reason, I shall delay a consideration of the (very complex) issues involved till later in this
chapter,[9] and continue for the time being to use the account in
our search for procedural principles in morality. Now though the
account itself defines moral judgements in purely formal terms,
the implication of the underlying notion of equality suggests at
least one obvious procedural principle for at least one area that
we usually call 'moral': perhaps the most important, or the most
typical, area. This is the area of interpersonal morality: that is,
the area where the wants and interests of individuals living in
society conflict, or may conflict. The procedural principle is
simply that the *sort of justification* needed for a moral view in this
area must relate to the feelings and interests of other people (just
as the sort of justification needed for a scientific view must relate
to observed empirical facts, experimental results, and so forth).
This is not to say *either* that moral or scientific views must have a
particular content – that we can dismiss *a priori* certain specific
views as not moral, or not scientific – *or* that you can rationally
hold any moral view you like. It is simply to say that a moral
view, to count as rational, must be backed up by certain kinds
of reasons.

Thus, suppose a man said that he believed that we ought to
kill everyone whose name began with a Q on Tuesday night,
whilst they were sleeping. He might hold this in a way which
satisfied all the formal criteria for a moral view; yet in itself it
seems a very odd view to hold. But now suppose he explains as
follows: 'Well, you see, I happen to know that every Wednesday
from now on Martians will descend and torture everyone whose
name begins with Q – Martians don't have the letter Q in their
language, and they hate it so much that they can't stand hearing
it spoken: and the torture will be so horrible that it would be
better for them if they were killed painlessly in their sleep on
Tuesday night'. Now this becomes intelligible as a moral view.
What makes it intelligible is that he is relating it to the interests

of other people, those whose names begin with Q. It is ultimately because they have those interests – because they would prefer to die painlessly rather than under Martian torture – that he holds the view, not *just* because it is a Tuesday or because their names begin with Q.

This is not an argument for assigning a particular content to morality, in the sense that we can give any purely descriptive or empirical specification of things that would be always good or bad, or actions that would be always right or wrong.[10] It is rather an argument for assigning particular criteria of relevancy, or a particular mode of justification, to morality. Suppose, in the example above, I replied to the man by saying: 'Ah, but actually the people whose names begin with Q *like* being tortured: they're rather looking forward to the Martians coming, as a matter of fact', and he replied 'Oh, well, I don't care what *their* attitude to this is, I still think we ought to kill them'. Suppose, that is, he could not base his view on the wills of other people, but based it simply on some personal preference of his own (perhaps he couldn't stand the thought of them being tortured). Then what he had might still be a moral view, but it could not be a rational one.[11]

One could dispute whether this sort of view should be called moral or not, but I'm not sure whether the issue would be a substantial as against a terminological one. Imagine a man who thinks that the preservation of works of art is more important than saving human life. This principle might certainly be an overriding one (in the sense of our fifth criterion; see page 77). Is it a moral principle? We could say yes, just because it's overriding, because it's about what he thinks to be most important, what ultimately governs his behaviour.[12] Or we could say that it depends on how he defends it. If he says (i) 'Well, future generations of men will gain pleasure and profit from these works of art, so it's worth preserving them even if it costs human lives', then it counts as moral because it's about other people's interests: if he says (ii) 'Well, they just are so beautiful and marvellous, even if no human beings existed they should be preserved', it isn't moral.[13]

But whichever criterion we use, the significant point here is that when it comes to defending views of this sort, a rational defence has to relate to human interests. The second defence (ii) offered by the art-lover above sounds implausible; we feel inclined to say 'But what's the *point* of keeping all these pictures if there are no human beings around to enjoy them?', and hence more generally 'What's the point of *anything* apart from its relation to someone's interests and desires?' We allow people to use different criteria of justification when engaged in other activities (aesthetics, etiquette, science, mathematics, and so on); but this is partly because these activities as a whole either do serve human interests, or at least do not militate against them. But when it comes to overriding opinions, those which ultimately settle how a man behaves in relation to his fellows (even if he does not himself consider that relationship), we demand that these opinions be justified in the light of human interests. For when somebody holds up a rule of behaviour as something to be followed (by the use of words like 'good', 'ought', and 'right' that have a universal application), as opposed to merely expressing a selfish or personal desire or intention, then he *ipso facto* submits it to the judgement of all of us.

Not moral or not rational?

We may still feel uncertain whether beliefs of this sort are entitled to be called 'moral' at all: and this involves a brief discussion of how we are to categorize beliefs in general. To take a parallel, suppose a child in a mathematics lesson puts down wrong numbers in his book because he is not paying attention, or because his memory is bad, or because he has misunderstood the point, or because he copies them from the book of a friend who has also got them wrong. Are we to say in these cases that the child is not doing mathematics at all, or that he is doing mathematics but doing it badly? Perhaps we should say different things in different cases. Or, again, someone might hold that a painting was beautiful for some reason that most of us would regard as wholly irrelevant – because he owned it, for instance, or because it depicted horses. Is this an *aesthetic* belief? Or someone might believe the earth to be flat because the Bible said so: is this a *scientific* belief?

We have to distinguish between (i) holding a moral belief, and

(ii) using the methods and type of reasons that are relevant to moral beliefs. Whether something is a moral belief or not depends on whether the believer says things like 'It is wrong to do X' or 'One ought not to do Y' *and means them*: that is, whether he commits himself to universal rules in the way described on page 77. People may hold moral beliefs without (ii), using appropriate methods and reasons to arrive at them: they may just pick them out of a hat, so to speak. In the same way, so long as statements like 'This poem is very moving' and 'The earth is flat' are meant in their normal senses – i.e. as aesthetic and empirical judgements, rather than in some kind of distorted, or poetic, or unusual sense – then they are aesthetic and scientific statements, even though the speaker may not have used the methods appropriate to aesthetics, or scientific method, to arrive at them.

In practice it is often very difficult to tell whether a speaker really does mean what he says: and of course his reasons for saying it may be a guide to what he means, even though they must be distinguished from it. Thus a child might be told to add two and two, and consistently write the number seven: and he might even say 'Two twos make seven'. But if it turns out that he thought to put down a 7 after 2 x 2 for some non-mathematical reason (perhaps because a 7 looks rather like a 2), then we should wonder whether he really believed that two twos *made* seven: for it seems that he does not understand the implications of 'two twos' and 'making', i.e. the operation of multiplication. So he may have a belief, but not a *mathematical* belief. In the same way, someone may say 'God spoke to me' or 'An angel appeared', but these hardly seem to be scientific or empirical beliefs, since it usually turns out that words like 'speak' or 'appear' are not used in their normal empirical sense.

Thus one way of finding out what people mean – what sort of belief they have – is by checking upon their reasons. It is because the child gives the reasons he does that we suspect that he does not understand what he is saying when he says 'two twos are seven', and hence that he does not intend anything mathematical. The kind of belief characteristically depends on the kind of reasons. But people are often irrational – they use the wrong sorts of reasons for their beliefs. A man may say 'I believe that horse will win the race – I just have a hunch about it'. This is a

Assumption: that articulation is
adequate medium for "reasons"

perfectly genuine belief, although we might not think his reason
to be a very good one. He means what he says, and will no doubt
act on it (by betting on the horse, for instance).

Belief and reasons for belief are thus connected, via the meaning of what a person says when he expresses a belief. If I say
'You ought not to smoke' and defend it by saying 'because it will
give you bronchitis', I probably mean something different from
'You ought not to smoke' defending it by 'because it upsets other
people in the cinema'. The first is a prudential, the second a
moral, belief. But it is perfectly possible to hold overriding
beliefs which are not defended by reference to other people's
interests: as in the case mentioned earlier, of the art-lover who
wants paintings preserved for no reason connected with such
interests. If he really intends such beliefs to be understood as
satisfying the formal criteria for a moral belief – as prescriptive,
impartial, and overriding – then it would be difficult not to call
them 'moral'. We may prefer to call them 'arbitrary', or describe them as 'whims' or 'caprices', but this to evaluate such
beliefs on some scale of rationality, not to reclassify them under
some other heading than 'moral'. We could only refuse to call
them 'moral', if we *defined* 'moral', not just as 'relating to other
people's interests' – for all overriding beliefs do in practice affect
such interests – but as 'defended by relating to other people's
interests'. And there seems no sufficient reason for such a definition.

Much of the difficulty here, however, is caused by the simple
fact that people say things without knowing exactly how they
intend them. It is unrealistic to take a statement in the abstract
and claim to know whether it is a moral belief or not: we have to
find out just how the speaker intends it. In the course of our finding out, by asking him his reasons and hence trying to discover
whether he really intends it as prescriptive, impartial, etc., the
speaker may well come to mean something much more specific
than anything he had in mind before we began our inquiry: or he
may have meant one thing, and come round to meaning another
when we begin probing. It is just because people are not clear
about the criteria of a moral belief that they are characteristically
not clear what beliefs they intend by the words they say. Thus
often a man may say 'It is good' or 'One ought', but really mean

'I like the idea of' or 'I feel guilty about'. Or again, in quoting an authority as reason for his belief, it is not clear (even to him) whether he is really giving a reason, or just repeating the belief. ('Why do you think it right?' 'Because it's the will of God.' Is this a reason or a repetition? It would take time to find out.)

When we say, then, that it is 'perfectly possible' to hold over-riding beliefs which do not relate to human interests, we can be safe in meaning that it is not contradictory to do so. Further, we can be safe in meaning that people do in practice hold beliefs which overridingly govern their actions, and which they cannot in practice defend by reference to human interests: perhaps even which they do not want to, or do not appear to feel any obligation to, defend in this way. But we have to remember that much depends on the context in which such beliefs are questioned. What it is 'perfectly possible' for people to maintain is a function of the empirical situation – who they are talking to, what rules of procedure they have been brought up to follow, how clear they are about the meanings of words, and so forth. Thus there is a very great difficulty in applying our distinction in practice. But this difficulty is counterbalanced by an encouraging fact: that getting people to clarify what they actually do mean is itself a way of morally educating them. Many people imagine that they hold moral views, where some attention to what they themselves say would persuade them that they do not: and such a realization would be likely to influence their opinions and behaviour.

C. 'PRUDENCE' AND 'MENTAL HEALTH'

There is a whole host of other decisions and opinions which do not fall under this description of morality. Some of these may be plausibly described as 'ideals': others are perhaps more in the nature of prudential choices and beliefs. I have in mind here such questions as 'Shall I marry or stay single?', 'Shall I be a stockbroker or a philosopher?', 'Shall I spend my spare time keeping fit or learning Greek?', and so on. Many of such questions are certainly important: a lot of people would certainly *say* that some of them were moral questions: yet we would not, and in some cases could not, answer some of them by reference to other people's interests. I am sure that we should consider these to be moral questions also, though of a different logical status, partly for the kind of reasons given by Professor R. M. Hare.[14] But there are additional points which need bringing out in the context of moral education, if only because a person's behaviour in the 'prudential' area may be more or less governed by the second-order norms of rational morality which we are trying to elucidate: that is, a person's ability to attend to these norms may be as apparent in our 'idealistic' or prudential opinions as in our inter-personal morality. Moreover, there may be an important sense in which a man's interpersonal morality *flows from* his ideals and his general view of life,[15] which themselves may be capable of assessment by the second-order norms.

There are many different categories of opinions and behaviour which fall under this heading: I shall take an example from just one. Suppose that we know a married couple, of which the husband is a pronounced sadist, and the wife a pronounced masochist. Both get what they want in their private life, and they restrict their 'perversions' to this, so that there is a sense in which neither behaves immorally: yet we might still think there was something wrong. But the kind of wrongness here is different. If we wanted to argue the case, we should have to try to show that they would be happier, or have a more enjoyable and fruitful relationship, if they were not perverted. And this is like arguing that someone ought not to smoke, because it is not in his own interests: because it will give him bronchitis or cancer. This is a prudential argument, not (in a strict sense) a moral one. We try to show that his wants are irrational: that they are not 'really' in accord with his interests, with what he recognizes (or can be brought to recognize) is good for him.

Although these two types of argument, the strictly moral and the prudential, can be logically distinguished, it is in practice very difficult to know which type we are entitled to use in a particular case: and this is an additional reason for not excluding prudential views from our criteria of a 'morally educated' person. For it can plausibly be argued that there are, in reality, few if any cases where what a man does has no effect on the wants and interests of other people. If I get drunk, drive and kill somebody, this is plainly a moral issue: but what are we to say about the cases when I get drunk and (a) speak crossly to my wife, or (b) have a bad headache and work less efficiently the next day, or (c) thereby miss the chance of reading some improving book which will help me to become more morally educated? We might be tempted to say that all choices which might put you in a better or worse position to behave morally were in principle moral choices:[16] that the concept of morality was, in this way, infinitely extensible. But we need not attempt to solve this problem here.

We must be careful to distinguish between this 'prudential' kind of 'wrongness', in which we view what the person does as a *mistake* – as something which will do him harm or which he ought at once to avoid – and as the kind of 'wrongness' that may be purely symptomatic rather than causative.[17] For instance, suppose we are trying to persuade a boy that it is wrong to seduce girls. Then we might advance three kinds of arguments:

1. That what he is doing is against their wants or interests. This is an argument that what he is doing is (in the narrow sense) immoral.

2. That what he is doing damages himself in some way (makes him lazy, 'decadent', etc.). This a prudential argument.

3. That, although his behaviour damages neither himself nor other people, it is not the sort of thing a 'morally educated' person would do: it is, perhaps, symptomatic of a neurosis, a compulsive desire to conquer women, or whatever.[18]

Now the kind of argument advanced in 3. does not give any reasons for the boy *simply stopping* doing what he is doing (unlike the arguments in 1. and 2.): indeed, it may do him harm if he does stop, or is prevented from doing it.[19] But it does give reasons for him taking *some* thought and some kind of action about his unsatisfactory mental or moral state. (Perhaps he should try to understand himself better, or go to a psychiatrist.) This is not only true if he is acting under compulsion (and hence not liable to a particular kind of praise and blame), but also if he could stop it if he wanted.

We have here, therefore, a category of moral inadequacy which is very like some notions of mental ill-health:[20] not because he might not be able to help what he is doing, but rather because he is damaging neither other people nor himself, and yet there is still something morally – or psychologically, if the word be preferred – wrong with him. This category is very important: partly because we may sometimes confuse it with other categories, but also because a great many types of inadequacy which we should want to remedy under the title of 'moral education' may be of this sort, rather than taking the more striking form of damage to other people or oneself.[21]

Which phenomena are cases of moral inadequacy in this sense we have outlined, deriving from lack of awareness of and control over one's own feelings, and which are cases of a different type which could not, by any stretch of language, be called 'moral', is of course an open question. Somebody who had a brain tumour, which made him behave in ways which a 'morally educated' person would not, could hardly be said to be *morally* inadequate; he is, rather, physically ill, and needs to be cured, rather than educated. Much depends here on the kinds of causes that operate. I should be inclined to say that moral inadequacy covers those deficiencies of character that in principle require various forms of *conscious* or *rational* learning to remedy them, as opposed to deficiencies that can be wholly dealt with by surgery, the injection of hormones, electric shocks, or whatever.[22] There are many problems here which need to be tackled: but it will be enough for our purpose simply to be clear that there is this category of moral inadequacy, which is not fully covered by the notions either of strictly 'moral' or strictly 'prudential' incompetence.

Rationality and one's own interests

We have seen that moral actions and beliefs have to be defended by reference to the interests of other people: so that the 'morally educated' person must, of course, be aware of those interests. This will be one of the kinds of rationality which such a person must possess. But we have gone on to consider two other kinds of moral inadequacy: the 'prudential' kind, when a person does something which damages himself (drug-taking, suicide, etc.), and the 'mental health' kind, when a person's actions betoken some kind of mental or moral deficiency, but are nevertheless not causative of harm or damage to his interests. Something must be said about our criteria of rationality in reference to these last two cases.

We advanced a quite practical argument[23] for including the 'prudential' cases under the title of 'moral education': the argument that it was difficult, if not impossible, to delimit with any firmness the field of actions which affected other people. This argument applies also to the 'mental health' cases. If a person is morally inadequate in any of the three ways mentioned, his state of mind is likely to affect other people adversely. This becomes clearer when we remember that we can fail in our relationship towards others not only by doing something which is against their interests, but by not doing things that are in their interests: that there are sins of omission as well as of commission. Thus the person whose mental illness takes the form of feeling compelled to touch every lamp-post, or to keep washing his hands, may neither be harming other people in any obvious way, nor yet doing something which damages himself. But even this person, by not being as mentally healthy or rational as he might be, is in a quite obvious sense failing in his relationship towards others. He consumes much of his energy in acting out his compulsions, energy that might be devoted towards better ends; and he may fail in some quite specific moral duty because his attention is occupied in this way.

But the kind of irrationality that the 'prudential' and 'mental health' cases display is also very closely linked with the irrationality of the strictly 'moral' cases. This last includes ignorance of the feelings and interests of other people, and/or the failure to make up and act on moral principles based on those feelings and interests. The connection here is that awareness of other people's feelings is (both conceptually and in practice) bound up with awareness of one's own feelings. By suppressing or failing to be aware of our own feelings, we distort our perception of other people: we inevitably force them into a pattern which may fit us but does not fit them. Because we keep some of our feelings out of our consciousness, we limit the range of feelings which we are aware of, and hence are unable to recognize them in other people. Similarly, we are unable to learn more sophisticated and accurate descriptions of feelings unless we can match these descriptions to our own experience: and this involves admitting our own feelings in order to match them properly with the descriptions.[24] To put the point in more conceptual terms: awareness of feelings involves being able to give correct descriptions in a public language. We learn this language well or badly: and if we have learnt it badly in the case of our own feelings, we shall also have learned it badly for those of other people. The two are part of the same process.

This is to give only a very brief indication of why it seems to us correct to include these cases under our general title of 'moral education', and why they may be able to be subsumed under the different criteria of moral rationality which we are trying to sketch out. There are of course many problems raised by the 'mental health' cases in particular, which we cannot try to solve here. The introduction of these cases may, however, vitiate the whole approach to moral education, if we are not aware of three temptations, which need to be clarified at this point.

1. First, we must not renege on our decision to identify cases of moral inadequacy by failures in rationality, as opposed to identifying them by overt behaviour or the content of what is done. We cannot immediately say whether a particular act is 'wrong', or 'evidence of moral inadequacy', or 'neurotic': we want to know why the person did the act, whether his perceptions were distorted, whether he had lost control of himself and so on. It may, of course, be true that some particular actions often or always correlate with irrationality on the part of the actor, so that these actions would be a good *guide* to this irrationality; but this is not to *define* moral inadequacy in terms of the actions alone.

2. Nor must we assume that there is a single behaviour-pattern of moral adequacy for all people. Some writers[25] have attempted to evolve a distinction between a basic morality which is the same for all, and a diversity of 'ideals' or types of life which may and perhaps should vary very widely from person to person. This does not preclude the possibility that an individual may make a mistake – in an important sense, a *moral* mistake – about his own 'ideals', or in other actions and beliefs which are not subject to generally agreed moral rules of an interpersonal kind. A man who is infatuated with an unsuitable girl, marries her, and lives unhappily ever after, makes a moral mistake. But different people require different marriage partners: there is no single

overt form of moral adequacy for all. The only general criteria
are the criteria of moral rationality.

3. Nor again must we suppose that such behaviour is reducible
to a single dichotomy, 'rational' or 'irrational', 'prudent' or
'imprudent', 'mentally healthy' or 'neurotic'. It is plainly a
matter of degree. For some practical purposes, we may delimit a
class of 'morally educated', or 'rational', or 'sane' people: just
as psychologists sometimes talk of some people as 'normal' and
others as 'mentally ill', and just as for purposes of practical
living we make the concept of moral duty extend only over a
certain area (see p. 120, note 16). But in reality we can only say
that some people are more rational than others, in certain respects, and in certain contexts.[26]

Contexts for following rules of procedure

We must distinguish between what I have vaguely called 'rules
of procedure' and real-life contexts in which these rules are supposed to be followed. The rules of procedure are formal: that is,
they define the rationality of a particular activity. In morality, we
must be logical, know the facts, use words correctly, be aware of
our own and other people's feelings, desires and interests, and
count other people as our equals. What contexts actually enable
us best to obey these rules of procedure is a much more open
question. Thus it is, I think, a fairly safe bet that in order to learn
very much about our own feelings (or, indeed, the feelings of
others, since perception of the latter is very much dependent on
perception of the former), we may have to go in for some intense
form of interpersonal communication, one example of which we
may describe rather vaguely as 'psychoanalysis'. But this is an
empirical question. It could be argued that we can learn all we
want to know in the silence of our own room, or in the confessional box, or just by reading books: though I doubt it. In the same
sort of way, though perhaps to a lesser extent, my guess would be
that interpersonal communication of a different kind – what goes
on, or is supposed to go on, in discussions, arguments, tutorials,
etc. – is a much better context for learning to be logical, to respect the facts, and to be clear about what one is saying, than

solitude is. All rules of procedure tend to be followed more effectively if we are not the only person present: for the rules are
themselves impersonal, and the temptation to distort them for
our own personal advantage is very great.

In the last chapter[27] we sketched very tentatively some of the
features of morality, and laid particular stress on those which
were concerned with the development of perception, awareness
of feelings, imagination, and human understanding. It is these
features (amongst others) which differentiate rationality in
morals from rationality in other human activities, such as mathematics or science; and it is these which allow us to go beyond the
notions of logical consistency and 'facing facts', in the normal
sense of such phrases. For awareness of our own and other
people's interests is obviously dependent on them. Although
such notions as 'perceptivity' and 'imagination' are very slip-
pery, and although it is much more difficult to tell when someone is being perceptive than to tell when he is being logically
inconsistent, we do in fact recognize certain rules of procedure as
being relevant to such notions, and certain contexts of communication as forming a loose but significant framework in
which such rules can be followed. In other words, we recognize
standards which define and certain methods which enhance these
rather vague abilities, just as we recognize the form and methods
of a factual discussion and a logical dispute: a form which defines what it is to be reasonable in the realm of factual and logical
beliefs, and methods which may enhance our rationality therein,
if properly practised.

There are, of course and as usual, certain conceptual problems
about the notion of becoming aware of one's own and other
people's feelings. We are not, for instance, entirely clear about
what it means to say that somebody 'really wants' or 'really
feels' something and 'only thinks he wants' (or 'feels') something
else. At the same time there is not much doubt that it means
something. Not only in psychoanalysis, but in plenty of other
contexts, we commonly become convinced that 'we didn't know
what we really felt' or had in some sense 'seen the situation
wrong'. How do we become convinced? Is it that our attention
is drawn to facts that had escaped us, or is it that we come to see
that we had been misdescribing facts which we knew already?

To make a common instance, suppose a man says he loves a girl but behaves sadistically towards her. He may later become convinced that what he really feels towards her is not love, but (say) a desire to possess plus a desire to hurt. Now is it (a) that he knows quite well what the word 'love' means, is shown that the way in which he behaves and feels is inconsistent with that decription, and hence changes his mind? Or is it (b) that he means by 'love' something different from what we mean, so that he has to learn a new meaning for the word partly (though not only) *by* having his attention drawn to facts and feelings he has overlooked?

This is to do no more than raise, in very incoherent forms, some of the problems which seem especially relevant to the general and crucial rule of procedure under discussion. Even if we were clear about the conceptual difficulties, it must be admitted that there would still be difficulties in trying to cash out the rule of procedure described as 'awareness of feeling' into practical contexts. We feel, and ought to feel, uncertain about what exactly, in practice, these contexts are. Thus it may be denied that the study of literature or social anthropology improves our understanding of other people's feelings: that psychoanalysis makes us more aware of our own feelings: that paying attention to the meanings of words, which is part of philosophy, lessens the chances of our deceiving ourselves with our own language. In order to overcome such denials, we should have to produce some kind of tests, which were conceptually tied to the notion of (say) 'understanding other people's feelings', and which showed that people scored more highly in these tests if they (say) studied literature. (Perhaps they would be better able to predict what other people would say or do, or perhaps they would be less shocked or surprised by what they did, or be more capable of living in harmony with them or whatever.[28]) But I do not think this practical difficulty is fatal to the general point I am trying to make, which is that the range of contexts relevant to rationality extends further than those which concern logic and empirical observation.

Another way of putting this might begin by pointing out the way in which most of what we call 'moral arguments' fail to be effective. They fail because we too often treat them either as arguments only about fact and logic, or as excuses to express our own emotions. We fail to create contexts, and to follow general principles, designed to elucidate just what it is that we feel and why: and to elucidate how we see other people, ourselves, and the world in general. Occasionally it happens, either in the course of conversation, or by reading a book, or as a result of our own immediate experience, that something clicks. We become masters of a new description which enables us to see things in a different light, which helps us to understand and hence to control what is going on. Here we have hit on a context which is profitable to us. Though these cases may seem like accident, or pieces of pure good luck, we do in fact have a fairly clear idea of what sort of contexts are likely to be useful: it is just that we fail to engage in them. And it is one of the marks of such failure that we often try to pretend that morality is something other than it is, something which is easier to do.

D. 'Being Reasonable' in Morals

A summary

From these scattered points, which relate to a vast and complex subject, I hope that the reader will be able to glean the general trend of our argument. But it may help if its main features are summarized at this stage:

1. We wished to avoid giving an account of the morally educated person in terms of *content*, and hence began with the questions 'What is it to be "good at" morality?', 'What counts as being reasonable (sane, sensible, unprejudiced, etc.) in the moral sphere?', etc. We hoped to find certain skills, abilities or other characteristics which defined the morally educated person: and we mentioned some of the more obvious of these (having regard to logic, attending to the facts, etc.).

2. This led us (p. 77) to consider one account of morality which was conceived not in terms of content but in *formal* terms (overridingness, prescriptiveness, etc.) This account suggested one rule of procedure relevant to moral thinking: namely, that the reasons offered should relate to *other people's interests*.

3. We then considered (p. 80) whether we should regard this

kind of reasoning (in terms of other people's interests) as a *defining* characteristic of morality. But we ended by rejecting this (p. 82): we allowed that people could hold moral views which were not defended in this way, but claimed that such views would not be rational. So long as their views satisfied our formal account – so long as they were genuinely intended as impartial, prescriptive, overriding, etc. – they could fairly count as moral.

4. We then noticed two other categories of belief and action, where the notion of other people's interests did not seem to apply: first, there were what we called 'prudential' or 'expediency' cases (concerned with a person's own interests); and second, what we called 'mental health' cases. We distinguished these two categories from 'morality' in the narrower sense of inter-personal morality. But we saw that there were good reasons for including them under a wider sense of 'moral', and that they were relevant to our picture of the morally educated person. We then went on (p. 89) to consider some of the rules of procedure which might apply to all three categories, and the contexts in which those rules might best be followed.

We now need to see how far we have got in attaining the objective mentioned in 1. above – that of listing the skills, abilities or other features of the morally educated person. This will take the form of trying to summarize the ways in which, and the senses in which, a person's thought and action can be called 'rational' or 'irrational' in the moral sphere.

(a) There is first the basic sense of 'rational', which we considered in Chapter 1 on pp. 48–52, the sense in which a person must act for a reason (rather than just as a result of causes). Someone who did not act for a reason would certainly not be acting in the *moral* sphere: indeed, he would not be *acting* (in the full sense) at all. (This also includes the case of the person who is rationalizing: i.e. who may say that he is acting for a reason, but in whom the reason is not actually operative).

(b) In the sphere of interpersonal morality, where other people's interests are strongly affected, there is the person who acts for a reason, but whose reason has nothing to do with other people's interests and is therefore not appropriate. The thought and action of such a person would not be rational, because he is not following the rules of procedure relevant to this sphere of morality.

(c) There is the person who (in his moral thinking) is logically inconsistent, does not know all the relevant facts or refuses to face them, or does not sufficiently attend to the meanings of words (p. 76). He is irrational in terms of those rules or principles which enter into other kinds of thinking as well as into morality.

(d) There is the person who does not use sufficient psychological awareness, perceptiveness or imagination, and who is hence no good at identifying his own and other people's feelings. He is irrational in terms of those principles which go beyond the principles in (c) above, and which are peculiarly essential to morality.

One very important point must now be noted. The above list is not *simply* a list of skills, abilities or competences. In (c), for instance, we talked of the man who 'does not know all the relevant facts or refuses to face them': and these are two very different things. Similarly the man in (d) who 'does not use sufficient psychological awareness' may *either* not have the skill or ability to know what other people are feeling, *or* he may *have* the ability but *just not use it*. In other words, we have not distinguished in this list between (i) a person being morally educated in the sense of having the relevant skills and abilities, and (ii) a person being morally educated in the sense of actually using these skills and abilities in his moral life.

The latter connects with what we said earlier (pp. 74–5) about *people* being reasonable or unreasonable. We have to recognize that a man may be quite reasonable, and yet be unable to use the relevant skills and abilities (perhaps simply because he has not been taught them): and conversely, that a man may be possessed of all the skills and abilities, and yet himself be unreasonable (and hence not in fact use them). We are all familiar with people who have at least some of these skills – who are highly intelligent, know a great many facts, are good at logic, and so on – and yet rarely bring them to bear when they actually make their moral decisions. Their emotions get in the way, or they are lazy, or in one way or another *they* are unreasonable in their moral living: even though they may be extremely rational in other areas (they may be very good scientists or politicians, for instance). Equally we are familiar with people who are extremely reasonable – they are open-minded, anxious to learn, unmoved by misplaced fears or impulses, and so on – but who yet cannot reach reasonable moral beliefs simply because they are uninstructed. Neither type of person is fully educated in the moral sphere.

The notion of *people* being reasonable or unreasonable comes into the matter in yet another way. We may regard the list above as characterizing the person who not only has certain skills, but actually uses them in making his moral decisions. But there is still a gap between decision and action. A person may be wholly rational in making up his mind what he ought to do: he may be logical, perceptive, know all the facts, etc., and he may actually use all these abilities when presented with a moral problem: but he may still *act* irrationally. There may be a fatal disjunction between his thought and his behaviour. Inappropriate emotions may intervene, not before or during his moral thinking, but before or during his actions: he suddenly becomes afraid, or yields to impulse, or grows apathetic. We need therefore to add to our list by mentioning

(e) The person who has and uses all these skills, but fails to translate them into action because he is himself unreasonable in this respect.[29]

This summary will show, I hope, that it is at least possible to establish some general criteria for the morally educated person. But the last item on our list, (e), which dealt with the notion of a *person* being reasonable or unreasonable, shows that there is a lot of water still to be charted. We showed earlier that the notion of morality could fairly be held to include what we called 'mental health' cases: and we can now see that questions normally discussed under that title are significant for other categories of morality as well. Thus the kind of irrationality that appears in the 'mental health' cases is crucial for interpersonal morality also: for unless a person is himself reasonable, he will not be able to *use* the skills and abilities we have outlined.

Consider, for instance, the example of learning to drive.[30] The pupil requires factual information (where the brake and accelerator are), rules of thumb ('Don't switch on when in gear'), and practice. If he is to be a good driver, in the sense of being considerate as well as skilled, he also has to know something about the feelings of other road-users (e.g. that it is annoying to be held up by a slow-moving car on a narrow road). But this is by no means all. As we know only too well, road accidents may be partly or even chiefly caused by deficiencies which have little or nothing to do with what we may have taught the pupil so far. The real trouble may be that the pupil may sometimes become unreasonably aggressive, dislike being overtaken, drive too fast, forget what he has learnt about driving (if 'forget' is the right word – it's not that his *memory* is bad), and in general act unreasonably as a person. There are plenty of other cases. The lunatic who thinks he is Napoleon may be told all the facts, and may even be intelligent enough to understand them: the point is rather that he won't *face* the facts, or perhaps that he won't even *listen*. These and other such signs are the marks of unreason.[31]

We are dealing here with unreasonable *emotions* and *attitudes*: and it is important to realize in what way 'mental health' may be a misleading title under which to consider such cases. If a man is overtaken by an epileptic fit, foams at the mouth and shouts, or if he has a heart attack, or falls asleep, we do not describe him as *unreasonable*. His behaviour is neither reasonable nor unreasonable, for he is not acting as a human being in the full sense at all. He is, rather, being acted upon. Some 'mental health' cases may be like this: but many others are not. 'Having a neurosis' or 'being neurotic', for instance, is not like having bunions or being anaemic: nor, again, is it like having a gun in one's back or being pushed. Neuroses are not diseases which overtake you: nor are they genuine, full-blown cases of compulsion. If they were, one could not describe neurotics as unreasonable. Like many terms used in 'mental health', they are to be taken as descriptive of a certain type of irrationality, a very deep kind of unreason.

It is appropriate to speak of reason and unreason here because of the connexion between emotions and beliefs.[32] When we talk of the reasonableness of a person's emotions, we most naturally think in terms of whether the person may have some false belief as regards the object of the emotion, or (more generally) in terms of whether the emotion is directed towards its proper object.[33] The criteria of what is to count as a 'proper object' of an emotion require more attention than we can give them here: but we can see how the notion of *unconscious* beliefs is highly relevant. Thus X may be hostile towards Y because he thinks that Y has done him an injury: and when he learns that Y has not, his hostility ceases. But there is also the case where X does not (consciously) believe that Y has done him an injury, but acts as if he did. (Perhaps Y unconsciously reminds X of his father whom he hated.)

Looking back at our summary, we might be tempted to say that we can divide the task of moral education into two parts. First we should educate people so as to give them the skills, abilities and knowledge required for rational moral decision (these would be (a)–(d) in our list): and then we should 'give them the motivation' to put these into practice ((e) in the list). But 'giving them the motivation' does not really cover what we want to achieve in (e). We could in some sense 'motivate' people to put the skills into practice by threats, bribes, drugs or some form of conditioning. But this would not make them into more reasonable *people*, and would not count as *education*.[34] We need rather some way of educating (to say 'curing' may mislead) people so as to improve this deep and subtle form of rationality. This is why the case of psychoanalysis is of interest. For it suggests that, partly by enabling a person to get rid of certain profound misconceptions, his energies may then be freed for rational behaviour. He finds his own motivation, rather than being given it like a drug. And this, as well as avoiding difficulties about conditioning and indoctrination, is very much in line with what we want from (e) in our list.

We are here, of course, very much on the borderline between cases of profound unreason and cases of actual disease: and the vague phrase 'mental health' ought, indeed, to be broken down into these two very different parts. Which cases fall into which part must depend on a very close study of the individual cases themselves. But to fight free of the medical and clinical implications of the phrase 'mental health' may make us realize the very large number of cases which come into the first category: that is, which are cases of unreason rather than disease. For the reasons given above, it would be a great pity if moral educators failed to devote all the attention to this very important category which it deserves.

Also case of "redemptive" conversion

Types of irrationality in interpersonal morality

In that narrow but central sense of 'moral' which is concerned with interpersonal relations, we have seen that the rationality of an action or belief depends on the kind of reasons that a person has in mind, and that are actually operative in him (i.e. not rationalizations). What we might call self-generated or 'autistic'[35] reasons (or what appear to be reasons) fail in one of two general ways. Either they are merely prudential or 'selfish': or else they are merely forms of words which express the speaker's obedience to an authority. For instance, suppose I appear to be doing something which might be described as 'giving money to a beggar'. One set of reasons for doing this might be, e.g. 'Because my friends will think better of me', 'Because I shall avoid the embarrassment of passing the beggar without giving him anything', or 'Because my soul will be saved by such actions'. Another set might be 'Because my father told me to', 'Because my religion enjoins it', or 'Because the President approves of this sort of thing'.

For a reason to be a good moral reason,[36] it must point to some facts in the external world which make it reasonable to commit oneself to a universalizable rule. These facts must relate to the interests of other people. Neither a 'selfish' desire, e.g. for one's friends to think well of one, nor the psychological impressiveness of an authority, e.g. one's father's commands, can by themselves count as moral reasons. Either may, however, *correlate* with good moral reasons. Thus it may be the case that when I feel desire X, or when an authority says Y, the feeling of desire or the existence of the authority may be signs that there are good moral reasons for X and Y. So far as my own rationality goes, everything depends on how these facts are *used*. Thus my instinctive reaction to my wife's suffering (I want to comfort her) may be a sign that comforting her is right: but the *reason* or justification for comforting her is not that I have this instinctive reaction, but that the reaction correlates with what my wife needs. Similarly, what the Pope says may correlate with what is morally right. If I have reason to believe that it does correlate, which involves some prior knowledge of what *I* think is right so that I can know what it is supposed to correlate *with*, then to use these signs is quite reasonable. Thus if I say something like 'I just feel that A knows best', this must break down into (i) a feeling of being impressed, overawed, etc. by A; (ii) entertaining some proposition about the relation between what A says and what is right. For the belief to be a moral belief, or the choice a moral choice, there must be some element of (ii).

Thus, suppose that I am wondering what to think about birth control. Then I might accept some authority about the facts: say, a person who has been to China and seen suffering there, knows the country, can assess the consequences and so forth. I might *also* think that he is a perceptive, wise, sympathetic, etc. person. Then if he says 'Birth control is a good thing' I might rationally go along with this. But what makes this a moral opinion, and may make it a rational one, is my initial judgement that he is wise, perceptive, knows the facts, and so on: and the rationality of *this* judgement will in turn depend on whether I have good reasons for thinking all these things to be true of him. I am, in effect, using him as a very complex tool – as a computer, one might say, that I believe to be programmed not just with factual knowledge but also with a number of guiding evaluative principles that I approve of.

Although what I have called 'selfish' reasons and reasons derived from authority are psychologically distinguishable, they fall into the same logical category when contrasted with proper moral reasons. We experience desires, fears, sudden impulses, feelings of guilt, or pricks of conscience, or we have a tendency to admire or look up to some authority. None of these in themselves are moral reasons: for by themselves they are not reasons at all, though we may make them into prudential reasons of the form 'I couldn't live with myself if I did this, *so* I won't do it', or 'I want very much to do that, *so* I will do it', 'I feel awful about having done the other, *so* I won't do it again', or 'I feel an urge to act as he commands, *so* I will'.[37] We enter the moral arena, not when two feelings which we might call 'selfish desire' and 'conscience' or 'a sense of duty' conflict, but when we make an effort to decide, by reference to *other people*'s feelings and to the facts, which of these feelings (if either) should be followed – or to what rule or moral principle, in this situation, we ought to commit ourselves.

'Conscience' and 'moral authorities'

These considerations may help to evaluate the very popular notion of 'acting according to one's conscience', which may be briefly mentioned here. The notion of conscience is a compound of two logically distinct elements, (i) what one might describe as a 'raw' *feeling* of guilt, fear, taboo or whatever, and (ii) some kind of propositional *belief* or judgement about what is right.[3] Now if we ask the general question 'Should one act according to one's conscience?', this may mean (i) 'Should we follow our 'raw' feelings of guilt, etc.?': and the answer to this is obvious, namely 'Sometimes we should and sometimes we shouldn't'. Alternatively, it may mean (ii) 'Should we do what we believe or judge to be right?', to which the answer is equally obvious, namely 'Yes, of course, what else can we reasonably do (even though we may sometimes judge mistakenly)?'.

It is also perhaps worth while trying to spell out the relevant points about the notion of a 'moral authority'[39] somewhat more clearly. They amount to the following:

1. Somebody may have 'moral authority' in that sense of 'moral' which really means having some kind of psychological hold or power over others. When people appear to be giving reasons for their moral actions, such as 'I felt compelled to follow him', or 'He impressed me so much with his presence that I felt I ought to do what he said', or 'I was driven by the power of Jesus/the magnetism of Hitler/the deep sincerity of Gandhi to do so-and-so', they may well be admitting to a compulsion rather than quoting a reason.

2. People may also pose as 'moral authorities' in another sense, i.e. as people who by some method 'know the right answer' to moral problems. Whether they can be accepted as real authorities depends, not on whether they happen to get what we later come to regard as the right answer, and certainly not on whether they make some kind of psychological appeal to us, but simply on whether they have shown themselves better than other men at using the skills, and hence at fulfilling the criteria of rationality, which are appropriate to morality.

3. It is probable that various people will be, in this sense, authorities in *different* aspects of morality. Thus, some will be

good at attending to the hard facts, others at the meaning of words, others at knowing what people feel, and so forth. It would thus be rash to accept anyone as a moral authority without quali- fication: the temptation to do so would derive from the idea that moral knowledge depends on some single quality of intuition or apperception.

4. To be a moral authority is not to be good at communicating or teaching morality, for which other skills and talents are also in- volved: in the same way as to be a good historian is not necessarily to be a good teacher of history.

5. It may be reasonable to accept the word of a moral authority, but the choice to accept a moral authority is still our own choice: and the reasonableness of accepting the authority's word depends on the reasonableness of accepting the person as an authority in the first place.

6. Even where it is reasonable to do this, there are still good arguments for preferring that, as far as possible, people should themselves directly perceive the appropriate reasons for their moral views at first-hand.

Possible arguments here are:

(a) because this will result in a more secure psychological basis for their morality, a basis which they have appropriated for themselves and by their own efforts:

(b) because part of the point of morality is to adopt the right attitude towards other people within oneself, not merely to do the right thing.[40]

7. Hence we should do best to regard moral authorities as primarily useful in the following ways:

(a) as people whose skills we can attempt to emulate:

(b) as people whose precepts may help us to do the right thing (even if we do not outselves see why it is right), which will at the very least keep us from actively disturbing the interests of other people:

(c) as people whose precepts may give us a framework of action, which we can use to develop the right attitudes which are central to morality.[41]

E. CAN THESE NORMS BE JUSTIFIED?

We have painted a picture which could be called something like 'the liberal theory of morality'. Basically what we have tried to do is to draw a distinction between our first-order moral principles and some second-order norms or rules of procedure: things like self-awareness, facing facts, developing imagination, being consistent, attending to logic, and so on; and we are saying that following these norms is the ultimate objective of 'moral education' and its many preconditions. But however strongly or clearly we delineate this picture, there may yet be people who feel like saying 'But why should we accept these second-order norms? Why should we educate people to become like this rather than like something else? Are you not really imposing your own values in a rather subtler, second-order form?'[42]

This demand would require a number of different answers, depending on which of the second-order norms we were being asked to justify. Very roughly, we may make a distinction between (1) questions about why we should accept the norms that apply to interpersonal morality in particular – why, for instance, we should take account of *other people*'s interests at all: and here it may be that part at least of our answer must be empirical – that is, dependent on psychological facts: (2) questions about why we should frame our norms in terms of *interests* at all: why, for instance, we should not derive our judgements – at least in 'prudential' or 'mental health' cases – from some vision or ideal of a quite non-utilitarian nature: and (3) questions about why we should face facts, attend to logic, etc., where we should most naturally want to give a conceptual answer of some kind – that is, to show that the questions were in some way unreal or incoherent. We must now say something briefly about all of these: although it must be stressed that we cannot begin to do justice to the complexity of the issues involved.

1. Is there any point in bothering about other people's interests? Does virtue pay? Is justice profitable? Is it worth while being good. These Platonic questions[43] seem to take it for granted that, if their answers are negative, there is some sense in which the foundations of morality have been shaken; and certainly many

ordinary moralists and men of religion have gone out of their way to try to prove that the answers are not negative – that, if you are virtuous, it will pay off in some coinage or other: somehow, somewhere, perhaps in the next world if not in this.

(a) It is plain that, if a man has already committed himself to some attitude or rules of procedure which relate to other people's interests, then he is able to find a reason within that attitude or those rules. Thus if you genuinely love somebody, this makes it in itself satisfying to seek that person's good: if you agree to abide by some rule of procedure, such as voting or spinning a coin (instead of just grabbing what you can get), then you necessarily have a reason for going along with whatever is voted or decided in this way – even if you are outvoted or lose the toss. Although the analogy with morality is in important respects deficient, we may regard the situation as like that of someone who has decided to play a particular game. Having decided, he necessarily has a reason for accepting whatever the rules of the game enjoin, even if they enjoin losses or penalties. Thus a person who said 'I will be just, except where it doesn't pay me to be just' is like one who says 'I will abide by the toss of a coin, unless of course I lose the toss'. The former would not really have decided to be just at all, but only to pretend to be, just as the latter would not really have agreed to abide by the toss. In both cases the acceptance of a set of rules involves the *exclusion* of arguments about profit and loss in particular cases.

(b) But this is different from the person who wonders whether to play the game *at all*: who asks in a quite general way 'Why should I go in for justice, or virtue, or moral goodness – or for specific virtues, such as truthfulness or courage?' Some philosophers[44] have argued, I think successfully, that certain norms are logically necessary to the concept of a human society; for instance, the norm of truth-telling, without which communication (and hence society) would be impossible. But I am not clear that arguments of this type give us all that we want here: for the person who questions the necessity of morality may well question the necessity of a 'social order', in the sense of that phrase which the argument requires. If, indeed, a person has already made the move of accepting a social order or a form of life in which other people are regarded as equals,[45] then we are back to (a) above:

once he has asked the question 'What rules shall *we* have?', he has already taken the crucial first move. But even if he rejects completely that form of reasoning that regards others as equals, it is not yet clear that he is thereby denied the possibility of reasoning at all about his actions. For he may, obviously, still use the reasons of self-interest: he will use whatever means most readily serve his wants and desires. It is true that his wants and desires are partly determined by the conceptual descriptions he has learned in his society; and also that he would not have learned a language at all if he had not learned those impersonal rules without which language could not exist. But the fact that he is using the moral or linguistic capital of his fellows does not logically entail that he has to treat them as equals.

Certain other arguments, however, may be advanced relevant to this point:

(i) If such a person is seriously questioning the necessity of *any* kind of interpersonal rules at all, it may be possible to argue[46] that his position is not logically coherent. Briefly, the argument is that the concept of 'giving a reason' or 'having a reason' entails granting the validity of that reason to other people in relevantly similar positions. Thus if a man argues 'I ought to get as much money as possible, by any means I can, because that will make me happy', he thereby allows that other people ought to do the same if it will make them happy. The kind of reasoning here is (one might say) prudential rather than strictly moral: but even a prudential reason is only a reason if it is valid for other people. Hence reasoning itself implies a kind of embryonic morality, inasmuch as anything that could count as a reason must be impartial as between one person and another. Thus a policy of total self-interestedness may not be logically viable, since anything that would genuinely count as a policy must be based on impartial reasons.

(ii) The notion of having a reason is connected with human wants, needs or desires in general – perhaps particularly with pleasure and pain – and may indeed first be learned in this connexion.[47] If I have a headache and take an aspirin, my reason for taking it is that aspirins relieve headaches. Taking the aspirin gets me what I want. If someone asked me why I took the aspirin, and I gave an answer which had no connexion with my wants at all, what I said would not count as a reason. Thus I might reply 'Oh, I always do on Tuesdays': and this might turn out to connect with my wants, e.g. if a weekly dose of aspirin prevented the pain caused by excess acid. (Here I should have given a reason for taking an aspirin weekly; something additional would have to be said to justify taking one on *Tuesday*.) But it might not have any such connexion: and then I might in some sense have explained my behaviour (my friend would know what to expect on Tuesdays), but I could hardly have given a *reason* for it. Not just *anything* can count as a reason.

These arguments may certainly help us to disqualify *some* moral (or apparently moral) opinions (or what may be advanced as moral opinions). The first, (i), may disqualify the man who says, for instance, that his being hungry is a good reason for his trying to grab all the food, *if* such a man objects to other hungry people trying to grab all the food too: for it is (at least *prima facie*) being hungry that he must offer as a reason, and not *his* being hungry. The second argument, (ii), may disqualify the man who (for instance) gives as his reason 'Because I'm stronger than you' or 'Because I'm of royal blood', *if* he fails to show that 'being stronger' or 'being of royal blood' has any connexion with human wants or needs; the man who quotes these facts may more easily be understood as *arrogating* the right to take the food rather than *showing that he has* the right – that is, explaining why he is doing what he does rather than justifying it: 'I shall take it, because I'm stronger' rather than 'I ought to take it, because I'm stronger'.

But it would be a mistake to suppose that these arguments give us all that is required; or even, perhaps, to suppose that these kinds of arguments could ever do so. For too many cases escape our net. First, we are confronted with those whose wants or ideals are (to our eyes, at least) unusual: the sadist, the Jew-hater, the man who loves animals or pictures but is indifferent to human beings, and so forth. We have also those who seem, not so much to have unusual wants, but to lack the usual ones: the manic-depressive, the extreme ascetic, or the potential suicide who suffers from no obvious external disasters but who nevertheless 'sees no point' in anything. Secondly, we are confronted by those whose wants are perhaps *not* unusual, but are nevertheless not very closely related to other people's interests. A person may genuinely and coherently advocate a policy of *laissez-faire*, or a free-for-all, rather than one which we should recognize under such titles as 'loving your neighbour', 'helping other people', or 'considering other people's interests'. It is certainly plausible to represent this as a question about the *content* of morality rather than about whether there should be such a thing as morality (in the sense of interpersonal rules) at all.[48] But he may still ask, as it were, why we should not act like egoists rather than altruists. Is it not a good thing to be a tyrant, to have absolute power? Is it not so good a thing that we ought to be prepared to take the risk of failure, the risk of ending up as a slave, in order to have the chance of success as a tyrant? Indeed, may it not be that we are so constituted as human beings that the roles of tyrant *and* slave may fit us better than the relationships of equality and fraternity that sentimental moralists try to urge upon us?

In order to deal with the very wide variety of these cases, it seems to me that conceptual arguments of a quite different kind may be required. One may indeed point to certain very general criteria of rationality, and show how such wants may conflict, or be impermanent, or be impossible to satisfy. But there seems to remain a basic and genuine question about how far one ought (as a matter of social or psychological expediency) to identify with or care about other people: how much feeling one should invest in them. It is easy to make vague general remarks[49] about this problem; but the question of how far the problem merits conceptual (as opposed to empirical) arguments seems to me very obscure. It may be that a proper analysis of such notions as 'happiness', 'satisfaction', and 'what a man really wants' on the one hand, and of certain concepts in the field of mental health (particularly the notions of 'communication' or 'relating to other people') on the other, would yield a purely conceptual argument for altruism: an argument, that is, not just for doing altruistic actions, but for being the sort of person who takes pleasure in being genuinely altruistic. Such an argument would show the importance of 'considering other people's interests' in a much stronger sense:[50] but (so far as I am aware) modern philosophers have not yet given most of these concepts the attention they deserve.

On the other hand, it may be that the problem also calls for empirical evidence from psychology; and indeed it seems that certain unalterable facts about the child's world and his up-bringing indicate a close connexion between personal happiness and a strong regard for the interests of others. Many psychologists have written a great deal about the importance of love, relationships of equality, 'maturity' and so forth, which I will not venture to repeat here.[51] I must leave it to the reader to decide for himself, on the evidence, just how strong the case is; but it does not seem possible to doubt that it is strong enough for the practical purposes of moral education.

2. Considerations of this sort may give us some kind of guidance in dealing with our second question – the question of whether we have any right to disqualify those who derive their morality from some ideal, or vision, or picture of the world which is not conceived in terms of *interests* at all. The case in favour of such people, and against those philosophers who (perhaps somewhat incautiously) have seemed to imply that a liberal morality is the only possible morality, has been powerfully argued.[52] But it is possible, I think, to maintain our criteria of rationality (summarized earlier, pp. 93–7) whilst granting all that the case demands.

We may grant the following points:

(i) That if the liberal view of morality and our criteria of rationality are intended as a *description* of how many people in fact think morally, then they fail to do justice to those who think in a quite different way: perhaps in terms of 'dignity', 'honour', 'the will of God', etc.[53]

(ii) That purely conceptual arguments – that is, arguments derived solely from the use of particular terms (e.g. the argument derived from the concept of 'having a reason' in (1) above) – are insufficient to give us all the methodology we need for morality;

(iii) That the area of morality is wider than the area of actions

for which we allot a particular type of praise or blame: it includes also our general attitudes, feelings, ways of looking at
the world and at other people, etc. (this indeed we have
noticed earlier; see pp. 59–66 and pp. 86–9);
(iv) That 'interests' may be too 'utilitarian' a word to describe
moral ideals and visions which may, nevertheless, be perfectly
justifiable. Thus one might accept that granting independence
to a very backward people was, at least in one sense, 'against'
their interests' (because of the economic chaos, civil war, etc
that would ensue), but still reasonably maintain that they
ought to be independent (and here one might talk of 'human
dignity', 'freedom', 'self-respect', etc.).

But it does not follow from any or all of these points, that
there are *no* criteria of rationality to be followed by a person who
opposes, say, an ideal of dignity or honour to some more
'utilitarian' ideal conceived in terms of pleasure or satisfaction.
To talk in terms of 'interests' is not necessarily to commit oneself to some ignoble or hedonistic ideal. It is simply to say that
reasons offered for personal ideals, as well as for interpersonal
actions, can be good or bad reasons: that their goodness or bad-
ness is connected with human wants and desires:[54] and that the
kinds of skills we require here are those to which we refer when
we talk of awareness, perceptiveness, insight, and so forth. The
man who sacrifices wife and children to avoid 'loss of face', and
the man who remains entirely at the pig-like level of food, drink
and sex, do not merely offer us interesting examples of different
ways of life, between which there is nothing to choose. We would
naturally suspect that both men were blind to important facts
about themselves; or, if this be too crude, had failed to connect
certain of their desires or intentions with other of their desires or
intentions, or with important experiences in their own life-
histories. Of course we should have to prove this; and such
proof would not necessarily be only a matter of conceptual clarification.[55]

It is possible, indeed, that too narrow a conception of philosophy may tempt us to concentrate unduly upon purely conceptual
arguments; as if, so to speak, one could prove a person's irrationality by logical or linguistic deduction. It might be more profi-

table to pay greater attention to what actually happens in different types of discourse which we could call 'arguments' or 'rational persuasion'.[56] There is, in fact, quite a lot of discourse (and some things that could hardly be called 'discourse' at all) which comes within the general area of 'rational persuasion'; we need only consider such obvious instances as reading a novel, relating a parable, making use of paradoxes, irony, overstatements, or sudden remarks that seem to act like squibs on our moral sensibilities, or showing someone a leper colony. There is a whole range of activities, which stretches from what we might call offering 'raw experience' at one end to deductive argument at the other. All these have their uses, their purposes and their rules of procedure.

Philosophers often write as if people already accepted the merits of certain forms of discourse and the rules governing those forms, so that whatever they prove within those forms would thereby be acceptable; and it is at this point that practical people feel inclined to object that the whole thing is 'too academic'. This objection may not be without point. It is groundless, indeed, if the implication is simply that people are not in fact reasonable, and that we need more than philosophy to make people good: this philosophers would be the first to grant. But it may be well grounded: the implication may be that the merits of a particular type of discourse have to be demonstrated, if any proof or demonstration within that type of discourse claims any solid title to rationality. Certainly, it is one task actually to employ such discourse, and quite another to comment on its point or purpose, its rules of procedure, and its merits; and no doubt the second of these tasks, not the first, is the philosopher's. But it may be that it is the reasons for the acceptance of these types of discourse, or of certain forms of communication, which would most reward our attention: and these reasons are not necessarily deductive.

Nevertheless, it is too slick to say simply that nobody can tell us how we *ought* to think in the area of morality without thereby imposing their own ideas of morality on us. For what the philosopher does (or ought to do) is to *remind* us, as it were, of criteria of rational thought which we all accept; or else to show us that we ought to accept these criteria by explaining to us how they follow from higher, second-order criteria which we already accept but which we have failed to apply. This process of 'assembling reminders' may take a short time or a long one, and it may succeed or fail: but it is a reasonable process, and not a matter of bullying.

3. To this extent, then, our second-order norms seem to be supported by reason rather than by any desire to impose a partisan morality on our children. Few of us, indeed, seriously doubt this – when we think seriously about the matter at all. This applies also to the other norms with which we have not yet dealt, those which involve what appear to be basic principles of rationality, such as facing facts or attending to logic. Many people – more, perhaps, than some philosophers or other academics seem to imagine – question (or appear to question) such basic principles.[57] One practical difficulty that arises is to know how far such questions are seriously intended as questions,[58] i.e. whether the person is genuinely seeking an answer, or merely using the question-form as some kind of emotional attack on what he takes to be unjustifiably authoritarian requirements. For many the unconscious train of thought appears to be 'reason = rules = the tyranny of adults/elders/schoolmasters'; or indeed 'reason' may symbolize to them restraints of a less obvious kind, which it would require a psychoanalyst to uncover.

We may begin our discussion with one such example. Once I had a philosophy student who contradicted herself. I said 'Look, you've contradicted yourself: you said A was X, and then that it wasn't X'. She said 'So what? Why shouldn't I contradict myself?' I said 'Well, you *can*, of course, but then you'll find that you won't have *said* anything: thus if you say things to me like "I've read the book and I haven't looked at it", you won't be making any sense, and we shan't be able to talk'. She said 'Well, I don't see any point in talking anyway'. I then changed the subject. Now what is being challenged here is something which we all normally take for granted, the law of non-contradiction. One could equally well challenge other rules of procedure. I might say to a lunatic 'Look here, you're not Napoleon, because he died some time back, and see, here's a portrait of him ...' and so on, and he might reply 'Oh, facts, facts, who cares about facts?' And, after all, why *should* one care about facts?

Sometimes this sort of move results in the person's being unintelligible. If you say 'I'm Napoleon, but I don't care what the facts are', there is an implied contradiction – not so much in your actual words, but between your utterance of them and the words themselves. The utterance of 'I'm Napoleon' is normally intelligible only as a statement of fact, and implies that it is made as such, in good faith: so that if you then say 'but to hell with the facts', one feels baffled. Perhaps one begins to think that it is meant in some odd way, like 'I'm a Dutchman' or 'I'll eat my hat'. In something like the same way, the person who says 'Why should I have a reason for doing anything?' sounds odd, because 'why' normally asks for a reason, and yet the whole apparatus of having reasons is just what he's challenging. But it is always possible not to face facts, not to be intelligible, or to contradict oneself. Whether it is possible to have a consistent and coherent *policy* along these lines, is more doubtful: for the notions of consistency and coherency seem to imply things like intelligibility and the normal laws of logic. But even if this isn't coherent, people could still *do* it. They could just *not have* a policy at all: they could just *not be* reasonable. (This happens a great deal as it is.)

Why is it psychologically odd to take this line? Roughly, because human beings want to satisfy their desires. They want (in a second-order way) to get what they want; they want to adopt means to achieve their ends. This means that they want to exercise control over themselves and their environment. It is in this sense that everyone wants to be rational: not in the sense that everyone wants to think hard and logically all the time. The second-order norms we have outlined are, in effect, simply very general principles that we have always found helpful in gaining such control: using language in accordance with certain rules, facing facts, and so forth. To be human and conscious, to be a person, *is* to play this game. It is a difficult game, and one we often temporarily resign from. (Sometimes we resign from it permanently by committing suicide or going mad.)

Another way of putting this is to say that our second-order norms are not themselves moral values or opinions of any kind, but rather represent the necessary foundations for *any* moral or empirical belief. Thus part of what we mean by an empirical belief, a judgement about something in the world, is that it concerns itself with the facts: a person who did not attend to the facts at all could not seriously hold any empirical beliefs. In the same way somebody who paid no attention to human feelings and desires, the external facts, and the laws of logic, could hardly be said to have moral principles. Again, to initiate people into these second-order norms could not intelligibly be described as *indoctrination*,[59] or as the imposition of a particular set of values or beliefs on them: it is, rather, initiation into those general principles which are <u>characteristic of a certain form of human</u> thought.

Self-awareness and Moral Knowledge

The complexity of these matters may well make some people feel that only the very intelligent, or the very sophisticated, have any hope of being good at morality. This is so far from the truth that it is worth stressing the opposite point; that we frequently use our intelligence and sophistication as a defence against having to engage in contexts of communication which, *as we know quite well*, will in fact improve our rationality. We may raise philosophical and empirical questions about morality *ad nauseam*: 'What does it mean to talk of a moral "mistake"?', 'Can we prove that psychoanalysis cures people?', 'Do the statistics show that maternal security is important for children?' and so forth. Of course these questions must be answered; but the difficulty of answering them must not be used as a kind of academic defence in depth against being honest. There is a quite straightforward sense in which it is easier to be sophisticated than to own up. It is far from clear that there is any correlation at all between sophistication and rationality, sanity, honesty, the ability to love or anything which we think to be important in the moral sphere.

This is why the notion of self-awareness is crucial. Of course a great deal may be gained by attention to rationality in the more simple senses of consistency and logic: and we cannot tell just what percentage of moral difficulties and disputes require other methods, though I suspect it is higher than some philosophers are apt to imply. But in any case, the practical difficulty is not that people are not clever enough or have not spent enough time studying formal logic or academic philosophy, but rather that they are not willing, or just do not try, to engage in contexts of communication which aim at satisfying these standards. It's not that they can't, because of intellectual deficiency, play these games: it's rather that they don't want to, or are frightened, or out of practice, or lack encouragement. Self-awareness is important, not just because it is fashionable, but because it is the only means we have of tackling these basic difficulties.

Most of those who (like myself) have stressed the importance of freedom in morality, under such philosophical headings as 'autonomy', 'prescriptivism', etc., have really been concerned to block some intuitionist view of morality whereby moral truths are regarded as factual truths, only somehow grander or more difficult to see: or else to shoot at certain abuses of the notion of authority in morals. But, as we have seen, this is not to deny the possibility of moral rationality or moral knowledge. It is no part of this book to say what I or anybody else would regard as the content of that knowledge, though I should be more than willing to grant that it would include most of the usual propositions about the wrongness of killing, lying, stealing, breaking promises, etc. There is no doubt a corpus of moral knowledge, handed down by tradition, of whose validity we have every right to feel certain: and no doubt there are certain facts, contingent but not purely accidental, about the nature of human beings which can be used as a basis for the 'primary rules' in morality, or could be called 'natural law'.[60] From this point of view the kind of criteria we have put forward are unlikely to result in anything very revolutionary.

In a sense, indeed, our line has been to stress the implications of moral *knowledge*. Knowledge entails being *entitled* to believe: it is not a matter of just believing and happening to be right. Educating people so that they know things entails educating them to derive their beliefs from good grounds, not just teaching them in such a way that they repeat truths correctly. This is not so much a point about morality, but about any form of rational education: and this is why we have stressed the notion of the criteria of rationality, and the notion of moral skills or aptitudes, rather than attempting to discover some general 'basis for moral-ity' by combining features common to most moral codes into a mélange which might be publicly acceptable – at least for the time being, and for some societies if not others.

Reason and Emotion

My choice of words like 'rational' to express these second-order norms may still arouse misgivings, perhaps particularly on the part of those who feel that justice has not been done to what are sometimes (misleadingly) called the 'irrational' elements of human nature. The following points may help to prevent mis-understanding:

(a) Words like 'rules', 'reasons', 'logical' and 'rational' on the one hand, and 'imagination', 'feeling', 'emotion' and 'com-mitment' on the other, may be used to present a false picture, a picture of mythical conflict of 'reason versus emotion' or 'faith versus logic'. Being rational or reasonable, however, does not mean disregarding one's feelings, but trying to assess, guide or direct them in some coherent way. If we make any sort of judge-ment at all about our feelings, commitments, etc. we cannot do so except by reference to some kind of standard, or rule, or prin-ciple: and words like 'right', 'justifiable', 'wise', 'sensible', 'authentic', 'unprejudiced', 'perceptive' and many others are tied to the notion of such standards. Hence, while it is correct to say that one's rules and standards must be one's own, and not accepted uncritically from authority, it is not correct to say that one can do without standards altogether – unless one wishes to resign one's humanity and live at random.

(b) So far from disregarding feelings and emotions, therefore, we have to do them justice – but in the right sort of way: and this is not to regard them as (on some mystical grounds) authori-tative, but to understand them with a view to our being able to use and control them for our own benefit, rather than being controlled or compelled by them. Now there may be all sorts of other descriptions which would, in practice, fit the idea of a 'morally educated' person, or some aspects of that person. We could talk sociologically of the 'autonomous' person, who is not governed purely by tradition or by the norms of his contemporary society:[61] we could talk psychologically about 'having a strong ego', or 'being mature':[62] we could borrow from various moral or religious traditions and talk in terms of 'love', or 'justice' or righteousness': we could borrow from the existentialists and talk of 'authentic' or 'genuine' moral commitments, and so on. So far from having any quarrel with these descriptions, I welcome them as attempts to cash out the notion of rationality into practical terms, with an eye on the causes and preconditions necessary for the existence of rationality. But since they are not intended as *logical definitions*, they run the risk of being partisan by including within themselves some first-order norms or moral values which might reasonably be challenged. Thus one might reasonably ask 'Why be what the *psychologists* call "mature"?', 'Why be what the *existentialists* call "authentic"?', or 'Why be what the *Christians* call "righteous"?': whereas one cannot reasonably ask 'Why be reasonable?'. Certainly one can ask 'Why be what the *philosophers* call reasonable?': but if philosophers have given a partisan definition of 'reasonable', rather than one which we all accept or can be brought to see without being bullied, then they are just bad philosophers.

(c) Hence there is nothing wrong with suggesting that what I have called 'rationality in the moral sphere' and 'being morally educated' are, in practice, functions of some more general description or set of descriptions ('having a strong ego', 'autonomy', etc.). Indeed I have no doubt that this is so. But we have to *test* these descriptions against the notion of rationality, or any better logical definition of 'moral education' that we can find. We have to know that these phenomena actually produce rational people and not something else (people who just conform to their society, or who just rebel against it, or whatever). Again, it may well be that most of the factors relevant to a child's moral education concern features of child development, or of the social system, which we might be tempted to call 'non-rational', meaning that nothing much could be done about them by having logical discussions with children, or persuading them to think very hard: perhaps even that there is very little we can do about them by any methods. A respect for these hard facts is perfectly consistent with my thesis: indeed it is part of any such thesis that facts should be respected. We have to recognize them, understand their importance, and use them as far as we can for our own purposes. This *is* precisely 'doing justice to the irrational element in human nature'.

As far as I can see at present, I would say that abandoning these norms means resigning from being a person. One may say 'Well, why be a person?': but any answer to this would have to be given in terms which already imply the concept of a person (or any other rational, rule-following, reason-giving entity: Martians are included). Insofar as an entity is still a person – particularly, insofar as he (or it) is prepared to talk, then rationality has a foothold, and we can do business. If it is not a person, then we can perhaps help to make it into one, as we do every day with new-born infants. If we make life such hell for it that it wants to resign from being a person, temporarily or permanently, then something has gone wrong and it is our fault. It is just because things so often go wrong in this way that philosophical description is not enough: we need not only to describe rationality, but to find out and produce the psychological and social factors that make rationality tolerable and, if possible, enjoyable.

1. I don't want to imply that this is the fault of 'literate people'; it may well be largely the fault of philosophers.

2. That is, he may accept the facts (that *we* count as evidence), but not accept them *as* evidence.

3. See, e.g., my *Logic and Sexual Morality* (Penguin Books), pp. 48–9.

4. See pp. 110–12.

5. In the sense already discussed in Chapter 1, pp. 48–52.

6. For example, if somebody says that he did a certain thing because he would get a lot of money for it, this is probably not an impartial reason; for there is no indication that he would wish anybody else to do the same sort of thing to him. Thus if the act in question was that of defrauding somebody, he would not want somebody else to defraud him in this way. It might be a man's principle to get as much money for himself, always, as he could; but he would not prescribe such a principle impartially for everyone else.

7. Perhaps most of us have a lot of prescriptive opinions in matters of aesthetics or etiquette which, if they came into conflict with morality, would be overridden – put into cold storage, if you like – in order to do the morally right thing.

8. See R. M. Hare's *Freedom and Reason* (O.U.P.), from which I have borrowed freely here and elsewhere (though I don't want to imply that Hare would necessarily agree with anything I have said). This is not the place for a discussion of technical philosophical issues often hung on such pegs as 'descriptivism', 'autonomy' and so forth. But since it does affect our thesis to some extent, the following points may be worth making:

(i) It has been argued by some that this formal and 'autonomist' kind of analysis (a) can have no claim to universal validity, since it would not apply to the moral thought and language of a very primitive or restricted society, and/or (b) could only have been made in an 'open' society such as our own, i.e. the possibility of philosophers and others giving this kind of account is causally dependent on a certain type of society. (b) seems to me true, but (a) – insofar as I understand it – either false or misleading. There is always a logical possibility of any human being choosing to value different things from what his fellows value, and for different reasons: and also the logical possibility of his expressing this choice in language. It may be that members of certain very restricted societies do not realize this possibility: it may also be that in practice they cannot, e.g. because they are unaware of alternative standpoints, conceptually hidebound, heavily conditioned or indoctrinated, or whatever. But to say that this analysis is invalid on these grounds is like saying that it is 'invalid' because it does not fit the 'moral language' of children, or that modern descriptions of 'scientific method' are invalid because they do not fit the 'science' of the Babylonians or the ancient Greeks. (See also pp. 346-7, note 7.)

The point is rather that when (for whatever sociological causes) individuals become aware of alternative standpoints, they have to be able to choose between them if they are to behave rationally. Indeed these alternatives *exist*, whether or not certain cultures are aware of them; and the analysis (or at least some analysis which takes account of this) is necessary for the rational man. What has been called 'the autonomous standpoint' or 'the individualist framework' is thus not *just* one standpoint amongst many, except in the quite simple sense that many people do not (perhaps cannot) adopt it. It is forced on *us* by our awareness of alternatives: but awareness of alternatives – of the possibility of using *different* criteria – seems to be one of the distinguishing features of a rational man in any society or conceptual system. As one author says, 'it seems that to envisage a choice between frameworks of evaluation is in effect already to opt for the autonomist or individualist position' (Alan Montefiore, 'Fact, Value and Ideology' in *British Analytical Philosophy*, edited by Bernard Williams and Alan Montefiore, Routledge & Kegan Paul, p. 201). But this does not imply that we opt for this *arbitrarily*, any more than it is arbitrary to adopt a new scientific theory to deal with new facts. J. L. Austin pointed out that this kind of clarification '... is as much a matter of making clear distinctions as of making already existent distinctions clear' (*How to do things with Words*, O.U.P., p. 72). 'Making clear distinctions' is certainly a rational activity.

It may nevertheless be better for certain societies and individuals – or even for all societies and individuals at a certain stage of development – if their awareness of alternatives is restricted. There is nothing particularly paradoxical about this, for awareness of alternatives is only one of the characteristics of a rational man: another characteristic, which might be very relevant to such cases, is his ability to withstand temptation. On this see pp. 155-64.

(ii) Other philosophers have raised questions in relation to this account, which may be crudely summarized as doubts about (a) whether the account has an *exclusive* right to the title of 'moral thinking': (b) whether it may *include* or admit some types of thinking that we would *not* call 'moral': (c) why, in any case, people *ought* to think in this way. The meaning of these questions (no doubt there are others also), and the actual issues involved, still seem to me very obscure, and I am not sure that the extant literature (quoted below) has yet made them very much clearer. I do not feel competent to discuss them fully here, though some of what follows in this chapter may be thought relevant to them. But I do not think it can be shown conclusively that they debar us from using Hare's account, at least as a starting-point, *for the purposes of moral education in this society*. The question of how one ought to define areas of discourse perhaps partly turns on the context within which one wants a definition, and on the kind of purposes one has in mind. (See Chapter 3, pp. 126–8.) I hope at least to be sufficiently lucid, in what follows, for the philosophically minded reader to be able to detect if and when any questions are being unfairly begged, or any grossly partisan viewpoint being adopted.

The literature on this topic is enormous, but the reader may find it easiest to take up the references (particularly to the work of P. R. Foot) given in the article 'On Morality's Having a Point', by D. Z. Phillips and H. O. Mounce (*Philosophy*, October 1965); see also A. C. MacIntyre's 'What Morality is Not' (*Mind*, 1957).

9. See pp. 102–10.

10. I do not want to say that we cannot do this. It may be – perhaps obviously is – a contingent fact that everyone or nearly everyone has some constant wants, such as to avoid pain or death. It may also be that some wants can be shown to be conceptually necessary to satisfy other wants: for instance, the ability to talk, think and act seems to be a prerequisite of satisfying almost any want. But we need not enter these waters here.

11. Of course this may be disputed: see pp. 80–83.

As this example shows, there is a problem about whether our concern as moral beings is with other people's *wants* or *preferences* on the one hand, or with their *needs* or *interests* (in a sense in which a man's 'interests' or 'best interests' might conflict with his 'wants') on the other. I incline to think that, in the area of interpersonal morality that we are here considering, it is the former: that morality in this sense is concerned with a kind of basic social contract, designed to institutionalize conflicting wants by agreed rules, which it is our moral duty (as individuals) to obey. This raises other problems about which rules *are* agreed, or which rules really express what people want (as against rules which just happen to be there or are imposed by authorities): and about how, in general, you verify what a person wants. (People want different and incompatible things at different times, for instance, and sometimes they don't know what they want.) The question of what we (collectively) *ought* to want – what rules to have – or of what our 'true interests' or 'real needs' are seems to me to fall under a wider sense of morality, which we shall consider under 'prudential' and 'mental health' judgements, in later sections of this chapter. (See also p. 66 in Chapter 1.) But since I believe all these can, in practice and from the angle of moral education, be subsumed under certain general criteria of rationality, I do not think we need do more than note these problems here.

12. The desire to stick to the criterion of overridingness in the case of morality is not unreasonable. If we are interested in a man's morality, we are usually interested in what he will *do* (rather than just in what he believes, and how he defends his beliefs), in a much stronger way than in the case of other forms of life, such as science or aesthetics. To talk of 'moral behaviour' makes more sense than to talk of 'scientific behaviour' or 'aesthetic behaviour'.

13. Perhaps what we ought to say is that the art-lover's view is 'aesthetic' in the sense that it derives from feelings about colour, form, and other qualities in works of art: but that it becomes a *moral* view if and when he uses those feelings to propound principles of action that are overriding, impartial, prescriptive, etc. – i.e. when (in (ii) above) he says 'they *should be* preserved'.

14. See his *Freedom and Reason* (O.U.P.), pp. 146–56.

15. See pp. 105–10 and pp. 178–9.

16. 'If only I had studied psychology before, I could have understood myself and my teenage son better and not driven him to suicide. I didn't know what I was doing' (a father): 'If only I had drunk less I could have driven more carefully and not killed him: I didn't know what I was doing' (a motorist). We might say: 'Ah, but motorists know quite well that drink leads to careless driving'. Yes, and fathers know quite well that ignorance of psychology leads to uninformed handling of teenagers. The assignment of praise or blame seems partly to depend on how much, in practical living, we can reasonably expect of people that they should do by way of informing themselves, taking precautions, being aware of themselves and other people, and so forth. But that they should do these sorts of things is certainly part of a general moral duty.

17. Of course some actions are often both symptomatic and causative: in a sense, since all actions have some effect, they are always so. But not all actions are causative of *harm*, either to others or to the actor. It is this class I am talking about.

18. I am not, of course, saying that any of these arguments are valid for this particular example.

19. There is an important practical question here about when we

should stop people acting out various forms of moral or psychological inadequacy. The relevant points seem to be:

(i) If he damages other people thereby, we should want to be sure that stopping him from acting would damage him more, if we were going to allow him to act.

(ii) It could be argued that even if it does neither him nor anyone else any harm, it will still not do him any good, since he is not likely to acquire any more rationality (in the form of insight) by the mere acting out.

(iii) On the other hand it might be true (a) that if we stop him, a worse or more damaging symptom will take its place, and – more interestingly – (b) that unless he does act it out, he will not be in a position to objectify his own mental state at all: that is, by acting out he may acquire no more specific or detailed insight, but at least he may be able to see what sort of person he really is, or that he needs treatment.

All this of course belongs to the domain of psychiatry, and needs further investigation at an empirical as well as the conceptual level.

20. Those framed in terms relating to rationality (see R. S. Peters' essay in *Aims of Education* (bibliography)): not those which make mental health conceptually parallel to physical health.

21. And also for the deeper reason that the concept of mental health may underlie prudential and interpersonal morality: see pp. 106–7.

22. See pp. 61–6.

23. pp. 84–5.

24. There are no doubt *some* basic feelings which it would be difficult for any human being not to be able to recognize, or the descriptions of which he would not be able to understand, (love, hate, jealousy, guilt, etc.) These feelings seem to be necessary features of human life (perhaps of all animate thinking creatures), and because they pervade so much of life it would be hard to conceive of a person who had totally suppressed them and had hence wholly lost his grip of the descriptive terms. But (a) there are other feelings whose descriptions may not have been adequately learned in childhood, and (b) even the common feelings may not be acknowledged or properly described in certain contexts, or in reference to certain objects. See pp. 96–7.

25. E.g., Professor Strawson (see reference under *Christian Ethics and Contemporary Philosophy* in the bibliography).

26. See Part II (A), pp. 233–41.

27. See pp. 59–66.

28. See pp. 195–6.

29. We normally list such cases under two headings: (a) those who are blameworthy, and could have acted rightly if only they had tried: (b) those who are not to be blamed because they couldn't help it. 'Unreasonable' can apply to cases of both types: not only to those who are weak-willed, but also to the neurotic and other 'mental health' cases. The well-known problems about blame and free will are of course connected with our general thesis, but I don't think we need wait on their solution: they are not the *same* problems as problems about what is meant by calling people 'unreasonable'.

See Professor Strawson's *Freedom and Resentment* (O.U.P.).

30. I have borrowed this example, and some of the points, from R. M. Hare's *The Language of Morals* (O.U.P.), pp. 62–68.

31. See for instance John Lucas, 'The Philosophy of the Reasonable Man' (*Philosophical Quarterly*, 1963).

32. On emotions generally see Anthony Kenny's *Action, Emotion and Will* (Routledge) Chapter 3.

33. On this topic see Bernard Williams' *Morality and the Emotions* (op. cit.), particularly p. 20: also Mary Warnock's 'The Justification of Emotions' (*Proceedings of the Aristotelian Society*, Supplementary Volume, 1957).

34. As we observed at some length in Chapter 1, pp. 45–56.

35. The word 'autistic', as used by psychologists, has a technical descriptive sense (though exactly *what* sense seems to be disputed and obscure). I use it here and elsewhere in a wider, but I hope still intelligible, way.

36. Again, in the narrow sense of 'moral', referring only to inter-personal morality.

37. But we must not forget that such prudential reasons do not offer us a complete excuse. It may be right for me, *being the sort of person I am*, to do or not to do certain things: but it may still be wrong for me to be the sort of person I am. Thus if I have very strong feelings of guilt, horror, etc. about (say) sex or war, it may be prudentially right for me not to engage in these activities; and it may even be morally right, in the sense that other people's interests might not be served by my engaging in them if my strong feelings are going to cause too much trouble all round. But I might still have a moral duty to try to change those feelings, if other people's interests (and perhaps my own best interests also) demanded it. See my *Logic and Sexual Morality*, p. 63 (bibliography).

38. See pp. 47–8.

39. See pp. 17–18.

40. See R. S. Peters, *Authority, Responsibility and Education* (Allen & Unwin) – Chapters 1 and 2: also his *Ethics and Education*, Chapter IX.

41. For a further discussion of this, see p. 131 ff.

42. Readers who feel no temptation to say this at all may wish to skip the next few pages.

43. See particularly Plato's *Republic*, Books I and II, and P. R. Foot's 'Moral Beliefs' (*Proceedings of the Aristotelian Society*, 1958).

44. E.g. Peter Winch, 'Nature and Convention' (*Proceedings of the Aristotelian Society*, 1959–60).

45. In practice, those who wish to throw morality overboard are precisely those who refuse to regard others as equals: they may or may not admit certain similarities with themselves, but in any case their interests do not *weigh* with them. Thrasymachus' metaphor of a shepherd who uses sheep for his own profit (*Republic*, Bk. I, 343–44) is the first philosophical example of this: 'race prejudice' is perhaps the most topical illustration nowadays.

46. See R. S. Peters, *Ethics and Education* (bibliography), Part Two, particularly pp. 120–26 and 170–77.

47. Moreover, the giving of reasons characteristically comes to an end here. In the example which follows, my friend might say 'But why do you want to relieve your headache?' It would be pretty odd for him to say even this, but I might think he wasn't very well-informed about headaches (or didn't know what 'ache' meant), and reply 'Headaches are painful'. For him to ask 'Why do you want to avoid pain?' would be very odd indeed, if he meant to ask for a reason. A great many answers, such as 'For fun', 'I just enjoy it', 'It hurts', 'It gives me pleasure' act as stopping-points to demands for reasons. One may even say 'Oh, I don't know, I just felt like it'; and here the borderline between giving a reason (in the sense of a justification) and giving a psychological explanation is very blurred. See also pp. 107–10.

48. See A. Phillips Griffiths and R. S. Peters, 'The Anatomy of Prudence' (*Mind*, April 1962), particularly pp. 178–80.

49. 'To identify with other people, to regard and treat them as equals, to count them and their interests as having equal validity with oneself and one's own interests are necessary preconditions for the satisfaction of one's own desires. To hate, to feel superior or inferior, to adopt master-slave relationships rather than relationships of equality is to place oneself in a hostile and unsatisfying world. To put it in the least high-minded way I can think of, you *get more out of* people if you identify with them: and, incidentally, not only out of people but out of animals and even inanimate objects. Woolly notions like "a respect for life", "doing good to others", "giving rather than receiving", etc., may thus be firmly sponsored by psychological facts'. (From my *Logic and Sexual Morality* (Penguin Books) p. 53.)

50. See my *Equality* (Hutchinson's) pp. 137–68 – though I am far from satisfied with the arguments there put forward.

51. See, for instance, A. Storr's *The Integrity of the Personality* (Penguin Books).

52. See Iris Murdoch's essay in *Christian Ethics and Contemporary Philosophy* (bibliography).

53. Philosophers may indeed have regarded their task partly as one of describing how people think morally; though they could hardly suppose this to be a task for them alone, since the variety of such thought would require the assistance of (at least) the historian and the sociologist.

54. It is hard to know just *how much* can be proved by the argument connecting reasons with wants in 1 (ii) above (p. 104). Suppose a man, living in a society whose criteria of morality are mostly utilitarian, who says that it is his moral principle to kill people on Tuesdays. We ask him to establish some connexion with the common stock of human wants and desires in that society; he does not even try to do this, but instead says that Tuesday is the third day of the week, that the number three is sacred, etc. Then he has certainly given a reason in his own terms: that is, 'because it's a Tuesday' is a reason within his framework, and can itself by supported by 'because Tuesday is the third day in the week', which may in turn be supported by other reasons, until we arrive at his ultimate end – which is, perhaps, to promote as much excitement as possible connected with the number three. What could we say here? We should have to say that he has given a reason, or has a reason: for he has a particular desire or end (to cause excitement in connexion with the number three), to which killing people on Tuesday is a means. We could say that, if those are the kind of reasons he has, then they are not those which govern what we normally call moral discourse: but this need hardly worry him, unless we can show him, by reasons which he would accept, why he ought to engage in this kind of discourse. We could say that it would be 'odd' or 'paradoxical' for him to offer such reasons: but this seems to mean either (i) that it is contradictory or unintelligible, which is surely not the case: or (ii) that it is an empirical rarity in that society for people to talk thus; and this cuts little ice, since it may be quite common in other societies, and in any case the man is not necessarily unreasonable just because he is in a minority. The trouble is rather that his wants or desires seem unreasonable: and hence the chief part of the problem seems to lie (as we suggested earlier, p. 106) in discovering the criteria by which we may be entitled to demonstrate this.

55. See also pp. 106–7.

56. As some writers have already done: see, e.g. John Wisdom's

Philosophy and Psychoanalysis and *Paradox and Discovery* (Blackwell's); also C. L. Stevenson's *Ethics and Language* (Yale University Press).

57. It may be particularly common among young people at the present time, but is certainly not confined to them.

58. See R. S. Peters, *op. cit.*, pp. 164–5.

59. See pp. 168–76.

60. See. H. L. A. Hart, *The Concept of Law* (O.U.P.), Chapter IX.

61. Cf. D. Riesman, *The Lonely Crowd* (Anchor Books): see under 'autonomy' in his index.

62. Our second-order norms are almost exactly paralleled by the descriptive account given by J. C. Flugel in his *Man, Morals and Society* (Penguin Books), Chapter 16. See particularly pp. 307–10.

CHAPTER 3

PROBLEMS IN MORAL EDUCATION

A. How Do We Justify Our Methods?

THE reader who has followed us so far will now be aware of some of the most important conceptual points about the notions of morality, intention, rationality and so forth; and he will, I hope, be convinced at least that there is more to the notion of 'moral education' than might appear at first glance. But he may still feel that we have pitched our interpretation of moral education too high: that we are asking too much of children and their teachers: in particular, perhaps, that in stressing the notion of rationality we have failed to do justice to the essential groundwork of moral education, which must surely consist (at least in part) of quite simple notions like the training or conditioning of the child's behaviour, making the child accept a number of basic rules, and so forth. So before we proceed it is important to get clear about how these things fit together.

Education and Standards of Rationality

First, we must remember not to be misled by the sense of 'moral' or 'morality' mentioned earlier (Chapter I, pp. 144–5): that is, the 'sociological' sense whereby the 'morals' or 'morality' of a society means simply the current *mores*, the behaviour-patterns which members of that society follow. In this sense, it is true that even the most primitive societies, or very young children in Piaget's 'heteronomous' stage[1], can be said to have a 'morality' – that is, a code of behaviour – even though this code was derived simply from authority and was not supported by anything we could seriously call a moral *reason* at all. In the same way, we could also talk about the 'science' or the 'historical beliefs' of primitive peoples, even if their 'science' was based on superstition, and their 'history' consisted of stories invented to increase the prestige of their great men.

As soon as we bring in the notion of moral *education*, however (or scientific or historical *education*), we have to use the concept of a set of standards or criteria. We begin to think about how to help them to get their morals (science, history) *right*. Here the above sense of 'morality', 'science' and 'history' is of no help: for in this sense these words refer simply to the outlooks and behaviour of the people concerned, and not to the *merits* of these outlooks and behaviour. Hence we were driven to the notion of morality, science and history as *forms of rationality*: that is, as different kinds of beliefs, each with their own proper set of standards. They are, as it were, different games which you play with different rules.

Once we have this notion, we begin to wonder in what sense we were right in calling certain beliefs and actions among primitive peoples or young children 'moral', 'scientific' or 'historical'. A savage believes, say, that the earth is supported by an elephant, which is supported by a tortoise. Is this really a scientific belief, or do we only call it so because we think the savage is doing the same sort of thing (namely, science) as we are, only doing it badly? A child believes that he musn't steal, otherwise his father beats him. Is this really a moral belief, or do we only call it so because we think the child is engaged in morality just as we are, only less competently? I have argued (pp. 80–83) that questions of this sort turn on what the savage or the child really *means* when he says 'The earth is supported by an elephant ...' or 'I mustn't steal'. And what he means is often best demonstrated by the kind of reasons he is prepared to give.

On this view, many beliefs and actions which appear to be 'moral' or 'scientific' – that is, to be derived from those rules and standards which define these activities – are not really so. But I still have no quarrel with those who want to call them 'moral' or 'scientific', as long as they realize what they are doing. Thus to call the child's belief 'moral' because it is in fact an overriding belief which governs his behaviour (however unreasonably), or to call the belief of the savage 'scientific' because it is (if it really is) a belief about what keeps the world up, is quite acceptable. We can also talk quite sensibly about 'the morality of ancient Sparta' or 'the science of the Hopi Indians' as sociologists. But from the point of view of *education* – that is, of our desire to improve a person's 'morality' or 'science' by getting it to conform to a non-partisan set of standards – this way of talking is inadequate and may be misleading.

Educational Practice must be justified by the Standards

But in the second place, I want to make it absolutely clear that the criteria of rationality of which I have made so much are not the be-all and end-all in moral education. There is even a sense in which these criteria may not be the most important feature; but we must be clear about what this sense is. Suppose we are trying to educate people in science. Then we must start by being clear about what science is, and what criteria and rules of procedure we must use to arrive at and judge the merits of scientific beliefs; and we need a rough definition of an ideally 'scientifically educated' person in terms of those criteria. Now there is a sense in which this is the most important feature of 'scientific education': that is, we have constantly to refer our educational methods to this goal – we have to try to produce people who are as 'scientifically educated' as possible, as defined by these criteria. But there is also a sense in which these criteria may not play a predominant part in our educational *practice*, in the actual arrangements we make for teaching children. The arrangements must be geared to, or focused on, this end: but we might in fact spend most of our time doing things which had no direct or obvious relationship to the end.

To use another parallel: if we want to teach someone to play football, we have to be clear about what counts as playing football and what counts as playing it well. If we are not clear about this, we simply do not know what we are doing. But the largest part, in a sense the most 'important' features, of 'football education' would not necessarily consist of explaining the rules of football or giving the child a grasp of tactics. They might rather consist of making the child take plenty of exercise, preventing him from smoking and drinking, giving him the right sort of equipment and playing-fields, and so forth. In deciding exactly what to do in practice, we should have to defend our arrangements by showing that they were necessary to produce a person who could play football well: but most of our time would be spent on the arrangements themselves, and not on explaining the rules of football.

I hope this will lessen the temptation to misinterpret what we have said about rationality, or to think (as I suppose somebody still might) that we have been talking about *how* you should educate children morally, instead of about *what it means* to educate children morally, and how one would have to *justify* various methods and arrangements for moral education. Of course the child needs what we might call training, conditioning, enforced rules, a firm framework and so on: he needs to accept – indeed, in his early years he can probably do no other than accept – a certain code of behaviour, parental commands, traditional rules, etc. The child also needs other things, such as love, emotional security, food, warmth, enough sleep and so forth. All these things, as well as a framework of rules, are necessary if we are going to be able to produce people who are 'morally educated' in the sense already described.

There is a difficult question, which I shall say something about in the next section, about how to describe these various necessities or arrangements. But it is already obvious that to describe them all as moral *education*, without further qualification, may be very misleading. Preventing a child from smoking and drinking may be a necessary arrangement if he is to play football well, but would hardly be properly called 'education in football' or 'physical education'. It is, rather, a *precondition* which is necessary if our physical education is going to succeed. In the same way the early training, emotional security, and so forth which we need to give children may best be regarded as preconditions rather than as educational processes in themselves. This does not make them less important, but it puts them in a different category.

It would, of course, be extremely silly for educationalists in any field to disregard some essential precondition on the purely linguistic grounds that the precondition is not, strictly speaking, an *educational* process. Certainly we shall include all the preconditions – whatever they may be, for we cannot know what they are without further research – under the general title of 'moral education'. But the distinction between education and its preconditions is nevertheless very important, chiefly for the reasons which follow.

The crucial point is that, in considering what preconditions to establish or what arrangements to make in moral education, our criteria of justification must be taken from a neutral and nonpartisan definition of a morally educated person *and from nowhere else*. When children are young, we make them do various things – we give them toilet training, make them sit up at table, tell them to say 'please' and 'thank you', prevent them from hitting each other, and so forth: we may also say things like 'It's wrong to tell lies', or 'It's breaking the law to steal': and we may punish them if they hit each other, or tell lies, or are dirty. Now how do we justify these arrangements? Briefly, we must *not* try to justify them by saying 'It's obviously bad to tell lies or be dirty', or 'All decent societies tell the truth and are clean'. This would put us right back to square one, where we are trying to justify certain specific *first-order* moral beliefs or actions. What we must do is to inspect the arrangements, and ask whether these arrangements generate those preconditions which are necessary for producing people who are morally educated in the *second-order* sense of being rational, sane, 'reality-orientated', autonomous, capable of loving, or whatever general descriptive expression we care to use.

Whether a precondition is necessary is emphatically *not* a matter of whether we ourselves happen to approve of it. It is not a matter of counting heads, or going by the majority verdict; in morality just as in science weight of numbers goes no way at all towards establishing truth. It is a matter of whether or not the *facts show* that a particular arrangement does actually result in giving the child a piece of essential equipment. This is why it is important to regard these arrangements as preconditions rather than as educational processes, or morally educational processes. For if we give them the latter description, we shall be tempted to think that we can judge our arrangements on some first-order, partisan basis. For instance, suppose we are deciding whether to allow children to bite their nails or not. We have not to decide whether nail-biting is in itself 'good' or 'bad', but rather to decide whether by stopping it or allowing it we shall best be able to increase the child's security, his capacity for moral thought and action, the strength of his ego, his ability to relate to other people and consider their interests, etc.

Moral Training

This example will show that very often we simply do not know the right course: but this will vex only those people who expect moral education to be easy. There will of course be many cases where we can feel confident that our arrangements are substantially correct, and do generate necessary preconditions: but even here it is difficult to know what *sort* of preconditions are the crucial ones. It is an open question, for instance, how far some kind of 'moral training', in the sense of getting children to obey rules and regard certain actions as 'wrong' or 'naughty', is important, as against those preconditions which might be generally described as giving emotional security, regularity of life, opportunities for personal attachment and imitation and so forth. Those who are impressed with the notions of 'ethics' or 'a moral code' may instinctively favour one line: those whose orientation is psychoanalytic another. The important thing is to realize our own ignorance.

Our chief point here, however, is the way in which we should evaluate or assess these arrangements; and one more example may help to clarify it beyond doubt. Suppose we decide to draw up a code of moral behaviour from some source or other, make children study it, and make them act in accordance with it. This arrangement might establish a very important precondition for moral education, in that it might give the children some idea of what a set of rules was, and what it was to obey them. It might help them towards a later stage, in which they come to accept or reject rules of their own free will, to see the point and purpose of rules in general and so forth: and at this stage, i.e. when we help them by various methods to formulate and abide by their own rules, we can properly talk of a process of direct moral education. Now the only *point*[2] of the earlier arrangement is that it may be of use for the later stage (just as the only point of doing a special set of breathing exercises is that it may be a help for long-distance swimming); and we would have to consider what sort of code to make the children learn and follow *with this in view*.

We can see that what this would mean in practice is a very open question; and it is *not* to be decided *only* by asking what is 'the right' code to make them learn and obey. For, to put it briefly, what may be right for us may not be right for them. We must have a concept of 'the right code' which is formulated on quite different lines: we must ask rather 'By learning and obeying which code they will be most likely to grow up into independent and rational adults?' The answer to this question may vary, depending on the age, social and cultural background, prejudices, intelligence, family environment or even the sex of the children concerned. Everything depends on what sort of results are produced by making children learn and obey this or that code.

This would be true even if we were (wrongly) content to ensure merely that children behaved in specific ways, rather than morally educating them. To make the point in an extreme way: if a certain type of adolescent is going to do the opposite of what we tell him or whatever code we make him study, we would be better advised to make him study some satanic set of principles, hoping with reason that he will act like Lucifer only in reverse. In fact, what we are interested in is not the degree of conformity to or rebellion against some particular code, but the extent to which he has a rational moral code of his own and lives up to it. To achieve this purpose, no doubt it is important that he should be confronted with *some* code and trained in it: but the content of the code may matter less than other factors, such as the type of training, the personality of the teacher, his own family background, etc.

Thus it is plausible to maintain that teachers and parents should confront the child with their own moral codes in a very clear and definite manner, so that, whether he accepts or rejects a code, at least he knows *what* he is accepting or rejecting. Certainly this seems preferable to a general muddle in which the child is presented with no moral code at all – not only because the absence of a clear and definite code of rules (whether moral or not) generates anxiety and insecurity, but because unless the child is given the chance to inspect one moral code at least, it will not be easy for him to learn what a moral code *is*. But this too is a point about the clarity and manner of presentation of the code, rather than about its content.

However, it does not follow from this that we should not make our own code of moral behaviour as rational as possible: indeed, it is of the utmost importance, for all sorts of reasons, that we should do so. The child whose moral education has been successful will, of course, end up with a particular set of moral principles. By using the relevant skills which we have called by the general title of 'rationality', he will reach particular conclusions such as 'Stealing is wrong', 'One ought not to tell lies', etc. If we like, we can call these 'the right answers': it is a little dangerous to do so, because we may be tempted to suppose that as long as the child gives the 'right answers' it does not matter how he arrives at them – and this would be as silly as a mathematics master who did not mind about how his pupils got the right answers to their sums (even if they looked them up in the back of the book), so long as they wrote them down. But, in cases where we are quite sure about the rationality of a particular moral principle, there is no harm in saying, as it were, 'Look, this is the answer you'll almost certainly get, if you apply the moral skills correctly', 'or Well, an awful lot of rational people think your answer is wrong, we'd better go over the working again'. There are parallels here with teaching science or history or most other subjects. We don't *just* want the pupils to get the right answers: but we recognize also that we can *use* what are commonly taken as the right answers to educate the children in the relevant skills.

Habit and 'going through the motions'

A great many of the methods and practices which, in Chapter 1 we may appear to have dismissed rather airily under such titles as 'making children go through the motions', or 'conditioning', will therefore have an important place in moral education. It is obvious that in the case of young children in particular these methods and practices will be quite essential.[3] We must beware, however, of thinking exclusively in these terms. It is possible to be bewitched by a picture of this kind: 'When they are young, children are stupid and can't think for themselves. So you make them "go through the motions" of moral behaviour. Then as they get older and more reasonable they will be able to think for themselves, and then you can discuss and argue with them about morality, and then perhaps they will develop their own autonomous moral code'. This picture assimilates morality too much to purely rule-governed activities like science or mathematics. The 'irrationality' of young children in the moral sphere is not solely, perhaps not even chiefly, a matter of being stupid or incapable of reasoning logically. It is largely a matter of not being *emotionally* developed; and though of course the two are closely connected in practice, we must distinguish between them. Thus a young child can be a calculating genius, or very good at physics or Latin: but there are different and deeper reasons why he cannot be very good at morals.[4]

The extent to which it is profitable to make children 'go through the motions' in other subjects, e.g. by making them learn lots of facts by heart in science, is nowadays regarded as very doubtful by many educationalists; and in the case of morality we need to preserve an even more open mind. Thus for many maladjusted children notions like 'obedience' or 'moral training', in the sense of making the child obey a set of what are (from the adult viewpoint) moral rules, seem to be out of place: whereas the child's emotional relationship to adults, and the ways in which we can help him to handle his inner life of anxiety, fear, guilt, aggression and so forth seem to be much more important. Over-simple notions of 'moral training' may be tacitly based on naïve pre-Freudian views of the 'natural child' whose mind is a 'tabula rasa', who needs only to be taught to make moral motions, as it were, and who (as a potentially rational being) will naturally come to understand the point of them later. But on any serious psychological view the emotional development of even the youngest child is so complex that such 'training' may not be the only, nor even the most important, requirement.[5]

The comparison with learning-methods in other fields is an interesting one, and though much more research is needed before any specific conclusions can be drawn, it is worth our while to pursue it briefly from the conceptual point of view. Consider, for instance, the teaching of mathematics or science. Here we may contrast two general types of methods:

(a) those which we might call 'drill', 'rules of thumb', 'making children go through the motions', 'learning by heart', etc., e.g. parrot-learning of the multiplication tables, reciting Boyle's Law, and so on.

(b) those designed to give the children understanding of what they are doing, and of why the truths of mathematics and science are true.

Now (*pace* some very 'progressive' educationalists) it would be doctrinaire to say that we should *only* use the methods in (b). For there are obviously many occasions on which it is extremely useful for the child to be able to calculate automatically, in his head and on the spot, without the use of blocks, coloured rods or adding machines, and without taking time off to wonder why the right answer is right. The child will need to be able to make sure he gets the right change, to know what happens if he joins two electric wires together, and so forth: it is not necessary to enter on these occasions into the conceptual foundations of mathematics or the real nature of electricity. It *may* be that the methods in (b) will enable him to do these simple, habit-based things just as well as those in (a): but this has to be shown. But the *reasons why* we may need (a)-type methods are of two quite different kinds:

1. They may be useful, as initial drill-movements, to give the child a proper basis for being 'mathematically educated' or 'scientifically educated' in the sense that (b)-type methods aim to achieve.
2. They may be useful for reasons that have nothing at all to do with *education*, but rather (as hinted above) with quite practical objectives, like getting the right change or not getting electric shocks.

In just the same way, habits, drill or 'going through the motions' may be useful in education:

1. As psychologically essential groundwork for becoming 'morally educated' later on:
2. For other reasons, such as to keep the child out of trouble, prevent him coming up before the magistrates, stop him from offending his elders, and so on. These *need* not have anything to do with moral *education*, any more than teaching someone not to touch electric wires has anything to do with scientific education.

In both cases, we can see that there are other objectives in bringing up children besides strictly educational ones: we want the child to remain healthy, not to be cheated, not to be put in prison, and so forth. Only a very silly and doctrinaire person would regard these as unimportant. But we can also see that the dangers of not teaching the child habits that will enable him to avoid these misfortunes can be minimized, if the misfortunes turn out to be partly of our own making. Thus, if you have an irrational monetary or spelling system, or unsafe electrical equipment that gives you a shock if you touch it, then you will have to work quite hard to give children the right habits: whereas if you change to a decimal system and reform the spelling it becomes easier. Similarly, if we have to teach children a lot of complicated moral habits simply because the adult world reacts irrationally, then we shall waste a lot of time that might be better spent elsewhere.

But what the comparison chiefly shows is that success in using *any* methods is heavily dependent on knowing what we are trying to do and knowing what counts as doing it well. It is chiefly because we *know how to do* mathematics and science that we can experiment successfuly with various educational methods and techniques: and the child, too, can get the hang of the general aims, logic and criteria of the subject at a fairly early age – partly because we ourselves are clear about them. We can say 'Put down so-and-so, and such-and-such, and I'll show you why and how it works in a minute'. But in moral education, although we can certainly *say* 'Do x y and z, and when you're older I'll show you why it's reasonable', do we really feel any confidence about being able to show this? The fault does not lie with morality: it lies with ourselves unless and until we have worked hard enough to get as clear about the methodology of morals as we are about the methodology of science. At present we are still in the 'alchemy' stage of morals; and it is not surprising that we tend to convey to our children an impression of a field of discourse where much may be reasonable, but much also arbitrary, relativistic, tyrannical or just plain feeble-minded.

The Variety of Morality

As we have already hinted, the kind of preconditions and methods which we often assume to be useful can usually be seen to follow from the kind of picture which we have of morality. Perhaps the most common picture, in our own culture at the present time, is still the one which interprets morality as a matter of following interpersonal rules, in the way described on pp. 76–83. If we stick exclusively to this picture, and fail to take account of the 'prudential' and 'mental health' aspects of morality (pp. 83–9), then we shall naturally make much of the analogies with learning science or mathematics. It will seem inevitable that children must first acquire certain habits, go through certain motions, and perhaps learn a particular code – just as they must first learn their tables or accept certain formulae if they are to do arithmetic and algebra: and we may find it natural to draw a distinction between 'basic skills' or 'basic knowledge' on the one hand, and a proper grasp of reasons, concepts and justification on the other.

This is not a false picture; and if we have to rely upon only one such picture, it is certainly this one which most naturally springs to mind when, in our society, we talk about 'morality'. But if we give full weight to the others, which I have attempted briefly to describe under the titles of 'prudential' and 'mental health', but which are very commonly in the minds of those educationalists and others who talk of 'human relations', 'learning to live', 'creativity', and so forth, then we may be able to avoid too narrow a view. In terms of these other pictures, the analogy of mathematics or science might be supplemented by an analogy of learning to paint or to act. Here the importance of habit, going through motions, or learning a code seems more uncertain. Similarly, where the first picture stresses such interpersonal situations as stealing, lying, cheating and so on, the other pictures suggest such situations as marriage, friendship, doing a particular job, living with one's parents, bringing up one's children, etc.: and the preconditions for success in the latter may well look different from the preconditions for success in the former.

Some writers (including, if I understand them, certain existentialist philosophers) seem to have painted these wider pictures of morality in such bold colours as to convey the impression that moral thought and action can be arbitrary, purely 'creative', a matter of 'spontaneity' or 'genuineness', and not rule-governed at all. We need take no such view. If we are to act as human beings, purposively and not at random, there must be standards, principles and rules of procedure which govern our thought and action even in those situations which are the most elusive and difficult to describe. Our moral progress in these situations seems to me to depend, indeed, on our ability to elucidate the criteria of rationality which apply to them more fully than I have been able to do here (pp. 92–5). The whole business of being aware of one's own feelings and those of others, of giving a correct and full description of those many situations which cannot easily be subsumed under a general moral rule about stealing, lying or whatever, is essentially bound up with following the rules of a public language: it cannot be used as an excuse to stop thinking altogether.[6]

B. IS 'MORAL EDUCATION' A SUBJECT?[7]

People ask questions like 'Is moral education a subject?', 'Do we teach it by itself or do we smuggle it into other subjects (such as religious instruction or English)?', 'Is it suitable for children of all ages?', 'Is it something you can teach at all?', and so forth. If we are now clearer about what we mean by a morally educated person, we may at this point be able to tidy up some of the muddles that underlie these questions. Many of the muddles are the result of very deep-seated confusions which I have not space to deal with fully: but the following points may be of some help.

Suppose a 'morally educated' person is someone who has abilities or characteristics a, b, c and d (for instance, someone who considers the interests of others, knows what they feel, makes up moral rules appropriate to the situation, and abides by those rules). Then a particular educational context (A) might be ideal for developing one of these characteristics (a); and this context might already exist in our curriculum. 'English literature', for instance, might be ideal as it stands for developing awareness of other people's feelings (a). But for the development of another characteristic (b) we might need to invent a new context (B): thus the subject that we call 'ethics' or 'religious instruction' might be very bad for helping children to make up moral rules. We might find that teaching the children anthropology or psychology, or giving them personal experience of social classes or groups different from their own, or making them play certain kinds of games, was much more efficient. Or we might find that it did not much matter what you taught them, but the way in which you taught them was very important. Or we might even find that no *direct* attempt to develop these characteristics was much good – that their existence depended more on how the school was organized, or the personality of the teacher, or how much their mothers had loved them in infancy. Hence we might end up with a lot of contexts or arrangements (B1, B2, B3 etc., C1, C2 etc.), some of which might be the same as existing subjects, or part of existing subjects, some of which represented quite new subjects, and some of which were not subjects at all.[8]

In other words, some of the most important factors which *produce* a morally educated person may have little to do with any *direct process* of moral education, or even with any *educational* process at all.[9] Those that can be institutionalized into an educational process may fit some already existing subjects or disciplines, or they may not: or they may partly fit and partly not fit: or they may fit if the subject or discipline were to be taught in a different way, but not fit as the subject is taught at present. Suppose – purely for the sake of example – that we can list the following factors as necessary for producing a morally educated person:

(i) That he should be of a certain physical type, or have a certain minimum I.Q.;

(ii) That his mother should love him in infancy, or that his schoolteachers should be of a certain personality-type;

(iii) That he should be taught to read;

(iv) That he should be taught English literature;

(v) That he should be taught history, but in an unusual way;

(vi) That he should be taught some new (intellectual) subject, (say) psychology;

(vii) That he should be taught some non-intellectual skills, already institutionalized, (say) mime or painting;

(viii) That he should be taught some non-intellectual skills which we have not institutionalized: i.e. we need to introduce some new activity, perhaps some new kind of game, or psychotherapeutic sessions, or social work, or whatever.

Now of these, (i) is something we can as yet do nothing at all about, either by education or anything else. We can do something about (ii), but it would not count as education. (iii) is education,

but would not normally count as specifically *moral* education.
(iv)-(viii) might count as moral education, but their variety
shows that we cannot assume any particular correlation (or lack
of correlation) either with existing subjects or disciplines as
against ones we have to invent, or with intellectual subjects or
disciplines as against non-intellectual skills.

Any educational process can count as moral education if it is a
deliberate process and directed towards producing (or perhaps
just produces)[10] the skills or characteristics of a morally educated
person. Suppose English, as normally taught, produces one of
these skills. Then a question like 'Shall we teach the children
English or morally educate them?' is silly, because teaching them
English *is* morally educating them: just as it is silly to say 'Shall
we have pigs or animals?'. To the extent that an existing subject
or discipline morally educates, teaching that subject or discipline
is moral education. Again, if I try to make people think logically,
then what governs my teaching is the laws of logic: I try to get
children to follow these laws and *thereby* (incidentally) contribute
to their moral education. Even if we have to change the style of
certain subjects, or invent quite new ones, it might still be misleading to *call* them 'moral education'. For each subject or discipline would still be trying to develop its own particular skills or
abilities, so that (from the point of view of someone doing or
teaching the subject) it is in a sense accidental that these skills
are characteristic of a morally educated person. We have to rid
ourselves of the temptation to think that there is a *thing called*
'moral education' which exists over and above particular activities designed to elicit particular skills.

What counts as a precondition?

We can now also distinguish between processes of moral
education and the preconditions of such processes. These
preconditions may be of three logical types:

(a) The features mentioned in (i) and (ii) above are preconditions: they could not themselves count as moral education
because they are not educational processes.

(b) Other preconditions may be achieved by educational processes which are not (or not primarily) morally educational. Thus

iii) above, the ability to read, may be a necessary precondition, but is not specifically a process of *moral* education.

(c) An elementary form of moral education may be considered as a necessary precondition for a more advanced form: just as having learnt O Level mathematics may be a precondition for doing A Level mathematics successfully.

The general distinction between the preconditions and the process of moral education itself is best understood by keeping our eye on one particular piece of moral education. Thus, suppose we want to lay on a particular course for children, designed to improve their awareness of other people's feelings by a study of English literature. Then the preconditions of doing such a course successfully might be:

a) That the children admire the teacher, and that the class should not be too large:

b) That they should have learned to talk and to read:

c) That they should have done some English literature at a more elementary level already.

Different pieces of moral education will thus have different preconditions.

There could, of course, be other classifications of preconditions besides this one, designed to fulfil other purposes. We could for instance classify them under such general headings as: (1) psychological, which would include features of child development, emotional maturity, individual skills mastered by the child, and the personality of the teacher: and (2) sociological, including such things as the organization of the school, the child's home background in its social setting, the child's future expectations of society, the 'staging' of the lessons or activities, and so forth. But it seems premature to select any particular classification scheme before we know a good deal more than we do about the relationship of any of these preconditions to the effectiveness of particular processes of moral education. I mention them only to reinforce the point that effective moral education may depend as much (or more) upon one or another class of preconditions as upon any deliberate *educational* process.

C. What about Discipline?

If the preceding points have been properly established, we ca
begin to see our way through one dilemma which has trouble
both theoretical and practical educationalists. This dilemm
arises from a feeling of tension between two desires: on the on
hand, the desire to ensure that our children have a solid frame
work within which to live, perhaps a 'faith to live by', and tha
we do not let them run wild, thereby losing the advantages of
process of socialization which has been built up over many gener
ations: and on the other hand, a desire not to indoctrinate o
condition, sometimes expressed as an unwillingness to interfer
with their 'natural development'.

What we have to realize is that these two elements in educatio
will fit together quite happily so long as we do not think that w
have to build our own moral values into the framework, or tha
this framework alone will morally educate the child. Moral prin
ciples and actions are things which, as we have seen, the indivi
dual can (logically) only believe and do for himself. He can b
helped, but not forced. Thus the framework may consist of rule
which we ourselves morally approve, or it may not: or it may be
mixture. In any of these cases, it is useful for the child to hav
such a framework, not because obedience to its rules alone ca
ever make the child into a moral being, but for other reason
One such reason may be that the framework initiates the chil
into the whole concept of a set of rules which are thought (thoug
by somebody else) to be moral rules – that it gives him an idea o
what morality is like, even though he may wish to reject tha
particular morality.[11] But there are other reasons for such a frame
work, on which I want to concentrate here.

'Ground rules' and 'keeping the ring'

In the light of these other reasons the framework appears, not s
much as a part of moral education, but as creating certain of it
preconditions. One way of looking at some of these precondition
is to regard the rules of the framework as what we might ca
'ground rules'. These ground rules are, as it were, workin
social principles which make it possible for moral educatio

(and other forms of education) to occur. I am thinking here of such situations as this: suppose we wish to lay on some context of moral education, such as a group discussion or some film designed to increase insight into the feelings of others. It is an obvious precondition of such a context that Johnny does not hit Mary whenever she tries to speak, or that all the children watch the screen instead of throwing bottles at it. There must, therefore, be ground rules to prevent this. In much the same way, in a liberal society, we might say that the laws laid down by the state kept the ring for the benefit and freedom of individuals, rather than attempted to do their morality for them: they set the stage, as it were, or provided a context of communication in which a moral life could be led – just as the rules of a public debate are not themselves opinions or information, but make it possible for opinions and information to be exchanged.

It is here that the desire for a firm and definite policy comes in. For if we are quite sure that these preconditions *are* necessary to produce rational and independent adults, rather than just products of our own values, then of course, we must be as firm and authoritative as possible in ensuring that they exist. Feelings of guilt about being too 'tough', or 'imposing our own values', or 'not respecting the child', are out of place here. To try to impose values is immoral, but to fail to create frameworks within which people can choose their own values is just as bad. To take a parallel, freedom of speech depends (a) on restraint – we must not think that we know so much better than other people that we have the right to shut them up: but also (b) on enforcement – we must ensure that the rules of debate are kept, so that everyone has a chance to say something, and so that the conversation does not degenerate into a shouting-match or a fight.

What 'ground rules' should we have?

The general question 'What sort of "ground rules" should we have?' can be given the general answer 'Those which are necessary to produce rational and independent adults'. But this is to give only the general justification by which to measure particular decisions, on questions like 'Shall we make the children sit up at

table?', 'Ought we to make children go to bed at 6 o'clock?', and
so forth. About particular questions of this kind I want to say
only that we can give no satisfactory answers if they are not
based on adequate empirical evidence. It is, perhaps, partly because in many cases we do not have this evidence that people are
so often tempted to treat them as moral questions, and to answer
them by the wrong method.

I do not want it to be thought that we are underestimating the
importance of such questions, and the general importance of
ground rules which derives from the importance of habit and
tradition in morality. We are not underestimating them, because we are not estimating them at all: any estimation is an empirical business. The way in which habit and tradition can fit
into a liberal conception of moral education has, I hope, already
been made clear not only in this book,[12] but by other writers.[13]
The rest is up to the fact-finders. Any theory of moral education
which implied that we could treat children of all ages as rational
adults, who only needed to be reasoned with in order to become
morally educated, would of course be grotesque in the light of
facts. Our concern here is rather with conceptual mistakes that
might be made whilst considering the facts.

One such mistake is to suppose that some naïve notion of
'keeping the ring' will cover *all* the ground rules that we need.
Those who adhere very closely to a J.S. Mill-type theory of politics, roughly to the effect that we are not entitled to stop people
doing things unless they interfere with or harm other people,
may feel tempted to transfer this bodily to the education of children. That is to say, they may argue 'So long as children do not
interfere with adults or other children, we must let them do what
they want'. This will cover the case of Johnny hitting Mary: but
there are many cases which it will not cover. Children may stay
up instead of going to bed, use fingers instead of forks to eat
with, be dirty without being positively unhygienic (in the sense
of seriously increasing the possibility of disease), and so on – all
without actively interfering with anybody else. What are we to
do about such cases?

On our view, we have to find out whether stopping children
from doing these things, and making them do something else,
contributes to our educational ends or not. If it does, our man-

late[14] over children entitles us to take this course irrespective of whether the children are interfering with other people or not. Many people are tempted to an extravagant liberalism by the non-interference theory, because they have been understandably exacerbated by a lot of rules, perhaps particularly about hygiene, tidiness, sex and so forth, which they call 'Victorian' or 'puritanical'. They unconsciously argue: 'If the child *does no harm* by staying up late, being untidy, etc., then let it carry on'. But we have, of course, to consider the development of the *child*: and some of his actions which may affect nobody but himself may nevertheless be crucial for his development. Which actions these are is a matter for psychologists.

To take an example: in the film (and the book) *Lord of the Flies*[15] there is a scene in which the children, having killed and cooked a wild pig, tear bits off it with their bare hands and eat it. Such behaviour hardly interferes with anyone else: indeed they all enjoy it. Yet to many people this scene seems a crucial point in the moral degeneration of the children: one is tempted to react by saying 'Ah, they've really become uncivilized: now they'll do anything, it'll be murder next' (as indeed it is). The point here is that we do not know whether such behaviour is *causative* of the subsequent real moral degeneration (i.e. murder), whether it is *symptomatic* of a degeneration that has already occurred, or whether it has nothing to do with it at all.[16] If it were causative, then we might (begging a lot of questions) have reason to suppose that we were justified in making children have some kind of able manners, in their own interests.

In other words, there is a confusion in the issue at stake as between the doctrinaire liberals who say 'Leave them alone if they're not doing any harm to anyone', and the doctrinaire authoritarians who say 'It's just wrong to eat with one's bare hands, they must be stopped'. We have to consider the facts. It may well be that our own culture is (or was) over-impressed by the virtues of tidiness, toilet training, good manners, regular hours, etc. But it may also be that some of these things, as instantiated in quite simple forms for the child, are essential if he is to develop habits and standards which are necessary as preconditions to true moral thinking. One might reasonably guess that this was true of areas which, because the child's world is inevitably

limited, formed a central part of his interests: his food, sleep,
play, the cleanliness of his own body, and so forth.

On the other hand, if it cannot be established that making a
child conform to certain ground rules is not necessary in this
way, it may be not only reasonable but important to let him do
what he wants. This may be so, even if what he wants to do
might be symptomatic of an unsatisfactory development rather
than (so to speak) totally unexceptionable. Thus, suppose that
spending a vast amount of time listening to pop music, or wearing
extravagant and peculiar clothes which are disapproved of by
the school authorities, or eating at irregular hours, or behaving in
an experimental/promiscuous way about sex, do not seem either
to interfere significantly with other people, or to cause any extra
difficulty about their developing into rational adults, we might
still think that these were symptomatic indications of some form
of insecurity, maladjustment, irrationality or whatever. Now it
might be extremely dangerous to check or repress these symptoms. They might be, as it were, the best the children or teenagers could do by way of finding some kind of identity or
achieving some temporary form of security:[17] a pretty poor best,
we might think, but to them very important. Nothing may be
gained, and a great deal lost, by adopting any attitude towards
them other than one of benevolent interest. It is not only that
we must be very cautious in regarding them as symptoms of
some 'unsatisfactory' condition (for after all, by what standards
can we objectively judge dress, length of hair, 'good' music,
'decent' manners, or 'satisfactory' sexual relationships?): it is
also that only a very foolish educator would try to demolish
the *symptoms* of mental ill-health, just as only a very foolish
doctor would try to repress the symptoms of a physical ailment,
when it is only by having those symptoms that the patient
manages to survive at all.

'Moral myths'

Again, it is claimed by some that the child's framework must
include someone who at least poses as a moral authority, or
some accepted moral myth, if individuals are not to feel lost or
become neurotic. This strand of thought runs from the 'noble

lie' in Plato's *Republic*[18] to Devlin's *Enforcement of Morals*[19] and onwards. But once our basic points about morality have been made clear it is not too difficult to see what we should say about this. First, it is not at all certain that a *moral* pose is essential to the framework: the vital features may be much more connected with economic and emotional security, close personal relationships, and quite other factors. Secondly, if this moral pose is necessary, it can only be necessary as a precondition: and this makes no difference to our general theory. If children and other individuals not only want someone else's morality rather than their own, but actually need it, then by all means let them have it. Suppose, for instance, that without it they will kill themselves or go mad. Then we should say something like 'Well, we'd better give it to them as a stop-gap, but let's think up some other methods of making them feel secure enough to think for themselves: perhaps when they get older or more mature we can get them to stand on their own feet'.[20]

But even these arguments are misleading, because they do not go far enough. Insofar as, under the aegis of this 'moral authority', the child does not think and decide for itself in the moral sphere; insofar, that is, as the child's reasons for his actions are of the form 'because so-and-so says so' or 'because that's the rule': then to that extent the child is not thinking *morally*, in the full sense of the word. What we are doing, then, is to prevent or save the children from having to find appropriate moral reasons: we are allowing or encouraging them to take orders rather than think – in other terms, to remain in the 'custom' or 'tribal' stage of morality, rather than advance into the 'autonomous' or 'rational' stage. How far this is desirable, for various children at various ages, is partly a matter of empirical psychology. But to show that it is desirable, in certain cases, is not to show that the person who lays down the rules must pose as a moral authority. This would be tantamount to saying that rule-makers cannot do their job, nor commanders give orders effectively, unless they themselves believe that their rules and commands have the status of moral truths: in effect, that they must be conceptually confused about the logic of morality if they are to operate efficiently.

Such a suggestion, which perhaps lies at the psychological

roots of many Devlin-type theories,[21] is for that reason not to be dismissed too casually. There are indeed many people whose confidence and emotional security might evaporate if they could not maintain a semi-metaphysical belief in the certainty of intuited moral truths: just as there are many people who, perhaps, could not bring themselves to fight or kill unless they were persuaded that their enemies were in all respects wicked, representatives of the Devil, etc. (Some English people refused to play Beethoven during the last two wars against Germany.) How such people should be handled in practice is as much a matter for the psychoanalyst as for the philosopher. Here I am only making the point that this kind of misguided confidence is unnecessary. Because of their other merits, such people may be excellent teachers, even excellent 'moral educators'; but these merits need not depend on bad logic.

What is to be learnt from all this, however, is that if you have a system which depends on the acceptance of authority for 'moral' behaviour, and you then remove the authority without replacing it by other methods, a good deal of chaos ensues. To describe this by saying that people then behave 'less morally' is misleading, for they were not really behaving morally before. They were just obeying, and now they cease to obey. What we have here is not an argument for replacing authorities, but for filling in the gap by other methods. If people will not take orders any more, they must be taught to discuss as equals and reach their own conclusions. To remove the props and put nothing back does not make them less 'moral', but it may make for so much chaos and anxiety as to be extremely cruel. This is why we need to be very firm about non-moral rules, another purpose of which is precisely to diminish the child's anxiety, or recast it in a manageable framework – another essential precondition for 'moral education' proper.

When to be strict

I am very much concerned to make it clear that what we have said about the connexions between morality and freedom, so far from implying a general policy which might be described as one of 'less discipline', 'not being so strict', or 'treating the children as equals', in fact suggests that in certain aspects of our treatment of children and adolescents we ought to be very much tougher. There is a good deal of evidence, not all of it exaggerated, which testifies to the lack of confidence which parents, teachers and others of us display in this situation. It arises, in part, because many of us still mistakenly feel that we can only enforce discipline, obedience or conformity if these rest on some secure first-order moral basis. Questions like 'Should we allow boys to have long hair?', 'Should we allow students to be promiscuous?', 'Ought girls to wear lipstick when they are twelve?', 'Should I stop my boys playing pop music all day?' and many others are treated as moral questions. Since we feel increasingly uncertain about what the moral answers to them are, we tend to dither and make uneasy compromises. But if we regarded them like the general question 'What forms of behaviour are necessary psychological or social preconditions of moral education?', we might be clearer about the answers.

Of course, as the more progressive of us will be quick to point out, a lot of behaviour stigmatized as 'immoral' (or 'not respectable') among the young cannot be shown to destroy these preconditions: it is not clear, for instance, that dress, hair, musical taste, or sexual behaviour do so. But others of us, perhaps particularly those who have had practical experience of children, will want to point out the very many varieties of behaviour which do fall into this class. Notions like 'obedience', 'respect for the rules', 'playing the game' and so on do not stand for nothing. Moreover, the ground rules that are required will vary from society to society and context to context. Long hair will not do in the machine shops, because it is dangerous. More importantly, the need for survival in a competitive world may necessitate that a lot of rules and skills are built into our educational system that might otherwise be needless: rules about hard work, the ability to play one's part in a modern technology, and so on. Some of these may be inimical to moral education, in the sense that we would prefer a world in which such dangers or realities did not exist, so that we had more time to do other things. But you can't educate people morally if they're starving or dead. The important thing is to preserve a very firm distinction between the ground rules and the education of human beings.

Different types of rules

Some, perhaps many, of the rules with which children are faced may be unjustifiable: and this not because of dangerous phenomena over which we have little control, like disease or a hostile army, but because of human beings who are irrational. Thus there are some laws in any society which no rational educator would want the children to approve of, either morally or as necessary ground rules. (Nor, of course, would he make the children disapprove of them: he would help them to form their own opinions.) In these cases, he presents these rules as deriving from natural phenomena which, rightly or wrongly, form part of the furniture of the child's life. Fires burn you, lions eat you, and if you run around naked and swear, people don't ask you to tea. These are some of the facts: they can be changed, perhaps, but they must be recognized. Children can be made to keep these rules, to respect these facts, without being turned into hypocrites: the notion of 'hypocrisy' in this context itself stems from a falsely monolithic view, the view that all rules fall into the same (moral) category. But they do not.

Perhaps an example may clarify these rather dislocated points. Take tidiness. Within a certain area, tidiness is a justifiable ground rule: if a child's desk, or exercise book, is in total chaos, an essential precondition for his learning may be destroyed. In another area, it may be an unjustifiable ground rule: the person whose house or school it is may just dislike a muddle that is in fact harmless, and get very angry if the child is untidy. The child has to know this and respect the fact: 'Aunt Jemima hates a mess' is a perfectly good reason for the child's being tidy in Aunt Jemima's house (or even in the child's own house), though it is a different *kind* of reason from the first. In another area, it may be a moral rule which the child has to learn to see for himself: 'If you make a mess which somebody else has to clear up, isn't that unfair? How would you like it if . . .' and so on. Not only rationality and freedom, but discipline and obedience, are encouraged if we keep these separate, and help the child to keep them separate too.

Since the right of the educator consists solely in his mandate to turn infants into rational adults, the rules he makes must be defended at this bar: and these defences are thus more naturally conceived of in terms of efficiency towards that end, than in what we would normally call 'moral' terms. All the rules he enforces must admit of such defence. But *some* of his rules may also admit of a truly moral defence, as in the case of Johnny hitting Mary. What is important is that he should himself distinguish between the two classes. His right to enforce the rules is the same in both cases, but unless he distinguishes between the different *point* of the two types of rule he is unlikely to succeed either in creating an efficient educational context or in transmitting a reasonable moral code. This failure has, in effect, created the moral and social chaos in many societies today.[22]

As we have said, it is no doubt highly desirable that children should be initiated (by imitation, the force of example, compulsory rules and other methods) into a particular moral code or tradition, parts of which they may later fully appropriate for themselves or reject. It would be dishonest and grotesque, as well as inefficient, for teachers to pretend that they themselves do not have such a code, or to be over-hesitant in telling children what it is: and for this reason alone it is obviously important that teachers and other educators should attempt to make their own beliefs as rational as possible. Getting children to 'go through the motions' of a moral code, the point of which they may later come to see for themselves, is not the whole of moral education, but it is no doubt an essential part: and it is no doubt preferable if they 'go through the motions' of a rational rather than an irrational code.

But it is equally important that the 'ground rules' should be understood and defended for what they are. Most schools (and indeed most adult institutions) have rules whose silliness is the result of the incapacity to distinguish in this way. If educators made a serious and honest attempt to answer the question 'What ground rules do we need to achieve our ends?', without getting involved in first-order morality, a great many rules which in practice serve only to bring the whole of school discipline into disrespect would no doubt disappear. (Consider some of the rules about dress, hair, 'bad language', some conventional behaviour, wearing ornaments and so forth.) Equally, other rules which are quite essential would be more efficiently[23] enforced (consider bullying, disobedience to the teacher, destruction of property, assault, etc.); but they would be enforced as they are justified, as rules of the game rather than as the moral opinions of the teacher. We could then get on with the important business of teaching *moral* rules; some of which will be coextensive with the ground rules, but some of which will not.

The adult's attitude

To make our general point yet again in another context, let us consider the attitude of the rule-making adults, rather than the kinds of rules they should make or their efficiency in enforcing them. It is often said, perhaps most often by progressive parents who have tried to bring their children up in a liberal way but who seem (at least to themselves) to have been misguided in doing so, that children and adolescents really want adults to 'take a strong moral line', or show themselves to be shocked and offended on certain occasions, in order that the adolescents should 'have something to rebel against' – something to cut their teeth on, so to speak. There are even some who, strongly desiring that adolescents should become non-conformist and critical, suggest that the best way to achieve this is to put them under a strict discipline in a moralistic atmosphere, so that they will then react against it. How do such views fit in with our general theory?

Plainly there is a great deal of truth in them.[24] It is certainly quite conceivable, and may indeed often occur, that for lack of a firm framework, or a clear lead of any kind from adults, a child whom the parents intended to become a critical and autonomous adult may turn out to be desperately conformist. He wants something to hold on to; and if his parents keep saying words to the effect of 'Well, *I'm* not going to tell you what to do or think, that would be illiberal and unprogressive', then he may well grab the nearest piece of conformity and hang on tight. But this is simply to point again to what may well be an essential precondition for autonomy: namely, that the child and adolescent must be given a clear lead, and a chance to rebel against it. My guess is that only an adult who was very unsure of *his own* moral principles, and very muddled in the kind of way I have been trying to clear up, would fail to give such a lead.

To put it another way, we can say in general that the child needs to grow away from his parents – to rebel, if we must put it dramatically. We can, if we like, describe this as a need to fight with or measure himself against his parents, to display aggression towards them in order to establish his own identity. This means (1) that he should be able actually to *do* this – that we must not pretend that he is adult already or that he will grow up in any other way (and this is where the liberal or progressive parent can be unrealistic): but it also means (2) that the *way in which* we enable him to do it must be as efficient as possible, and geared to the ideal of producing an autonomous adult. Thus a father might achieve (1) by fighting physically with his son, until the son was big enough to beat him: but if that were all the father did, he would not have contributed much towards the son's moral education. He needs to find an institutional form in which the aggression may be expressed and dealt with in a more constructive way: a way in which the son may *learn* something instead of just establishing himself as an adult.

Conversely, a liberal father might suppose that it would suffice for his son to argue with him or play chess with him: and this may be psychologically naïve, in that the form is inadequate to bear the weight or force of the aggression that needs to be expressed. The father might have his eye on the right *aims*, those of producing a rational adult: but he would be tacitly denying the extent to which his son needed to rebel in some more overt and demonstrably successful way.[25] (Most children tend to lose arguments and chess games.) One might say that, as so often with liberals, he gives far too nice and mealy-mouthed a description to himself of what the son really feels: he denies the existence of hostility, hatred, murderous impulses, and all the other things for which these words may not be such over-dramatized descriptions as the casual observer would suppose: particularly if the casual observer has a vested interest in suppressing these impulses in himself.

But here yet again we need much more empirical research before committing ourselves to any specific views about what preconditions are necessary. Liberals may often be psychologically naïve: but this is not an argument against liberalism. For liberalism is defined by reference to its aims, not by reference to any

specific methods used to achieve those aims. A parent or teacher
may have the most liberal aims, and yet use forms of upbringing
which might appear very tough-minded and authoritarian: thus
he might give stern orders, be shocked, use corporal punishment
and so forth. What makes him a liberal is that he will assess these
various forms in the light of his objective – his desire to turn his
children into real adults who can think for themselves.[26]

Different contexts of teaching

There is a further practical distinction, with which most intelligent teachers and parents are already thoroughly familiar, between contexts in which rules are obeyed, without argument and
preferably quickly, and contexts in which one can discuss reasons
for rules. These two contexts also tend to get muddled up in the
crise de foi, so that many of us vacillate between a process of enforcement and a process of reasoning, ranging also over the
in-between processes of bribery, threats, emotional pressure, coax-
ing, lamentation and so forth. It is very desirable, even in
command-and-obedience situations like soldiering, to talk about
what we are going to do and why, both before and after the doing
of it: but it is chaotic to muddle up the talking with the doing.
Both suffer in consequence.

We need not, therefore, feel guilty about familiarizing the
child with some very clear-cut command-and-obedience situations. These are useful, not just because they are often the only
situations appropriate to young children, but also because a
rational adult needs to be able to obey quickly when obedience is
necessary, and needs also to be able to recognize those situations.
Many situations are best handled by a command-and-obedience
mechanism, and not by the more sophisticated but also more
long-winded mechanisms of democratic procedure: there are
many occasions when we need to recognize authority, captaincy,
or the special ability of an expert – more occasions, perhaps, than
academical thinkers and writers tend to suppose.[27]

This is not to say, of course, that when a child is learning to
do something, whether it be in the area of morality or in any
other area, the giving of orders and the giving of explanations
(plus any discussion that may arise) may not in practice go hand

in hand. If you are trying to teach someone to sail, for instance, you may have to shout at one moment 'Pull that rope!' in order to prevent the boat capsizing: and then, directly afterwards, you explain why the boat capsizes if he doesn't pull it. In the same way when teaching mathematics, you often say: 'Look, put down $(x-y) (x+y)$, never mind why for the moment': and then on some other occasion not too long delayed, you explain. But it is a great advantage if the learner can distinguish between the two contexts, even if they succeed each other rapidly: by the tone of voice of the teacher, or some other formal device.

What should be common to both morality and any other form of learning that involves thinking or rationality, however, is that the drill-movements through which the learner is put – the orders he obeys – both have, and are seen to have, a point and a purpose: that they are not, nor seem, merely ritualistic or dead. If they appear so, they are bound to be regarded by the learner as an imposition, either stupid or positively malevolent, on the part of the authorities. They have got to make sense as part of the learner's ends: and that is why the authority is only an authority in the sense of someone who the learner trusts to establish the ground rules, the essential preconditions of learning. The real authority consists of the impersonal canons of rationality that are relevant to whatever is being learnt. The mathematics master mediates the impersonal rules of mathematics for the child: whatever is right for the child to do in mathematics is not right because the master says so, but because the rules are what they are: his authority is that of a mediator. If the child wants to do mathematics, the master can help him – though if the child does not want to do mathematics, the master is unlikely to be able to help him very much: which is why so many educationalists rightly stress the importance of child-centred education in general, an importance particularly relevant to the learning of morality.

D. MORAL EDUCATION VERSUS OTHER OBJECTIVES

There is not a lot to be gained by discussing here *how far* any person or class of people can be expected to progress towards autonomy. It may be thought that, however great our efforts as moral educators, there will always be large numbers of people who 'cannot think things out for themselves', as it is said, or who 'need to be told what to do', or 'are too stupid to decide intelligently'. We must be careful about saying this sort of thing, because we may be unconsciously making any of at least four mistakes:

(a) thinking that we have the right to decide what is good for other people (without a special mandate to do so),[28] which is certainly not true in any straightforward sense:

(b) thinking that we can put people firmly into one of two classes, those that can think for themselves and those who can't: whereas obviously it is a matter of more or less ability to do so, and we must try to help everybody to increase this ability as far as we can:

(c) thinking that moral autonomy is largely a matter of *intelligence*, and that we can hence easily identify those who 'cannot think for themselves': whereas the whole business is far more complicated than that, and our personal judgements about other people's abilities in this field are liable to be emotionally biased:

(d) thinking that the autonomous or rational person has to be very self-conscious and logical all the time, ratiocinating furiously, always wondering about reasons, and so forth: an error which I hope to have cleared up earlier,[29] but which may still persist.

What results we can expect to achieve by way of making people autonomous depends on many unknown factors. It depends on how much we learn about the relevant psychological and sociological facts, how imaginative we are about inventing new forms of moral education, how well we can train teachers and others to conduct such education, how much resistance there is in our society to the principles of such education, and many other things. Briefly, we don't know how much we can achieve, because we haven't tried very hard so far: so it is not just starry-eyed to set our sights fairly high. What is fatally inhibiting to discovering and mastering the relevant factors is any kind of doctrinaire or simple-minded theory.

None of this, however solves a problem that may still be worrying the reader. The problem arises from the application of non-rational processes to children which cannot, it seems, be justified by saying that they establish essential *preconditions* of rationality. It may still be felt, for instance, that there are many children who will never become rational at all, or for whom the possibility of any real autonomy is so remote that it may be discounted. 'What about mongols or autistic children?', the reader may say: 'won't we at least have to condition or indoctrinate *them*? And if we must, how can you defend it by saying that these processes are necessary as "preconditions" of moral education? For, in the case of such pupils, there is no possibility of any truly moral education for them to be preconditions *of*.'

We must distinguish here between two sorts of cases. First, there are those children (and indeed adults) that have no hope at all of autonomous morality. I do not think these cases are particularly worrying. Insofar as such people cannot be helped to think for themselves (and this means that they cannot be helped to think morally, in the full sense, at all), then we have to persuade, force, condition or otherwise non-rationally induce them to behave in ways which will be beneficial to them. This is nothing new: it is essentially the same situation which applies to all very young children. We prevent them from harming themselves, get them to do things which they will enjoy, try to teach them simple things which will make them happier, and so forth.

We do this because their lack of rationality gives us a mandate to tell them what to do. They cannot decide for themselves, so that we have to decide for them. There is no tyranny in this, and no necessity to pose as a moral authority. We have simply to determine what is best for them. It would be misleading to say simply that we 'make their moral judgements for them', for we have seen the sense in which a person can only make his own moral judgements: it is better to say that we tell them what they (acting not as moral agents but as obeyers) ought to do. Of course, this will depend on our own judgement about what will keep them happy, stop them from being too much of a nuisance to others, and so forth: but then we have to make this judgement, since they cannot make it themselves.

The real difficulties arise not so much here as in another class of cases where there is some hope of developing increased rationality. If our object in conditioning and forcing them in certain respects is simply to establish the necessary preconditions for rationality, there is no particular conceptual problem (though of course many practical ones): but often we are not sure what can be called a precondition, and what must rather be regarded as (so to speak) a piece of 'moral training' or conditioning in an area which the child will *never* learn to work out rationally for himself. Here there may, in practice, be a genuine conflict between the two different objectives (a) of establishing a precondition and (b) of keeping the child out of trouble, happy, etc.

To use an example, suppose we have a girl of six years old whom we wish (a) eventually to educate so that she becomes 'morally educated' about sex, holding her own views and acting on them rationally, and also (b) to protect from seriously traumatic experiences which might destroy her ability to do this. Now if we believe that there is very little chance of our ever obtaining objective (a), because the girl is too mentally handicapped, we might well think it right to condition her very strongly against ever talking to strangers, particularly if we lived in an area where the incidence of rape was very high (perhaps Epping Forest). But if we thought that she might be able to reach the 'autonomous' stage of (a), we might hesitate. Certainly we do not want her to suffer rape: but if we used *very* strong methods of conditioning (perhaps electric shocks) which could not be reversed, this might prevent her from behaving rationally in the future: thus, she might be unable to talk to strangers when she was grown up, and miss the chance of meeting an excellent future husband.

Such examples (however implausible) show at least the possibility of cases where the educator has to balance the possibility of harm or unhappiness against the possibility of preventing an increase of rationality. Plainly his decision will be largely governed by the facts (insofar as we know them in any case). If there is a very great possibility of harm, and a very slender chance of rationality appearing at all, he will jump one way: if the harm is unlikely, and the prevention of rationality very probable, he will jump another. One would hope to solve most problems at the practical level by finding methods which avoided the conflict: i.e. which effectively prevented harm, but which did not inhibit rationality. In particular, we would try to avoid irreversible processes of conditioning.

We cannot deny, however, that there is a conceptual problem here which may be briefly discussed: though I cannot hope to solve it.[30] This is the problem of determining by what standards we are to weigh the two desiderata, of rationality on the one hand and the avoidance of harm, pain, emotional insecurity and the like on the other. The educator has a mandate to decide issues in this area for children, but this still leaves open the question of the standards on which his decision should be based. To put it dramatically, he may have to choose between producing a full but tormented consciousness, and producing a contented but narrow one. Ultimately, it is not good enough to say simply 'we have to compromise', if we do not know how to judge the merits of one possible compromise as against another.

This is, in essence, the same problem that the psychoanalyst faces when he has to decide whether to continue a treatment situation in which new and very disturbing feelings may be aroused in the patient, or to let sleeping complexes lie. The first alternative may eventually result in the patient becoming a wiser, fuller person: but if the new feelings cannot be properly handled and brought under conscious control, he may become too anxious to make it worth risking. In the psychiatric situation, the patient is supposed to decide this for himself: it is up to him to continue or break off the treatment as he wishes. But even here the patient's decision will be very much influenced by how the analyst has handled the treatment up to that point: and in the case of children, the educator has to decide for them, so that we cannot use that particular escape route from the problem.

This example suggests that practical solutions are possible if we can create forms and contexts of education, as of psychotherapeutic treatment, which serve the double purpose of diminishing the possibilities of harm or misery and also of increasing – or at least not inhibiting – rationality and a fuller consciousness. But it is worth reminding ourselves here of a common type of case, in which a slight or partial increase in rationality in an uncontrolled situation may get somebody into serious trouble. There is a point in such remarks as 'a little learning is a dangerous thing', or even in 'you're not paid to think': namely, that unless the institutionalized forms and contexts are adequate to keep serious trouble away, such slight increases in rationality may be in practice undesirable. In the same way we may err badly by giving control over the environment (e.g. mastery of physics) without backing it up by control over the inner self (enough sanity not to start an atomic war). And in general, if we cannot create enough controlled contexts, then our problem remains.

How the educator should decide

If the educator is dealing with a rational (or potentially rational) being at all – and this excludes those cases mentioned earlier, where the child is so mentally handicapped that he cannot be in any sense rational – then his mandate is to decide what is best for the child, not just as a created object, but as a potentially rational being. Suppose that if he acts in one way he will produce, on the expiration of his mandate, an adult of type A, not very rational but fairly contented: and that if he acts in another way, this will result in an adult of type B, highly conscious but to some extent tormented. It would, I think, be dangerous for him to settle this by asking the question, 'Which of A or B do *I myself* think is the more worthwhile person?', for the temptation to impose one's own values is here too great. Some of us are prejudiced on the side of playing for safety (A), others on the side of adventure, consciousness, 'touching the heights and depths of experience', and so on (B): '... for who would lose, Though full of pain, this intellectual being?'[31] But of course manic-depressives might opt for some such loss, and suicides do opt for all of it, and who is to say they are wrong? He must rather ask some question as 'If a person could, as it were, try out A's life and B's life, which would he prefer? Would A prefer to be B, or B to be A?'

But this procedure may not give us a clear answer. For our own decision about whether to produce adult A or adult B may still remain crucial, since adult A may well make one choice, and adult B another: so that, in effect, we still have to decide on our own criteria. When we educate children we form their own wants and their ends, so that we cannot escape responsibility by saying that we should decide such matters by reference to the preferences of the child, or to the preferences of the adult which the child is to become (and which are hence our own product).

We are again tempted to fall back on the hope that we can find methods of bringing up children which will enable them to shape their own lives, and do not irreversibly condition them one way or the other. But as we have seen, we cannot escape so easily. Ultimately, it seems as if the educator is forced to decide the matter himself. This need not be too worrying, since it is still possible for him to make a rational choice about whether adult A or adult B is preferable. He has to imagine himself as A and then as B; and then to consider whether, *as somebody who can be A or B, but not anything else*, he would more reasonably choose to be the one or the other.

Another example of the same kind of choice may help to show the sort of approach the educator should adopt. Suppose you are a doctor, and your patient has a crippled leg, which sometimes gives him pain and may cause him to fall over and break his neck. Then you have to balance the loss of a leg (which means that the person may not be able to walk properly) against the unpleasantness or dangers of having a crippled leg. In this case, you would naturally refer the decision to the patient, having told him all the facts. The patient might decide unreasonably, in your view: he might for instance be unduly scared of pain and demand an amputation, or unduly scared of losing a leg and refuse the operation. But now suppose your patient is an orphaned child, so that you have to make the decision yourself. Suppose further that (being a bit of a psychologist) you know that children who have crippled legs always wish they had had them amputated, and those with amputated legs always wish they had retained their crippled ones. How do you make your decision?

It is no good saying 'I will do whatever the child, when it grows up, would prefer that I had done', because your decision may dictate the child's preferences. It is also no good saying 'I will do whatever *I myself* would prefer', because you can't be sure that your personal and immediate preference would be right. So you have to say 'I will do what is, by some neutral standard, preferable': and one way of getting at this neutral standard is to consider both alternatives from the point of view of what the rational person would prefer: if we are asked for a further explanation of 'rational', we can only refer again to the general criteria of rationality for making moral decisions – awareness of feeling, attention to fact, and so on. There appears to be no escape from this.

To put this another way: the educator can make a (rational) decision about how far he is, in any particular case, entitled to inhibit rationality. For rationality itself is not the only good thing in life, and cannot be treated as a sacred cow. We saw earlier (pp. 110–12) that the notion of rationality even in regard to such basic rules of procedure as facing facts, or such basic laws of logic as the law of non-contradiction, required some sort of defence in terms of human interests. There is not much point in being rational if it does not get us what we want. Of course in general it does, and to abandon it totally would mean abandoning our humanity. But this only shows that any deliberately *anti*-rational policy is likely to be logically incoherent: it does not show that there are not some cases where it may be rational to inhibit rationality, just as there are cases where it may improve a person's physical health if we cut off his leg or drug him.[32] These are cases where, for lack of ideal techniques which do not force us to choose the lesser of two evils, we have to compromise.

It is tempting to extend the notion of rationality, the different features or senses of which we have outlined on pp. 92–6, so that it becomes logically contradictory to say both (a) that we have inhibited a person's rationality, and (b) that his state of mind is better as a result. It is true that our mandate over children involves that they should eventually be able not just to think for themselves and entertain doubts, but to feel secure enough to do these things without severe anxiety or unhappiness. The notions of sanity and mental health certainly include the ability to relate to the real world without undue torment, not just the ability to relate to it. Indeed a psychoanalyst might say that a very insecure person, however consciously rational, was not 'really' or 'completely' relating to the real world: that there was a part of him which was failing to do so.[33] We too might be tempted to say that a tormented person was not 'really rational', thereby bringing under the heading of 'rationality' all those things which we think it good for a man to be or to possess.

But this would be to renege on the way we have been using the concept of rationality, and would make the concept useless for practical purposes by extending it too widely. It is plainly possible, in our vocabulary, that a person should be morally rational in the narrow sense (aware of the interests of others, possessed of moral principles based on those interests and constantly acting on those principles), and even that he should be rational in the prudential and 'mental health' senses (pp. 83–92), but that he should not be as happy, or certainly not as contented, as a less rational person. As other writers have pointed out,[34] neither rationality nor mental health includes all that we think desirable in life. Sometimes the educator may opt for contentment, and think it worth producing an adult who is more like a satisfied pig and less like a dissatisfied Socrates: and sometimes he may think that increased rationality is worth some discontent, perhaps particularly if the rationality is exercised in some activity which we think to be especially worth while, such as the cultivation of personal relationships or certain intellectual and cultural pursuits.

This is simply to grant that moral education as we have outlined it is not the sole consideration of the educator. The child himself has (or will have as an adult) other interests besides the cultivation of rationality and mental health. Further, it may be that society as a whole can make legitimate demands on the individual which tell against the possibility of an ideally liberal upbringing. One could imagine, for instance, a situation in which a nation could survive only by heavily indoctrinating or conditioning its children. Hitler may have believed that the survival of Germany was dependent on a highly-indoctrinated Hitler Youth Movement. This example should, of course, make us be very cautious before deciding to indoctrinate or condition. But there are other examples. Thus it might be true that, unless children were indoctrinated with the notion that hard work is always a good thing, a nation might fail to cope with economic competition, and starve. The ancient Spartans or the Romans of the early Republic may have depended on indoctrinated values, or conditioned behaviour, for their survival amidst so many enemies.

Some liberals are apt to regard the (apparently) secure position of some modern societies as historically typical, and to assume that general principles can easily be laid down about such matters: the distinction between private and public morality, how far the law should interfere with the individual, to what extent indoctrination or conditioning is acceptable, and so forth. But in fact situations for different societies vary very widely: and the liberal society of the western world, which has generated the liberal notions of rationality and autonomy which we have made so much of, is certainly a rare case and probably a precarious one. Hard facts about money, power, war, economic efficiency and many other such things form the basis of any kind of education: to disregard them would be to saw off the branch on which educators are sitting.

Here again, however, it is vitally important that we should make a distinction, both in theory and in educational practice, between morally educating children, on the one hand, and bringing them up with quite different purposes in mind on the other. What we have seen in this section is that not *all* these other things can be justified as establishing preconditions for moral education: though we would still hope, because of the importance of moral rationality and autonomy, that we should be able to justify as many as possible in this way. We would hope, that is, to find means of satisfying our other criteria – national survival, the avoidance of damage or misery to the individual, and so on – which did not inhibit rationality, indeed which helped to establish it. But if we cannot, then at least we can be clear in our own minds what sort of objectives we are trying to achieve at different times. If we have to indoctrinate or condition children for certain purposes, at least we can be clear about what those purposes are: we can try to make sure that they are justifiable purposes: and we can stop pretending that we are educating them as rational human beings.

Society and the Educator

I hope that some of the points made above may help teachers and others to see their way through another dilemma which often afflicts them. Often this dilemma is stated in some such form as 'Ought we to bring up our children to conform to the morality and values of society, or to bring them up in what we take to be the right values?', or 'How far is it our job to reflect social values, and how far to counteract them?' This sort of question is commonly raised with one eye on certain social phenomena of which teachers disapprove (commercial advertising and the values of the market-place are popular targets), but it obviously has a wider application.

The correct initial reaction to these questions is to reply 'Neither. Your job (as a moral educator) is to bring them up to be rational and to form their own values: to instil respect for, and capability at applying, the second-order principles relevant to morality, and neither to produce conformity nor to encourage rebellion. Of course, you may also have other tasks. Society may (perhaps rightly) ask you to indoctrinate and condition, for the sake of national survival: and you may also rightly want to do other things besides moral education, things which may actually conflict with your role as a moral educator, for the sake of the children themselves. But keep these other things distinct from the task of moral education.' A clear grasp of this point, which I have belaboured until its screams must by now be wearying the reader, should help the educator over most difficulties. Its acceptance does not of course imply that the educator tacitly condones certain social values, any more than that he tacitly approves them. No doubt it is his duty to encourage his pupils to seek means of changing those features of society which the pupil disapproves of: and getting young people to do this rationally, rather than merely make flamboyant gestures, is a large task in itself. Similarly he will encourage the pupil to respect, and try to extend, those social phenomena of which the pupil approves. This *may* result in producing a generation of pupils who take part in protest marches against some government decision, or who decide to teach maladjusted children instead of going into advertising, or who think that living in caves is nicer than living in large conurbations, or almost anything. In one sense, concern with all this is not the teacher's business. His business is to make the pupils realize the intellectual difficulty of deciding what to do, whilst not allowing the springs of action to dry up: to help the pupils to avoid both gesture-making and apathy.

Insofar as teachers and educators want to campaign for something, it would be better for them not to bring in their partisan commitments (whether for or against particular social values). What they should campaign for is the right to do a non-partisan job: that is, the right to bring up their children as free and rational adults, insofar as this is consistent with other objectives of equal or greater importance. Here indeed is material enough for the most ardent reformer. Few, if any, societies grant teachers this right in full: they have to make obeisance to the prevailing political party, church, or social values, to parental prejudices and local standards of morality or convention. Sometimes this may be, *per accidens*, justifiable, and we are not of course saying that teachers should be given a monopoly of power over children: to this all parents and society as a whole would rightly object. But one can limit a teacher's power without distorting or crippling it: at least one can clarify its extent and nature.

At the very least, educators themselves could make some effort to produce a coherent policy based on these principles. If the pupils of some institution tend to behave in ways which society regards as immoral, unconventional, or whatever, the institution has to make its mind up about whether this behaviour impedes the rational development of the pupils, or assists it, or neither. Suppose the institution decides that there is no evidence to show that the pupils' development is impeded. Then it can say so, for a start: and it can go on to try to persuade society either to allow it to continue educating them in accordance with the criteria of rationality, or else to prove that this would be disastrous in terms of other objectives. It may be that society will refuse: but at least we should know – and, more important, the pupils would know – where we were. The educators could then visibly dissociate themselves, in the eyes of their pupils, from the demands of society in the relevant cases, while continuing to enforce these demands if society insists on them: for, after all, it is society which pays for most educational institutions, we live in a democracy, and campaigns for freedom and the right to educate rationally do not always necessitate revolution or secession – though sometimes they may.

It is in some sense an acceptable excuse for educators that they themselves are not clear about these principles, and hence still play around with their own first-order values, which of course confuse the issue. But insofar as they are clear, or could try to get clear, it is difficult to find any excuse for not facing the problem squarely. Perhaps this is another instance of the empirical approach at its worst, involving a tendency to muddle through and not raise any issues of principle which might cause trouble. But if educators muddle through, they must not be surprised if their pupils just muddle. Whatever the contractual relationships between an educational institution and society, it is better that everyone should be clear about them. Of course there is a temptation to let sleeping dogs lie: that is, to avoid raising issues which might not be decided in one's own favour. But to yield to this sort of temptation is to add plausibility to the view, common amongst the young, that in practice adults are hypocritical, whatever they may say in theory.

If the educator takes the sort of attitude to society I have outlined, it does not of course follow that he should fail to equip his pupils to survive in society, or to be able to compromise with it. The idea that you should always 'stand up for what is right', or 'practice what you preach', is on one interpretation a pernicious idea. If it implies merely that you should be clear in your own mind what state of affairs you think it right to bring about, and should work as effectively as possible to bring it about, then of course it is unexceptionable. But if it implies that, in the course of this work, you should never compromise with the facts, so to speak, then it testifies to a kind of internal compulsion often miscalled 'integrity'. To take an example we have used before, there is one kind of pacifist whose conduct may be guided by reality or the facts – who genuinely believes that, if he personally refuses to fight, the resulting situation will be better than if he fought. But there is another kind who appears to think that, from the proposition that war is wrong, it follows that he should himself never take part in it. (I say 'appears to think', because it is more likely that he does not really think at all, but just 'stands by his principles'.)

People who act in this compulsive way have a kind of definitive uprightness which is very attractive to those who are themselves so torn by doubts, or so conscious of failing to live up to their own (perhaps rather more sophisticated) principles, that they welcome any easy answer or any clearly-defined father-figure. But such monoliths are not what we must teach a young person to admire. We have to teach him to accept the complexity and the irrationality of society, to be secure and flexible enough to act intelligently upon the social order, and to be sufficiently clear and determined about his own reality-based principles to ensure that he does not get bogged down by his task or sell out to the prevailing values. Such teaching can only be effectively done, in any coherent form, by educators who are themselves clear about the criteria of moral rationality – though they will need much else besides.

E. INDOCTRINATION AND FREEDOM

One way of expressing our general thesis is to say that we do not have absolute moral rights over children (including the right to make them accept our moral values), but only a *mandate* over them. We protect and educate them so that they may grow up into free adults. Questions may be raised about what gives us the right to assume this role: but to some extent it appears that we cannot avoid doing so. Newly-born infants are not rational people: to make them so, we have to teach them to think and talk, to formulate their wants and purposes, and in general to acquire the equipment of a fully adult person who has rights of his own. Questions may also be raised about how long this mandate should last: what do we do about a boy of fourteen who wants to run away to sea, for instance, or a girl of fifteen who wants to get married? These questions are partly conceptual, but I cannot deal with them here. It is the way in which the mandate should be used that we shall consider.

It is clear enough, as we have shown earlier, that this mandate includes the right to use *force* or *compulsion* on the children, and the right to *condition* their behaviour to some extent. I am thinking here of such things as making a child go to bed, inducing feelings of fear or guilt about touching dangerous electrical equipment, and so forth. These methods are necessary partly in order to establish the preconditions for moral education. But it may help to clarify our thesis if we consider the question of *indoctrination*. Are we entitled to indoctrinate? Can we help indoctrinating? And, first of all, exactly what is meant by indoctrination?

Indoctrination as opposed to conditioning and force

We must distinguish indoctrination from conditioning[36] and both these must be distinguished from straight-forward force. Roughly, if I illegitimately (whatever this may mean) persuade a child to think that God will punish him for masturbating, this is indoctrination: if I simply give him a feeling of fear and repulsion about it, this is conditioning: if I tie his hands behind his back, this is force. It is peculiar to indoctrination that the will of the person is not *directly* overridden. Someone conditioned may say: 'I have an irresistible feeling of repulsion about doing X, though I know it is perfectly all right to do it'. Someone physically forced, or commanded under the threat of force, may similarly remain free in his beliefs, and even in his feelings. But the indoctrinated person subscribes to a belief. For the concept of belief, more is required than that a person should utter certain words and behave in a certain way. It is required that he should be able to offer some sort of reason, however bad, for his belief: and that the belief should be intelligible.

One might now feel inclined to ask 'How is indoctrination logically possible?' For a moral belief, or any belief for which the believer has reasons (not just causes), is something which you can (logically) only accept for yourself.[37] The notion of 'making someone agree to something', or 'making someone accept something', may seem logically incoherent. The rough answer to this is that indoctrinated beliefs are those which a person may think that he has accepted freely, for good reasons, but which in fact he has accepted when his will and reason have been put to sleep or by-passed by some other person, who has some sort of moral (as we significantly say) hold over him, by virtue of his authority or some other power-bestowing psychological factor. The indoctrinated person, as Sartre would say, is in a state of self-deception: he is sleep-walking, or (in extreme cases) double-thinking. His belief cannot be totally irrational, i.e. non-free and non-reasoned, otherwise it would not be a belief – and perhaps some utterances which we take to be beliefs are not really so; but it is irrational to the extent that it is indoctrinated. (Of course it may also be irrational for other reasons: because he is stupid or misinformed or neurotic, for instance: what characterizes indoctrination is that another person is responsible for implanting the belief.)

Aim, method and content

Indoctrination is an intentional activity: you cannot indoctrinate by accident, and it would be odd to say that physical objects, or a particular kind of environment, or even robots could indoctrinate people (unless the robots had been specially programmed by men, in which case it is really the men behind the machines who are indoctrinating). But indoctrination is not wholly to be defined by the conscious aims of the indoctrinator; we should call some of the things that Roman Catholics or Communists (justly or unjustly) are supposed to do 'indoctrination', whatever description they gave, however sincerely, of their *aims*. They might say, and believe, that they were helping people to form their own beliefs rationally and freely; but this might not be what they were in fact doing. To be an indoctrinator, a person must certainly intend his pupil to arrive at a certain belief, but he need not specifically intend that the pupil should always maintain the belief in the face of reason, or that he should reach it as a result of bowing down to the indoctrinator's authority, or anything else of that kind.

This is simply to point out that what a person says to himself that he is doing is not the same as what he actually *is* doing. If I thought that some food was common property when in fact it was private, and with this belief took it away and ate it, I should have stolen it. Although I am acting intentionally, neither my aims nor my intentions can be correctly described by the word 'steal'; but my actions can be so described. So too with 'indoctrinate' and many other words.[38] It is thus possible to indoctrinate without knowing that you are indoctrinating: and it is also possible to try to indoctrinate but fail, without knowing that you are failing. Many (perhaps most) people, indeed, might have no very clear idea of the method or process they were using when they taught their pupils to hold certain beliefs. We might often be able to guess that their aims and intentions were indoctrinatory, if their actual behaviour suggested it: but a person's aims and intentions (except perhaps for his unconscious intentions) are not wholly to be verified by observing his actions.

Besides this (non-specific) intention, it is also logically necessary to the concept of indoctrination that the indoctrinated person arrives at the belief by non-rational methods. The indoctrinator must (consciously or unconsciously) be using such a method, thereby implanting a belief which is causally motivated (by a desire to obey authority for instance) rather than rationally motivated. Any such belief will necessarily be (so to speak) dogmatic: that is, either the believer will not be able to give relevant reasons for it at all, or else the reasons he gives will not in fact be the true motivators of his belief – they will be rationalizations.[39] This might apply, for instance, to a person who had been taught by a very sophisticated indoctrinator to parrot what were in fact good reasons for a belief, but who, nevertheless, did not really *found* his belief on those reasons. It is not surprising that the word 'indoctrination' implies that the beliefs are usually of a certain kind, namely, those that might properly be called *doctrines:* for these are the kinds of beliefs to induce which, because of our ignorance of how to use rational methods of teaching, non-rational methods have commonly been used instead – par excellence in the case of political, moral and religious beliefs.

There is, in this way, a logical as well as a practical connexion between the methods of acquiring a belief and the rationality with which it is held. Somebody who has never faced the facts or thought for himself cannot, I think, be said to hold a belief rationally: the belief may be (accidentally, as it were) true, but part of what we mean by a rationally-held belief is that it is causally based on the real world, and will change only if the world changes (as opposed to if some authority changes its mind, or if the believer's inner feelings change). For much the same reasons only a certain type of process – namely, a process which brings the pupil up against the real world, and helps him to control it by the use of language, perceptions, and logic – can teach the pupil to behave rationally; that is, to follow rules in virtue of which his behaviour will be more than that of an automaton, and his beliefs more than parrotted words. There is a concealed contradiction in supposing that you could condition or 'programme' somebody to carry out any rational activity: I take this to be a truth of logic that remains true however clever your conditioning or 'programming' might be.[40]

Indoctrination occupies a kind of half-way house between

conditioning and rationality. As we have seen,[41] a completely conditioned person could not strictly be said to have beliefs since he could not *mean* the words he was conditioned to utter. Indoctrinated beliefs, if they really are beliefs, must be meant: what distinguishes them is that they are irrational. We have also seen[42] that the content of such beliefs may in reality be very different from what the words of the belief suggest: that is, the person may mean something different by them from what he appears to mean. Often he may not be at all clear what he *does* mean: and sometimes, no doubt, he may not be using the words to state a *belief* at all – it may rather be (for instance) an expression which merely signifies a willingness to obey authority.

Is indoctrination always wrong?

If we say that indoctrination implies that a person is implanting certain types of beliefs by non-rational or illegitimate methods, we intend some criticism by the word 'illegitimate'. Suppose, however, that it is sometimes right to make children believe certain myths in order to give them more security – even, perhaps, to fulfil the ultimate objective of bringing them up to be free and independent adults. Thus we might persuade a child to believe that 'Daddy will stop anything nasty happening to you', 'Mummy will always be there', or 'Jesus will always protect you': and suppose that we do not give the child any real evidence for these beliefs, but just encourage his wishful thinking.[43] This process is illegitimate, not in the sense that it is a morally wrong thing to do, but rather in the sense that the methods used in relation to these beliefs are non-rational, or logically inappropriate. If it is sometimes morally right to use such a process as this, we have two options: either we continue to call it 'indoctrination', remembering that 'illegitimate' does not here imply 'morally wrong': or else, if we feel that 'indoctrination' has always to be a word of moral dispraise, we can refuse to call it 'indoctrination'.

The normally pejorative element in 'indoctrination' might also make us want to withdraw the term from some such case as this: Suppose a child believes something for very bad reasons indeed, e.g. that he ought to steal something because his gang-leader says so. Now suppose I persuade him to believe that he ought not to steal something by saying things like 'Doesn't your conscience prick you?' or 'Don't you feel guilty about it?' Assuming the second reason to be a slight improvement on the first, we should certainly have helped the child in the direction of rationality: but at the same time our methods would have been far from ideally rational. Here too, if we wish to approve of such cases, we might not want to call them 'indoctrination'.

The important point here, in my view, is not so much whether we call something 'indoctrination' or not, but whether a particular process increases or diminishes rationality. What we need is a good phenomenological account of indoctrination, or (more widely) of rational or sane thinking in general as opposed to rationalized or compulsive thinking. One reason why the borderline between indoctrination and other kinds of compulsive thinking is so hard to demarcate is that there are all sorts of ways in which we can compulsively direct another person's thinking. Granted, inculcation of feeling is conditioning; and of beliefs, indoctrination: but what are we to say, for instance, of the sets of verbal descriptions which we make available to children, and the built-in implications of value that parts of our language inevitably contain? Suppose we describe certain behaviour as 'dirty', 'uncivilized', or 'inhuman', or say of some misfortune that 'these things are sent to try us'? It is we, or our neighbours, who teach children to *see things in a certain way* via the descriptions and language we offer them. Is this indoctrination or not? Whatever the linguistic issue, I should be inclined to say that the substantive question has partly to be settled, in any particular case, by empirical psychology, and that the test is 'Does this way of seeing things, this sort of language, increase or diminish the child's rationality, in the sense of his appreciation of and control over reality?'. This question is extremely vague but I do not see how we can avoid it.

No doubt the linguistic issue in such cases depends on whether we can be said to be giving the children a *belief* of a certain kind (as opposed, perhaps, to particular feelings or particular concepts). If we take our stand here, as we must if we are to retain any clarity for the concept of indoctrination, then we shall be prepared to admit in principle that there can be justifiable cases

of indoctrination. The word will still carry pejorative implications, since we shall probably think that a diminution of rationality in beliefs is for the most part to be deplored: but as with
other pejorative words ('stealing', 'lying', etc.), we shall be
prepared to make exceptions. If we take this line, however, we
must take care to be aware of the particular dangers of indoctrination, which are worth a brief mention here.

If I force or condition a child, by making him go to bed or
giving him guilt-feelings about dirt, at least I have not tampered
with his *intelligence*. He is still able to say 'Well, I've got to go to
bed' or 'Well, I just feel I must clear up this mess', and add
'but I think it's jolly silly, and when I'm grown up I shan't
bring up my children like that'. But if you deliberately indoctrinate somebody, knowing what you are doing, you are *pretending* that certain reasons, which are in fact bad reasons, are good
ones which the child ought to accept. Even if you indoctrinate
without meaning to, which I have claimed to be a possible situation[44] you still act as if this were true: you convey to the child
the impression that a certain type of (invalid) reason is valid.
This may be because you yourself are muddled about what types
of reason are valid; or it may be because your technique in
communicating with the child is so inefficient that you fail to
make clear what these valid types are, so that the child (for instance) believes something just because you say so rather than
because he sees the merit of the reasons you advance. In all
these cases you have (to put it rather baldly) given the child a
false impression of how to think morally.[45]

Now it may be true, as we imagined earlier, that there are
cases in which we would be prepared to give the child this sort
of false impression in order to save it from a worse fate; and from
these cases I would not want to withdraw the word 'indoctrination'. But to allow the child to remain under this false impression, or to create or sustain it except when absolutely necessary,
seems to me dangerous in a way in which force or conditioning
are not. For here we have taken over, or put to sleep, a central
part of the child's personality – his ability to think rationally
in a certain area. To put it dramatically: there is always hope so
long as the mind remains free, however much our behaviour
may be forced or our feelings conditioned. But if we occupy the

nner citadel of thought and language, then it is difficult to see
now a person can develop or regain rationality except by a very
lengthy and arduous course of treatment. To indoctrinate is to
take over his personality in a much more radical way than anything we do by way of force or conditioning: it is, in effect, to
take over his consciousness.

I hope that this very brief analysis will at least lessen the temptation to claim that all ways of bringing up children are equally
impositions – that 'you can't help indoctrinating'. Of course in
practice our education will not be 100% free from unjustified
imposition: but the reasons for this will lie either in our own incompetence or in hard facts about the world which may make it
desirable, and not in any logical inevitability. Briefly, if you bring
children up to think for themselves, it is not intelligible to say, in
general, that you have indoctrinated them: because 'indoctrination' is opposed to 'thinking for oneself' – it is not a word which
we apply to *any* context or system of education. If I use my
commanding presence, an admixture of fear, and constant parrot-
like repetitions to make a child believe that stealing is wrong, then
I have indoctrinated him: but if as a result of unprejudiced discussion and his own personal experience he comes to believe, for
good reasons, that it is wrong, the word 'indoctrination' is out
of place – if one called *that* 'indoctrination', the word would have
lost its meaning.

But we must be careful to remember that our mandate over
children in this respect is not adequately fulfilled merely by
avoiding such things as indoctrination. Indoctrination and the
imposition of our own values is only one of many possible enemies to rationality. Another enemy is within the child himself, and
consists of his own (largely unconscious) fears, desires and other
feelings which may dominate his conscious mind in just as
tyrannical a way as any external indoctrinator: indeed, it is
roughly true to say that external indoctrinators could hardly
succeed if they did not play on these inner fears and desires for
their own advantage. The external enemy is no doubt easier to
identify and easier to shoot at: but the inner is probably the
more important. Indoctrination should be regarded not so
much as a wicked attempt to interfere with the child's 'natural'
development, but as a boring failure to tackle the problem at all.

Finally, a word of caution. In this part of the book we have
been concerned only with the drawing of certain very basic
conceptual distinctions. We opposed rational to non-rational
methods of education, and of the non-rational methods we have
tried to distinguish indoctrination from conditioning and force.
Some of these terms, e.g. 'conditioning', are used by psychologists to refer to certain specific mechanisms: I have used them
rather to make distinctions which may or may not correspond to
differences in psychological mechanism by which these phenomena are produced. I think that the connexion between certain
mechanisms and certain types of phenomena is not purely contingent: for instance, that rational thinking can only be generated by particular kinds of methods. But there is still a great gulf
between the technical terms used by empirical scientists for a
particular purpose, and general terms (sometimes signified by the
same words) in common use which nevertheless need a more
precise definition.

There is a great deal of work that needs to be done here by
way of bridging that gulf. Thus one would want to distinguish
between the sense of 'action' in which psychologists sometimes
talk of a 'reflex action' (as in the behaviour of Pavlov's dogs),
and the fuller (intentional) sense in which a person will go off to a
restaurant if he is hungry. It would be interesting to see how far
one particular type of learning-mechanism correlated with one
particular type of phenomenon as described in more general
terms. Again, our very brief discussion of 'indoctrination' is
only a nibble at one of the concepts in this area. We would need
to consider a whole range of non-rational processes, including
overt force, threats, different kinds of 'influence' or 'persuasion',
'propaganda', 'hypnotism', 'suggestion', 'brain-washing' and
many other such. But this is beyond our present scope.

F. RELIGION AND METAPHYSICS

We have had a great many enquiries about this Unit's attitude to
religion and religious education, and many readers will no doubt
be wondering how they fit into the criteria for moral education
which we have outlined above: so we must give a brief account
of this. I must make two points plain at the outset. First, this

account cannot begin to do justice, either to any particular set of religious beliefs, or to the very complex philosophical questions that arise about the nature and verification of religious belief in general. Second, what I shall say is intended to apply to all religions or systems of metaphysical belief, not just to Christianity or any particular version thereof.[46]

One motive for establishing this Unit was the feeling, now widely shared, that religious education alone could not provide a completely satisfactory framework for moral education. The reasons for this are obvious enough. In our society there are people of many religious creeds and of none: it would be difficult to identify a particular set of religious beliefs that could be regarded as 'established' in any but a purely political sense: and in any case, there is much uncertainty amongst religious believers both as to the interpretation of their own beliefs, and as to the way in which these should enter into anything that we might call 'religious education'.

This might lead us to suppose that our Unit is totally neutral in relation to religion and religious education; and there is a sense in which this is true. We are certainly not committed, nor should we be committed, either for or against any form of belief or disbelief, or any particular sect, church, or metaphysic. But it plainly does not follow from this that we can merely leave the whole matter on one side. For certain religions or metaphysics, like Fascism in Nazi Germany (to use a fairly uncontroversial example), may both in theory and practice collide head-on with the criteria for moral education we have outlined in previous chapters. Here we cannot be neutral without resigning from our task altogether. Thus we cannot say, in effect, 'A morally educated person must base his moral views and actions on other people's interests, awareness of the facts etc., but of course if some religion or metaphysic says that they can base them on something quite different, *which may conflict with this*, such as what the Führer (or the Koran or the Bible or Karl Marx) says, that's perfectly all right with us.'

The sense in which we want to be neutral is something like this: We hope to have established criteria for morality which should commend themselves to anyone who will take the trouble to think about the matter intelligently: that is, criteria derived

from the concept of morality, not from any partisan belief or disbelief. These criteria will almost certainly *cut across* the partisan
categories in which most of us are still accustomed to think. Thus
if we summarize our criteria in terms of 'rationality' ('lack of
prejudice', 'awareness', etc.,) then so far as morality goes there
will be more or less rational (and irrational) Christians *and* agnostics, Buddhists *and* atheists, and so forth. We are concerned
only that these criteria should be preferred to any partisan set of
values, whether religious or anti-religious. There will be forms
of religious belief which meet our criteria adequately, and other
forms which do not: but we do not expect, and certainly do not
presume, that there will be any correlation between those forms
which are adequate and those forms which are the particular preserve of any single faith or sect.

I do not think that this *need* generate any very violent conflict.
Whatever view may be held by religious believers of such notions
as 'faith', 'revelation', 'authority', 'conscience' etc., or of the
logical status of their belief in general, I would hope that most
believers would not regard these notions as being essentially *in
opposition to* the criteria for morality that we have suggested.
This for two reasons. First, many religious believers would
grant that, whatever the importance of the 'faith' or 'revelation'
which they have, there is still a need to work out particular moral
problems by our criteria: i.e. by attending to the facts, to people's
feelings, to logic and so forth. Secondly, and more importantly, a
believer might want to say that his religion is justifiable and
valuable partly and precisely *because* it instantiates and supports
the criteria. Thus the commandment 'Love thy neighbour',
which is indeed as good an injunction as any to deploy the moral
skills we have commended, plainly should not conflict with anything we have said. The commandment, and the religious belief
of which it is a part, may be thought justifiable precisely because
it indicates the right way of going about morality; and (in
general) religious revelations, commandments and authorities
may be regarded as acceptable because they fit human nature
and the human condition – they are not accepted arbitrarily, but
because they are good sense.

Nor need we fail to do some justice to the general importance
of metaphysics, or what we might more generally call 'outlooks

on life', in relation to morality. We all of us have a stake in maintaining some outlook or other, some way of looking at the world. The kind of outlook we have is often a function of our mental health or ill-health and our conscious and unconscious minds in general, even though these themselves may be the creations of society as well as of our personal experiences as children and individuals. Certainly to rob people of this by force is as unwise as to inculcate it forcibly. What we have to do is to help people formulate *their own* way of looking at the world. We are very much in the dark about how to do this, just because we are very much in the dark about what criteria to use in assessing one outlook as against another: here I point only to a vast area of uncertainty, an area in which this Unit has much work to do. For the sense in which a man's morality flows from his metaphysical outlook is plain enough.

Thus it has been pointed out by many authors[47] that a person's metaphysical standpoint, or even the use of imagination which shapes the world in a way which is not overtly 'metaphysical', may in an important sense already have impregnated the empirical world with value before those operations which we describe under the headings of 'reason', 'will' or 'desire' come into play. But although this is both true and important I doubt if it substantially affects the present issue. As we have said elsewhere,[48] rationality in morals involves more than attention to logic, language and the overt facts. It involves attention to one's feelings and *controlled* use of imagination. Without imagination, morality would be sterile; but without the control, it would be irrational – and ultimately not *our own* morality at all, but merely the result of the workings of our unconscious minds and other such factors. To abandon this control, as we have said earlier, is to resign from being human.

The assessment of what we might generally describe as 'non-empirical world-building' – that is, the different ways in which people view the empirical world, colour it, impregnate it with value, and perhaps subsume it under large-scale metaphysical systems – seems to me to lead one, most naturally, at least in the first instance, to a consideration of psychological cases. Psychoanalysts are familiar with such concepts as the 'projection' of one's own feelings (consciously or unconsciously) onto the world, and the kind of 'expectations' one has of the world; they are familiar, partly through a study of pathological cases, with the way in which paranoids or schizoids or manic-depressives may invent their own reality or reject ours, and the way in which more 'normal' people function. What needs to be done here is to consider the whole range of phenomena with an eye on the *criteria of success* which we should use to evaluate these different constructions. To do this, we should have to do more than consider the internal workings of religious language and statement: we should have to get clearer about what *sort* of thing, socially and psychologically, people were doing when they used this language in general – to put it roughly, what the *point* of the whole game was. But we cannot pursue this here.

As I have said, we hope that any serious conflict can be avoided by the considerations set forth above. But there may well be many, perhaps particularly those who maintain a very firm allegiance to some religious authority, who feel that I have skated over the matter, and that there is still a real conflict between their own allegiance or beliefs and the criteria we have outlined. This is not the place for me to argue the matter in full: all I can do is to ask such people, if, on reflection, their allegiance and beliefs are really such as to challenge our presuppositions. Do they really want to maintain that any religious or non-religious authority can *in itself* act as an acceptable basis for morality: that commandments must be obeyed *just* because they are commandments? Do they not rather believe that God (or the Church, or the Party, or whatever authority it may be) ought to be obeyed because he says what is right or good, rather than *just* because he is God?[49] And if so, will not what the authority says about morality turn out to be justifiable in terms of our own criteria, so that they need have nothing to fear from their application? Do they not think that they are *justified* in accepting the authority – that they accept it for some *good reasons*, rather than as a completely wild leap in the dark, a leap which (unless backed by some kind of good reason), would be logically indistinguishable from leaps made by Fascists, Baal-worshippers, or lunatics? And if all this is so, can we not agree to find common ground, at least so far as morality is concerned, on the basis of those reasons for morality which we all accept as primary?

It would, I think, be little short of tragic if some such plea as this were to be made wholly in vain. Only a very foolish person would be prepared to write off, without further investigation, all the things which religious belief brings out more obviously than most other forms of discourse – perhaps particularly the psychological insights contained in its doctrines, myths, stories, parables and ritual. Our fear is rather that, due to a lack of communication and a lack of clarity about that common ground of rationality which must underlie all beliefs, believers and disbelievers may expand their energies in a sterile war.

Fortunately, there are signs that this problem is being tackled. Those teachers and writers on religious education who have experience and insight into what is psychologically healthy for a child advocate a form of religious education which is, in practice, non-authoritarian in the sense described above. They want, in the words of one of the best of them, to make 'the authoritative transmission of a received tradition ... give way to the open search for living truth.'[50] This means a child-centred form of teaching, using (in effect) the criteria of maturity, mental health and rationality as the measures of success.[51] Although these criteria are vague, it would not be too rash to predict, or at least to hope, that the future of religious education, as of moral education, will follow this path, and that the two may merge rather than conflict.

In other words, though we may not yet be able to agree about the criteria by which we should assess religious belief, we may at least agree about the methods of communication and teaching which we should use. Most believers today would, I think, be prepared to support a concept of religious education which implied that we should help children and adolescents make up their own minds about religion, rather than forcibly condition or indoctrinate them into one particular creed. It could be shown, indeed, that genuine religious belief, like genuine moral belief, was something which could not (logically) be forced, but had to be freely chosen. Such a concept of religious education at least entails certain general intentions and methods which would not be entailed by brainwashing or the use of various kinds of non-rational pressure.

Of course there may still be people who so strongly desire to hand down a particular religious belief to their children that they would prefer that this belief should not be discussed, or criticized or compared with other beliefs, either at school or elsewhere. This is no doubt true of moral beliefs also. But here too I would hope that they would not, on reflection, feel entitled to adopt this as a serious policy. There are beliefs about which each of us feels very strongly: but if we value truth above our own beliefs, we are bound to value those methods which we know to be helpful in finding out the truth (such as discussion and mutual criticism) above our own feelings, however strong.

This is not at all to say that we can leave aside the question of how to assess religious belief. For unless we can get clear about this, the whole concept of religious education must remain very obscure. Unless we can answer questions like 'Just what is a religious belief, as opposed to other kinds of belief?', 'Can religious beliefs be shown to be true or false, or is it just a matter of different beliefs suiting different people?', 'What does it *mean* to talk about God, or the supernatural, or life after death?' and many others, then we can hardly know what religious education is supposed to be *about*, or whether we are doing well or badly. Thus one might argue that children should know about the Bible because of its important effect on literature, that they should know about Christianity because of its contemporary social effects, that they should know about the Church because of its historical importance in our culture, and so forth. But this is to teach the history, or the literature, or the sociology *of* religion: it is not to teach religion. We may, if we like, make the child do some rigorous and hard-headed theology, in an endeavour to prevent the subject from becoming 'mushy'. But do we know whether there is any *point* in doing theology? Perhaps it is just another autistic academic game. What any intelligent person, even an intelligent child, will want to know is whether religion is true: or, if that word is inappropriate, whether it is *worth having*. He will want to know what are the criteria of success for religion – whether it is worth while playing the religious game at all, and if so, in what form. Failure to face up to this is merely to sidestep the whole problem.

These difficulties, which we cannot attempt to resolve here, may nevertheless be quoted as an additional reason for laying more stress on good methods of communication, and less on our own individual beliefs. As I have written elsewhere, 'we know quite well that many able and unprejudiced people are Roman Catholics, Marxists, agnostics, atheists, Muslims, and so forth. This should make us resist the temptation to claim any brand of religion or irreligion as *obviously* the most reasonable: for "obviously" is partly defined by the sort of thing that few intelligent people would be in doubt about'.[52] There are encouraging signs amongst many religious (and non-religious) bodies that the intellectual 'cold war' is thawing: signs of the recognition that to communicate is not necessarily to lose face, and that to indoctrinate argues fear of the truth rather than security in the possession of it. Religions and other metaphysics are so close, both logically and psychologically, to morality that moral education will be very much facilitated if this improvement continues.

Notes to Chapter 3

1. See p. 256 ff.

2. The only point, that is, relevant to moral education. Of course there are other educational objectives (see pp. 163–8).

3. This point is also made by Aristotle: 'It is the repeated performance of just and temperate actions that produces virtue', and again 'It is therefore quite fair to say that a man becomes just by the performance of just, and temperate by the performance of temperate, actions; nor is there the smallest likelihood of a man's becoming good by any other course of conduct'. (Nichomachean Ethics II, 4: see also II, 1). See also Michael Oakeshott's *Rationalism in Politics* (Methuen) pp. 1–36.

4. These reasons are also mentioned by Aristotle, when he claims that ethics cannot profitably be studied by a young person, because he is 'swayed by his feelings'. 'It makes no difference whether the immaturity is in age or character. The defect is not due to lack of years but to living the kind of life which is a succession of unrelated emotional experiences'. (*ibid.*, I, 3.)

5. Consider a parallel with a part of education related more to manners than morals. We commonly tell children to say 'please' and 'thankyou'. If we are simply out to make the children socially acceptable, it might be sufficient merely to inculcate this as a habit, so that they will automatically say 'please' and 'thankyou' in certain social situations. Even this might not work, however, since they might say these words in such a nasty tone of voice as to be socially unacceptable. (Think how unpleasantly one can say words like 'darling' when one is angry with somebody one is supposed to love.) So inevitably we are driven to consider the *point* of saying 'please' and 'thankyou', which is (roughly) to show recognition that you are asking or receiving something as a favour rather than as of right. This is what we really want children to appreciate. Now it may be that one good way of getting them to appreciate a favour-asking situation is to make them say 'please' in certain contexts, so that eventually they will recognize the contexts, and come to really *mean* 'please'. But it may be that this recognition depends mostly on quite other factors: thus if the child is neither spoilt nor insecure, he may be able easily to distinguish between favours and rights, and easily pick up some way of marking his recognition – perhaps by the word 'please', perhaps by saying 'Would you mind . . . ?', perhaps just by his tone of voice.

In this respect there is a similarity between 'manners' and 'morals':

bringing up a child to have good manners means more than bringing it up to make certain social gestures. He has to learn to understand the point of these gestures, in relation to other people's interests. Habit may be a necessary method, but will always be insufficient. 'Good manners' are important, but not merely in the purely descriptive, custom-bound sense of 'good manners'. We want people who are both aware of the interests of others, and can express this recognition in forms which others will understand. Many of these forms will no doubt be standardized ('please' and 'thankyou'), because standardization is useful for intelligibility: but they do not have to be, so long as they are intelligible. We all know people who have 'good manners' in the purely descriptive sense, but who are socially unpleasant: and we all know people who (one might say) would like to be courteous to others, but don't know how to express it. We need to incorporate both factors.

6. See pp. 110–16.

7. See also Note B.

8. We need to be careful about two points when we talk of 'subjects':

(i) A distinction must be made between individual 'disciplines', 'skills' or 'abilities' on the one hand and 'subjects' on the other. In the case of purely intellectual activities this distinction is reasonably clear. Thus I might choose to study the 'subject' of religion: and if I ask different questions about it, it will turn out that I need different 'disciplines' to answer them. A question like 'Is the Church of England an upper-middle class organization?' is a sociological question, and needs the use of sociological techniques to answer it: 'What did the Romans think about religion?' is a historical question, and needs the historian's techniques: then there might be questions like 'Is Communism a religion?' or 'Is religious faith contrary to reason?' which are partly conceptual or philosophical. The disciplines are different because of the logical difference in the questions asked, not because they are about different subject-*matter*. Most 'subjects' include questions which demand different disciplines: thus 'English' might include questions about the Shakespearean stage, about the meaning of Anglo-Saxon words, or about the merits of *King Lear*.

(ii) We can if we like reserve the words 'subject' and 'discipline' (and even 'education') for activities or areas which involve a good deal of intellectual work, or which are traditionally hallowed, or which are non-vocational or non-practical. This would cut out respectively swimming, or chess, or advertising as 'subjects'. It does not much matter if we do this, though I think normal usage is against us: those who wish to do it are usually making some kind of purist academic protest against the introduction of certain activities into schools or universities, by persuasively defining 'subject' and 'education' to suit themselves. (Some people even want to monopolize the word 'university' to mean an institution devoted solely or chiefly to traditionally-hallowed intellectual skills.) If we do this, we must be careful not to regard skills and abilities which are not primarily intellectual (and hence, by this definition, not 'disciplines' forming part of a 'subject') as in any way inferior. They are just different.

9. I don't want to imply that 'education' is the name of a set of 'processes': the matter is more complex than that. (See R. S. Peters, *Ethics and Education* (bibliography), Part One). But I hope the general point will be clear.

10. The verb 'educate' certainly implies a deliberate or intentional process, at least in its characteristic uses. But it is an open question whether the sentence 'He is educating the children morally' normally implies not only intention but also the intention to educate morally. A man who is deliberately teaching English but not deliberately educating the children morally thereby, though the result of what he (deliberately) does is in fact that the children become more morally educated, might intelligibly say 'I'm not doing moral education, I'm teaching English'. However, we might reply 'Ah, but you are morally educating, although you don't know it'. I don't think it matters much which way we jump here: but it is important to realize which way we *are* jumping when we jump, because lack of clarity underlies a lot of confused argument about who is morally educating and who isn't.

11. See pp. 131–6.

12. See pp. 131–6.

13. See R. S. Peters' article in *Moral Education in a Changing Society* (bibliography).

14. See p. 168.

15. William Golding.

16. See p. 85.

17. See Part II (B), pp. 339–42.

18. Bk III, 414–15.

19. P. Devlin (O.U.P. pamphlet, 1959).

20. See also pp. 156–64.

21. I do not, of course, imply that Devlin falls into this category. It is quite possible to argue for the necessity of a common set of social *mores* in the interests of national survival, or on some similar grounds. But this is not an argument for *morality* in the full sense: it is an argument for the expediency of the members of a society having certain laws, psychological reactions or behaviour-patterns; as if one were to

say 'Without the censors and a belief in the gods, Roman soldiers won't fight properly and Rome will fall'. It is a sociological argument, and would have to be examined by considering the facts of each particular case.

22. I have no objection to anyone calling the ground rules 'moral' if he really wants to. Certainly they are maintained for an end – to help children to become free and rational adults – though I would want to maintain (in much more detail than in this book) that it is not an end anyone could reasonably reject. But they are not maintained for a specific or first-order moral purpose. Again, the ground rules may be regarded as incorporating 'values' or 'social norms' or what you will; as long as the essential distinction is preserved, this doesn't matter very much.

23. 'Efficiently' doesn't necessarily mean brutally or toughly. Of course there is a problem about how you get children to obey the ground rules, which is part of the problem of moral education as a whole: but to solve the problem we need to do a lot more empirical research.

24. Of course these views are here very vaguely expressed, purely for the sake of example. I suppose one might be saying at least three things:

(i) That the parents (or other adults) don't *have* any clear moral views:

(ii) That they don't present, in their own persons, any clear image of such views to the child:

(iii) That they don't give the child an arena in which to fight against or dispute such views.

No doubt other interpretations are also possible.

25. See p. 410.

26. These and connected points are very well put by R. M. Hare in his 'Adolescents into Adults', in T. H. B. Hollins' collection *The Aims of Education*.

27. The merits of an apprentice system, one might guess, are partly that the adolescent apprentice can see very plainly that his master is more skilled than he, and more skilled in an area which is of considerable practical importance to him – his future job. In a complex modern society a special effort has to be made to bridge this gap.

28. See p. 168.

29. See pp. 50–51.

30. See pp. 160–68.

31. Belial in Milton's *Paradise Lost*, Bk. II, 146–7.

32. Briefly: you can't *not* value rationality, but you can value other things as well. And rationality is necessary, at least for some of us, in

order to be able to decide this very problem. We have to be aware of facts and feelings, pay attention to logic and language, and so forth, in order to balance the possibilities sensibly.

33. Something like this is required to meet such arguments as those advanced in I. Berlin's 'From Hope and Fear Set Free' (*Proceedings of the Aristotelian Society*, 1963–4). But the whole issue raises many difficult questions about how much of the human personality we count as 'the person' in particular cases, about the notion of unconscious intentions, and many other interconnected issues which I cannot deal with here.

34. See R. S. Peters 'Mental Health as an Educational Aim', in T. H. B. Hollins' collection *The Aims of Education*.

35. For some discussion of this topic see R. M. Hare's article in *Aims of Education* (ed. T. H. B. Hollins), and Antony Flew's in *Studies in Philosophy and Education* (Southern Illinois University, U.S.A.), to both of which I am much indebted.

36. It will be seen that I am not using the word 'condition' in any of the specialized senses familiar to psychologists, but in a looser and more general way.

37. See pp. 69–70 (note 11).

38. See p. 186 (note 10).

39. See pp. 51–2.

40. *Pace* A. Flew's attack on A. C. MacIntyre in *Brain and Mind*, ed. J. R. Smythies (Routledge and Kegan Paul).

41. See p. 169.

42. See pp. 82–3.

43. I don't myself think this supposition is necessary in practical education (see pp. 158–60), but it is logically possible. Another case might be this: in the jungle it might be best to indoctrinate soldiers to believe that their officers always knew the way, were sure about where the enemy were, etc.: otherwise they lose confidence and cohesion, and everybody gets killed.

44. See p. 170.

45. Of course there are many different types of case. One thing the indoctrinator does very often is, not so much to offer invalid reasons as valid, but rather to inhibit the child from reasoning at all: so that the child becomes as it were more subject to causal compulsion in his thinking, and less guided by reasons in general.

46. Of course the borderline between what is 'a religion' or 'a metaphysic' and what is not is difficult to determine; but we intend to include, for instance, the Marxist, the Buddhist, the Christian Scientist, and so on. In a broad sense we should include all those who call themselves a something-ist, or say they believe in a something-ism,

where the 'something' is a creed which they believe to have some kind of authority over their whole way of life.

47. e.g. by Iris Murdoch: see her essay in *Christian Ethics and Contemporary Philosophy* (bibliography) and a review article in *Encounter* (July 1966).

48. See pp. 95–7.

49. See pp. 98–9.

50. Harold Loukes, *New Ground in Christian Education* (S.C.M. Press) p. 175.

51. *ibid.*, pp. 176 *et seq.*

52. *Philosophy and Religion* (O.U.P.) pp. 10–11.

CHAPTER 4

ASSESSING THE
'MORALLY EDUCATED' PERSON

IF the neutral and liberal picture of morality and moral education that I have painted has to be accepted, we are committed to a programme of research which might otherwise be very different. For instance, if we defined a 'morally educated' person as somebody who did certain easily-verifiable things (like giving money to charity), or held certain easily-verifiable beliefs (such as that it was wrong to steal), we could then proceed to discover the causes that produced 'morally educated' people in this sense. Apart from the fact that any such definition would be partisan, however, we have seen that even this would be less simple than it sounds. For the concepts of action and belief are not so easily turned into operational definitions. We would want to know, for instance, that a person was really doing something which we could rightly and relevantly describe as 'giving his money to charity', as opposed, say, to just avoiding super-tax or getting rid of a feeling of embarrassment when he met with beggars: that he really believed that it was *wrong* to *steal*, as opposed to believing (say) that it is nasty when his father beats him for taking money from the till, or that it is bad to pinch from one's friends but perfectly all right to diddle the income tax authorities. In fact, however, the object of our concern is at once wider and more difficult to verify. It is wider, because what we want to know is the extent to which the moral thought and action of an individual is *rational* (in the senses described in Chapter 2[1]) or sane, and why it is: and it is more difficult to verify, because motives and intentions will play a far larger part in such verification than they would in any definition of 'moral' education' which is tied down to particular beliefs and actions, difficult though they too might be.

We have in fact two tasks, which must be distinguished:
(i) Producing an operational definition of a 'morally educated' person; and

(ii) Discovering the preconditions and causal factors which produce such a person.

Both these tasks are enormous, but I want particularly to stress the first, which is apt to receive less than its fair share of attention. After what we have said earlier, we may now be conceptually clearer about what counts as a 'morally educated' person; but we are still a long way from being able to identify such a person in practice by means of tests, measurements, or any kind of verification-system. Yet until we can do this, our work on the preconditions and causal factors will be handicapped by our not being sure *what* it is we want to find the causes *of*. In other words, we want to be able to show that certain types of education produce 'morally educated' people: but unless we can first identify a 'morally educated' person, it will be hard to know what types of education to look for.

The general effect of what we have said in previous chapters has perhaps been to enlarge our notion of moral education – to compel us to take into account various features which are essential to morality, and without which our picture of moral education would be dangerously one-sided. We can summarize the points very briefly as follows:

1. Overt behaviour by itself – 'going through the motions' – is not sufficient for the notion of morality. A moral action is connected with intention and with acting for a reason: so that we have to know, not just what people do, but why they do it.

2. Only certain kinds of reasons will count as good reasons. We can't say 'Any reasons will do, so long as they lead to the right action': partly because we may have serious doubts about what in fact the 'right action' is, but chiefly because of the close connections between actions and reasons.

3. Good moral reasons must be based on a rational consideration of other people's interests: authority ('because so-and-so says so') or selfish desires ('because I feel like it') won't do by themselves.

4. A 'rational consideration' does not necessarily involve a great deal of conscious deliberation, but it involves such things as regarding other people as equals, knowing what their feelings are, respecting logic and the facts, not being deceived by

linguistic confusion, and having moral rules or principles based on all these.

5. Finally, a man must have the ability to act on his moral principles: indeed, this would be one of the tests of whether he had really *committed* himself to the principles in the first place – whether they were really *moral* principles for him, as opposed to principles to which he paid only lip-service.

A. A LIST OF MORAL COMPONENTS[2]

What we need in order to make further progress is something like a phenomenological description of morality, which can be broken down into a number of components, each of which has some chance of being assessed in neutral terms. We have made some progress towards doing this, and the following scheme – though it is both vague and logically shaky – may be of interest. We have used the first few letters of a number of classical Greek words to give names to our components:

(a) PHIL refers to the degree to which one can identify with other people, in the sense of being such that other people's feelings and interests actually count or weigh with one, or are accepted as of equal validity to one's own. Different PHIL ratings might refer to the degree to which people are able to identify, and also to the range of this ability. Thus some people may identify very highly with, say, other gang-members, and not at all with old ladies: other people may identify very poorly with those of another class or colour, and so forth. (The degree with which one *ought* to identify in particular situations is of course in question here: but the general principle is that one ought to identify sufficiently to think and act in such a way as always to take their interests into account, regarding them as on an equality with oneself.) Like the other components, this is a matter of whether, in principle, one accepts others as equals: not a matter of how far one loves them, feels for them, etc.

(b) EMP refers to awareness or insight into one's own and other people's feelings: i.e., the ability to know what those feelings are and describe them correctly. A distinction might be drawn between self-awareness (AUTEMP) and awareness of others (ALLEMP). EMP does not of course logically imply PHIL, though as a matter of psychological fact it may be that one cannot develop in such a way as to have much EMP without also having PHIL. (Thus one can imagine a tyrant who, having EMP, could manipulate others cleverly, without regarding them as equals: but how many such cases exist in practice is a matter for further research.)

(c) GIG refers to the mastery of factual knowledge. To make correct moral decisions, PHIL and EMP are not sufficient: one also needs to have a reasonable idea of what consequences one's actions will have, and this is not entirely a matter of EMP. Thus a person might have enough EMP to know that negroes felt pain as much as white people did, and enough PHIL for this to count with him in making moral choices: but, through sheer ignorance rather than lack of EMP, believe that (say) because negroes have less nerve-endings or thicker skulls they do not get hurt so easily. Similarly Marie Antoinette ('let them eat cake') *may* have lacked GIG rather than EMP or PHIL.

(d) DIK refers to the rational[3] formulation of EMP and GIG, on the basis of PHIL, into a set of rules or moral principles to which the individual commits himself, by the use of such universalizing words as 'good', 'right', etc., where these rules relate to other people's interests. There may be people, good at PHIL, EMP and GIG, who nevertheless do not put all these together to make a set of consistent and action-guiding *principles*, or who draw their moral (or pseudo-moral) principles irrationally from elsewhere.

(e) PHRON refers to the rational formulation of rules and principles (whether we call them moral or not) relating to one's own life and interests. Thus a drug addict or a suicide makes decisions which may affect virtually no one's interests but his own. There are, I think, reasons for saying that these choices are in some sense 'irrational', 'mentally unhealthy', or whatever.[4] Such a person would be lacking in PHRON rather than in DIK. For PHRON, EMP (or at least AUTEMP) and GIG would be logically necessary. Whether PHIL is necessary – whether people can get to be aware of their own feelings, or even of factual consequences, without identifying with other people – is, as a *psychological* question, quite open. But logically they are distinct.

(f) KRAT refers to the ability to translate DIK or PHRON principles into action: to live up to one's moral or prudential principles. (One could distinguish between DIKRAT and PHRONKRAT if required. A person might be very conscientious towards other people but show a good deal of 'akrasia' or weakness of will about himself.) In talking of KRAT one is of course talking of the person who has genuinely decided on a principle, whether moral or prudential, but who is in some sense compelled to act otherwise: the model case is the addict.

Thus a typically 'morally educated' person would act as follows: he is driving a car, for instance. He identifies with other people sufficiently for their sufferings or inconvenience to count with him (PHIL). He knows how aggravating it is if a road-hog crowds one into the side of the road, or if one is held up by an unnecessarily slow driver (EMP). He knows that if, say, he drives his car at a steady 30 m.p.h. on a crowded main road, most people will want to pass him, because most cars cruise at more than 30 m.p.h. (GIG). Putting these together, he formulates and commits himself to a rule ('It is not right to drive at only 30 under these circumstances [sc. either for me or for anyone else]'), or ('One shouldn't crowd people into the side of the road') (DIK). He is then capable of acting on this principle, not carried away by fear of going too fast, or a desire to be obstructive or anything of that sort, and increases his speed (KRAT). Some average of these might perhaps be made to give a general 'moral education' rating (ARI).[5]

Though this framework is certainly extremely crude, and may have important logical gaps, I quote it here chiefly in order to show the general direction of our thinking, which is (it seems to me) the direction that any such large-scale enquiry which is not based on partisan values must take. It should not be beyond our powers to devise some means of assessing the ratings of these various components. We should then be in a position to do a number of interesting things; for instance:

(i) One could detect just which components were missing in certain classes or groups of people e.g. delinquents, teenagers, etc., or particular sub-groups of these: and conversely with groups that might have a high ARI rating.

(ii) One could detect what measures increased what ratings

(e.g. it is a reasonable guess that the use of films with discussions, etc. would increase EMP).

(iii) One could make a more intelligent guess about what sorts of things schools ought to try, once one knows more precisely where the weak components are.

It goes without saying that the general findings of psychology and sociology would give us at least a clear lead as to the causes of high or low ratings and there would be interesting comparisons with social class, I.Q. and many other things.

The status of the components

Though we are not indissolubly wedded to the details of this outline, I believe that it can stand as a reasonable basis for future research. What is important, at this stage of our work, is to be clear about its logical status and function. It amounts in practice to little more than a brief explication or enlargement of the various ways in which moral thought and action can be rational or irrational, as described earlier. Thus the component GIG (factual knowledge) is a necessary feature, because the person who was ignorant of important facts relevant to a moral situation would think and act unreasonably. He would need, for instance, to be aware of the nature of his society or institution, of the laws or rules that governed it, and the results of breaking them. (It is under this heading that one might be interested in teaching children about citizenship, the way their country is governed, the ethical codes of particular professions and social groups, and many other such things.)

These components are, then, merely a first hesitant step towards bridging the gulf between our criteria of rationality and any specific recommendations that might eventually be made for moral education. It is important to realize just how wide this gulf is. Take as an example a component which perhaps seems at first sight to hold out most hope of being cashed out into practical measures; awareness of one's own and other people's feelings (EMP). Then we must distinguish between:

(a) What we *mean* by EMP, which is logically connected with the way in which EMP is normally verified. Thus awareness of feelings is logically connected with a person's ability to state correctly what so-and-so feels, and to predict what he would feel, in certain situations.

(b) Operational tests or verification-methods for EMP i.e. a specific method which would act as a good guide for whether a person had a high or low EMP-rating in his everyday life. Thus one might think of presenting a person with a set of stories, and asking him what he thought that certain of the characters felt in particular situations: this would be a good test if his score on it correlated with his actual EMP as normally verified in real life.

(c) The various *causes* or *preconditions* of developing EMP. Here it must be realized that the particular components, as I have hinted in discussing some of them, do not necessarily correlate with particular *psychological* or developmental factors or abilities. Thus one particular factor – say, security in early childhood – may be an essential precondition or cause for a good performance in all the components. Another – say, linguistic ability or intelligence – may be relevant to some components (perhaps to GIG, DIK and PHRON) but not to others (PHIL and EMP). So too with the sociological factors. The business of relating these empirical factors to the components and to their operational tests is obviously immensely complicated; and it is only when we are clear about this relationship that one can go on to the fourth stage:

(d) The methods one might use to increase EMP in children. Here we have to distinguish between:[6]

(i) Factors that, in a given school situation, we can do nothing about: for instance, the child's basic I.Q. or his experience in infancy;

(ii) Factors we can do something about, but not by *education* in the strict sense: e.g. we may be able to influence the child by choosing teachers of a certain personality-type, or organizing the school in a particular way;

(iii) Factors we can influence by education: e.g. by showing him films, having discussions about other classes and cultures, getting him to read novels, etc.

In practice, the factors in (iii) above are obviously most likely to be of immediate interest to ordinary teachers, and those in (ii) to education authorities, training colleges, headmasters and others. But these distinctions are, of course, relative: the factors in (i) which 'in a given school situation we can do nothing about' may be reclassified into (ii) or (iii) *if we change the school situation*. Thus certain conditions which may now be regarded as unalterable in the case of certain schools – for instance, the necessity that the children pass certain examinations, or that parental opinion should not be offended in certain respects – can, in principle, be altered. If it is shown that this alteration is necessary for effective moral education, the authorities then have a choice: the choice will presumably depend partly on how important they think moral education to be.

Difficulties in verification

I want now to draw attention to a further difficulty regarding the operational definitions and test-procedures for these components. All the components involve human thought and action. Remembering what was said in Chapter I about the importance of reasons and intentionality in this area, we may well appreciate the difficulties involved in verification. For – to put it crudely – we are out to get at what actually goes on in people's heads: and their overt movements, or even their spoken words, may always be misleading. This is because these movements may not represent intentional actions of the kind we imagine them to be, and the spoken words may not really represent effective reasons – they may not be *meant*. These difficulties apply particularly to such components as DIK and PHRON, in which we are trying to discover a man's moral or prudential principles and his reasons for holding them. How are we to be sure, when considering what he says in a questionnaire or an interview, that he really means what he says? He may be simply repeating what he has been told: or saying what he thinks he ought to say when on record: or saying what he really believes when talking to one person or answering a questionnaire, though he may believe quite different things in other contexts (e.g. with his peer group, or his parents, or sitting on a committee, or in the privacy of his bedroom, etc.). Quite serious problems, some of them at least partly philosophical, are raised when trying to discover what a man 'really' believes, or what his 'real' moral principles are.

To overcome these difficulties involves a good deal of work which might be described as social anthropology: and if the test-procedures are not to be hopelessly naive, it is essential to get some idea of how far, when practically applied, they actually correspond with the facts. The really serious problems here are not, I think, the standard ones of recognising overt dishonesty in answering questionnaires, or making allowance for the kind of expectations the subject thinks he has to live up to. They relate rather to the more subtle effects of observer upon observed, which in the case of rational behaviour are impossible to avoid. There is for instance a problem, which I hinted at earlier, about incoherent or confused beliefs. Partly owing to the immense possibilities of self-deception when using language, it is very common for people to utter words which are supposed to represent beliefs, consistently and in all seriousness, and yet for the beliefs to be logically incoherent. Often the beliefs are of a different logical type from what they suppose, so that in a sense they do not believe what they think they believe: sometimes it may even be that the beliefs are meaningless, so that in a sense there is nothing for them *to* believe, even though they utter words. Not infrequently, for instance, certain religious or metaphysical beliefs, which believers may take to be factual, may actually seem to operate in a quite different way – as expressions of hope, puzzlement or despair, as a sign of some decision or commitment or sometimes even of a language-ritual which may not, in one sense, *mean* anything at all.

A serious observer would want to discover, not just how people who uttered these words behaved, but what it was that these people actually believed: in other words, what they *meant* when they uttered the words. But, as we have known from Socrates onwards, asking people what they mean by things very often results in their changing their minds: or, more precisely, becoming more aware of the incoherence of their beliefs, and perhaps subsequently framing more adequate or intelligible ones. Hence the observer's investigation may change what is being observed. This is, of course, no news to many research workers, perhaps particularly those who try to combine psychotherapy with observation: but I think the problems in assessing beliefs are particularly acute. This does not, of course, mean

that they are insoluble – or that this influential effect of such
investigation may not itself be of considerable interest.

For example, suppose we attempted to test DIK by asking
certain questions. We want to find out how far a man's moral
views are based on other people's interests, and his regard
for other people as equals. So perhaps we ask 'Do you think
it right or wrong to use obscene language?' He says 'It's
wrong'. We then say 'O.K., now why is it wrong, in your eyes?'
He says 'Well, it just is'. Various versions of this last reply –
'It's a rule', 'You just oughtn't to', 'Because it *is* wrong, that's
why' – may be quite common answers. Now there will be great
difficulty here in finding out (a) whether the person has a reason
at all for this (apparent) belief, and (b) what the reason is, or
(if there is no reason) what the cause of his uttering these words
is. We might then press him as follows: 'Come, come, surely
you think there's *some* reason why you shouldn't use obscene
language', and then perhaps he says 'Well, I suppose it gives
offence'. But one might interpret this answer:

(i) as showing a genuine reason, which is also the cause, of his
    having a principle of not using obscene language:
(ii) as showing a reason, which he could have given in the past,
    but which was not a cause, but only a rationalization (perhaps
    the real cause is that he has been conditioned against using
    obscene words – he just can't bring himself to do it):
(iii) as showing a reason, but a reason which he has only just
    thought up in order to satisfy our questions, and which he
    has never thought of before.

Even this is over-simplified; but it may be enough to show
some of the extra difficulties that arise if we wish, as we must,
to distinguish between reasons and causes, and more generally
to find out what is going on when people utter words in particular situations. Of course one would hope that other con-
vergent verification-methods would shed light on the problem:
for instance, if a man constantly said that obscene language was
wrong, but nevertheless constantly used it without apparent
reluctance, one might reasonably suspect that he did not mean
what he said – that he did not really mean 'wrong', but perhaps
just 'generally regarded as wrong or unconventional by this
society'. In making people aware of distinctions by asking

such questions as 'Do *you* think it's really wrong, or just that it's generally *thought* to be wrong?', or 'Do you mean you actually *think* it's wrong, or just that you *feel* a bit guilty when you do it?', we come back to the problem raised earlier – the effect of observer upon observed. But it may be that a man's ability or inability to make distinctions of this sort is itself very relevant to our general enquiry.

Contexts of communication

By insisting on the notions of autonomy and rationality in moral education it may be that we have conveyed the impression of underestimating the essentially social nature of morality. This is of course far from our intention. Autonomy and rationality appear precisely *in* a man's relationships with his fellows. In trying to assess the components, therefore, we shall obviously be very much concerned with the way in which a person relates to others in his social group. 'Having good relationships', which is a general title for what are perhaps the most important features of being 'morally educated', must be assessed in terms of our components: but in order to assess them for each individual, we have to look at the individual as a group-member. This is particularly true of those components which most obviously refer to the individual's action in reference to the group: one could hardly verify KRAT, or at least DIKRAT – his ability to live up to his interpersonal moral principles – without looking at how he actually behaved towards his fellow men.

But the importance of these relationships comes out in another way also. The ways in which moral education is carried on may be considered as contexts of communication. To take simple examples, we may try to educate a child morally by teaching him about the laws of the land: or by discussing his personal problems with him: or by getting him to play games, or criticize films and novels, or help to govern his own school, and so on. All these activities involve relating to other people in a particular context, in order to bring about a certain result – perhaps to acquire factual knowledge, clarify his own feelings, develop awareness of the feelings of others, learn how to act decisively, or whatever. These contexts of communication[7] should result in the individual improving his rating in one or more of our components: a discussion about a particular moral issue might help to improve his DIK, of a film or novel his EMP, and so on.

Now if it can be shown that certain contexts do or can help in this way, it is of great interest to discover which individuals can take part in such contexts effectively and why: in other words, who is good at *learning* to become more morally educated. I must make it clear that this is not at all the same as verifying who *is* morally educated (in terms of the components). It is a matter of finding out who is able to join in and benefit from particular *methods* of moral education. Such an enquiry may seem to be premature, since we are not clear about whether this or that method is in fact any use. But I think it would be over-cautious not to pursue this line of enquiry. For certain methods of moral education seem to follow very plausibly from the concept of a morally educated person. For example, it seems that a person must be capable of taking part in a context of rational discussion with his fellows, if he is to stand much chance of becoming clear about his own moral principles (DIK). Similarly one might reasonably guess that someone who found it hard, in any context, to learn about other people's feelings via the media of literature, drama, or films would be handicapped in trying to acquire more EMP: someone who had never been able to learn the importance of accuracy in factual knowledge (GIG) via the study of some kind of scientific or fact-orientated subject might be at a disadvantage; somebody who had never taken part in rule-governed games or social systems, and hence was unable to see the point of rules in general, might not have much chance of acquiring PHIL, and so on.

One can hardly avoid remarking on the importance of one particular kind of communication, which consists in the use of conventional signs or descriptive language. Much practical work in moral education, as in psychotherapy, could no doubt be described as an attempt to enable the individual to substitute this sophisticated and consciously-controlled form of communication for the type of 'communication' which consists of impulsive actions, unconsciously-expressed signs of fear, anger, love and so forth. Hence it would not seem unduly rash to attempt some kind of enquiry into the abilities of individuals to partake in and benefit from <u>linguistic communication</u> in various contexts, since we have every reason to believe that the effective use of these contexts is not only a sign of the morally educated man, but a useful means of moral education.

Thus we might take the notion of 'being good at rational discussion'. Even in this vague form, i.e. without tying it down to rational discussion in a specific field (politics, or sex, or literature), there are certain marks of rationality which we all recognize. Thus one such mark is <u>to listen</u> to what the other person says <u>and reply to it,</u> rather than continuing a monologue. This is in fact a comparatively rare phenomenon: in much of what passes as discussion, either A talks and B does not listen, and then *vice versa*: or else either A or B dominates throughout: there is a good deal of disconnected *talk* but not much discussion. Other criteria include not shouting, not interrupting, not being irrelevant, not using loaded words, being able to speak intelligibly and briefly, seeing the other person's point, and so forth. With carefully framed operational definitions, it would be difficult but not impossible to verify abilities of this kind in a more formalized and effective way than we do at present.

Here again much of the work is conceptual: that is, it is a matter of being much clearer about what we *mean* by 'rational discussion', 'being sympathetic', 'understanding other people' and so on. Whilst not underestimating the immense difficulties of producing quick, easily-applied, and totally objective tests for such abilities, I am optimistic enough to believe that a clear conceptual grasp of these matters will in itself prove a guide to some useful kind of verification-system, and also to the general methods which might be used for moral education. To use a parallel, we might want to know how to teach literature or history, and to be able to verify which students should be given the best marks in these subjects. In order to do this, we have first to get clear about what exactly it is that we are trying to do when we do 'literary criticism' or 'history'. But getting clear about this will also help us to settle the other question. Thus we might assume that 'literary criticism' is a matter of very detailed analysis of certain passages in authors, or that it is a matter of knowing the dates of particular literary works. These would plainly suggest different verification-systems and teaching methods in either case; in the first, there might be a lot of group discussion, perhaps after the manner of Dr Leavis, whereas in the second there would have to be a lot of memorizing of dates. In the same sort of way a concept of morality which was based on such notions as making a contract, choosing freely, facing facts and so forth would in itself actively suggest not only very different criteria for the 'morally educated' person, but very different methods of moral education, from what would be entailed and suggested by other concepts, such as 'abiding by the law', 'doing what the Church thinks is best', 'doing good to others', or 'developing the qualities of leadership'.

B. SOME DIFFICULTIES FOR RESEARCH[8]

Existing tests or verification-methods may be very useful for research in this field, even though they may not have been designed to assess the moral components we have outlined. But it is important to note both the possibilities and the difficulties here. For instance, under (b) in the last section we spoke of operational verification-methods for the EMP component, and we mentioned the possibility of a very 'direct' method of verifying EMP, by presenting people with a set of stories and asking them to say what the characters felt. I call this a 'direct' method, because it is obviously closely connected with (a) in the last section, namely what we *mean* by EMP. The test-procedure here is little more than an attempt to cash out, in a particular form, what we mean by the general quality of EMP. We would hope that those who scored highly in giving a correct account of what the story-characters felt would be those who were in general, i.e. in other situations also, good at knowing what the feelings of others are.

However, we might be disappointed in this hope. The story-character test might be a very bad guide to EMP. On the other hand, suppose that a test existed which was designed to measure how religious a person was, or how prejudiced he was about negroes or those of a different social class. Now it might be that this test was in fact far the best indicator of

EMP. Of course we should have to prove this, just as we would have to prove it of any test, however 'direct': that is, we would have to show that those who scored highly in it were, in fact, those who were in general good at knowing what other people felt. But if we could show this, then the test would be very useful.

But there are difficulties here. Suppose we found EMP to correlate highly with (say) being religious: then we might think that by laying greater stress on religious education, we should be able to increase EMP. The first difficulty is obvious – that there might be correlation without any causality: i.e. a third and quite different factor might be responsible *both* for people being very religious, *and* for their having a lot of EMP. This is a standard problem in any research of this kind, and we need say no more about it. But secondly, it would not necessarily be true that high scores in the 'being-religious' test had anything very much to do with what we normally *meant* by 'being religious'.

Here the difficulty of bridging the gulf between the normal meaning of a concept and particular tests or verification-methods, a gulf which we have to some extent measured in this book in specific reference to morality, reappears in another context. In other words, even if we could be sure that 'being religious' as operationally defined by a particular test was a cause of people gaining EMP, this would still not justify us in saying anything about 'the importance of being religious for EMP-development' in any *general* sense of 'being religious'. A great deal of conceptual work would have to be done by way of analysing the operational or test-definitions of 'being religious', and seeing how near or how far they were from the normal meaning. And in this particular case that would be very difficult, since it is not at all clear what the 'normal meaning' of 'being religious' actually is.

Since this point affects (or should affect) the whole research procedure, not only of this project but of a great deal of other work, it is worth going into more fully. For it cuts deeper than might be supposed. To take an example more or less at random: Michael Schofield, in his excellent survey *The Sexual Behaviour of Young People*,[9] breaks down sexual activities into categories of the following type: dating, kissing, deep kissing, etc., up to 'sexual intercourse'. For his specific purposes this is no doubt quite satisfactory: but it would be premature to assume that we can use the results of his survey to talk generally about 'the sexual behaviour' of young people. This is not because the survey is in any way misconceived as a piece of sociological research: it is rather because of the gap between his operational definition of 'sexual behaviour' or 'sexual activity' and the general meaning of such terms. Schofield is not to blame for this gap: it is a gap which has to be filled by philosophers. But it exists. Suppose, for instance, it were the case that many young people engaged in such activities as watching strip-tease shows, masturbation, homosexuality, reading pornographic books, and having sadistic sexual fantasies: should we not count these into the general meaning of 'the sexual behaviour' of young people? Conversely, how do we know that the 'dating' category is always a *sexual* category? What do we mean by 'sexual activity' anyway? These are questions which we must answer if we are to say anything *in our normal language* about 'sexual behaviour', or if we are going to apply research results to some form of practical action, such as 'sex education'.

Again, much research has been done under the title of 'aggression'. But are we clear about what counts as aggression and what does not? If a man knifes someone, that certainly looks like 'aggression'. But suppose he does it by mistake, what then? Or suppose he just threatens to knife somebody? Is boxing an 'aggressive' activity, or is it not aggressive because it's institutionalized? What about fencing? Chess, or other war games? Are arguments 'aggressive' if they're conducted acrimoniously, and not 'aggressive' if they're conducted amicably, or with the desire to find the truth? Is it the intentions of the agents, or the kinds of feelings he has, or just his overt behaviour?

The moral to be drawn from this is not, of course, that research workers should cease all work until all these questions have been answered. It is rather that their *results* cannot be applied until *certain* questions are properly answered. All tests in the social and psychological sciences are supposed to be tests of *something*, in which case work has to be done to settle the question of what exactly it is that they are tests of: or else there is an important sense in which the tests used in these sciences may at no point touch the ground. Of course they may be justified simply as predictors of behaviour, much in the manner of some high-level theories and instruments in the natural sciences: and in so far as we are out to predict human behaviour in the same way that we want to predict the behaviour of atoms, they would be very useful. But often the kind of behaviour we are interested in is not of this sort: and then the gulf-bridging work I have spoken of has to be done if we are to be sure that the tests are relevant to our interests.

The difficulties with sociological and psychological research which is not based on or linked to conceptual work of this kind may be stated a little more precisely as follows:

1. Call the 'subject' of the research X: thus X might be 'social class', 'voting', 'lying', 'being aggressive', etc. Now for the normal meaning of X, the conscious intentions or rule-following actions of a person may be:

(a) Neither a necessary nor a sufficient condition for X. Thus what we normally mean, in most contexts, by 'class' or 'social class' is not connected with intentions or rule-following, but with multiple criteria relating to overt behaviour or overt characteristics, such as (perhaps) having parents of a certain type, speaking in a certain way, having a certain income, having attended a certain kind of school, and so on.

(b) A necessary if not a sufficient condition for X. Thus 'lying' is something which you have to do intentionally, though it is also tied to certain overt behaviour (namely, using verbal or other signs in a way which does not correspond with the facts). Many concepts, like 'bidding' at an auction, are almost wholly intentional, in the sense that almost any sign or piece of behaviour would count as bidding, if it were intended and understood as such.

2. Now if the research worker is not concerned with intentions or rational behaviour, his attitude to X may be:

(a) That his operational definition of X just *is* what X normally means. This might be true in the case of (a) above, though it is unlikely: for the criteria governing most concepts (e.g. 'class', are usually more complex than operational definitions.[10] It cannot be true in the case of (b) above, since here X is tied to the notion of intention.

(b) That his definition of X is *part* of what X normally means. This may be true but very misleading. We may be tempted to move from saying that, because Y is 'part of the meaning of X', therefore someone who is Y is partly X. Thus we might argue 'Saying what is false is part of the meaning of "lying", so someone who says what is false is partly lying', which is obviously silly. The idea behind this is that there is a thing called 'lying', which we can (as it were) get at a part of, by finding out when people say what is false. So too it would be silly to say that a person was 'partly upper-class' just because he satisfied some of the criteria for the meaning of 'upper-class' (e.g. perhaps, having a duke for his father).

(c) That his operational definition of X – call this 'X (op. def.)' – has nothing to do with the normal meaning of X – 'X (normal meaning)'.[11] He may say, for instance, 'Of course I'm not saying anything about what most people mean by "religious", or anything about religion in general at all. All I'm saying is that this particular test does so-and-so and correlates with such-and-such. If you don't want to call it a test of "being religious", call it the abracadabra test if you like'. This is, I suppose, what most sophisticated research workers would say.[12] But the dangers here are very considerable. It is not so much that laymen will undoubtedly assume that X (op. def.) *does* have something to do with X (normal meaning): that is not the research worker's fault, and perhaps we could educate people to be cautious about making such assumptions.[13] It is rather that the gulf has to be consciously bridged whenever we want to take some *action* as a result of the research. For here our initial interests will be X (normal meaning): and if we use X (op. def.) we may fail to satisfy our initial interests, but succeed in doing something which we did not mean to do at all, and which may be disastrous.

If our interests do not lie in the direction of rationality, but rather with getting people to be certain things or behave overtly in certain ways (e.g. to be richer, or to buy more Thunderball Pills), then the danger is less because at least we know what we are doing. Research workers may show that X (op. def.) is caused by Y (op. def.) and Z (op. def.): so if we want X (op. def.), we generate the other two and get what we want. Even here we may mislead ourselves in wanting X (normal meaning) but unconsciously using – and hence eventually getting – X (op. def.). Thus we might want, rather vaguely, to get rid of 'class distinction', and use some operational definition of 'class' (in terms of income variation, status of occupations, and so on): we succeed in abolishing 'class' in these terms, only to find that we have 'class distinction' based on new criteria (perhaps I.Q., or age-groups, or personal beauty). We then belatedly realize that our initial interests had much more to do with personal feelings of being under-privileged, general segregationist tendencies among human beings, and so on, than we originally thought: and it may even be that the subsequent 'class distinction' was worse than the original one, so that we should not only have failed to improve the situation in which we were initially interested, but actually have made it worse.[14]

But if we are interested in rationality, then the dangers are far greater. For *all* we can do, if we stick solely to any X (op. def.) which does not take intentions and rationality into account, is to produce overt behaviour or perhaps also to generate certain 'raw' feelings. This will inevitably fail to satisfy our interests, and may also go against them by diminishing rationality rather than increasing it. We have tried to make this clear in the case of moral education, but it applies to all forms of operational research which does not take this problem into account. Briefly, if we value individual human beings, and are interested in promoting their rationality and freedom, then it is excessively dangerous to look at their behaviour only from the outside, so to speak. We have to ask what they are doing, in the sense of how they intend their own actions and what they are trying to do, in a manner more like the historian's or the anthropologist's than the scientist's.[15] Only then can we understand what they are doing from a viewpoint which will enable us to help them, rather than from one which will enable us only to manipulate or cause changes in them. For although research into non-intentional or non-rational behaviour is plainly very relevant to improving rationality, we shall not know how to apply the results of such research unless we marry up the operational definitions with the original concepts.[16]

This, incidentally, is why there is a sense in which psycho-analytically-orientated research is particularly relevant to the problems of moral education. Despite the mystique which still surrounds some forms of psychotherapy, and despite the difficulty of satisfactorily verifying any of its claims, it seems nevertheless to be true that its methods are primarily concerned with an increase in rationality rather than with merely effecting *any* kind of change in the individual. This is no doubt due to certain non-scientific features in its past and present history as a form of therapy (although Freud himself was muddled about the logical status of his own views, and may even be said to have conceived them as 'scientific' in the sense that the natural sciences are scientific). Of course the logic of these views and of the therapeutic techniques are still very obscure, not least to their practitioners. But there is at least some reason to believe that the intentions of many therapists, and the way in which they conceive their rôle, are pretty well in line with our criteria of the morally educated person.[17]

'Hard' and 'soft' facts: the concept of proof

These difficulties have not been raised merely in order to administer warnings or rebukes to the experimentally-minded, but rather to achieve a little more clarity about how, in practice, certain kinds of research should proceed. For the 'kind of research' may not be (as in our own case it is not) dictated solely by one or more particular approved *methods* or *techniques* of research, but rather by the need to answer a particular *question* or to shed light on a particular *topic*. Thus one might understand phrases like 'research in psychology', 'research in the social sciences', etc. primarily by reference to certain research techniques, or at least to certain disciplines or methods. But one could not understand 'research in education' in this way, since here 'education' names a topic rather than a discipline.[18]

It is not appropriate here to enter into the question of how much research should, in practice, be demarcated or allocated by reference to topics rather than disciplines, or of what conditions must be satisfied for such research to be successful.[19] We need only to note that, when the task of a research team is in fact demarcated by a question or a topic, there is no *a priori* certainty about what particular disciplines will be required. For it is not immediately clear what disciplines will help to translate the 'normal meaning', enshrined in the question or topic, into a set of demonstrable 'facts' or 'proven hypotheses' which will be useful to us.

There is however one important point that still needs to be made. We have tried to show (a) the importance of appreciating the gap between the normal meaning of a word or phrase and their 'operational definitions' in general, and (b) the particular relevance of the gap to questions and topics concerned with human action and intention. When this is grasped, however, we are sometimes tempted to state it as a distinction between what can be proved and what can only be guessed at, between 'hard' and 'soft' facts. We may feel something like this: 'Yes, I see, we can do proper scientific research on physical objects like planets, and get some hard results: but when it comes to the intentional behaviour of human beings everything is going to be much more vague and imprecise, and we can never really be certain of our conclusions. Some work in psychology and sociology – controlled experiments on rats, or statistical correlations about social class – will produce solid results and proofs: other work, which perhaps we ought not to call "psychology" or "sociology" at all (as perhaps Freudian researches or "sociological novels"), can be interesting or illuminating, or provide a useful quarry for more precise hypotheses, but that's all'.

But it is a mistake to suppose that scientific proof is the only kind of proof. Thus, we know that historians can be certain of some things, and can prove them, even though they do not prove them by scientific methods. I can be certain that Churchill did not intend to give in to Hitler and I can be certain that the reason why my wife went to town yesterday was to buy a hat – not because of any scientific procedure, but (briefly) because they said so and there is no reason to suppose them insincere: moreover, their behaviour gives me supporting reasons for what their intentions were. (Of course there are disputes about

historical facts, but so there are about scientific facts.) In other
words, our accounts of human action can be just as well-based
as our scientific accounts: it is just that the basis is different.
Words like 'evidence', 'probable', 'certain', 'true', 'conclusive',
'demonstrate' and 'prove' have their place in this sort of enquiry,
just as in scientific enquiry; but it is a different – not an inferior
– *kind* of proof, certainty, etc. It is not even correct to say that
research into human behaviour is necessarily always more
difficult than scientific research: everything depends on what it
is that you are trying to find out. Thus, finding out whether
there is life on Mars or Venus may be easier than finding out
whether Julius Caesar intended to make himself king of Rome,
but harder than finding out about Churchill's reasons for not
giving in to Hitler.

We may be tempted to say that it is impossible to *generalize*
about human action and intention, in the way we can generalize
in science. But this is not true either. It is indeed often the case
that those who are interested in explanations in terms of intention restrict their interest to particular instances: a historian
may be interested in Churchill's reasons and not in those of
war-leaders in general, and a psychiatrist may concern himself
exclusively with the motives of his patient Joe Bloggs and not
with those of other manic-depressives. But, as these examples
show, there is nothing to prevent us from making generalizations about what sort of intentions or motives particular classes
of people are likely to have in certain situations. Indeed, if we
were not able to do this already, it would be very hard for us
to conduct ourselves properly in society at all; for we should
never know, without prior and intimate knowledge of each
individual with whom we came into contact, how in general
our fellow men would react.

None of this implies, of course, that certain general methodo-
logical principles which we often include under the heading
of 'scientific method' are irrelevant to this kind of research. Nor
is this only because non-intentional behaviour is causally
related to intentional behaviour.[20] It is also because many of
these principles are necessary for establishing any kind of
useful generalizations, or relating one such generalization to
another. The techniques of random sampling, statistical analysis,

control groups and so forth are plainly required if anything is to be conclusively demonstrated. The distinction between 'hard' and 'soft' facts, then, can be maintained as a distinction between facts (or indeed theories) which are conclusively or adequately demonstrated on the one hand, and those which are not (it may be that the observer is biassed, or that what he is observing is atypical); and indeed we might not want to describe the second class as 'facts' at all. But this distinction has nothing to do with what *kind* of facts they are, or what kind of evidence they require: it is rather a distinction simply between adequate and inadequate evidence of *any* kind.[21]

Some of the difficulties of verification which I have stressed throughout this chapter, therefore, should perhaps be taken with a pinch of salt. For it is not clear that *all* these difficulties are inherent to the topic, or arise simply because we are here dealing with human behaviour. It may partly be that, owing to an excessive preoccupation with the methods of the natural sciences, the research techniques suitable to human behaviour have not been properly developed. But of course this lack of development itself constitutes an important difficulty, and emphasizes the necessity of developing adequate research instruments before any very useful results can be obtained.

Other methodologies

It is partly because of the points raised in the last section that our own methodology will be different from some others which have been put forward. Whether or not I have succeeded in establishing all these points in detail, I hope to have said enough to show that their general force implies a verification-system very different from those which (consciously or unconsciously) we often apply. There are, of course, other reasons as well – which we have tried to make clear in the course of this book[22] – why we feel inevitably led to our own methodology: and we may conclude this chapter with a brief glance at the kind of difficulties which other methods of approach seem to face.

Here for instance is a list, whose items are culled more or less at random from the pronouncements of educationalists, Government committees and so forth, of criteria for a 'morally educated' person:

1. Carrying out the duties and responsibilities of a citizen.
2. Obeying the law.
3. Having a firm faith to live by.
4. Understanding and accepting the ideals of Christianity.
5. Displaying the qualities of leadership, independence and initiative.
6. Helping other people.
7. Being imaginative and creative.
8. Obeying one's conscience.
9. Acting in accordance with the public morality.
10. Adjusting to one's environment.

Now it would be difficult to quarrel with most of the items in this list, or to claim that (as they stand) they represent principles that are thoroughly perverted or vicious. We might add items taken from more obviously partisan programmes of other countries,[23] such as 'Helping to maintain the revolution' or 'Being loyal to the Party'; but even these need not be interpreted as positively wicked – in practice they may turn out to amount to much the same as some of the items on the list above (1, 2, 3, 9 and 10, for instance). Yet it still appears that this is not the right way to go about verifying who is 'morally educated' and who is not.

This is partly because any such item, on closer inspection, turns out to be either dangerously partisan or unhelpfully vacuous. Take 'obeying the law' (2). Either this means 'always obeying the law', in which case the usual objections apply (surely one oughtn't to have obeyed Nazi laws, and anyway if it's to be a moral action one must obey for a reason, not just obey): or else it means 'obeying the law when it's right/rational/morally desirable to do so', in which case the item is not very helpful, because it doesn't really offer us a criterion at all – of course we ought to do what's right/rational/morally desirable but we know that already. Or take 'having a firm faith to live by' (3). Either you have your eye on some particular creed or creeds, so that you're saying in effect 'You must be a Christian/Buddhist/Marxist' (as opposed to an agnostic, for instance), in which case this is partisan: or else you're just saying 'People ought not to dither or be neurotic, they ought to know what they think, be consistent, have some firm moral values, etc.', which we're more or less bound to agree with, but which doesn't spell out any criterion very clearly. Or again, 'the quality of leadership' (5) either refers just to a tendency to take the initiative and be the leader, in which case there are times when we might want to call this 'bullying' rather than 'leadership': or else it means 'taking the initiative when it's appropriate to do so', which is unexceptionable but also unhelpful.

Items of this sort can be useful in pointing to *contexts* or *spheres of activity in which* a person's moral worth may appear, but they do not go very far towards any *general* verification of a 'morally educated' person. Some people, impressed with the dangers of indoctrination or a partisan approach, are inclined to despair at this point, and hence to backslide into a kind of vacuous neutrality. Thus they may suggest that the child should be presented with a number of different ways of life or moral codes and allowed to choose between them. This suggestion is more common (and is not uncommonly put into practice) in the field of religion, where the child is taught about different creeds, usually under some such title as 'comparative religion', in the hope that we shall avoid forcing him to become Christian. Such a notion is not so much dangerous as inadequate. It amounts to a form of window-shopping, in which the child can buy whatever happens to appeal to him: and it indicates the bankruptcy of our thinking about morality and religion. What we are failing to provide is a set of *standards*, or a set of criteria of rationality, which are appropriate to the subject and which we can help the child to apply. If we do not do this – and in the case of religion we have notoriously failed to do it – we cannot be said in any serious sense to be educating the child: we are merely amusing him with a number of different pictures, which he cannot evaluate intelligently because neither he nor we know how.

To take another topical example, the concept of 'Christian ethics' is very commonly put forward as a basis for moral education. People say things like 'Even if we don't all accept the Christian religion, at least we all agree with the main ideas of Christian ethics', sometimes remembering to add 'in this society, anyway'. But here again, either we are going to bring in particular and partisan Christian beliefs (e.g. the value of monogamy and pre-marital chastity), or else we mean only to stress certain general principles found in Christian ethics (and no doubt elsewhere), such as treating people as equals, having regard to their interests, being aware of their feelings, and so on: and these are much more properly seen, not as a particular *kind* of ethics, but as part of what it is to have *any* system of ethics or morality. It may be true that these general principles are more adequately emphasized, or more imaginatively illustrated, in Christian writings than elsewhere: but that is another question.

A similar way of approaching the problem would be to make a list of 'virtues', and try to assess how far different individuals were 'morally educated' in these terms: thus we could see how far they were loyal, honest, truthful, hard-working, just, courageous and so forth. This approach might seem to avoid both the danger of being partisan and the danger of being vacuous. But although some valuable and interesting work has been done in trying to classify various types of virtues and moral 'functions',[24] there are a great many difficulties in using this general approach as a basis for verification and for future research. About this I can only speak very briefly here.

The basic difficulty with this approach is that we cannot be sure – certainly not without an immense amount of conceptual work – just how far the common English words which we use in talking about the 'virtues' really represent what we are out to achieve in moral education. Even if we were sure about the correct meaning of the words 'honesty', 'loyalty', 'thrift', 'justice', etc., which would be an immense task in itself, we should then need to fit these words unambiguously into some conceptual classification: and even if we could reach agreement about such a classification, we should still be uncertain about whether its categories were in any sense psychologically distinct.[25] For example, it might be that such virtues as truthfulness, honesty and promise-keeping came into a conceptual category which we might call 'rule-keeping virtues', and determination, courage and patience into a category called 'executive virtues'. But even this distinction is artificial: all virtues require both the notion of rule-following and the notion of execution or putting into practice – indeed, they require the use of all or most of the components we have outlined. More obviously, the psychological abilities may cut across these categories. Whatever makes a man loyal may also make him just: or, conversely, one thing might make him loyal in one context, and another thing in another.

Another difficulty, perhaps of prior importance, is to know how much we can take commonly-mentioned virtues for granted. This comes out in two ways. First, different societies have different lists of virtues. Consider the English notion of 'gentlemanly behaviour', the Greek *megalopsychia*, the Roman *gravitas*. The position is further complicated by the fact that many 'virtues', like the above, are or were regarded as appropriate only to a particular social class: and still further by the fact that many concepts connected with particular virtues might well be radically questioned today – such concepts as 'reverence' or 'blasphemy', for example. Secondly, while it might be possible to extract from some co-ordinated list of virtues certain common elements to which nobody could rationally object, this would certainly involve an immense amount of dispute, both philosophical and empirical. Consider the difficulties of reaching agreement about the meaning, and correct criteria of application, of such terms as 'chastity', 'thrift', or 'indecency'.

Some words that might be taken as names of 'virtues', such as perhaps 'justice', 'benevolence', 'love', 'righteousness' and so on, seem rather to describe qualities of mind or dispositions which are necessary if a person is to think and act morally at all. These very general 'virtues' remind us of the criteria of rationality outlined in Chapter 2, and could be broken down into the components mentioned earlier.[26] But there would be great difficulty in distinguishing them from other general virtues, such as courage or temperance, which might be thought necessary for any morally educated person, and which seem to enter into a great many moral situations (one can be courageous *in* being just, and temperate *in* loving): and also in distinguishing them from specific virtues of a more questionable kind, such as patriotism, humility or nobility.

Again, if we were out to verify the degree of moral education in a particular conceptual area – say, loyalty or honesty – then either (i) we should just be observing specific (overt) behaviour in particular contexts, in which case (a) we don't know, at least in all cases, if this behaviour is really rational or even really moral, and (b) we don't know whether it is really *his* (autonomous) behaviour, which he will transfer to other situations because it is backed by his own good reasons: or (ii) we should try to get at the different components, both rational and non-rational, which constituted loyal, honest, etc. behaviour, in which case we would eventually be driven to make some such list of moral components as we have already made.

None of this should be taken to imply that research work done on some other conceptual basis would be profitless, and it would be foolish to be polemical about any methodology which will produce useful and interesting results. Further, the practical problems of verification, and of the empirical research work itself, are likely to reflect back upon the conceptual basis, and to raise difficulties about the components we have outlined. Many additions and distinctions at least will no doubt have to be made. But, whilst we anticipate the necessity for such changes, we do not feel unduly uncertain about adopting the general method of approach which I have outlined. A shortage of time, space, and quite possibly ability makes me more than usually hesitant in putting it forward as anything like a water-tight basis: and I am very much aware of gaps, loose ends, and unsolved problems. But I hope that it will be of some value to other workers, as well as to practising educators; if not as a completely solid methodology, at least as a set of preliminary notes or prolegomena to one.

Notes to Chapter 4

1. pp. 92–5.

2. The word 'components', here and elsewhere, should be understood in the sense of *logical* components, one might say, a set of *attributes* of the morally educated person. They are not psychological components, or specific psychological skills or abilities. It is precisely the relationship between these logical components or attributes and the psychological abilities, skills or other factors that enable people to possess these attributes which we will have to investigate in future research. The points made earlier, on pp. 114–15, should be borne in mind. See also p. 195 *et seq*. below: also Note B.

3. As outlined in pp. 92–5.

4. See pp. 83–9.

5. The index-names of these components (PHRON, DIK and ARI, etc.) are intended neither as witticisms nor to add a spurious air of classical authority: they are simply a convenient device, which may incidentally help the reader to keep them clearly fixed in his head.

6. See pp. 138–41.

7. Of course it is extremely vague to describe all these simply as 'communication'. There are different (logical) types of communication, and a proper analysis of the concept would require a book in itself. For the use of the concept particularly relevant to moral education, however, see S. H. Foulkes and E. J. Anthony, *Group Psychotherapy* (Penguin Books), p. 224 *et seq*.

8. On this topic see G. H. Bantock, *Education and Values* (Faber), p. 153 *et seq*.: also Professor Ben Morris in J. W. Tibble's collection *The Study of Education* (Routledge).

9. Longmans, p. 25 *et seq*.

10. Some seem bewitched by the idea that some one or more features *must* form necessary conditions for applying the concept, whereas in fact it may be that there are (say) ten criteria, any three of which have to be satisfied, but not any *particular three*. (See J. R. Bambrough, 'Universals and Family Resemblances', in *Proceedings of the Aristotelian Society*, 1960–61).

11. The research workers may also be interested in some feature as a possible *cause* or *determinant* of (say) 'class', rather than as part of the definition. This is a complication which we need not discuss here: it can be subsumed under this heading (c).

12. Actually different research workers say very different things, and far be it from me to say which of them are 'sophisticated'.

13. Though they can be pardoned for the assumptions, if the two Xs are designated by the same word.

14. See, e.g., Michael Young's *The Rise of the Meritocracy* (Penguin Books).

15. See pp. 56–9. To take a quick autobiographical example: my wife held Conservative views, I held Labour views. We both voted Liberal, because (a) we knew that either the Labour or the Conservative candidate would win, (b) if one of us voted (Conservative or Labour) the other would also vote and cancel it out, (c) we liked the Liberal candidate and thought he ought to have some more votes. The gulf here between 'voting behaviour' and *why* we voted as we did is a wide one.

16. A brief note on a vast and complex problem: In case any social scientists are worried, I do not think that any of this implies that intentional or rational behaviour is always unpredictable. An X (op. def.) that did not cater for intention and rationality could not be *translated* into an X (normal meaning) that included such notions: but in principle the former could include all the observable *correlates* of the latter, and there are causes (as well as reasons) for rational behaviour itself. So there is no *unbridgeable* gulf between this kind of research and our practical interests: the point is rather that, to bridge the gulf, we have first to be quite clear how we identify X (normal meaning), in order to see how far the correlates in X (op. def.) really do correlate (or – if X (op. def.) points to causes of X (normal meaning) – what the causes are causes *of*). See R. S. Peters' *The Concept of Motivation* (bibliography), pp. 15–16 and elsewhere: also A. C. MacIntyre's 'The Antecedents of Action', in *British Analytical Philosophy*, ed. Bernard Williams and Alan Montefiore (Routledge & Kegan Paul).

17. See also p. 125 (note 62).

18. See Chapter 3, pp. 185–6 (note 8).

19. But see Note A, pp. 441–6.

20. See note 16 above.

21. Of course social scientists may distinguish between 'hard' and 'soft' in other ways, for practical purposes of research, and I am not questioning the usefulness of such distinctions. But the accounts they give of them vary from one author to another, and even the account of a single author is often far from clear: see for instance Barbara Wootton's *Social Science and Social Pathology* (Allen & Unwin), p. 309 *et seq.*

22. See also pp. 72–3.

23. Actually, lists of moral rules for pupils in Communist countries sometimes seem depressingly Victorian. William E. Barton, in his Swarthmore Lecture *The Moral Challenge of Communism* (publishe

by the Friends Home Service Committee), quotes (pp. 40–41) the 'twenty standard "Rules for Pupils" in Soviet Schools', among which are:

'To obey the instructions of the school director and the teachers without question',

'To come to school clean, well-groomed and neatly dressed',

'To keep his place in the class-room neat and tidy',

'To sit upright in the lesson . . . to listen attentively',

'To stand to attention when answering the teacher',

'To be polite to his elders',

'Not to use coarse expressions, not to smoke, not to gamble for money or other objects'.

This is worth mentioning because it is just possible that we may be stampeded by the success of some of the (officially) 'Communist' countries to revert to an outlook of this kind. To make our general point yet again in this context: a country may be successful in achieving such objectives as economic prosperity, law and order, unanimity of belief, 'social cohesion' and so forth, but very unsuccessful in helping its individual citizens to develop as sane and rational people. Of course we have to try to do both.

24. See particularly R. S. Peters and W. K. Frankena in Scheffler's collection (bibliography).

25. Of course this latter difficulty applies to our own components. But my point is that the difficulty is likely to be less if we ask the question 'What is (conceptually) necessary for the making of moral decisions in general?', and try to break this down into as many components as possible, than if we ask 'What makes people honest, loyal, just, thrifty, etc.?', which would tie us down unduly to particular moral concepts.

26. pp. 192–4.

WHAT CAN THE EXPERTS TELL US?

THE RELEVANCE OF PSYCHOLOGY AND SOCIOLOGY

THOSE who are concerned with moral education, either as practical workers or from some more distant standpoint, need not of course try to become professional philosophers, psychologists or sociologists. On the other hand, as I shall argue later,[1] it would be fatal to assume that practical workers and other interested people can simply 'take over' or 'apply' the 'conclusions' of psychology and sociology, or 'put into practice' what they have 'proved'. One reason why this would be a dangerous assumption, which is also the reason why I have put these words and phrases into inverted commas, is that it misrepresents the nature and function of the two disciplines. This is not the place to consider the precise logical status of psychology and sociology, but there are one or two points that need to be made if the reader is to find this Part of the book helpful in the way we intend.

First, these disciplines are important, for the practical worker and other interested people, as much for the way in which they offer new categories in which to think – new ways of viewing practical situations in the classroom and elsewhere – as for any 'scientifically-proved' conclusions. There is a great deal in psychology and sociology, as in philosophy, which is a matter not so much of proof as of something more vague but equally important: a matter of guidance, 'illumination', a new orientation, a new set of concepts. Thus – to anticipate some of the points – the concepts of the superego, of a multi-dimensional assessment of morality, and of 'folk' and 'mass' society may in themselves represent some advance on comparatively simple ideas of (respectively) 'conscience', 'good men' and 'bad men', and the 'virtuous villager' and the 'decadent big city'. How well these concepts relate, or could be related, to experimental and other empirical evidence is, of course, a more open question: and we hope, by describing some of the evidence, to give the reader some idea about this question also.

Secondly, anyone who is going to use these disciplines either for research or for practical purposes needs to have some idea about *how* they relate to a particular topic. He needs, that is, not only to be able to recognize a piece of psychology or sociology if he meets one on a dark night, so to speak, but also to be able to see the relevance of it to what is ultimately a practical problem. For this purpose, a simplified introduction to each discipline[2] as a whole would be inadequate, and might convey the impression (understandably common amongst laymen) that academic disciplines had better be left to academics: perhaps in a hundred years they will be able to tell us something useful, but until then there is not much point trying to 'learn a new subject'. This is so far from the truth, and yet such a natural reaction, that it is very much worth while trying to show how, in general as well as in particular instances, these disciplines are relevant.

Thirdly, enough is known in these fields (let us not say 'proved') for us to be able to extract some practical suggestions, albeit of a very general nature, for moral education. This we shall do in Part III. Much of what is known – the ground which has already been gained by the psychological or sociological approach – is far from new, and will of course appear unexciting to professional workers in those fields. But it needs to be shown how relevant this is to 'moral education' *as that phrase ought to be understood*. The reader must constantly bear in mind that the material in this Part takes its cue from the conceptual points made in Part I. Considered in that light, there is (as I shall say in Part III) quite a lot that we can do about moral education already with reasonable confidence. Here again, it is not so much a matter of experimental proof as of drawing practical conclusions from those considerations in the disciplines of philosophy, psychology and sociology which are (or ought to be) common knowledge.

To put all this another way: what we are primarily concerned with here is a general orientation of those who are interested in moral education, by taking those concepts and findings of psychology and sociology which seem especially relevant to the way in which moral education ought to be conceived. Briefly (and immodestly), this is how we think people *ought to be thinking about* moral education. This task, one might say, represents the first stage in our work: a very critical stage, because unless it is effectively accomplished no organized attack on the topic, however scholarly or original, is likely to cut much ice.

In this context it is perhaps worth enlarging briefly on a point made earlier.[3] While. attempting to select, from the mass of psychological and sociological material, those concepts and findings which seem most relevant to moral education as here defined, one cannot but be very conscious of the degree to which psychology and sociology have developed as independent disciplines. It is thus not surprising that those areas of research which have produced the most solid results, or the most impressive findings, are by no means coextensive with the areas which relate most obviously to a properly-defined concept of moral education. For example, the results obtained by those psychologists who are concerned with the conditioned reflex and with 'behaviour therapy', or those sociologists interested in the equalization of social opportunity by educational selection, however important, are plainly at least one step further removed from our own interests than (say) Piaget's work on the moral judgement of the child, or Talcott Parsons' on the importance of the school as an inculcator of social values and Coleman's on intergenerational conflict.

This is not to say, of course, that results of the former type are simply irrelevant. But the kind of relevance they have suggests that we ought to work back to them, rather than start from them. Their importance as preconditions for the development of rational morality may turn out to be very great: but it seems more sensible to try to get a clearer picture of more obviously related factors and concepts before turning to possible causes which, if perhaps more basic, are also more remote. Because of this, we may seem to have done somewhat less than justice to certain segments of psychological and sociological research – perhaps in particular to English (as opposed to American) sociology, and to the more experimentally-oriented psychologists: but at least our reasons for doing so should be clear.

To make the same point in another way: Psychologists and sociologists are very properly anxious to confine themselves to what they conceive to be their proper disciplines. But the roles which they give themselves in this way cannot, as they stand, always be transferred *in toto* to the study of moral education.

For the gap between these roles, and the areas to which the concept of 'moral education' points, is sometimes too great. Thus one leading sociologist[4] writes:

For the sociologist the problem of moral education is the problem of social integration or consensus – the preparation of individuals for participation in social life and acceptance of social rules: in short the problem of role allocation and socialization.

(The reader will by now be aware of how far this notion of moral education differs from our own.) Of course this *is* a sociological problem (or cluster of problems), which may be highly relevant to moral education as we understand it. But it may not be: it is certainly not the only problem: and the fact – if it is a fact – that sociologists regard it as '*the* problem of moral education' (even for sociologists) must not be allowed to dazzle us too brightly. The particular game we are playing must be kept more open.

It would not be too misleading, perhaps, to regard this as an interim report; and certainly the reader must not suppose that we are offering more than a general orientation of the kind described. The major part of our task lies in the future, and the reader will remember from Chapter 4 of Part One just how difficult this task will be. The devising and assembling of test-procedures for the components of morality (PHIL, EMP, DIK and so forth) represent one crucial aspect: equally important is a clearer view of the general preconditions, in schools and elsewhere, which are relevant to the development of such components. These will only result from many years' work in tests, surveys, experiments and patient observation. But it is perhaps not too hard to see how the points made in this Part (II) are directly relevant to this general task, and how it would be impossible to proceed with any confidence unless they were taken into account.

J.B.W.

Notes to Introduction

1. See Part III, pp. 426–30.

2. Of course, it is misleadingly simple even to talk about 'the two disciplines', as if each title ('psychology', 'sociology') stood for only one clear-cut and acceptable method of working.

3. pp. 30–31.

4. A. H. Halsey, in *Moral Education in a Changing Society* (bibliography), p. 35.

Part II (A)

What the Psychologist has to Say

INTRODUCTION

PART I of this book approached the question of moral education from the conceptual standpoint. In order to consider the contribution of psychology, it will be necessary to reorientate oneself to some extent. The psychologist has a different task from the philosopher, and different methods. He is concerned with attempting to account for observed phenomena by the application of scientific methods: though there is some divergence of opinion amongst psychologists as to what counts as 'scientific'. There have been, broadly speaking, two main approaches to the tasks of psychology, two main traditions of work. Firstly, there has been the *clinical* approach, in which the conclusions are based on prolonged and detailed observation of individual subjects, sometimes over a very long period of time. Such work has necessarily relied very heavily on the subjective judgement of the clinician. At the opposite extreme, we find psychologists who have relied on stricter *experimental* methods, 'scientific' in a narrower sense of this term; such psychologists would frequently not regard the work of the first group as being, properly speaking, scientific at all. However great the disagreement between such approaches may appear to be, there is one basic assumption among all psychologists, namely an agreement about the need to start from the same basic data – observed and recorded behaviour. Concepts, theories or hypotheses must always be linked to this starting point; they are advanced to account for phenomena which have been really observed; the process should never be reversed.

This point could lead to a number of difficulties in dealing with our subject from the psychological point of view at this stage. In the first place, it might be thought premature for the psychologist to write anything at all. Normally, the process would be one of observation, and the formation of hypotheses which could be tested by experiment. In this instance, as has been explained in the general introduction, there are good reasons for giving a preliminary account of the initial problems, but it must be stressed that there is a sense in which the work that is possible at this stage must inevitably be only a kind of literary, or bibliographic, or 'philosophical' pyschology, which will only be fully significant insofar as it leads to objective findings verified by the future work of the unit. We are at this stage dealing essentially with hypotheses and concepts, and any reader of science fiction knows that there are more concepts than there are realities to correspond to them.

This is not to say that the philosopher's analysis of the concepts involved is not relevant to psychological research in this field, but rather that the disciplines involved (and this point applies equally to the sociological aspect of the work) have different functions and use different tools, and that there must be a process of interaction between them. If we are given the task of investigating moral education, or moral development, then it is clearly necessary to know what kind of behaviour counts as moral. Investigation carried out without such a framework runs the risk of being about something quite different from its intended topic. Thus, there has been a great deal of important psychological research on such topics as social adjustment, conformity and mental health. Such research, however, is not in itself about *morality*, unless morality is defined in these terms. This does not mean, of course, that we are in any way questioning the validity of the findings themselves. They remain a record of something that really happened, and any principles deriving from these events remain exactly as valid as they were previously; and they may, of course, be highly relevant to morality, even though they do not take the concept of morality as their starting-point.

Reference to objectivity and scientific method is a little misleading. Although the psychologist must attempt to be entirely neutral and objective and must avoid passing judgement or bringing his own prejudices to the subject under investigation, this is not always possible in practice – particularly when plan-

ing an exploratory work of this kind, which is to a large extent
peculiative, and which cannot rely wholly on experimental
ndings. Absolute neutrality is an aim, not a reality. Although
ve may avoid the more obvious and naive forms of ethnocen-
ricism, it is difficult, if not impossible, to rid ourselves of per-
onal and cultural prejudice. It is therefore as well to state at the
utset that what follows relates especially to work carried out in
Vestern societies. I am not equipped to consider how far it may
e applicable to people who have grown up in other cultures.

What can the psychologist hope to contribute to the study of
noral education? At this preliminary stage, it is not possible
o attempt more than a very general definition, which will con-
ist principally of outlining those questions which have to be
nswered. Nevertheless, such questions fall into relatively dis-
nct groups, which relate to different activities or phases of
esearch.

1. First, we must find out what we can about the nature of
noral behaviour. By this phrase, I do not mean the philosophical
xplication of what the concept must imply; this question has
lready been extensively discussed in Part I. I refer, rather, to its
psychological nature. If it is granted that morality must be de-
ned as it is above, there still remains the task of establishing
vhat kind of thing we are dealing with in terms of the individual
ersonality. What kind of model can best be employed to explain
s working? Are we dealing with an ability, like intelligence, or
vith some personality trait, like introversion? Or is it better to
egard it as a number of patterns of learnt behaviour? Or as a set
f conditioned responses?

2. The answers to these questions will enable us to begin deal-
ng with the important question of moral development. It will
carcely be possible to work out a scheme of moral education
rithout at least the beginnings of a developmental framework.
To what extent is moral development determined by congenital
r hereditary factors, and to what extent by the environment?
How do aspects of the environment and the growing child
nteract, so as to bring about his moral development? What
inds of moral activity are related to various ages or levels of
evelopment, and how does this line of development relate to
ne general development of the personality?

3. We must also turn our attention to the practical implications, those which relate to moral education proper rather than to the psychological nature of moral behaviour. In what ways can we facilitate the child's moral development? Are some environments more favourable than others? What are the parts played by the family, the school, and so on?

4. Finally (and this will present very great difficulties), we must attempt to discover methods of assessing moral development. These will serve to verify our hypotheses experimentally, to assess the effectiveness of different approaches to moral education, and to make predictions about the development of individual children.

Our concern in this Part of the book will be chiefly with (1) and (2) above. Even here it will not be possible to answer all of these questions, or most of them, in a book of this kind. The answers must depend upon extensive research of various kinds, and it will be many years before they are covered in anything like a comprehensive way. But we can at least bear in mind, examine and extrapolate from previous work done by a number of psychologists. Sometimes this work has not primarily been concerned with morality, but with another field which has a direct bearing on the subject. This will serve to give us a preliminary orientation, an indication of the kind of results which we can expect, unless our findings run contrary to the whole trend of psychological investigation of child development over the last thirty years.

One difficulty is the relatively small amount of work which has been done on this topic in the past. It is, perhaps, not small in absolute terms, but it is small in comparison with the amount of work which has been carried out on other topics. In spite of the expansion of interest in topics like the present one, the amount of work being carried out remains small. In the period 1961–3, for instance, there were more researches in progress on television in schools than on the moral development of children.

We must also remember that the task of explaining human behaviour is not, and never has been, the sole preserve of the psychologist. Much that could count as explanation has been embodied in the works of playwrights and novelists, who have often shown a great deal of intuitive insight into the human personality. Similarly, in our everyday lives, we can only make sense and order out of our dealings with other people if we attempt to organize our experiences into some coherent pattern. Many of the impressions which have been formed and recorded in this way have been accurate and by no means in conflict with the more recent findings of psychological research: a fact which has often led to the supposition that psychology merely restates, in long-winded jargon, what everyone knew already in everyday language. Such agreement is not always found, however, and there are many popular theories about personality, which do not at all fit in with the evidence brought to light by psychological research.

SOME COMMON PREJUDICES

Before starting to examine what moral education may be, it is probably worth while to take a look at some of these widespread misapprehensions. These commonly stem from our tendency to put very simple labels on to people, or to sort them into pigeonholes – usually the fewer the better. This is the sort of thing we may be doing when we refer to someone as 'a good man', 'a bad man', 'a nervous man', and so on, as though there were some definite borderline between the categories of people we are referring to. Such a process is, of course, naive in the extreme, and we are not dependent on any particularly psychological insight to reject it; but, since such equally naive expressions as 'an instinctive blood tie' or 'a moral imbecile' still make their appearance from time to time, a closer look at this question is perhaps worth while.

No matter how much we pay lip-service to findings to the contrary, many of us still tend to talk about 'a moral person' and 'an immoral person', as though they were separate kinds of people, with nothing in between. This seems to be a fairly widespread tendency, which has been applied in the past to other aspects of the personality not concerned with morality. In dealing with intelligence, for instance, people used to consider that children of very low intelligence formed a special category, which was rigidly demarcated from the rest of the population.

There were thus two pigeon holes, 'normal' and 'subnormal', a view which is still officially fostered in some of the Communist states. It was partly in connexion with this that Binet began his famous work on intelligence scales, which demonstrated that there is no such sharply-drawn dividing line, and that intelligence can be represented as a scale on which all measurements may occur in the population.

The tendency to put people in such pigeon-holes was also shown to be misleading in the case of those two well-worn categories, introversion and extroversion, which were at first visualized as separate boxes, but which have since been demonstrated to conform to a very different model, a model which has much in common with Binet's intelligence scale. The two terms are seen as the opposite ends of a continuum, so that it is more correct to speak of a person's *degree* of extroversion or introversion. If this dimension of personality is scored, and if a large enough sample of the population is taken, then every possible position on the scale will be found to occur.

But we do not always categorize so obviously. Consider the history of the word 'neurotic'. It was used at one time to imply that neurotics were a separate group of people, who differed qualitatively from the rest of the population. This view was attacked by Freud, and has more recently been demonstrated to be incorrect on quite different grounds by Eysenck, both of whom agree (though they use the term in a somewhat different sense) that the difference between the two groups is one of degree rather than kind. (It is pleasant to be able to record an area of agreement between these two authorities.) Eysenck has described it as a dimension of personality, to which he gives the name 'neuroticism'; and this conforms to the pattern of a continuum, along which any position is theoretically possible. Many similar examples could be quoted.

To consider human behaviour, then, in terms of separate categories of 'moral' and 'immoral' would be to suggest that this area of moral development is entirely different from any other which has been investigated. In other words, it would go against the whole trend of the findings of psychological research regarding the structure of human abilities and personality.

But it is unfortunately more complicated than this. Even when

ve are sufficiently sophisticated in our thinking to avoid the trap
f forcing people into discrete categories, we may still be guilty
f another kind of serious oversimplification. It is tempting to
egard a person's performance in any field as being governed by
 single ability, which is possessed by different individuals to a
lifferent degree. This is implied in our use of such expressions
s 'leadership', 'personality' and 'intelligence'. Here again, the
ctual findings of research do not fit in with this picture, no
natter how useful it may be for some purposes.

The psychology of intelligence gives an interesting example of
vhat I mean. We use the word 'intelligence' as though it were a
ingle overriding ability, which conforms exactly to the model of
ne single personality-dimension referred to above; and it is true
nat if we give a number of people the same intelligence test, the
esults will be arranged in a manner which is consistent with
1ch a model. However, if the same group of people is given a
umber of different tests, we find that we do not get precisely
ne same rank-order on each occasion. Now, a single intellectual
bility necessarily implies that those people who are good at one
ind of intellectual task are also good at another. This, of course,
 not the picture we see in a classroom, where a boy may be
ood at history and hopeless at maths, or good at modern lan-
uages and near the bottom of the class in chemistry. Analysis
f the results of a large number of intelligence tests led to some
nteresting conclusions. Although there is a general intellectual
ctor to which is given the name 'g', this is an abstraction, which
e do not often see, either in intelligence tests, or in real life sit-
ations. Our tests are in fact measuring a number of different
ctors, such as verbal ability, numerical ability, spatial ability,
emory and inductive reasoning. These factors tend to be asso-
ated with each other in the sense that people who do well on a
st of one of these abilities tend to have good scores on the
hers: but this association is by no means perfect. There is, in
her words, some tendency towards independence among these
rious factors of intellectual ability.

Let us apply this idea to the concept of 'a good man'. Let us
ppose that we avoid the trap of making rigid demarcations,
d regard his morality as being high on a continuous scale, an
ea which may be useful for many purposes. It does, however,

contain an assumption, similar to the misapprehension about in
telligence scales mentioned in the last paragraph. It implies that
if a man is 'good' in one set of circumstances, he will also be
'good' in any other; or conversely, that if we catch a person out in
one kind of immorality, he is to be expected to be deficient in all
other departments of moral behaviour.

This assumption appears to lie behind a great deal of our
thinking about moral behaviour. It has, at any rate, permeated
our everyday speech. 'If he'd do that, he'd do anything', I
overheard someone say recently; and, 'If anyone would stoop to
that, he'd be the sort of fellow that would strike a woman.' This
type of reasoning is not to be found only in our own language.
There is a German proverb to the effect that no one believes you
if you have told one lie. The dog with the bad name in the English proverb is an awful warning about the dangers of this type
of thinking, which is based on the idea of a single dimension
of morality.

But we need not necessarily adopt such a model for a structure
of morality. It is possible that, just as was found in the case of
intelligence, morality consists of not one, but a number of
separate factors. It could also be possible that, if this were so,
such factors might not be so strongly associated as is the case
with intellectual factors: in other words, a high level of performance according to one moral factor need not, in this case, imply
high ability in any other. It would follow, too, that it might not be
always possible to predict the degree of morality of a person's
response to one situation from his response to a situation of a
different kind. Before looking at the psychological evidence, let
us consider briefly such evidence as is found in our everyday
observations, or in the writings of non-technical observers.

If we are asked whether we trust such and such a person we
may reply that we would 'trust him with our chequebook', or
even that we would 'trust him with our own daughter'. A moment's reflection on our own acquaintances may show that these
two categories are by no means synonymous. We may say, in
fact, that, as far as concerns these two criteria, there are four
possible kinds of people, namely those whom we would trust
with both, those whom we would trust with neither, those whom
we would trust with our daughters and not with our cheque

books, and those whom we would trust with our cheque books but never with our daughters.

It is a matter of everyday experience that a person may be 'good' in one direction and 'bad' in another, that he will resist one temptation, and succumb to another. Truman Capote gives us a very clear example of this in his documentary novel *In Cold Blood*, in which he gives a detailed account of a particularly cold blooded murder in the American Middle West. The killer is a psychopathic murderer, who is, one would imagine, as low on any scale of morality as one could imagine. After he has killed, with no feelings of remorse, three members of the family, he discovers that his companion intends to commit rape on the 16-year-old daughter before she too is murdered. The killer will have none of this. He rejects the suggestion indignantly, because he will have nothing to do with immorality of that kind. I am not, of course, suggesting that the killer was in any normal sense a moral person. The point is that he is capable of an extreme of immoral behaviour in one direction, while remaining restrained in another, a striking example of nonspecificity of moral traits.

A similar picture emerges from examination of police-court records. The person who is an all-round degenerate is an exception: typically, a criminal is characterized by his own particular kind of crime. A bank robber is rarely guilty of offences against children: a cat-burglar rarely commits sexual offences: the man who floats fraudulent companies frequently lives an exemplary home life. I choose these examples of criminal behaviour, not because I wish to place undue stress on such deviant behaviour – we are, after all, primarily concerned with its opposite – but because subjects of this kind are the ones which, for obvious reasons, have attracted a great deal of attention in the past.

Material of this kind is illustrative, but does not prove anything unless it is backed by experimental findings. Fortunately, there are a number of investigations which have a direct bearing on this question. Probably the best known is one carried out by Hartshorne and May,[1] two American psychologists, whose findings were published nearly forty years ago. Their inquiry was concerned with the nature of character and dealt with a number of its aspects. The study was not only one of the earliest, but also one of the most thorough investigations of our topic, and its findings are still relevant to our work today. It will, therefore, be worth while to spend a moment or two in considering this work, with particular reference to its bearing on the question of generality of moral traits.

Hartshorne and May constructed a special battery of tests and ratings, which were designed to measure different aspects of character. Some were concerned with deceit and cheating, and of course with their converse, i.e. honesty. Some were concerned with stealing. Others were concerned with cooperation and self-control. The tests were very ingeniously constructed in that they not only conformed to the normal requirements of the experimental situation, but also appeared to the subjects to be part of everyday situations. This helped to avoid the falsification of results, which could arise if the children knew it was their honesty which was being tested.

A few examples will illustrate this. To test for cheating, an ordinary class test is administered. The children are later given an opportunity to mark this themselves, not knowing that there exists a record of the original answers, which enables the experimenter to check whether the mark is inflated, by altering some of the answers. A different test is the peeping test, which was even more simple and ingenious. The child was given a paper, on which were marked squares of different sizes. He was asked to draw a mark in each of the squares, keeping his eyes closed. It was possible to calculate the probability of getting it right without looking, and to show that any child who scored such-and-such in this test had certainly been cheating. The children were also put in positions where they had an opportunity to keep money which did not belong to them, apparently without fear of detection, and their response to this was noted.

Hartshorne and May postulated that, if honesty were a general trait, then we would expect the tests described above, and others used in the enquiry, to have high positive intercorrelations. This is to say that there would be a tendency for children who scored highly on one test to score highly on all the others, or, to apply this to moral behaviour in real life, there would be a high degree of predictability between one situation and another.

The findings in fact showed, among other things:

1. Whenever a test of honesty gave opportunity for a wide spread of scores along a scale, the children who were examined by that test tended to be spread out along the whole length of the scale. This observation confirms what we have thought likely about the distribution of moral traits, namely that they do not fall into discrete categories, but can be represented on a continuum, in which every position may be occupied.

2. Concerning the question of unified or specific moral traits, Hartshorne and May found only low positive intercorrelations. A child's performance on one test did not bear a very close relationship to his performance on the others.

Now there are two separate problems here. On the one hand, quite apart from the question of single or multiple moral traits, there is the question of whether there is any generality at all, or whether moral behaviour is not specific to particular situations. We could describe moral behaviour in terms of a large number of conditioned reflexes, established early in life, which consist of responses to particular kinds of situations. We might argue that, although there is some tendency for these responses to become generalized, this is by no means perfect, and that there is no need to postulate such a thing as generalized moral traits.

This argument has been questioned by H. J. Eysenck, who has shown in a recent book[2] that the experimenters were unduly pessimistic in their interpretation of the figures obtained, which were, after all, positive. Eysenck argues that these figures are sufficient for us to reject the specificity hypothesis, according to which we could expect intercorrelations of zero. But this does not imply that there is a *single* personality dimension of morality. If we suppose that moral behaviour is predicted by a number of different component factors, we have a hypothesis which is by no means incompatible with Hartshorne and May's findings. The situation would then be that the various tests tapped different components, either singly, or in combinations with each other in which the components had different weightings. If this were so, it would account for the fact that the correlations were positive, and also for the fact that they were low. What we are suggesting, in fact, is that the situation may resemble that which has already been described as applying to intelligence: i.e. we have a general factor, which operates and is tested in combination with a number of specific ones. The difference in the case of morality seems to be, according to the figures obtained by Hartshorne and May, that the general factor is very much less influential.

Such an approach has the initial difficulty that the concepts involved are, at any rate initially, not clearly defined. The word 'factors' gives us no idea about what sort of things we are dealing with, how they operate, how they develop, how they are related to each other and to other aspects of the personality. However, study of the existing literature of child development furnishes enough material to construct a hypothetical structure of moral ability and the beginnings of a developmental scheme.

Earlier in this section we discussed some of the popularly held views about the nature of moral behaviour. It happened that all the views mentioned were ones which did not stand up to methodical investigation. But this, of course, is not always so, nor is it the chief difficulty with views of this sort. Thus, if one asks a large number of ordinary people about the personality characteristics which, in their view, make for morality, they are likely to give an assortment of replies – 'having a conscience', 'possessing ideals', 'knowing right from wrong', 'self-discipline' and 'self-control'.

The trouble with such words is not that they are *wrong*. It is that everyone thinks that he knows so well what they mean that no one troubles to define them, and they are hence used in different ways. One result of this is that many people say, after reading an account such as is given in the following chapters: 'That's exactly what I've been saying all along. The trouble with these psychologists is that they simply translate what everyone knows into jargon that no one can understand.' Although the charge is sometimes justified, this is not really the point about 'jargon'. Words like 'conscience' and 'discipline' are highly charged with emotion. They often no longer communicate ideas, but merely act as a signal which switches on our prejudices. By using technical terms, we hope to avoid such emotional overtones. They are convenient, too, in that they have overtones of their own, relating to particular psychological theories and models of the personality.

The popular terms for the moral characteristics referred to above relate very closely to concepts which will appear in the following chapters, where they will be given psychological names – 'jargon', if you like. For some people, it may be true that this will simply re-state what they always knew, but this will not necessarily be the case. The emotional overtones of words like 'discipline' derive not merely from the words themselves; the associated feelings may be transferred to any new formulation, so that one's agreement, or disagreement, reflects pre-existing attitudes.[3] The attempt to inhibit this process through the use of carefully defined technical language is not always successful.

Notes to Part II(A) – Introduction

Hartshorne & May:

1. *Studies in the Nature of Character* (Macmillan's, New York).
2. *Crime and Personality* (Routledge & Kegan Paul).
3. It is sad (especially for the authors of books like this), but true, that your acceptance or rejection of a wide range of arguments connected with morality, politics, education and social welfare is related as closely to your personality type as to any other factor.

CHAPTER 5

FACTORS IN MORAL BEHAVIOUR

A. 'CONSCIENCE' AND THE SUPEREGO

'CONSCIENCE' is one of those words which we have just discussed;
it is so widely used that it has a number of quite different meanings.[1] Sometimes it refers to 'knowing the difference between
right and wrong', sometimes it means the power to resist temptation, or the feelings of guilt or of shame after one has succumbed
to it. We may offer descriptions, rather than a precise definition,
which will serve to direct our attention to the kind of phenomenon which concerns us here. 'Conscience', in the sense in which
we shall be interested, is the thing that makes us say, after listening to a careful argument which shows why it is really all right to
dodge income tax, or engage in a doubtful business deal, 'Well,
I dare say you're right, but I wouldn't feel right about it somehow.' It is the thing that makes us put a coin in the box of an
unattended newspaper stand, even when we know that nobody
is looking, or feel bad when we fail to do so, even though we
know we will not be caught out. In other words, we are concerned with an *internal system*, which operates without reference to
the opinions that other people may have about our actions, and
often without reference to considerations of reason, self-interest
or expediency.

There is a view that 'conscience' (in this sense) is playing a
smaller part in the personality structure of Western man, that
there is an increasing number of people who, in place of an
unconscious value-system and feelings of guilt, have a system
which relates to the attitudes of other people and the feeling of
shame – a kind of external conscience. Although this theory has a
direct bearing on our present topic, I shall not do more than
mention it here, since it is discussed in greater detail elsewhere.[2]

The most common psychological term to designate one aspect
of conscience is 'superego'. This has been defined as a 'term
employed by psychoanalysts to designate a structure in the

unconscious, built up by early experiences on the basis mainly of the child's relations to his parents and functioning as a kind of conscience, criticizing the thoughts and actions of the ego, causing feelings of guilt and anxiety when the ego gratifies, or tends to gratify, primitive impulses'. This term sometimes misleads people because of the fact that 'super-' usually implies the idea of 'higher', so that we might expect the superego to be more and not less conscious than the ego, or stronger than the ego. Nevertheless, having drawn attention to the anomalous construction of the word, we shall generally employ it below.

This topic has been the subject of a good deal of detailed work. For our present purposes, it will be sufficient to distinguish between two main lines of approach. Each of them has been developed to a point far beyond what can be explained here, and the reader should not imagine that the following gives a detailed picture of the work being done. All I can hope to accomplish is to indicate the main difference between the two opposing groups of theories concerned, to show that they have, in some respects, more in common with each other than might at first be supposed, and to argue that neither of the two sets of concepts comes entirely within the category of moral education as defined in Part I.

A. The first, and most widely employed of these, is a group of theories which make use of the idea of introjection. The term derives, in the first instance, from the original work of Freud, who suggested that the superego is formed by the *introjection* of aspects of one or other parent. That is to say, some parts of the parent are incorporated by the child into his own personality. The original Freudian theory suggested that introjection and superego formation are connected with the resolution of the Oedipus complex. The child's attachment to the opposite-sex parent, and his jealousy of the same-sex parent, result in an emotional crisis; the child has to give up the exclusiveness of his attachment, and at this stage is said to 'introject' aspects of the loved object which he has given up.

Many psychologists would regard this original formulation as being largely of historical interest: but there have been a number of recent studies, which have thrown light on the conditions under which introjection takes place, indicating that introjection and consequently superego formation take place most effectively where there is a warm relationship and strict discipline. Other studies have concerned themselves with attempts to provide an empirical demonstration of the mechanism by which introjection takes place. Such approaches have been in terms of identification with the parents and imitation of their behaviour; of defensive identification with a harsh parent; and of perception of other persons' reactions to one's own behaviour.

Whichever of these standpoints one chooses to adopt, certain observations about the way in which the superego functions remain constant, among which are the following points:

1. All of them see the conscience as being formed by parental attitudes or judgements being incorporated into the child's personality. Most of them agree that this does not happen at a conscious level. The child does not do it on purpose, nor does he usually know he is doing it, nor is it something which is intentionally induced by his parents.

2. The introjected material, or superego, remains fairly stable and unconscious, though the individual is aware of the feelings of guilt or anxiety which the superego may produce.

3. The introjected values may be at variance with those of the parents as consciously expressed. The superego is founded upon the *child's perception* of parental attitudes, judgements or behaviour, which of course is much wider than merely what the parents say to the child. Freud suggested that the child's superego is related to the superegos of his parents, rather than to their manifest behaviour. Whether or not this is so, superego formation goes much deeper than the parents' conscious attitudes and beliefs and their attempts at morally educating their child.[3]

B. An alternative way of approaching the question of conscience is to make use of the concept of the conditioned reflex. Psychologists who favour this approach suggest that conscience is simply a system of conditioned reflexes,[4] which do not differ in any respect from those conditioned responses that determine some other aspects of our behaviour. It is an approach which appeals particularly to those who favour a physiological or a strictly experimentally-based standpoint.

The possibility of the misuse of this term has already been mentioned. The conditioned reflex is properly confined to the following situation: Stimulus A elicits reflex X. The associated stimulus B is constantly associated with A. The 'conditioned reflex' occurs when B elicits X in the absence of A. To relate this to Pavlov's classic experiments: we are not simply saying that, when the bell rings, the dog knows his dinner is ready. We are dealing with a reflex action, an activity of the autonomic nervous system; it is a form of 'learning' which is not connected with what the subject consciously knows or does not know. Pavlov's dog may or may not have 'known' that his dinner was ready, but in either case, his response was involuntary. This aspect of conditioning becomes clearer when the response is measured in terms of such things as changes in the electrical rhythms of the brain, or in the conductivity of the skin. To take another kind of example: when I went to stay at a college where an electric bell was rung before lunch each day, it did not take long for a conditioned reflex to be established. Like Pavlov's dog, I salivated when the bell went. Common sense says that my mouth watered because I knew that the bell meant lunchtime. But in fact this was not the case, as was shown one day when I had to visit the dentist in the afternoon and was allowed no lunch: I *knew* that the bell meant lunch for everyone else, but not for me; nevertheless, the conditioned reflex took place and my mouth began to water. The point was, of course (to stress it once more), that responses of this kind take place in a part of my nervous system which is not concerned with *knowing* about things.

The principles of association illustrated by the operation of conditioned reflexes have some more general applications, but the utility of the idea of the conditioned response diminishes as one moves further from the original formulation. This must be borne in mind when applying the idea of conditioning to the development of morality. To account for the origin of conscience through a conditioned reflex theory, the following sequence of events is suggested, the essential part of the pattern being the same as in the formation of any other conditioned reflexes:

The child has to learn forms of behaviour which do not fit in with his own wishes. He has to learn bowel- and bladder-control, not to tear up his father's books, not to pull the cat's tail, or to beat the table with his spoon when people are talking. Such 'naughty' actions are punished by the parents. With the repetition of this punishment a conditioned reflex occurs, which is expressed in terms of the description given above. The slap (or other punishment) is Stimulus A, and the feelings of distress which it produces are Response X. The act, or the desire to carry it out (depending on the exact point in time when the punishment is administered), is Stimulus B, which becomes associated with the unpleasant feelings. This sets up in the personality a permanent inhibitory system with regard to the forbidden act. Next time the child feels inclined to tease the cat or steal some jam, the desire or the action produces some of the internal discomfort usually associated with a slap. There is evidence that, if the punishment occurs after the offence, then guilt results, but if the punishment is administered simultaneously with the offence, then temptation-resistance is produced with regard to that action.

It will be noted that, up to now, the situation described conforms exactly to the pattern of the conditioned reflex as it was originally formulated. The unpleasant feelings, the pain, the nervous tension and the distress, are produced through the operation of a part of the nervous system which is not subject to conscious control. Thus, we are not saying that the child *learns*, or *knows*, that if he does such and such a thing he will be punished. We are saying that the forbidden action, through the operation of a quite automatic sequence of events, comes directly to produce an unpleasant sensation, which is beyond the child's control.

This process is regarded as providing the basis of conscience, which can thus be regarded as being a network of a great many separately formed reflexes. As we saw in the last section, the possibility of specificity and uncoordination of response is in part diminished by the process of generalization, which tends to organize the responses into a pattern or network. This process is helped when the child's thought and language-patterns permit him to build up associated sets of concepts.

This thesis fits in very well with the facts of conscience as they have been described, and it seems to be remarkably simple and straightforward. But there are difficulties. In the first place, not as much experimental work is in unanimous support of this theory as one is sometimes led to believe. If conscience arises simply through avoidance-conditioning and punishment, we would expect that those children who are punished most frequently would have the strongest superegos. In fact, the reverse has been found to be the case. A further difficulty arises from an oversimplification of what is meant by the word 'punishment' in this context.[5] Let us see how it works out in practice.

Of course, for an event to be a punishment, in the sense of being something which can give rise to avoidance-conditioning, it need not be a slap or a scolding, or any other consciously-administered penalty. Any stimulus which is in some way unpleasant, and which leads to avoidance-behaviour, can properly be regarded as a 'punishment' in this sense. Intentionally punitive actions are far less frequent than actions of other kinds. They form only a very small number of all the possible stimuli which are constantly impinging on the child's perceptions, and which are available to contribute to the conditioning process. To consider only those unpleasant experiences, which might give rise to avoidance, we find that expressions of displeasure, the feeling of the child that his parents are angry with him, that they do not love him any more, the experience that he is left on his own, and so on, are, as a class, frequent occurrences. The 'punishing' stimulus will most frequently be some parental response to the child's behaviour. It is also clear that such parental responses must include a large number of quick emotional responses, involuntary reactions, outbursts of temper, and so on. Now responses of this sort need not be connected with our consciously-expressed principles, nor with our views on the proper way to bring up children; but they will nevertheless have a great effect on the development of conditioned responses.

It is no use saying 'It doesn't matter' to the child who is standing among the shattered fragments of a Dresden vase, if your anguish is written in every line of your body. It is no use claiming that we will bring up a child to have an 'enlightened' attitude about sex if we wince, or become gruff or embarrassed every time he asks an awkward question. Insofar as such responses are capable of arousing unpleasant feelings in the child, they are capable of setting up conditioned reflexes. Thus, the patterns we set up are likely to be related to our *actual* feelings and attitudes, rather than to what we *say* to a child, or how we set out to bring him up.

In practice, then, the conditioned-reflex approach to the formation of conscience visualizes a mechanism which is

(i) relatively permanent;

(ii) not amenable to conscious control, since it involves autonomic reactions;

(iii) both controlling and punitive; and

(iv) based in the first instance upon actual parental attitudes rather than parental teachings.

Thus it seems that there is little difference in the two pictures of the conscience or superego in action, one arising from the conditioned-reflex approach and the other from the introjection approach.

If one wishes to go further, however, and say that not merely conscience, but all moral behaviour, is the result of conditioned reflexes, then this approach becomes absurd. Whereas the theory of conscience outlined above is based upon the original formulation of the conditioned reflex, any generalization of the theory to include the whole sphere of moral behaviour involves so many different kinds of activity that the meaning of the term becomes extended to vanishing-point. Intellectual or cognitive processes – the weighing-up of moral principles, and the process of thinking purposefully about them – play a part in the moral conduct of at least some people. It is conceivable that one might explain such conscious processes in terms of conditioned responses (though it would be difficult), just as one might describe doing a crossword puzzle, or writing a book about experimental psychology, in these terms.[6] But it does not follow that this is the most convenient way of describing such events, or the easiest way to understand them. Nor is it necessarily the best way of communicating with other people, if one wishes to discuss the activity.

This point has a bearing on the question of which view of conscience we choose to adopt. The term introjection points to the relationship between parental attitudes and personality on the one hand, and the nature or content of the child's superego on the other. The theories which make use of it, while they do not account for the events in terms of a minutely described mechanism, nevertheless present this relationship in a way which can be grasped easily and quickly by people who are not experimental psychologists. It seems, then, that this approach has many advantages for the general discussion of moral education. It is not suggested that the Freudian scheme is merely a convenient myth; the point is that, even if it were nothing but a myth, it would still be the most suitable approach for many purposes. Whether we describe these processes in terms of the psychoanalytic institutions of the personality, or conditioned reflexes, we are, after all, dealing with models rather than realities.

But there is, in any case, a large measure of agreement between the two approaches when it comes to describing the manner of operation of the resulting structure. Both agree that the superego is a structure which originates from relatively primitive processes that operate at a fairly early stage of development, and which continues as an unconscious structure, not amenable to conscious control. It is not in any sense rational in its operation, nor is it concerned with reality. The self-punitive feelings which the superego can arouse do not necessarily relate to conscious moral beliefs. Most of us will have experienced irrational guilt at some time or other. Some people cannot be approached by a policeman without experiencing acute guilt feelings, even though their 'conscience' (using the word in a different sense) is entirely clear.

The superego is formed mainly at an early age; being unconscious, it remains relatively untouched by subsequent events. It is founded upon parental attitudes, as perceived by a four- or five-year-old child, and it remains relatively undiscriminating, making primitive 'judgements' about primitive impulses. Thus, the superego may simply 'say' that dirt, or aggression, or sex is wrong; there are no such things for it as extenuating circumstances or exceptional cases.

If my superego is not inclined to permit me to act aggressively, my feelings of guilt will not be diminished by the fact that, on rational grounds, I know that aggression is sometimes justified, or even morally desirable. For instance, I may know that a shopkeeper is persistently giving short weight to someone who can ill afford to be cheated, and I may feel that the only way to stop it is to say something extremely unpleasant to the man. Nevertheless, my superego, if it is as I have described it, will still attempt to prevent me from behaving in this way, and, if I manage to act in spite of these attempts, it will still make me feel unpleasantly guilty afterwards.

To sum up: Whichever of the explanations of the nature and origins of conscience one favours, it emerges as something which, though a most important instrument for socializing children and for controlling behaviour, cannot cover the whole of what we normally mean by 'morality': though of course it may provide some motive power for moral behaviour, through the discomfort of 'a guilty conscience'.

Amongst the various connotations of the word 'conscience' in addition to the guilt-producing agency which has been discussed above, we mentioned the power to resist temptation. It is commonly believed that these two aspects of conscience go together – that the person who does not fall prey to temptation easily is also the person most severely affected by pangs of conscience after he has given in. Recent experimental work has, however, suggested that the distinction between these two components of conscience is a valid one, in that they may be largely independent of each other.

One experiment was concerned with establishing a prohibition in young puppies by the use of a simple 'punishment'.[7] The puppies were faced with a choice between a plate of horse-meat and a plate of patent dog food. The object of the first part of the experiment was simply to train the puppies to choose the commercial food, to regard eating horse-meat as 'wrong'. Since (contrary to the claims of some of the pet-food advertisers) the puppies all preferred the horse-meat, this was a valid training task. The method of training was the ordinary one, used in many homes, of tapping the puppy with a newspaper whenever it made the wrong choice. As would be expected, an avoidance of the plate of horse-meat was built up in every case.

The next stage in the experiment consisted in leaving the puppies in a room with the plate of horse-meat when hungry and apparently unsupervised (the experimenter was in fact observing through a one-way vision screen). In human terms, the stimulus of the horse-meat exposed the puppies to a temptation to abandon their training. Since the avoidance of the meat was based upon a process of conditioning rather than on any understanding of the prohibition, it can be argued that this is a simple analogy to the situation which arises when the conscience is faced with a temptation.

There was a wide range of behaviour reported in the behaviour of the puppies in this situation. For instance, a simple measure of the strength of their temptation-resistance (the length of time which elapsed before they ate the meat) showed that some abandoned their training in a few minutes and some lasted out much longer – one of them, with a very strong 'conscience', fasted for more than a fortnight, upon which the experiment was stopped. There was also a wide range in the kind of behaviour reported. Some puppies circled the room, keeping their eyes turned away from the tempting object; others crawled towards it and retreated again.

One finding is particularly interesting from the point of view of our present topic. Two opposed patterns of behaviour were distinguished. Some puppies were apprehensive before eating the meat, but when they gave in to the temptation, they would eat it up with no sign of guilt at all. On the contrary, their tails would wag and they would be pleased to see the experimenter when he came back into the room. Others, often with a lower temptation-resistance, became very upset when they had eaten the meat: and when the experimenter came in they put their tails down and tried to avoid him. These two patterns, temptation-resistance and reaction of guilt, were found to be related to the *timing* of the administration of the punishment. If the punishment was administered as the puppy was approaching the meat, and before it had eaten it, temptation-resistance was developed. If, on the other hand, the punishment was delayed until after the puppy had started to eat, a guilt-reaction was built up instead.

These findings are very suggestive, and have clear implications for the effect of various child training patterns. Experiments have been put in hand to investigate the degree to which these findings apply to babies. The implication which is important for our present discussion, however, is that the two variables, which are sometimes lumped together under the name of 'conscience' – guilt and temptation-resistance – are, to some extent, independent of each other. In other words, the person with the greatest resistance to temptation is not necessarily the one who feels most guilty.

Of course, the term 'temptation-resistance' is in itself used to describe more than one kind of behaviour. The unconscious and unreasoned avoidance of certain kinds of behaviour, implanted in early childhood, is an entirely different phenomenon from that which is concerned, say, when a man decides to give up smoking and refrains from giving in to the temptation to smoke. This cannot be regarded as a conditioned response, nor (in most cases) as the operation of conscience in our sense. It is a function of an entirely different part of the personality, and, as such, will be discussed in a later section.[8]

B. Ego-ideal

So far we have discussed the superego as a punitive guilt- and anxiety-arousing agency, and the ability to resist temptations. There is a third question which is closely related to these. This is the question of 'ideals', which have much in common with the superego insofar as their formation and internalization is concerned. They also relate closely to our picture of ourselves. The question of the self-image will be discussed later in more detail: for the present it is sufficient to point out that each of us has some sort of internal picture of what kind of person we are. This picture is not in all respects satisfactory to us, and we have in addition to this an 'ego-ideal' which is variously described as an 'idealized image of oneself', a composite picture of the desirable traits which we would like to detect in ourselves, or a composite of internalized exemplars.

The 'ego-ideal' relates to the superego at the earliest levels, where it is initially formed. The 'ideals' are adopted from figures in the child's environment – parents, teachers and so on – but also to some extent from characters in books and comics and, increasingly in these days, figures seen on the television. In the latter case, however, it is far from clear whether the child adopts values from such figures, or whether the figures are used to exemplify or personify ideals which are already held.

We have, then, in conjunction with the negative, prohibitory aspects of the superego, a positive system of values to be aimed at. Thus we may, when assessing a possible course of action, measure it against such a picture of 'ourselves as we should be', asking 'Am I "ideally" the sort of person who would cheat the tax authorities, or drive dangerously, or take money from the collection plate at church?'[9] This provides a motivation for 'good' behaviour, since failure to live up to these ideals produces dissatisfaction and guilt; whereas, positively, the sense of having lived up to them produces a feeling of satisfaction, such as may be experienced by a small child when he receives his parents' approval.

The ego-ideal is limited in the extent to which it can be applied to the concept of moral behaviour. Many of the arguments already summarized in connexion with the superego could be repeated here. The ego-ideal is not, in itself, a rational instrument, nor do the values it represents necessarily relate to accepted moral standards. A child growing up in a delinquent subculture may build up, by a perfectly normal process of introjection, an ego-ideal and a superego which involve valuing highly qualities which the rest of the community regard as delinquent. A criminal may have an ego-ideal which involves being a skilful burglar. Less dramatically, many motorists see their ideal selves as intrepid characters, with nerves of steel, who take risks without batting an eyelid. (The question of the internalization of wrong values is not an academic quibble: Nazi Germany provided a very clear example of perverted 'idealism' on a national scale.) We are dealing again with a part of the personality which, for most of us most of the time, is an important instrument for controlling our behaviour, but which has no *necessary* relationship with *rational* behaviour.

It is convenient to refer to 'the ego-ideal' in this way as though it were a composite unified factor, operating in a single direction. This, of course, need not be the case at all. The ideals were based upon the perceptions of the behaviour of a large number of different individuals, all serving as models for our ideal personality: and their behaviour may not have been consistent. The individual may thus have a number of internalized ideals which are in conflict with each other, just as were the attitudes of the original models. If the person is unable to bring about a rational and effective solution of such a conflict, the defect of the ego-ideal will be in the direction of less efficient behaviour in his general life, as well as in the field of moral behaviour. Similarly, the ego-ideal must have some point of contact with the real personality. If the ideals are so high that there is no point of contact, that it represents an entirely unattainable standard of perfection, then this can be a damaging form of ego-ideal which will lead to unhappiness and even paralysis of action, when the individual gives up trying altogether. Jersild, writing about adolescents, said that the motto 'Hitch your waggon to a star' is a 'cruel motto, cruel to self and cruel to others. If an earthbound adolescent completely adopted this motto, he could expect no other return than guilt and self-reproach.'[10]

The nature of the ego-ideal goes far to determining the individual's reactions to his own deficiencies, to determining a realistic level of aspiration. The point was expressed as long ago as 1890 by the psychologist William James, in the following well known passage:

I, who for the time have staked my all on being a psychologist, am mortified if others know much more psychology than I. But I am contented to wallow in the grossest ignorance of Greek. My deficiencies there give me no sense of personal humiliation at all. Had I 'pretensions' to be a linguist, it would have been just the reverse. So we have the paradox of a man shamed to death because he is only the second pugilist or the second oarsman in the world. That he is able to beat the whole population of the globe minus one is nothing; he has 'pitted' himself to beat that one; and as long as he doesn't do that nothing else counts. He is to his own regard as if he were not, indeed he is not.

Yonder puny fellow, however, whom every one can beat, suffers no chagrin about it, for he has long ago abandoned the attempt to 'carry that line', as the merchants say, of self at all. With no attempt there can be no failure; with no failure no humiliation. So our self-feeling in this world depends entirely on what we *back* ourselves to be and do...[11]

Relate to "hope"

C. MORAL JUDGEMENTS: THE WORK OF PIAGET

When we talk of making moral *judgements*, or of '*knowing* the difference between right and wrong', we must not fail to distinguish this ability from the activity of the superego. We are dealing now with a *conscious* activity, a cognitive or intellectual process, quite different in character from that which was discussed in the last section.

To speak of this as though it were a single ability is no doubt an oversimplification. It would probably be more accurate to think of a group of cognitive abilities, concerned, for instance, with the formation of moral concepts, or the ability to reason in moral terms and to make moral judgements. We might say that we are dealing with a capacity for problem-solving in the moral sphere. It is necessary to bear in mind, too, that we are using the word 'ability' in a rather different sense from the way in which it is often used in such terms as 'verbal ability', 'numerical ability', or 'spatial ability'. 'Ability', in these examples, often refers to the level of *aptitude* in certain areas, rather than with an actual level of *performance* in skills which are related to that ability. (Thus, if you have a high level of numerical ability, it indicates that you would be likely to respond well to a lesson on extracting cube roots: it need not mean that you can do sums of this sort already.) By contrast, our cognitive 'moral abilities' imply actual performance, rather than aptitude: the term relates to the extent to which we *have learnt* to deal with actual moral problems at an intellectual level, rather than to our *capacity to learn* to do so.

These cognitive moral abilities have a clear relationship to other, more general, intellectual abilities; notably to verbal ability, since this must play a considerable part in the development of moral concepts. This relationship makes for difficulties in research: it would be quite possible to construct tests of moral thinking which simply measure intelligence, or verbal ability, or some similar factor.

The psychologist who is most widely known for his work in this field is the Swiss psychologist, Jean Piaget. His book, *The Moral Judgement of the Child*, appeared in 1932, but it remains the only child-centred work of major proportions which has been devoted to this topic. Unfortunately, many readers tend to

e intimidated by Piaget's writings: partly because of difficulties
of style and translation, and partly because of difficulties of ter-
minology, which themselves arise from a different way of
approaching the problem of child development, an approach
which needs the use of novel and unfamiliar concepts. Although
these difficulties are real, they are perhaps usually overstated,
with the result that one often still finds an ignorance of the true
nature of Piaget's methods and findings combined with an
uncritical view of the value of his contributions. In view of all
this, it will probably be as well to begin by saying a few words
about Piaget's work generally before considering that part of it
which is concerned specifically with the moral development of
children.

Piaget's approach is in marked contrast to any of the approaches to research which have been developed among English-
speaking psychologists. He is not particularly concerned with
experimental method in the stricter sense of the term, nor does he
employ much in the way of psychometrics, or methods of statistical analysis. His approach is in some ways nearer to that of a
clinician, since his findings are based upon the careful and detailed analysis of data gathered from a small number of subjects. It
is a method which resembles, in its painstaking observation, the
work of the naturalist; and in its conceptual analysis of the material gathered, it resembles the work of the logician. In contrast to
much of the psychological research with which we are familiar, it
uses only the simplest of equipment and the simplest of questions. This is perhaps illustrated best by some examples.

If you had been present at one well-known experiment, which
was concerned with the child's perception of volume and quantity, and the concepts he forms about these things, you would
have seen the child sitting at a table with the experimenter, who
had, as equipment, nothing but a number of jars of various sizes
and shapes, and a quantity of water. The water is poured from
one jar to another, for example from a low wide jar into a tall
narrow one, and the child is asked a number of questions. 'Is
there more water now, or less?', 'How do you know?', 'If I
poured the water into this jar over here, would it still be the
same?'. The experimenter is not following a rigidly-defined
scheme of questions: he is rather exploring the nature of the

child's responses to the material presented, and the thought-processes that lie behind them.

Other experiments concern themselves with the child's ideas about measurement and length. He is shown, for example, two pieces of wood of identical length, which are then staggered slightly. 'Which stick is longer, and why?': a simple question, but one which reveals a great deal about the development of the child's ideas about measurement and space. Children at different stages of development give various responses. 'That stick is bigger because you pushed it' ($4\frac{1}{2}$ years old). 'That one is smaller because it doesn't touch there' ($5\frac{1}{2}$). 'They're both longer. That one is longest at that side and that one is longest at the other side' (6). 'They're still the same; they can't grow' ($7\frac{1}{2}$). Piaget analyses the content of answers such as these, in order to throw light upon the kinds of concept used by young children and the line of development which these concepts appear to follow. Among the topics which have been investigated in a similar way are such things as the child's idea of number and space, his logic, his judgement and reasoning, his language and thought.

During the past forty years or so, Piaget and his collaborators have built up a theory of child development. Although this work is mainly concerned with the growth of intellectual and conceptual skills, its principles are not without relevance to our present topic. The theory emphasizes two aspects of child development in a way which may seem at first to be paradoxical. The continuity of the child's development is stressed, and, at the same time, it is suggested that the child's thinking is different in kind (not merely in degree) from that of the adult. These different kinds of thought-processes are embodied in Piaget's theory of developmental stages in conceptual development. Four stages are postulated, which succeed each other in an invariable sequence, though the stages should not be tied too rigidly to particular age-ranges.

A very much simplified account of these stages is as follows

1. _Sensori-motor stage_: (about 0–2 years). The child is learning to deal with his own perceptual and motor functions, and to fit these together, so that, for example, when he sees a biscuit, he (a) knows that it is an object in the external world, (b) can coordinate his vision and his hand-movements so as to pick up the

...iscuit and put it in his mouth. Activities of this kind, though ...ten apparently random, are the basic explorations of the nature ... the self and the outside world, the raw material from which ...e more sophisticated concepts of later life are built up.

2. *Pre-operational or representational stage*: (about 2–6 years). ✓
...he child learns to represent the world by means of symbols – ...pecially linguistic symbols; but he has no real concepts yet, and ... true understanding of such things as causal relationships, ...hich he tends to represent in an animistic, motivational way. ...he rain falls because 'the clouds are crying'; it gets dark 'be-...use the sun goes to bed'. He is not well able to separate goals ...d means.

BUT "UNFAIR"? "TAKE TURNS"? & STICK FIGURES

3. *Stage of concrete operations*: (about 7–11 years). The child ...gins to use genuine concepts and to apply these to situations ...d problems, but only insofar as these relate to the world as it ...n be immediately perceived. There is no generalization or ...bstraction.

4. *Stage of formal operations*: (about 12–15). Generalization, ✓
...bstract thinking and hypothetical reasoning become possible ...r the first time.

This general theory of stages in conceptual or intellectual ...velopment provides more than a mere background against ...hich to view Piaget's work on moral development. As will be ...en, the stages in some aspects of moral growth conform very ...osely to this pattern. Insofar as moral behaviour is regarded as ...ntaining a rational component, the theory of stages is highly ...rtinent to our understanding of the conditions of its develop-...ent. It may also determine which level of expectation we con-...der to be appropriate to children of various ages. The theory, ...e Freud's theory of personality development, emphasizes the ...cessity for adequate satisfaction of those needs which are ...propriate to the various levels of development. To expect ...rmal, abstract thinking on moral issues from a child who, irres-...ctive of age, is still at the stage of concrete operations, can ...ntribute nothing to the child's moral growth.

The methods of research used by Piaget to investigate the ...oral judgement of the child are no more complicated than ...ose used in his investigations of other topics. The first part of

the work is concerned with the child's use and understanding
of rules. To examine this, he substitutes for the sticks or jars of
water in other experiments the game of marbles as played in his
neighbourhood, which was Geneva. It may be thought that the
game has little connexion with morality, but marbles has 'an
extremely complex system of rules ... a jurisprudence of its
own'; this system of rules is dependent for its preservation solely
on the respect felt for it by successive generations of children. It
is argued that there is a close relationship between the child's
ability to understand and make use of rules of this kind and his
ability to deal with rules in the world at large. It will be noted
that coping with rules, though an important aspect of moral
behaviour, is not in itself the same thing as the making of moral
judgements, but Piaget sees general principles at work in the
child's use of rules; in the later part of the work, he applies
these to moral behaviour itself. This approach has the advantage
that the experimenters are able to compare what the child *says*
about the way in which rules work with what he actually *does*
when it comes to applying the rules of a game.

The experiments were quite simple and dealt with two questions. The first part of the investigation dealt solely with the
child's use and understanding of rules. The experimenter gave
the child some marbles, and asked to be taught how to play,
feigning ignorance, so that the child was obliged to formulate
and express the rules. Analysis of the responses of the subjects,
whose ages ranged from four to thirteen, led to the formulation
of a number of recognizable stages in the development of the
child's use and understanding of rules. These stages recall in
many ways the general stages of intellectual development described above, though it will be seen that they are not precisely
identical. The data gathered appeared to conform to the following pattern of four stages:

1. *The motor stage*. This corresponds to the sensori-motor
stage and occupies the same time-span, namely the first two
years of life. The marbles are handled largely at the dictates of
the small child's transient desires, or motor habits. His play is
not, however, entirely at random; he develops a number of rigid
patterns of behaviour, but it is doubtful to what extent it would
be correct to call these rules. Certainly, the child has not yet begun

to cooperate with other children; so, although these patterns modify, or even restrain his behaviour with the marbles, they cannot be rules in any collective sense.

2. *The egocentric stage.* Between the ages of two and five, the child begins to imitate rules which he sees in the behaviour of other children, but he does not as yet try to co-operate in any real sense. When a number of children are playing together at this stage, they do not make any attempt to arrive at a unified set of rules. In spite of the imitation, each child is playing separately. This phenomenon of 'parallel play' has been widely reported by other observers.

3. Overlapping with the second stage is the *stage of incipient co-operation.* By this, we mean that the children are now playing together in a real sense. They are trying to win, and therefore they begin to pay attention to the question of a code of unified rules; but their ideas of rules in general are still vague. They can usually manage, in an actual game; but when the children who took part are questioned separately, they may give contradictory accounts of the rules they have been following.

4. Lastly, somewhere about eleven or twelve years, comes the *stage of codification.* This is the stage where the rules are now fixed in detail, so that they have attained a form which Piaget can refer to as a 'jurisprudence'. The code of rules is known to the children's society as a whole.

All this applies to questions concerning the child's use of the rules of the game, his ability to explain them, and the *form* of his rule-following at various ages. More important, perhaps, are questions about the extent to which a child actually knows what rules are, and about where and how he acquires his ideas of rules and their operation. In order to find these things out, the investigators asked a number of simple questions.

The child was asked to make up a new rule of his own. When he had done this, he was asked questions, such as: 'Would it be all right to play like that with other children?', 'Would they want to play that way?', 'Is it a "fair" rule?', 'Is it a real rule?', 'Would your rule become the way everybody plays?', 'Do you think your father used these rules when he was a little boy?', and so on. These questions did not form part of a formal schedule to be administered in a given order. The investigators were free to follow up the child's remarks, to explore the underlying thought-processes and to discover the influences which determined his grasp of the question.

As with the earlier inquiry, the data gathered suggested the presence of an orderly sequence of stages, but these stages did not coincide with the first scheme, either in number or in age of occurrence. Three stages were defined:

1. The first stage coincides roughly with the motor stage and the first part of the egocentric stage in the foregoing scheme. At first, of course, the infant has no conception at all of rules. When towards the end of this stage, they begin to impinge upon his play, they are received as interesting examples, rather than as obligatory realities. They have no binding power or force.

2. The second stage begins towards the end of the egocentric stage and lasts until the middle of the third phase of the above scheme. At this level, there is a keen awareness of rules, which are, however, regarded as 'sacred and untouchable, emanating from adults and lasting for ever; every suggested alteration strikes the child as a transgression'. This phase is referred to as the *transcendental stage*.

3. In the third stage, the rule is looked upon as an arrangement which arises from mutual consent. At this level, it becomes permissible to alter rules, provided that the other players in the game agree. Piaget regards this final stage, arising as it does from mutual respect and co-operation, and from consideration of the rights of others, as being the phase which represents the achievement of a true understanding of the nature of rules, and the one which is most relevant to the question of genuine moral development.

The second and third stages present a striking contrast. It is not suggested, of course, that there is a sudden change in behaviour, a dramatic moment of enlightenment, as the child moves from one to the other. There is considerable overlap of stages, and the behaviour of children is at times markedly inconsistent. Nevertheless, these changes represent diametrically opposed attitudes to rules, and the question of how or why the child moves from the second stage to the third (and of whether there is any relationship between them) is of great importance. It is with this question of the progress from the transcendental stage to the stage of co-operation that Piaget is concerned in the subsequent sections of the work.

He goes on to explore the child's ideas about justice and fairness, about children's ideas on punishment, and about their understanding of such concepts as lying. He works partly by the method of telling children little stories and requiring them to make moral judgements about the situations presented. The following is an example:

(a) There was once a little girl called Marie. She wanted to give her mother a nice surprise and to cut out a piece of sewing for her, but she did not know how to use the scissors properly and cut a big hole in her dress.

(b) A little girl called Margaret went and took her mother's scissors one day when her mother was out. She played with them for a bit, then, as she didn't know how to use them properly, she made a little hole in her dress.

Again, there was no use of a formal schedule of questions. The children simply listened to the stories and then told the investigator which of the two children was naughtier, or which should be punished more severely, or what was the fairest course of action. The replies were followed by free exploration of the thought-processes which seemed to be involved, in exactly the same way as was done with the inquiries about rules.

The stories were rarely used in the investigations of the child's ideas about lies. This subject was dealt with directly by question and answer, e.g. 'Is it worse to tell a lie to an adult than to another child?', or 'Are lies which are wildly improbable better or worse than lies which might be believed?' The experiment also dealt with fairness, with stealing and a number of other questions to do with moral behaviour.

A number of interesting findings emerges from this part of the inquiry. The first of these is perhaps most clearly illustrated by reference to the two stories quoted above. Children at the transcendental stage tended to say that the girl who made the big hole was the more to blame, in spite of the fact that she was trying to be helpful. In another story, the boy who smashed a dozen cups, which were on a tray behind the door, was more to blame (although he could not have known the cups were there) than the child who broke one cup when climbing in the larder to steal some jam. The younger child tends to evaluate moral or immoral actions in terms of their actual consequences, and without regard to any question of motive. Not for him the excuse that 'he meant well'. The point is frequently made explicitly by the younger child: 'The one who wanted to help her mother a little is the naughtiest because she made a big hole; she got scolded'.

As the child grows older, there is a tendency for judgements of this type, which are said to embody the principle of objective responsibility, to be replaced by judgements involving subjective responsibility, which take into account intention and motive. The two features were not found to be separate and successive stages, however. Here, too, there was considerable overlap between them and it was found to be possible for the two attitudes to coexist in the same child.

Similar tendencies were seen in judging lies. At the transcendental stage, for example, a lie is worse if it is told to an adult than to a younger child. Similarly, and perhaps surprisingly to those who do not know young children, a lie is reprehensible in direct proportion to its size, no matter how great the resulting improbability. It is only during the stage of cooperation that we begin to see the more sophisticated argument that a lie is worse if it is more plausible. A similar process was seen at work in the responses to questions dealing with ideas of punishment and of fairness. The younger children thought in terms of retributive punishment, and an 'equal shares' idea of fairness. As they grew older, they began to take into account questions of motive and of individual needs.

In each of the areas of investigation, a similar change from one to another of two contrasting attitudes was observed. Transcendental rules gave place to co-operative rules; objective to subjective responsibility; rigid fairness to a fairness arising from individual needs, and so on. Piaget sees all these as different expressions of the same two tendencies which become manifest at different stages of the child's development, tendencies which are so much at variance – in conflict, even – that they are described as 'two moralities'.

The first is a 'heteronomous' morality, an authoritarian moral code, non-rational in character, imposed on the child by the adult world. It is characterized by moral realism: that is to say, the rules have a permanent and objective value, apart from the individuals who obey them. We can, in fact, if we are honest with ourselves, see a clear relationship between heteronomous morality and our approach to young children in our care. The child who blamed the little girl, who (with the best motives) cut the biggest hole in the dress, is probably giving an accurate reflection of the reaction of an exasperated mother. We must admit that we too would revert, at least momentarily, to ideas of objective responsibility when faced with a tray of broken teacups behind the door, no matter how we might deal with a similar situation if it involved another adult.

The second form of morality is egalitarian and democratic, based on mutual respect, and co-operation. It arises from the interaction between the child and his peers. Piaget sees nothing in the first morality which can give rise to the second. The 'sense of justice' is, in fact, largely independent of adult influences, and it requires nothing more for its development than the mutual respect and solidarity which holds amongst children themselves. It is often at the expense of the adult, and not because of him, that the notions of just and unjust find their way into the youthful mind.

A point which is not pursued by Piaget, but which merits further attention, is the question of the extent to which heteronomous morality survives as a factor in adult behaviour, and the form that it takes, if it does so. Some psychologists have attempted to identify this with the Freudian concept of the superego, and this, it must be admitted, is an intriguing attempt to bring together the two developmental schemes, at least at one point. There are two objections to such a view, however. According to the psychoanalytic theory, the introjected material is at once unconscious, and it remains so; this does not seem to apply to Piaget's heteronomous morality. It seems to the present writer that a more promising line would be to relate the concept not to the superego, but to Riesman's concept of other-directed people.[12]

We have dealt with this work in detail because of the great influence it has had on thinking in this area. Most of the experiments that have been carried out since its publication have been influenced, to some degree, by Piaget's work. Before going on to assess its contribution to a psychology of moral development, we should look at its limitations.

It would be wrong to claim for the book more than was claimed by its author. 'Readers will find in this book no direct analysis of child morality, as it is practised in home and school life, or in children's societies. It is the moral judgement that we propose to investigate, not moral behaviour or sentiments.' Although the book goes on to deal with an educational philosophy of morality in a manner which is perhaps beyond the limits envisaged by this modest disclaimer in the foreword, it is necessary to bear this distinction in mind. The capacity to make moral judgements is not at all the same thing as moral behaviour. It has yet to be shown that there is a high correlation between the two things. Certainly, an ability to make moral judgements must be necessary for moral behaviour, but possession of the former does not necessarily lead to the latter. We might find a child who is capable of the most refined discriminations in making value-judgements about which is the worst kind of lie; away from the experiment, however, he may lie consistently. A child may, in responding to one of the test anecdotes, show that he has passed the stage of retributive punishment, but this may not govern his behaviour towards another boy who has stolen his marbles. We are dealing with one important component of morality: this should not blind us to the existence of others.

It is apparent, too, that Piaget, in discussing what he refers to as 'moral judgement', is in fact talking about a number of different things. These include the ability to form truly moral concepts, as in understanding what is meant by the idea of a lie: the ability to make moral comparisons: the ability to have insight into the needs or the behaviour of other children: and in the case of the inquiry into rules, the ability to carry out rules in practice. The distinction between these various activities is not always adequately drawn. But this need not be a serious criticism of an exploratory work of this kind. Piaget has drawn our attention to the presence of conceptual and cognitive factors in moral behaviour, and has given some indication of the kind of developmental processes involved.

An objection which causes disquiet to many people, especially those accustomed to the methods of psychological research in the English-speaking countries, is the lack of controlled experiments and of statistical analysis of the results. This raises the important question of how far we are justified in generalizing from the findings. The work was based on small groups of Swiss children. The section dealing with rules was, for example, based on work with about twenty boys (*sic*), whose ages ranged from 4 to 13. How far would these results be applicable to children from other cultures, and with different social backgrounds?

On the other hand, in researches of this kind we do not look for precision in the sense of measurement of factors, and of the exact ages at which they develop. We seek rather a quality of insight into the nature of the processes which are going on, an insight which may enable us to frame hypotheses for further investigations, possibly of a more objective kind. Where the observations have been repeated in other countries, the results have tended to confirm the findings of Piaget and his collaborators. There have been experimental confirmations as well. While writing this, for example, a research report has come to hand, which is based on the more usual experimental and statistical approach; amongst other things, this research seems to confirm the presence and sequence of the heteronomous and autonomous moralities suggested by Piaget.[13] The absence of our familiar apparatus of scientific objectivity does not imply that the author is entirely subjective in his analysis. Whatever weight one attaches to the various defects which have been mentioned, Piaget's work still has great relevance for research in moral development.

Although the theory of the two moralities is, for many, the most striking aspect of this work, it is probably the least important for the purposes of enabling us to formulate a psychology of moral development. The phenomenon to which the theory refers has been observed by other writers and discussed in different terms. The educational conclusions – more self-government by the children, and so on – are perhaps more a reflection of the prevailing educational philosophy of the time than a necessary consequence of the observations reported.

What is perhaps more significant, and more fruitful, from the point of view of future developments is the general theory of stages. We have seen that the child's use of rules conforms approximately to this scheme. Insofar as there is a group of cognitive abilities, which are necessary for moral development (moral concepts, moral reasoning, value-judgements, etc.), it is at least possible that these factors will follow a line parallel to the development of other conceptual abilities which have been the subject of more detailed and careful analysis. The theory of stages would enable us to propose a solution to one very difficult problem connected with moral behaviour. This is the apparent discontinuity in certain aspects of moral development. Everyone who has had close contact with children will know that the primary school child's idea of 'fair', for example, is quite different from that of the mature adult. This is more than a difference in degree, or a matter of a higher level of sophistication. The primary school child's use of the term is different in its quality. What is there in the first to give rise to the second? It would surely be contrary to all that we have found about child development to suppose that there is a real discontinuity.

One answer may be found in Piaget's idea of a continuous process, which yet involves the necessity to work through qualitatively different developmental stages. This approach has been described as paradoxical. It may be a further paradox that Piaget's work on other aspects of concept development may be more relevant to the theory and practice of moral education than his work on the moral judgement of the child.

Since this work of Piaget's was first carried out, a large number of other workers have taken it up, either to attack the problem again, using methods derived from Piaget, or to subject his ideas to an experimentally more rigorous examination. A book of this kind is not the place to list these approaches. We shall, instead, move directly to a much more recent writer whose work is of particular interest.

Lawrence Kohlberg, working in the United States, used an approach which clearly owes a great deal to Piaget's pioneering study, but which at the same time remedies some of the deficiencies of the earlier work. His sample was much larger (72 boys,[14] aged 10, 13 and 16), more broadly based socially, and it was also selected in such a way that it was made up of equal proportions of popular and socially isolated children.

The study was based on long individual interviews, recorded on tape for subsequent analysis. The interviews centred upon moral problems put before the child in the form of little stories, each of which involved a conflict of values of a particular kind, namely conflict between 'obedience to legal-social rules or to the commands of authority' and 'the human needs or welfare of other individuals'.[15] The following examples will illustrate the form taken by this conflict in the experiment.

Joe's father promised he could go to camp if he earned the 50 dollars for it, and then changed his mind and asked Joe to give him the money he had earned. Joe lied and said he had only earned 10 dollars and went to camp using the other 40 dollars he had made. Before he went he told his younger brother, Alex, about the money and about lying to their father. Should Alex tell their father?

A woman was near to death from a special kind of cancer. There was one drug that the doctor thought might save her .... The drug was expensive to make, but the druggist was charging ten times what the drug cost him to make .... The ... husband, Heinz, ... went to everyone he knew to borrow money, but he could only get together about ... half of what it cost. He told the druggist that his wife was dying and asked him to sell it cheaper, or let him pay later. But the druggist said: 'No, I discovered the drug and I'm going to make money from it.' So Heinz got desperate and broke into the man's store to steal the drug for his wife. Should the husband have done that?

Each interview lasted about two hours. Attention was given not only to the solution propounded by the child, but also the reasons underlying this solution and a number of connected ideas.

The interview records, each of which contained from 50 to 100 'moral statements', were subjected to a detailed and complex examination, which dealt with such questions as the child's concept of rights, or justice, or his views on the importance of the intentions of an action as opposed to its consequences, and so on (30 such aspects of morality being distinguished for the purposes of this study).

Kohlberg's work led him to suggest that the child's moral development falls into six stages, which can be grouped into three moral levels. These are:

I. Pre-moral level

Stage 1. Punishment and obedience orientation. Rules are obeyed to avoid punishment.

Stage 2. Naive instrumental hedonism. The child conforms in order to obtain rewards, and so on.

II. Morality of conventional role conformity.

Stage 3. Good-boy morality of maintaining good relations. The child conforms to avoid disapproval.

Stage 4. Authority maintaining morality. The child conforms to avoid censure by authorities and resultant guilt.

III. Morality of self-accepted moral principles

Stage 5. Morality of contract. A duty is defined in terms of contract, general avoidance of violation of the rights of others.

Stage 6. The morality of individual principles of conscience. The child conforms to avoid self-condemnation.

Kohlberg's findings have particular relevance to our approach to moral education.

1. They provide statistical evidence (something which is not to be found in Piaget's work) for the hypothesis that there exists a genuine developmental hierarchy in moral growth, that is, a series of stages which must be passed through in a certain order, the attainment of each being a prerequisite for passing on to the next.

2. If we accept this view, then it becomes unlikely that we can explain moral development entirely in terms of internalizing outside values whether through socialization, introjection or conditioning.

3. Similarly, Kohlberg's findings must modify our views on moral education. Didactic moralizing and punishment become equally irrelevant, especially when they are carried out only with reference to the ultimate objective. Instead, the teacher's task becomes the much more practical one of helping the child to make the next step.

4. It is also interesting to note that Kohlberg's developmental scheme leads to a final stage which has characteristics of autonomous morality similar to those suggested elsewhere in this book.

D. THE PSYCHOPATH

So far, the component factors of moral development which have been discussed have corresponded to popular ideas of what is meant by morality. As we shall see now, there are other factors which are just as essential for correct moral development. There is, fortunately, a field of study which provides us with a great deal of evidence about that nature of these other factors. This is the great body of psychological literature which deals with the psychopathic personality and with the effects of deprivation in infancy.

To use cases of abnormal development as a means for throwing light on the normal personality is a method which is not uncommon in psychological research. The whole body of psychoanalysis was built up in the first place on such a basis, and a number of well known psychological tests originated in the same way. Of course, there are dangers in such a method: it is possible that there may be processes at work, in pathological cases, which are different in kind from those to be found in the normal personality. Nevertheless, it is a method which can be extremely fruitful in suggesting hypotheses for later investigation.

The danger of being misled by differences in the kind of mechanism at work does not seriously apply to the present topic, since it will be seen that we are concerned essentially with examining those processes which are absent in the pathological cases under discussion, but which are present in normal people. The particular advantages of approaching the problem from this standpoint are: firstly, that these cases highlight certain moral processes in a dramatic way; and secondly, that study of situations which may give rise to psychopathic states gives a number of indications about the origins and development of moral behaviour, relating this to the infant's developmental needs. Amoral and asocial behaviour are among the most striking and the most widely reported features of psychopathic behaviour.

This, too, indicates that studies on this topic are germane to the present study. It is also an advantage that the problem has been extremely well covered by a number of investigators of different backgrounds.

One preliminary difficulty is that the term 'psychopathic' itself is used in a number of different ways, which range from vague definitions like 'an individual, emotionally unstable to a degree approaching the pathological, but with no specific or marked mental disorder'[16] to detailed descriptions couched in terms of well-defined patterns of behaviour, and clearly-identified causal factors. We shall be concerned here with this latter, clinical line of thought.

As I have stated, the psychopath's amoral and asocial qualities are among the most striking features of his behaviour. It is these which are most widely known outside technical works on psychology and child development; such features figure sometimes in newspaper reports of criminal trials. My use of the word amoral, instead of immoral, is intentional. It serves to underline the psychopath's complete indifference to the rules of society, and to the needs and the feelings of other people. He appears to be without any sense of guilt. Every action is assessed in terms of personal advantage, and the world is seen as a place where jungle law operates. As one might expect from this description, the psychopath may be frequently observed in prisons, for he is often a habitual offender, who seems to be untouched by punishment. In short, he appears to be the very antithesis of the morally developed person, and as such is a phenomenon highly pertinent to our inquiry.

But although the psychopath's delinquent activities represent the aspect of his personality which cause the greatest concern to society as a whole, they do not by any means give the entire picture. Although they provide justification for our being interested in this question, they are not the aspects which are the most suggestive for our purposes.

The condition has been a subject of widespread study for a number of years. A large number of investigators[17] have studied its development and have related it to deficiencies in the earliest years of the child's life, and in particular to the deprivation of maternal affection. In the course of a large number of researches from the year 1913 onwards, there has emerged a consensus of clinical opinion about the picture presented by this condition, as regards both its manifestation in everday life and the nature of the deviant, or impaired, personality-organization which lies behind it. These observations go far beyond the question of amorality and delinquency, and are concerned with fundamental components of the personality.

The aspects of behaviour which have been almost universally noted are:

1. A marked deficiency in emotional development. This is variously described by different writers as 'shallowness of affect', 'an inability to feel love', a 'curious inaccessibility, frustrating to those trying to help', or, quite simply as an 'affectionless personality'. However expressed, there is nearly always a reference to the fact that the psychopath is unable to form deep and lasting relationships with others. He has no real friends; his contact with other people is superficial, and has the function of providing stimulation, or excitement, or enabling the psychopath to satisfy transient needs. He may spend a lot of time with another child in order to share his sweets or pick his pocket, but there is no question of the friendship going beyond cupboard love, or lasting for its own sake. The psychopathic child may form a superficial attachment: and the unwary, or inexperienced, adult may easily fall victim to this. The relationship flowers as long as it is fed by sweets or presents, or simply by attention; it vanishes with the first frustration.

2. The psychopath seems much less able to control his own impulses than are other people. One may describe this as a lack of self-control: and here we see again one of the popular ideas about the components of moral behaviour; although, as we shall see presently, the concept has rather wider implications than the usual idea of self-control. A psychopathic child is likely to help himself to sweets from a shop, or to make a vicious attack on another child, not because he is symbolically stealing affection, or acting out his jealousy of a younger brother or sister (though both of these could apply to some other kinds of children), but because he simply lacks the mental apparatus to control impulses of this sort. Of course, the world is such that it is not always possible, even for a psychopath, to gratify impulses

immediately. There may be external controls, which do the job of the absent internal ones. Situations like this give rise to frustration, and anger or aggressive behaviour is the normal response to frustrating situations. The normal person can control such responses; but this control too is beyond the psychopath, so that even quite trivial frustrations may result in an over-powering undirected rage in adults, or in spectacular tantrums in children. This kind of behaviour may be compared with the behaviour of very young children, of about $2\frac{1}{2}$ or 3; and this is a significant comparison, since children at this level of development have not yet been able to build up the kind of control we are discussing.

3. The psychopath lacks a sense of guilt. As we have seen, this may be described as a disordered or deficient superego, as a lack of conscience, or in terms of some deficiency in the formation of conditioned responses. It is not necessary to give further discussion on these topics; it is sufficient to say that any of the three formulations would be true of the psychopath.

4. A number of writers have commented on the psychopath's deficiencies in understanding causality and time. These deficiencies may appear as a lack in simple skills, such as telling the time, knowing the date, or understanding simple causal relationships in the world. More commonly, and more seriously, they appear as an inability to profit from his own experiences, or those of other people, an inability to foresee the consequences of his own acts, or his own contributions to any unpleasant situation in which he may find himself. He may be unable, too, to visualize himself in the future, and so plan towards a distant goal. It seems likely that these factors are related to the fact that the psychopath is so frequently impervious to punishment, and to psychotherapy of the usual kind.

5. Some writers have also suggested that psychopaths are deficient in their perception of the world around them – in psychoanalytic terms, their reality-testing is in some ways faulty. This is particularly true of the psychopath's testing of social realities. He is frequently quite unable to assess his role in a complex social situation, and act accordingly.

It is clear, then, that the complete picture is of a much more general group of disabilities than would at first appear. In the past, the label of 'moral imbeciles' has sometimes been applied to people like this; but such an approach is inadequate, since it throws no light on the question of what is meant by psychopathy or how it comes about, nor does it help us to explore the emergence of moral behaviour in the development of the normal individual.

Before going on to examine the possible causes of these various deficiencies, let us consider briefly the part that they play in determining the degree to which the individual is able to act morally, relating them to the salient features of the psychopath's behaviour: namely, his amorality. It will be immediately apparent that it is not possible to select any one of these as being the most important, since any of these deficiencies alone would be sufficient to produce amoral and asocial behaviour to a marked degree.

1. The fact of being affectionless is of fundamental importance, since it implies that other people are, in a sense, not real, and hence there is no reason to feel regret for stealing from them, beating them up, or even killing them. To say that other people are 'not real' does not mean that the psychopath does not know they exist. He is clearly well enough aware of them in a perceptual sense. It implies rather that other people are unreal in an emotional sense; that it is impossible to identify or sympathize with them. Other people have, perhaps, the quality of reality which a bird may have for a cat. Or to give another example: we can all perceive, and acknowledge, the existence of the spider in the bath, or the fly on the kitchen table. It is perceptually quite real, but since such a creature can scarcely be emotionally real (it is unlikely to be a potential love-object), we are not usually too distressed when we see the struggles of the former as it is swept down the plug-hole, or the writhing of the latter in a cloud of insecticide. Our attitudes to spiders and flies have something in common with the affectionless psychopath's perception of other people.

It is at once apparent that such an attitude is profoundly related to our moral behaviour. Given this lack of capacity to relate to others, there is no reason for not regarding people simply as objects to be used to one's own advantage. Questions

Is not the psycho's "logic" stricter than ours?

of self-control, or of conscience, simply do not arise; and this factor alone is sufficient to produce a marked degree of amoral behaviour. But, as will be seen presently, there is evidence to show that these other factors are in fact also deficient in the case of the psychopath.

2. The relevance of impulse control to moral behaviour is obvious. Even if one can relate emotionally to other people, identify with them and sympathize with them, one cannot be regarded as moral unless there is control of aggressive feelings, or desire for material possessions, or sexual desire. It is no use saying (even if you mean it), 'This is going to hurt me as much as it's going to hurt you', if you cannot help going on and doing it just the same.

3. The role of the superego in the development of moral behaviour has been discussed in an earlier section and will not be given further attention here.

4. Another impairment of moral development arises from the psychopath's deficient ability to make causal connexions, a disability which, it will be remembered, applies particularly to causal relationships to do with human behaviour. Insofar as it limits the extent to which he can see how his own acts have contributed to a given situation – say, his being in prison – it diminishes the possibility of social and moral learning. It also has a much more direct bearing on his behaviour; if one can imagine all of the above factors being present in one individual without the ability to think causally, then it will be seen that this disability alone is also capable of producing behaviour of an amoral kind. If one cannot predict that people may be hurt if they are attacked, that people will be impoverished if they are stolen from, then another possible behaviour-control is absent.[18]

5. Reality-testing is another factor which is necessary for moral behaviour. The fact that a person is unable to assess accurately the state of affairs in which he finds himself clearly impairs his capacity to behave morally. It has been reported that some psychopathic children are genuinely unaware of

delinquent or violent acts that they carried out. They are not telling lies. Their assessment of what has occurred, though convenient, is genuinely deficient. Similarly, in the sphere of social relations, if one is unable to understand the nature of social expectancies, or one's role with regard to others, or the possible reactions of other people to what one does, then the possibility of behaving morally towards other people must necessarily be impaired.

There is a difference, however, between the part played by reality-testing and that played by those factors already discussed. The use of moral concepts, the ability to reason about the consequences of our acts, and so on, are all activities which may contribute directly to the making of a moral decision. Poor reality-testing is a failure at a much more fundamental level, which leads not only to poor moral development, but to widespread general failures as well. The other factors are specific: reality-testing is general, like intelligence or adjustment, which, as will be seen, are also determinants of moral capacity. Factors in this group may be regarded as preconditions for moral development, rather than component factors.

But this field of study has more to offer than simply a number of component factors of morality. It offers us a number of useful clues to the developmental processes, whose malfunctioning leads to the psychopathic condition, and whose correct functioning leads to the morally developed individual.

The delinquent aspects of the psychopath's personality are so striking, and his lack of regret contrasts so forcefully with the behaviour of the rest of us, that one is at first inclined to attempt to account for the disorder in these terms, in spite of the evidence concerning the psychopath's widespread areas of personality-failure. Ideas of conscience have traditionally played a large part in our thinking about the genesis of moral behaviour, and this too tends to colour our approach. There have been attempts, including psychiatric and psychological attempts, to explain it in terms of an absence, or deficiency, in the superego, and to regard this as the central fact in the structure of the psychopathic personality. It must be admitted at once that the psychopath's superego is deficient or disordered; this has emerged from what has already been said. But to suggest that this is a cause of the condition is merely to beg the question, since to say this, is merely to select one of the factors as being pre-eminent without attempting to show how its absence leads to deficiencies in the others. Besides, we have seen in this section and in Section A that the role of the superego in the totality of moral behaviour is limited.

There are other approaches which suggest that psychopathic personality and normal moral development are closely related to the absence or presence of certain crucial early experiences. These experiences are frequently expressed as early developmental needs, and in particular as the need for love and the need for security; they are referred to elsewhere in this book in such terms. It is our purpose here to look at the question in a slightly different way, so as to see exactly what is implied by them, and how they relate to the developing personality.

The first of these needs is the need for love, the need for what has been described as the primary emotional relationship, which is basic to all others. This relationship is in normal circumstances, of course, with the infant's own, biological mother, but it must be stressed that this need not necessarily be so; the mother's absence, or death, need not lead to the disorders described above, since such a relationship can be satisfactorily established with a mother substitute. (There may be a limited time in which this ought to be brought about if damage is not to ensue). There are cases where such a relationship does not develop. Such cases of maternal deprivation may arise from actual physical separation, as when the mother or child spends a long period in hospital, or when the mother is dead; they may equally arise where there is no separation in the physical sense, e.g. when the mother, through physical or mental illness, is unable to meet the child's emotional needs. Earlier researches tended to obscure the point by making a wrong emphasis in stressing _maternal_ deprivation. Later work has shown that this does not lead to the affectionless personality as frequently as had formerly been expected. The point is that it is the _emotional_ deprivation which is damaging. Failure to meet the child's need for love may bring about the disorders described; if the need is satisfied – even in the absence of the child's own mother – then this aspect of the child's development can proceed normally.

There are various ways of describing the consequences of this deprivation. The simplest approach is to say that having missed this first and basic emotional experience, the child has failed in an elementary learning task, that he has not learnt how to love other people, and that therefore he cannot, in later life, transfer such feelings to others.

It is also possible, without contradicting such an approach, to look at it from the point of view of what the mother does for the child. She not only feeds him, and keeps him clean and comfortable, but she also plays with him, talks to him (even when he is too young to know what she is saying) and fondles and cuddles him. In cold psychological terms, all these activities may be regarded as providing sensory stimulation, which, it has been shown, is necessary for the proper development of the child's perceptual apparatus. We have seen that early sensori-motor activities have an important role in the earliest stages of concept formation. Deficiency of sensory stimulation may lead to widespread defects at a later stage, which may affect particularly ideas about causality and time, and the child's approach to the environment. The baby's future verbal ability, too, and consequently his power to reason (including his power to reason about morality) are closely connected with the quantity of verbal stimulation he receives. These things are all just as much related to maternal deprivation as is the emotional lack already mentioned, since who but the mother, or someone who is just as deeply and emotionally involved, has the patience and the persistence to go on and on 'providing stimulation'? – a small phrase for a long and wearying array of diverse activities.

E. THE EGO

But it is possible to approach the problem at a deeper level: and again such an approach need not be regarded as being at variance with either of the accounts summarized above. This approach is concerned with developmental tasks – with the most basic tasks of infancy: the establishment of a sense of self (and hence a sense of the outside world) and the building of the ego. The newborn child is equipped with a few behaviour patterns necessary for survival – responses like grasping and sucking and crying; there is little else. He is unable even to fixate objects, to perceive the environment with his eyes. The reader may remember James's description of the newborn child's world as a 'booming, buzzing confusion'. There is as yet no sense of identity, and no perception of a boundary between 'me' and 'not me'. One of the prime tasks of the earliest years of life is the establishment of this boundary.

This distinction seems to most of us to be such an obvious and elementary thing that it is possible to overlook the fact that it has not always existed. But, even in adults, it is not always so rigid and absolute a division as it may seem. Primitive peoples often regard hair, teeth, or weapons or clothes as being parts of 'me', even when the hair or teeth have been cut off from the body, or the weapons or clothes discarded. There is a sense, too, in which, in Western man, clothes and cars may be regarded as extensions of the self – this is particularly true in the latter case, where the boundary may become blurred in quite normal people.

The young infant may be said to work out this boundary in the first place not only in terms of sensory stimulation and exploration of his environment through unco-ordinated and random movement, but also in terms of an object relationship: i.e. in terms of the primary emotional bond, already referred to. Isolation in infancy, then, can be regarded as being more than the sum of the individual deprivations. It results in a total or partial failure in the child's achievement of a really fundamental developmental task. Not only is there the lack of a prototype for future relationships and an impairment in the child's conceptual and communication skills, but also the child's very sense of himself as an identity and his very perception of the validity of other people's existence are impaired; because the child, being, as it were, thrown onto his own resources too soon, has had to make a premature adjustment, crystallizing and organizing primitive forms of behaviour.

This idea of self is one which has been stressed by many psychologists, who have often approached the question of child development from different points of view. We see, for example, moral behaviour described in terms of a 'self-regarding sentiment', and we have already discussed the concept of the ego-ideal. The idea of self is necessary to moral development at all stages, though there are two periods where this is particularly important: the first stage of all, when it is being formed; and adolescence, when the identity, the whole perception of one's self, must be reorganized. If one is unable to perceive oneself as an object among other objects in the world, as a self among other valid selves, the whole mode of operation, the whole spectrum of relationships is drastically interfered with.

The study of psychopathy has suggested a number of assorted abilities, which are apparently related to moral development. It is possible to relate them to each other, and to the cognitive factors discussed in earlier sections, by regarding them all as part of the ego. There is a danger in introducing this concept into a discussion of morality, which is intended for readers who may not be familiar with its psychological usage. The word has crept into everyday speech, and, in doing so, it has acquired meanings and overtones which are rather different from its meaning in psychological literature. It is associated, in many people's minds, with the words egoist and egotistical, and is thus connected with notions of selfishness and self-importance, which can hardly be consistent with moral development. In what sense, then, can we say that the ego is a basic component of morality?

The term derives from psychoanalytic theory. It was first produced as a name for that part of the personality which is concerned with the realities of the external world. An example which has been quoted frequently to illustrate its meaning is that of a person who refrains from stealing: if he does it because he feels it is wrong, it is because of his superego; if it is because he knows he will be caught, the ego is responsible. But, of course, this latter reason is concerned with expediency, and not with morality, and examples of this kind appear to invalidate what has just been suggested concerning the ego's part in moral development. I shall suggest that this is because examples of this sort (I have quoted it because they are so common) oversimplify the picture to such an extent that they do not give us a true picture of what is meant by ego-functioning.

Although it is convenient to refer to this part of the personality by one short word, this must not be taken to imply that the ego is in any sense one thing. If we say more precisely that the ego has the task of modifying behaviour in accordance with the conditions which exist in the external world, then it is clear that we must be talking about a number of different activities. In fact, as a preliminary formulation, we must say that the ego has five functions, namely:

1. *Cognition.* This refers to thinking, reasoning, concept formation, 'knowing' about things, and all similar activities.

2. *Perception.* This refers to the operation of the sense-organs which bring information, both about the environment and about oneself: that is, the perception not only of houses and motor cars, but also of the fact that one is tired, hungry or angry.

3. *Voluntary movement.* This refers to all intentional movement (i.e. not reflexes), whether this is self-consciously directed or not. I may be deep in thought as I walk to buy a newspaper and not give conscious attention to what I am doing. It is nevertheless an ego activity.

4. *Reality-testing.* This is a term which comprises a number of activities connected with the boundary between self and not-self.

5. *Control.* This refers to the various mechanisms by which the ego checks, inhibits or redirects the expression of instinctive or impulsive behaviour. We shall refer to these various mechanisms collectively as ego-controls.

(This last term recalls the idea of self-control, which is popularly put forward as an adjunct of morality. Here again it must be pointed out that this is more than merely expressing a well-known truth in technical jargon. The point is that, whereas when we speak of self-control we are not committing ourselves to any kind of definite formulation, if we use the term ego-controls we are speaking of a number of known mechanisms, which have an extensive literature, and which are related to the developmental needs, discussed in this section. We are using the term as a short cut, a quick reference, which implies more than the idea of control itself; it implies that the controls came about in a particular way and operate through particular psychological mechanisms.)

It follows, then, that the picture of the ego which portrays it as operating solely at the level of expediency and being uncon-

cerned with morality is quite simply wrong. All of those activities connected with moral reasoning and judgement, such as
were described in Section C, are evidently to do with cognition,
and are therefore functions of the ego; this applies, too, to all the
factors discussed in this chapter, whose absence characterizes
psychopathic behaviour (with the sole exception of the superego).

There are a number of reasons why it may be convenient to
describe these aspects of moral behaviour in terms of the psychology of the ego:

1. The term relates the functions under discussion to each
other and to a comprehensive and widely understood personality
model.

2. The nucleus of the ego is laid down in infancy through the
medium of the basic relationship already discussed; its functions
are worked out within the framework of this relationship and
the security it provides, and, of course, as the child grows older,
the security provided by the family as a whole. We have seen
that in this early situation a variety of needs must be met, ranging
from sensory stimulation to the more complex emotional relationships. The way those needs are met is profoundly connected
with the development of the various ego functions. The theory
of ego-development thus connects with the views on child development already presented. It is a comprehensive theory,
capable of combining within itself other approaches, and of providing us with the beginnings of a psychology of moral development.

3. The idea of ego relates closely to the idea of 'rationality'
proposed above in Part I (see pp. 48–52).

But the concept of the ego is still regarded by many people as
being a relatively coarse conceptual tool. Although we have refined it to some extent, by postulating five separate functions, on
closer examination each of these terms is found to cover a variety
of activities. If we speak of defective cognition, or poor ego-
controls, we have only advanced a little way from the crude and
insufficient concept of a 'weak ego'.

One attempt[19] to refine the concept of the ego resulted in a list
of 22 different ego functions, all of which are jobs the normal ego
may be called upon to do. These functions include frustration

tolerance, temptation resistance, realism about rules and routines assessing social reality, learning from experience, and so on. It is not possible in the present state of knowledge to offer anything which even purports to be a final or exhaustive list of the functions of the ego. Certainly, no such claim was made by the author of the one mentioned above. But the point is not without relevance to the question of moral development. When considering those functions of the ego which are concerned with moral behaviour, it will be as well to regard these as being groups of related abilities, rather than isolated single abilities; and we should not close our eyes to the possibility of more refinement of such concepts in the future.

Notes to Chapter 5

1. See Part I, pp. 100–101.

2. Part II (B), Chapter 7.

3. It may indeed go deeper than that, and begin with the child's very earliest experiences.

4. We may here turn a blind eye to the philosophical outrage which such remarks seem to perpetrate.

5. It could also be claimed, on conceptual grounds, that the word 'punishment' can, strictly speaking, only be used in cases where the creature to whom unpleasant treatment is applied *knows*, or could in principle know, that it is breaking a rule. But we need not consider this point here.

6. Though even this possibility is philosophically doubtful: see Part I, pp. 204–9, and p. 219 (note 16).

7. It might be argued that an experiment in dog training has little connexion with human moral development. Of course a trained dog is not 'behaving morally' in any real sense, and it is extremely doubtful whether the term could in any circumstances be applied to animal behaviour. But we are only concerned at this point with the operation of the superego and the effects of conditioning. These are not 'moral' either, and the avoidance-behaviour which was developed in the puppies provides a simple analogy to the operation of the conscience (in our present sense of the word) in human beings.

8. See p. 271 ff.

9. This is, strictly speaking, metaphorical: often people do not *consciously ask* such questions: rather, they are moved by pictures or images of their 'ideal selves'.

10. A. T. Jersild, *The Psychology of Adolescence* (Macmillan's, New York).

11. *Principles of Psychology* (1890).

12. See Part II (B), Chapter 7.

13. Graham *et al: Some minor findings of a research in moral development* (Journal of Newcastle Institute of Education, March, 1966).

14. This was the core sample; the procedures were repeated with other populations, drawn from different age groups and cultures. D. Graham of the Psychology Department in Durham University is carrying out a confirmatory study in the United Kingdom, but the results of this work have not yet been published.

15. References to Kohlberg are all from: Kohlberg, L., *The*

Development of Children's Orientations Towards a Moral Order: Vita Humana, 6 (1963).

16. Drever, J., *Penguin Dictionary of Psychology*.

17. E.g., Bowlby, J., *Child Care and the Growth of Love* (Penguin Books).

18. Of course, these last two factors raise interesting questions of moral responsibility. If I genuinely do not know that driving a car at 90 miles an hour in a built up area is likely to result in someone's being killed, or that practising with a rifle in my back garden is likely to lead to the same result, then how far do these errors diminish my moral responsibility? It must be stressed here that such questions are not for the psychologist to answer. We are not concerned here with providing excuses for people who fail to behave in a particular way, any more than we are concerned with assigning blame. We are simply drawing attention to those factors which must be present if there is to be a possibility of moral behaviour, and amongst such factors must be listed the cognitive factors connected with perception of the world and understanding of causality, mentioned above. In the case of the psychopath, it is worth pointing out that these deficiencies lead not only to the impossibility of genuinely moral behaviour, but also to a greatly diminished chance of governing his behaviour by the principle of expediency.

19. Redl, F. and Wiseman, D., *Children who hate* (Glencoe Free Press, Ill.)

CHAPTER 6

MORAL DIMENSIONS AND DEVELOPMENT

A. The Component Factors

WE are now in a position to put forward a working hypothesis about the nature of moral behaviour, a preliminary sketch, based upon the various strands of psychological research and observation discussed in preceding chapters. For convenience, this will be summarized in a positive categorical form; the nature of these assumptions, the fact that they are essentially inferences based upon a number of sources, should always be borne in mind. The picture which emerges is put forward as a talking point, and as a possible framework for objective investigation in the future.

We have seen that there are several component factors involved in moral behaviour, and we have gone some way towards identifying a number of them. Each is best regarded as a group of similar abilities, or as an area of activity, rather than as a single factor, and it will be necessary to refine these concepts in the future.

These components may be summed up under the headings below; the factors listed under each heading should be regarded as examples, rather than as exhaustive lists.

(a) COGNITIVE FACTORS

(i) Abilities connected with the formation and use of moral concepts:

> The ability to reason morally and to make rational judgements: the cognitive aspects of the use and understanding of rules. (DIK, PHRON.)

(ii) Abilities connected with the understanding of facts and causal relationships:

> Concepts of causality: the abilities to predict consequences, both physical and psychological, and to learn from one's own or others' experience. (GIG, EMP.)

(b) OTHER 'ABILITY' FACTORS

(iii) The ability to relate emotionally to others, and, arising from

Abilities, as pointed out, have only something to do wi behavior; they don't "lead" to it.

this, the ability to identify and sympathize with other people. (PHIL.)

(iv) Ego-controls, both the defence mechanisms of the ego as defined by psychoanalysts, and other, conscious, means of inhibiting or redirecting primitive impulses. (KRAT.)

The relationship between these components and the logically-derived components of Chapter 4 (Part I) is still obscure: but I have listed the latter alongside the former, and the comparison is at least suggestive. Much of our future work will involve relating the two sets more closely.

(c) MOTIVATIONAL FACTORS

(v) The superego and feelings of guilt.

(vi) Social acceptance and feelings of shame.

(vii) The ego-ideal and self-evaluation.[1]

How about:
VII — gen'l health,
syl level, aggress
curiosity, habit
etc, here ?

The component factors under the first two headings are directly concerned with moral behaviour and can all be regarded as functions of the ego. Those in the last group have a quite different role. It would not be possible to give an account of the determinants of moral behaviour without mentioning them, but they are not sufficient for the development of true morality. It is true that they are powerful controls or modifiers of behaviour; but to be motivated entirely by the desire to avoid uncomfortable feelings, or to have other people approve of you, or to conform to a self-picture which may or may not be realistic or mature, is not in itself moral. The function of these aspects of the personality with regard to moral behaviour is probably simply to cause us to stop and examine a proposed course of action. The values they embody may be primitive; they may be irrelevant to the actual situation in the objective world. Genuine morality must imply the possibility of these motivational factors being overruled by the ego.

There are, too, a number of general preconditions which must be met before the possibility of moral behaviour can arise. These are all discussed elsewhere, and we shall therefore do no more than list them at this point.

1. Correct perception

(a) of objects and events in the outside world;

(b) of one's own motives, thought and feelings.

2. Reality-testing.

3. Intelligence – this does not imply that the most intelligent people are the most moral, but simply that there is a lower level below which the idea of rational morality does not apply.

4. Mental health, or adjustment – with the same qualification as intelligence.

The above represents the principal hypothesis concerning the nature of moral behaviour which will be tested in future research. Too much stress has been laid in the past on the investigation of single dimensions of morality. Our claim is that moral behaviour cannot be fully understood unless a global approach is adopted; unless it is seen as a multidimensional structure of traits or abilities, such as that which has been suggested above, though not necessarily identical with it. It is true that researches may have shown the existence of some common factor in honesty or morality. In stressing the need for a multidimensional model, however, it must be pointed out that (a) this factor is relatively weak – much weaker than the 'g' factor in intelligence, which is in some ways a close analogy: (b) although there is evidence for the *existence* of such a factor, it has not been named, nor has its nature been defined.

B. MORAL DIMENSIONS

It will be remembered that, in our introduction, morality was described as being distributed along a continuum, rather than as involving only simple categories of good and bad. We can now see that this, too, was an oversimplification. It is not simply a question of differences in the degree of morality lying between the extremes, but differences in the kind of morality. Of course, the idea of a single continuum was put forward as an illustration; it was not meant to suggest that an individual's moral achievement can be measured by a single yardstick.

Nevertheless, the idea of an overall moral placing on a 'scale of morality' is not without interest. If we are to attempt, in the future, to assess the effectiveness of different schemes of moral education, then the idea will, at least, have to be examined. The question is relevant to our present discussion, too, for the attempt

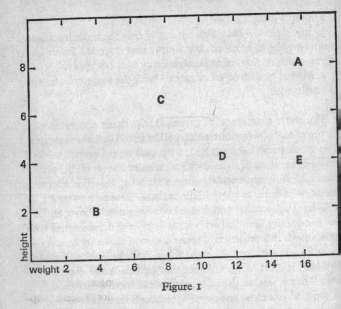

Figure 1

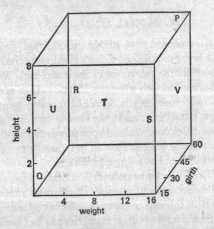

Figure 2

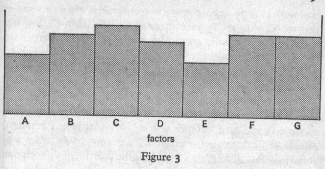

factors

Figure 3

to visualize or represent the differences and relationships between various degrees or qualities of morality throws a great deal
of light on the nature of the complex pattern of factors we have
suggested.

In dealing with a single factor, like the measurement of height,
the task of representation is simple enough: the individual's
position is indicated quite simply as a point along a straight line.
To deal with two factors simultaneously is still not difficult. Suppose, to take a simple example, we are dealing with height and
weight, and that we wish to combine these measures, to assess
people in terms of a new concept of 'substantiality'. (We are
doing something similar to this when we regard people as being
more moral, or morally developed, or morally educated.) We
cannot do this arithmetically, because the rank order we would
get would differ according to the units of measurement used –
inches and hundredweights, as opposed to feet and ounces. The
relationship between different individuals can be shown by a
simple graph, as in Figure 1. It can be seen that A is more substantial than B, and that C, D and E are all between these two,
but although we have shown a relationship, we have not drawn
up a rank order.

Suppose now that we add a third measure – say, girth – to our
combined assessment of substantiality. Whereas with two kinds
of measurement the relationship could be represented as points
in an area, with three it is a matter of points in a space. This can
be illustrated as in Figure 2. The situation now begins to resemble our multifactor theory of morality. Again we find that we

can make only an approximate rank-order. P is more substantial than R–V, who are in turn more substantial than Q, but any ranking of the middle group depends entirely on whether we choose to regard height, weight or girth as being a more important component factor of substantiality. This is approximately the position with regard to the component factors of morality.

But our picture of the structure of moral behaviour has suggested not three, but at least seven component factors. This raises difficulties of another order. To visualize the resulting relationships is within the imaginative compass only perhaps of some mathematicians, who would see the individual's position as being a point in a graph constructed in multidimensional space. That is, each of the seven factors is represented by an axis, each axis being at right angles to all the others. Concepts of this kind are beyond the grasp of the rest of us, and an overall pattern would probably best be represented in a rougher form by a profile, or histogram (Figure 3), such as is sometimes used to represent an individual pupil's performance in a number of unrelated school subjects. This type of figure is restricted of course to showing the pattern for one individual, or average for one class, and so on; it cannot place a number of individuals relative to each other.

Discussion of this topic is of theoretical interest, and it helps to illustrate the nature of the structure of morality we are suggesting. In practice, however, we are limited to assessing the development of individual factors; though, even here, caution is necessary, since it is not simply a question of quantitative superiority. A superego which is too powerful is as hampering to moral development as one which is weak. Over-rigid ego-controls do not bring a heightened capacity for moral behaviour; they simply mean that their possessor fails in a different way from the person with insufficient control. Even rational and constructive thought about moral questions can, in some people, be used as a defence against becoming emotionally involved with others. We are concerned primarily with the quality of the development, and with its effectiveness in dealing with the actual problems which the individual faces in his life.

C. MORAL DEVELOPMENT

Inevitably, in examining the nature of the various aspects of moral behaviour, we have formed some idea of the developmental processes involved. We have seen, for instance, the importance of early experiences, and in particular of early emotional relationships. We are now in a position to put these together to form an outline of the moral development of the child. In many ways, of course, this is parallel with the general development of the child. It is not possible in practice to isolate any one aspect of a child's growth and consider its development apart from the rest. Intellectual development rests upon emotional development, and many aspects of emotional development are in turn dependent upon the child's possession of normal abilities and capacities. A defect in physical development, leading perhaps to physical handicap, may have a profound effect on the development of personality, which in turn may influence the willingness or capacity to cope with intellectual tasks. Moral development is as intimately bound up with the total growth pattern as any of these, and our picture of it will therefore in some ways be a recapitulation of wider formulations of the developmental process. This very similarity implies the relevance of a number of general, preliminary principles, which are, in themselves, well known. All that needs to be done here is to draw attention to their application to the present topic.

The child's development is, in this sphere as in any other, to be viewed as a continuous growth-process, in which the earliest phases are relevant and necessary to the final outcome. It is a process which is essentially an orderly one. Anyone who has lived with young children will doubtless find the word 'orderly' a strange term to apply to a child growing up: it refers not to his behaviour, but to the succession of stages in relation to each other. There may be considerable variation in the ages at which different children attain various stages of development, but the order of the stages themselves is invariable. Each one is characterized by its own needs, or developmental goals; and it is necessary for the needs of each period to be satisfied, for the goals to be accomplished, before the child can move on successfully to the next. The growth of stages suggested by various psychologists is determined by the particular aspect of personality which is discussed; but, on this question of sequence, there is widespread agreement. Freud and Piaget, for instance, deal with very dissimilar aspects of child development, and their schemes of developmental phases appear to have very little in common; both writers stress, however, the need for adequate and appropriate experience at each level. The point can perhaps be illustrated most clearly by reference to some fairly simple learning process, like learning arithmetic. If a child fails to master, say, the multiplication tables, he will fail not only at this task but also at an ever-widening succession of subsequent arithmetical operations, each of which is dependent on his having mastered the previous one. This point raises important practical issues which will be discussed later in the chapter.

We must expect, too, that the same laws will govern moral development as govern the other aspects of the child's growth. There will thus be precisely the same interaction between in-born and environmental factors as is found elsewhere. For many years, controversy raged between those who held that heredity was the paramount factor in determining human personality and abilities, and those who held that environment alone provided the answer between 'nature' and 'nurture'. Such controversy has, of course, no place in current thinking. It is clear from a large number of very carefully conducted experiments that each of these plays a part, that the final outcome is determined by a process of interaction between the two, in which the environment is rather more heavily weighted.

This has a bearing on our topic. One still hears anxious or vindictive conversations about wickedness, or bad character being inherited. If the picture of moral ability which we have presented holds good, then there can be no question of bad moral traits, as such, being inherited, since all the factors which have been described arise from some form of relationship between the child and his environment. The relationship may be emotional, intellectual or perceptual, but, in every case, the component of morality spring from some such interaction.

That is not to say that hereditary or congenital factors play no part at all. It implies, however, that the part played by them is indirect. Thus, while one would not say that a child inherited tendency to be wicked, or to indulge in some particular form of immoral behaviour, like stealing, one might imagine the existence of a congenital deficiency which would prevent him from forming one or other of the components of moral behaviour. Severe intellectual defect may, in many cases, be congenital or hereditary. The child who suffers from this handicap may well be unable to build either concepts of right and wrong, or a sense of causality which would enable him to see the consequences of his acts. I am not, of course, in any sense disparaging or morally condemning children who suffer from this handicap; but it follows that their deficiency will disqualify them from becoming morally educated, as the term is defined here (a point of view which is embodied in the law of the land concerning criminal responsibility). To have the best chance of correct moral development, then, a child must be born with a normal endowment of mental and physical ability.

Not all handicaps lead to so pessimistic an outlook as that described above. Physical handicaps, such as blindness and cerebral palsy, to name only two, can be overcome; and, as everyone knows, people like Helen Keller demonstrate the possibility of impressive attainment in the face of extremely severe handicap. The point is not that this hereditary pattern, or that congenital deficiency, must necessarily lead to poor moral development, but that they will make it easier or harder for the growing child in his particular environment to develop this or that ability necessary for moral growth.

The prime need of the very young infant is acceptance and a warm continuous relationship. The developmental goals of this stage of life are to begin to define a sense of self and to begin to relate this self, both perceptually and emotionally, to the outside world. Failure to meet these needs, or failure on the infant's part to achieve these goals, is damaging to many aspects of development, not least to moral development in later years. It is not possible, in this context, to separate the idea of need from that of goals. They are simply different ways of looking at the same thing. The infant begins to define himself in terms of this relationship with his mother. He needs the security arising from acceptance, if he is to dare to explore his environment. Failure at this level may lead to permanent impairment of the sense of self, such as may be observed in psychopaths, or in schizophrenics. It is difficult to see exactly what this means. Its nature is, in a sense, beyond the imaginative grasp of normal people, whether or not they have a training in psychology or psychiatry. It is clear, however, that the behaviour of these severely disturbed people cannot be meaningfully discussed in terms of morality. If the child is failed at this stage of his life, the resulting damage may be long-lasting, if not permanent. That is not to say that it is entirely irremediable; where recovery is possible, however, it will occur as a result of difficult and drastic methods of psychological treatment.

The exploration of the environment, too, is necessary for many aspects of development. It provides both elementary tools and raw material for building concepts later in life about the nature of the world. Deficiency, or distortion, of these basic concepts gives rise to disabilities which go beyond the purely intellectual. As we have seen, one of the preconditions for moral behaviour is an ability to comprehend the real world; one of the component factors is the understanding of cause and effect, particularly as this relates to the consequences of one's own actions. Such abilities arise ultimately from the random movements, the primitive explorations, of the young infant.

Learning to walk marks the transition to a new stage; the child's environment is suddenly enlarged; the task of exploration, the building of intellectual tools and the formation of personality traits is dramatically accelerated. The goals of this phase of life are similar to those in the preceding one, except that they have increased in quantity and complexity. Not only is the environment larger, but the child's new-found mobility, the possibility for independent action, and the capacity to manipulate objects, all lead to a new range of relationships, which need exploring. Questions of texture, weight, movement and sound are fascinating (especially sound!). Such experience is intimately connected with the child's later ideas of causality and his ability to use concepts. More purely and obviously intellectual development begins to have an important place during this period. The appearance of speech expands the intellectual horizon in a manner which is comparable to the expansion of physical space, brought about by walking. There are new arts of communication to be learnt, and the beginnings of making more verbal concepts. None of these can be regarded irrelevant to the development of morality. At this stage, too, as we have seen, the child begins to form the superego and the ego-ideal by internalizing injunctions and prohibitions and the attitudes of his parents.

The need for emotional satisfactions continues through this stage. There is still the possibility of damage arising from emotional deprivation. It must be remembered, too, that though emotional deprivation is the failure most often discussed, there are a number of other deprivations which can have equally far-reaching results; these range from the amount of sensory stimulation provided by the environment to the quality and quantity of verbal experience and to the possibility of cultural deprivation. Impoverishment in any of these areas may lead to a lowered capacity to behave morally.

The next stage in the child's development coincides with the years spent in the primary school and ends with the onset of adolescence. At this level, the developmental goals are concerned with the perfecting of a large number of skills. These may be physical; you will have noticed how children in this age group love to do tricks, such as hand-standing, fancy cycling, and so on. They may be intellectual; this is the period when the acquisition of knowledge and of academic skills proceeds at its fastest rate. They may be social; the child moves out for the first time into a larger society, and has to learn how to deal with people of various age groups, who are outside the family. The problems and significance of this move, which on a social level represents as significant a widening of the horizon as learning to walk or talk, will be dealt with in Part II (B) of this book. The heteronomous morality of childhood is being replaced by autonomy based on egalitarianism in the children's society, and on mutual respect.

One important result of the expansion of the child's social world is the appearance of new adult figures, usually teachers, who will influence a child's moral development. Emotional attitudes, either positive or negative, may be transferred from the earlier experience with the parents to these new authority figures. The process of internalizing values and attitudes, begun at home, is continued into the primary school. The superego or conscience thus acquires at this stage new accretions. Our consciences are, it is true, based in the first instance upon the introjection of our parents, but we are not dealing with a closed system; they are modified through the influence of other people with whom we came into contact during the earlier years of middle childhood. This applies, too, to the building up of the ego-ideal. The period is also characterized by conceptual growth, the ability to manipulate concepts and to relate perceptions of the world in either causal chains or rational argument.

Adolescence brings a resurgence of interest in problems connected with morality, together with a feeling of urgency, a feeling of concern that there should be answers to the problems set by the sudden spurt in development. This rapid growth affects all aspects of development, physical, intellectual, social and emotional. The developmental tasks of the period are concerned with the establishment of personal identity and of seeing that one has adult skills and competences. The problems which have to be solved in a very short number of years, after so long a period of relatively tranquil development, amount to what some people call a reorganization of the personality. Certainly, there is a review of all factors connected with moral behaviour; and the adolescent, in re-appraising them, brings to bear on the problem intellectual tools which are almost at an adult level.

Let us examine some of the changes, to consider their bearing on our topic. There must be, in the first place, considerable changes in the young adolescent's perception of himself. These are brought about at one level by the sheer changes in actual size and strength, at another level by physical maturation, so that the adolescent has to take cognizance of new emotions and urges, not all of them directly sexual. This re-appraisal of his image of himself is reflected, too, in his perception of other people's changed perception of him.

Changes in his perception of his real self must be reconciled with the ego-ideal, which must have some point of contact with reality. This is not to say that ideals should be dropped at this age (though it is a period which is susceptible to disillusionment), but that some compromise must be arrived at, some modification of ideals and ambitions, in the light of what is actual and what is possible. A boy who has dreamed of becoming a policeman may now discover that he will be too short, and so must make a more realistic vocational choice. He may decide instead, for instance, to become a military policeman, or a security guard in a private organization. He may reorganize his vocational ambitions altogether and apply himself to something quite new. So, too, in the sphere of moral behaviour. The adolescent may find that his real self cannot measure up to his ego-ideal and cannot escape the censure of the superego.[2]

The superego, too, is the subject of re-appraisal. Of course, being unconscious, it is not directly amenable to modification. Nevertheless, the emergence of new aspects of the personality, in particular those connected with the adolescent's sexual awakening, bring about an urgent need for the adolescent to come to terms with his own feelings of guilt (or shame), and to relate these to moral principles, which should, at this stage of development, be becoming properly understood for the first time.

Guilt may be a powerful instrument of control; it may also be simply disabling. As we have seen, the superego is not concerned with the real world; any genuine morality must include a capacity for the ego to override guilt feelings of this kind. The skills or mechanisms of ego-control are during adolescence being subjected to tests which exceed everything that has gone on during the preceding years. This is a period when such abilities will be practised and consolidated. It is also a period in which deficiences, which have hitherto passed unnoticed, may become apparent.

On the more purely conceptual level, we find that there are equally important changes. It was stated above that the nature of moral concepts is beginning at this stage to be understood for the first time. The idea of 'formal operations' is of some help here in understanding the change that has taken place. The adolescent is no longer tied down to concrete situations. He is able to generalize, to see concepts as abstractions which can be applied in a large number of actual situations. This applies not only to his capacity for dealing with those concepts directly connected with the understanding of morality, but also of those connected with cause and effect, which are profoundly connected with our moral behaviour in practice.

D. PRACTICAL APPLICATIONS

Although it has been stressed more than once that this account of the psychology of moral behaviour is a preliminary survey and in no sense a definitive statement, there will doubtless be some who would like to see at this point a number of clear-cut techniques for moral education, which are generally applicable, in the sense that they could be put into practice by most of those who are concerned with the bringing up of children. 'Tell us what to do' is a frequent request; but it is doubtful whether it will ever be possible, or even desirable, to reduce moral education to anything like a rule of thumb.

One is often far more impressed by simple, practical accounts of empirically based practical methods of education than by any amount of theoretical discussion. There is an air of assurance and conviction about a writer who can explain in simple language, with no abstract nonsense about theory, how he got children through examinations, or improved their personality, or cured their delinquency, by rock climbing, or self-government, or the Dalton Plan. 'There's a man who is speaking from real experience', we say. Should we not try to offer something of this sort concerning moral education?

Unfortunately, such approaches are often very misleading. The accounts may tell exactly what happened at one level, but we frequently find that, in practice, it is not self-government or the Dalton Plan that is responsible for the success, but some quality of personality, or leadership, on the part of the writer, who may be much too modest a man to suspect the nature of the real reasons for his success. Other people are then quite unable to achieve the same results, even though they follow the instructions to the letter; their originator, on the other hand, would probably be just as successful if he used a method based on competition or programmed learning. We are not arguing that the method to be used is of no importance, but simply that practical methods of moral (or any other) education must be based on a clear understanding of the aims and the nature of the process.

It is not possible to separate the idea of moral education from that of moral development. The child's moral growth is not something that begins when the child goes to school, or when we can start talking to him about notions of good and bad. Moral education (or at least its preconditions) begins at birth, or even before. The effectiveness of any educational technique in this field, as in any other, must be assessed in terms of its relation to the total pattern of growth. Moral education is not something which can be superimposed on a basically insufficient personality.

It follows from this that moral development, and hence moral education, cannot be separated from the question of general development. Much has been written here and elsewhere about the crucial importance of the child's experiences in his family in the earliest years of his life. Here are the very roots of moral development, as of the development of so many other aspects of the personality. If the infant's needs are not met at this stage, then the task of moral education becomes infinitely harder, since it will be necessary first to meet these earlier developmental needs, allowing the child to achieve more primitive developmental goals, before further progress can be made.

There are two points which arise from this:

1. Critical periods

Firstly, this question raises the concept of critical periods.[3] By this is meant the possibility that there may be crucial or optimal times for the achievement of developmental tasks, and that if this period is missed, the task will be achieved only with very great difficulty, or not at all. We have already seen how early failures of this kind have a cumulative effect on later development. If this cumulative effect is taken in conjunction with the idea of critical periods, then the implications, when applied to our subject, are very grave indeed.

There is some evidence for the existence of such periods, though none of the work from which such evidence arises is explicitly concerned with moral development. The way critical periods work is perhaps best illustrated by reference to work with various kinds of animals.[4] It has been found that geese, for instance, need to have 'imprinted' on their minds the image of what a goose is, in order to behave in a goose-like fashion towards other geese as they grow up. They need to be able to follow a mother goose while they are goslings, and to follow their flight leader when they are full-grown. They need to be able to select a female goose for mating, and not some other species of bird. It has been shown that there is a definite period, lasting for a short time after hatching, during which this imprinting can take place. If the bird is raised in an incubator, and instead of its parent sees a human being, or a motor-boat, then the wrong imprint is made, and it is very difficult to do anything about this once the critical period has passed. Thus we have one rather sad account of a duck paying court to the motor-boat belonging to the staff of the Bird Sanctuary. Generalizing from animal to human behaviour has, of course, obvious dangers, and it is not suggested that anything quite like imprinting is taking place in the human infant: the example is simply one of the clearest ways of showing how environmental failure (in this case a very simple one) can lead to a developmental fault which is not corrected by later experience.

It has been suggested that something similar may happen in human development, though the evidence here is by no means as clear as it is with more primitive forms of life. The concept of a critical period has been advanced with particular reference to affectionless psychopathic children. This condition, as we have seen, is associated by most clinicians with the lack of adequate relationships in early infancy. Many of them claim that if this relationship, or a substitute relationship, is not formed within a critical period, then the chance is lost, and the resulting personality handicap is irremediable. On the other hand, there have been, during the last ten years, various therapists who have claimed good results in working with cases of this sort. Even here, though, the form of treatment is seen as difficult and radical, and certainly not the kind of experience which the psychopath would be likely to meet by chance in his everyday life.

We have seen that this aspect of development is essential for correct moral growth. It would be possible to argue, then, that here is at least one aspect of moral development to which the idea of a critical period may apply: if a child misses the necessary infantile experience, then he is not likely to benefit from any educational measures to which he may be exposed later (excluding radical psychotherapy of a kind not universally available).

A similar argument could be advanced with regard to some of the conceptual aspects of development.

Expressed in this way, the idea could give rise to a number of practical dangers of a serious kind. The chief among these might be a kind of resignation, or fatalism, that might come to appear in the attitude of teachers and others who are concerned with the child's development from middle childhood onwards. If it was all decided by events which took place when the child was eighteen months, they may ask, what is the use of bothering now? It is necessary, then, to re-formulate this concept in such a way that, while we underline the absolutely crucial nature of the child's experiences in the years before he goes to school, we do not, on the other hand, give the impression that everything that happens after this point is wasted.

There are several comments to be made here. As I have indicated, there has been some evidence that the operation of critical periods is not so absolute and irremediable as may be the case with lower forms of life. This, of course, is in line with what we might expect, in view of the greater flexibility of human behaviour. But those who have reported the existence of critical periods are clearly referring to something which they have observed. It may be that the best hypothesis is that of an 'optimal' rather than a 'critical' period, namely a period within which growth or learning can take place most easily and rapidly, and outside which the task is very much harder and takes much longer. Such optimal periods have been shown to operate, at different ages of course, for such things as learning to talk, learning to walk, or learning some of the basic school skills, such as reading and writing. Children who have failed to learn to talk for one reason or another at the proper age find great difficulty in learning to speak later in life, but it has been shown that the task is not entirely impossible.

Thus, though we may discover that there are optimal times for the development of those basic abilities which are components of moral development, it does not follow that there is nothing to be done once these periods have been passed. It is also important to remember that such periods are not confined to the very earliest years in life. There are needs connected with the child's conceptual development, with his rational thinking, which occur at later stages. We must not allow the fact that early experiences are so important to blind us to the crucial nature of later ones.

Paradoxically, the idea of optimal periods increases the urgency of anything we may be able to do for children who have been failed by their environment at such stages in their life. For moral development may be regarded as a cyclic process, whereby the attitudes, the personalities and the abilities of each generation affect the development of the next by determining the manner in which, or the degree to which, the next generation of parents will be able to respond to the needs of their children. Anything we can do to further the development of today's children will have an effect beyond what we can achieve for them. This is the sense in which we can say that moral education begins not only at birth but even earlier.

2. *'Mental health'*

The second point which arises from the interdependence of general personality development and moral development is the question of the connexion between morality and mental health, if this is regarded as being the outcome of proper personal development. These two concepts are not identical. If we assess a personality in terms of mental health, we are carrying out a different kind of activity from assessing morality.[5] It does not follow that the most moral person is always the best adjusted; but since, on the other hand, it is difficult to conceive of a well-adjusted, but grossly immoral, or amoral, person, the two ideas cannot be entirely separate. It seems likely that there is a certain minimal level of mental health, below which a person cannot be said to be able to behave in a moral fashion, even if only on the grounds that conditions of mental ill-health tend to decrease the individual's area of personal responsibility. The aims of nearly all methods of psychotherapy are concerned with freeing the patient from the control of unconscious or irrational behaviour-determinants, rather than with simply removing symptoms. Thus, there is a clear implication that anything we can do to further the mental health of the child, while not directly concerned with his moral development, is nevertheless extremely pertinent to it. In practical terms, this points to the usefulness in this sphere, too, of the provision of counselling facilities for a larger number of children than are able to profit from such services now; it points to a need for school counsellors, or social workers, who will have a wider concern than merely with those children whose problems are severe enough for them to be regarded as maladjusted.[6]

If moral education, as has been suggested, depends upon (amongst other things) the possession of a number of abilities, this has certain implications concerning the way we carry it out. Though these abilities may have their inception in the early stages of the development of the personality, it is not unreasonable to suppose that their development may be similar to that of other better-known skills. We might expect, for instance, that they will improve with practice. The ability to reason about moral issues will not develop in the absence of the activity of reasoning. Even those factors which come under the heading of ego-control may well depend upon practice and experience for their best development. If a child is never faced with the need to control his impulses, to postpone immediate gratification, or to cope with frustration, it seems likely that such abilities will remain at a rudimentary level. This is not an argument for the imposition of frustrations by a harsh authority; it argues that a great deal of moral development arises from the child's own activity and experience. Morality cannot be imparted only by formal instruction, or by little sermons and exhortations after a school assembly. Here, to an even greater extent than in many other kinds of learning, the child must participate actively in the learning process. We can perhaps best facilitate his moral development by giving opportunity for responsible moral decision and action.

Similarly, at a conceptual level, discussion by the pupils of problems in this area may be useful. By this, I do not mean that the teacher presents a suitable story and then persuades the class to produce the right answer. It is no more possible to develop adequate conceptual skills without experience of the genuine use and manipulation of concepts than it is to make progress in the sciences without handling laboratory equipment. In this connexion, it will be important for teachers to bear in mind

Piaget's work on the phases of the development of conceptual thinking, so that they do not expect the child to work beyond the phase which he has reached. Every good teacher knows already that one cannot expect the same kind of discussion from a primary school class as from a group of adolescents, and, as we have seen, this is more than being merely a question of level. The significance of Piaget's work is that it gives us some idea of the nature of these differences of quality. It is more difficult to visualize how opportunities for practice of other skills can be provided, particularly in schools. Such opportunities are perhaps more likely to arise in the course of other activities rather than from formal arrangements. Group projects may well have a part to play here, just as they do in the development of social skills. With younger children, there is probably some merit in the planning of long-term activities, provided that the goals are not postponed beyond the limits of the child's ability to look forward in time.

None of the component factors of morality can be treated in isolation. Some of them are causally related. For example, we have seen that the child's development of ego-controls arises in the course of his emotional development. It is impossible to conceive of dealing with either of these without also dealing with the other. But even when we are dealing with factors which do not have a close causal relationship, or factors which do not particularly correlate with each other in their incidence amongst a child population, we cannot afford to turn our attention to one at the expense of others, since the child's overall placing as a moral individual depends upon a minimal level of performance according to all of the factors. Thus, although moral behaviour, as it is defined here, is essentially rational behaviour, it does not follow that moral education is essentially, or exclusively, concerned with rationality. It would be useless (to give an exaggerated and obvious example) to try to impart an understanding of conceptual aspects of morality to a psychopath, no matter how intelligent he might be. Even if they could be made meaningful to him (and this is doubtful), his impaired personality would make him quite unable to translate these into behaviour. Similarly, although there can be no morality which does not rest upon the child's capacity to love, this alone cannot produce a

morally educated person, since we must be able to see the consequences of our actions, to understand what we mean by 'right'
and 'fair', and so on, before right feeling can give rise to right
behaviour.

Finally, there can be no question of anyone concerned with
child care, or education, abdicating responsibility for moral
development. It is not possible to say that one's job is to teach
reading, or arithmetic, or French. In all these activities we may
advance, or retard, the child's moral development; and we educate more frequently and more effectively by what we do and
what we are than by what we say. Parents influence their child's
moral development, not only by what they tell him about right
and wrong, and not only by the example they set, but by the
manner and extent of their meeting his needs and by their response to his behaviour. Teachers add their contribution to the
child's superego and ego-ideal, because of factors which are
frequently beyond their control and beyond the control of the
child. One does not say 'I shall make this child introject this
quality or that attitude'. The child does not consciously decide
to select a particular adult as a model. We are furthering or
hindering a child's moral progress every time we foster his self-
respect by giving real responsibility, or remain uninterested in
trivial problems that loom large to him, or make arbitrary decisions overriding his developing ability to think for himself.
We are all moral educators, whether we like it or not.

N.W.

Notes to Chapter 6

1. In a sense, the id can be regarded as a fourth factor in the motivation of moral behaviour. It provides the motive power for many moral acts, and is, in a sense, complementary to the ego controls, described above.

2. I am not arguing that high ideals are a bad thing. It is true, however, that in many cases discrepancy between ego-ideal and the perception of the self can lead to extreme and long-lived feelings of guilt, to depression and to an abdication of the struggle to behave morally. The ego-ideal is not (and probably should never be) the same thing as one's actual perception of the self, but there should be some concession to the actually existing state of affairs. If one's ideal has for many years been connected with the image of a quiescent, unaggressive saintly person, and one discovers at adolescence that one is possessed of a violent temper, it is probably preferable to adapt the ideal to include the concept of control, or of directing one's aggression into a good cause, rather than simply to be guilty and depressed about one's own lack of saintliness.

3. See also Part III, pp. 401–2.

4. Lorenz, K., 'The companion in the bird's word', *Auk* 54, 1937, p. 245. See also Tibergen, N., *The Study of Instinct* (O.U.P.).

5. At least in the narrow sense: see Part I, pp. 83–92.

6. This, of course, begs the question of what is meant by such words as mental health or adjustment. The difficulties involved in defining these terms are as great as those involved in defining moral education, and they are, to a large extent, similar in kind. To attempt a definition, however, would need the inclusion of a section as large as Part I of this book, and the reader is referred to sources which deal more specifically with this topic (see bibliography). It will suffice to say here that, in this area too, we are concerned with a manner of functioning rather than with conformity to norms or carrying out particular kinds of behaviour.

Part II (B)

What the Sociologist has to Say

————

INTRODUCTION

THE criteria of moral conduct, so far as we are concerned in this book, apply mainly to inter-personal or social situations. It is therefore necessary to take some account of the *social context* in which people act. Of course the way people behave is partly related to personality factors, such as how intelligent, brave, creative, or altruistic they are: and some of the basic factors have been considered in Part II (A). But we still find that people with similar personalities behave differently in different social contexts. The stern father may be a meek employee in the office; the brutal drill-sergeant may be a loving father and husband.

Suppose, for the sake of illustration, that it could be shown that the average bus driver was more courteous to other road-users than the average taxi driver. This would not entitle anyone to infer that bus drivers and taxi drivers differ in personality. To do this one would have to show that the one group was more courteous than the other in a variety of other situations too, such as when driving their private vehicles. It is quite possible that the difference in road conduct (assuming it really exists) is due entirely to the different social situations of bus and taxi drivers. The latter makes more money if he hurries, while the former does not. In other words, the courteous taxi driver loses money by waiting to let others pass: not so the bus driver. That difference is built into their social situations rather than their personalities.[1] Thus it is sometimes more illuminating to know about a person's rôle and social situation than about his personality, and always more illuminating to know about both.

1. The nature of the *larger society* in which an individual lives will affect the kind of social situations in which he acts; in

particular it will affect the amount of choice he is permitted to exercise, and the kind of alternatives that are most obviously open to him. It makes a difference whether one lives in Britain, the Soviet Union, Japan, or Borneo. If it were possible to transport a number of young adults who had basically similar personalities to each of these places and leave them to live there, one would expect that their lives would be very different: and these differences would include moral ones. One concern of a sociological analysis is thus to examine the features of social structure that vary from society to society, and the way in which they make it harder or easier for the average member of the society to act morally. This will concern us in Chapter 7.

2. Then again, personality is substantially affected by *early social experiences*. It makes a difference whether one grows up in a prosperous lawyer's family of two, or an unskilled worker's family of five, or in an orphanage. It probably makes a difference whether one goes to a tough Outward Bound school or a free-and-easy progressive school. This points to the other main sociological concern, the major one of this treatment, which is to try to establish what social experiences in early life make some people more likely to act morally in a given situation in a given society than others in the same situation and society. Chapter 8 deals with these points.

This leads me to try to define the function of this section of the book in relation to the previous two. In Part I a case was made for defining the 'morally educated' person in a certain way: and in Part II (A) we discussed some of the psychological components of this person, and the processes that are involved in his development. In this Part, as in Part II (A), we shall continue to use the definition established in Part I. If the reader is not already convinced of the adequacy of that definition, I shall not attempt to convince him here. The reader will remember that being 'morally educated' in this sense does not just mean doing or refraining from certain overt actions (such as going to church, giving money to charity, being kind to children), but involves doing something *intentionally*, for a specifiable *reason*, as a result of a belief which the actor wishes to be *universally* valid and *prescriptive*, and which takes account of the interests and desires of *others*.[2] Given that we are interested in this kind of behaviour, the sociologist's function is to discuss how different kinds of social factors or pre-conditions tend to make it more or less common.

Notes to Part II (B) – Introduction

1. Over a long time playing a certain rôle, however, it may happen that one's personality is moulded to that rôle, so that one carries over the same kind of behaviour into other rôles or social situations. Occupational rôles often have this degree of salience. So the taxi driver may become (after years in the job) an aggressive private motorist too.

2. See Part I, pp. 192–5.

CHAPTER 7

MASS SOCIETY AND YOUTH CULTURE

A. FOLK AND MASS SOCIETY

ONE of the earliest and most important intellectual tasks of sociology has been the attempt to analyse the changes brought about in social relationships by the economic and political upheavals that rose to a crescendo in the late eighteenth and the nineteenth centuries. Modern sociology was born, one could say, out of the industrial revolution and the French revolution, as men such as Tönnies, Durkheim, Karl Marx and Max Weber strove to comprehend the full implications of these changes for the nature of social relationships. Of course, the breakdown of traditional ways was not unprecedented. Several centuries earlier, social changes had provoked the observations and protests of Thomas More's *Utopia*, to give just one example. And now, a clear century after the zenith of the industrial revolution, we have still not sorted out the confusion, both intellectual and moral, which these great historical changes created. Indeed, one of this book's major contentions is that the conceptual and empirical assumptions that sufficed for the discussion of moral problems in earlier times will no longer suffice, and that this point is not widely enough appreciated.

Sociologists and anthropologists (who may be regarded as workers in the same vineyard who happen to belong to different unions) have given a great deal of attention to showing that different societies often have very different customs and ideas of right and wrong. In some societies a courteous host lends his wife to his honoured guest, in other societies not; in some societies people are expected to give financial help to many kinsmen, to aunts and uncles, cousins, second cousins, etc., and in other societies only parents and children are held to have such duties to each other. Not only do customs and moralities vary from place to place but they may also change over time in any one place. In England, for example, the last century has seen great changes in the position of the wife *vis-à-vis* her husband and in that of children *vis-à-vis* parents.

This notion of cultural variability is crucially important for sociology in general, but its importance for this discussion of moral education is rather more marginal. According to our present approach we cannot say that any one society has the 'right' standards and morality while another has the 'wrong' ones. Equally we are precluded from saying that people are acting morally so long as they conform to the standards of their own society. Our concern is rather with the reasons that people have for conforming or not conforming to the rules of their society. Thus I shall argue that certain changes in the nature of society, which have gone along with the great economic and political changes of the eighteenth and nineteenth centuries, have radically altered the probabilities that people will act in a morally educated fashion, as defined here.

In order to make this point, let us draw a sharp contrast between social life in two very different kinds of community: first, the small and fairly self-contained community with a primitive technology and no written language; secondly the large-scale community with an advanced technology, written language and a complex interdependence, both among groups within the community and across the lines that tenuously demarcate it from others. Let us call them 'folk society' and 'modern society' respectively. For example, the reader may think of the folk society as an anthropologist's remote island-community, and the modern society as a large, contemporary metropolis. In the ensuing discussion we shall begin by ignoring the great majority of actual societies that have existed, and just contrast these two extreme types. For the time being, therefore, we need not worry whether (say) an English village involved in the late-medieval wool trade should count as a folk or modern society. To begin with, we shall just consider cases that are fairly clear and only proceed to more complex and realistic ones when we have clarified a few points in this way. Here then are some salient points of contrast between life in folk and modern societies.[1]

In the folk society, family and kinsmen loom very large. A large proportion of people's time is spent in the company of kinsmen, both at work and leisure. Children generally work under their parents' supervision, so that the family is a unit of production and (as in mass society also) a unit of consumption. Not only parents and children but uncles, aunts and cousins are frequent companions of work and play. The choice of marriage partners is usually made by the parents and elder kinsmen of the young couple. Tradition lies heavily on the pattern of life, in the sense that most people feel that custom must be maintained. Any member of folk society, asked why he acted in a certain way, would invariably reply 'Because that is our custom' (or words to that effect). Tradition governs behaviour over a very wide area indeed, including not only how parents should treat their children or how the young should behave towards the old, but also economic aspects of life, such as when ploughing should be begun, who should help whom with how much, what is a fair reward for this assistance, what is a fair price for one's produce, and so forth.

Often there are religious sanctions reinforcing tradition: and often too there is a large element of religious and magical symbolism in daily life, with celebrations linked to the seasonal cycle of agriculture and the life cycle of man. There are communal celebrations of harvest festivals, baptisms, marriages, deaths. Members of such communities have a close involvement in the communal life and extremely little contact with the outside world. Since every member appreciates the overwhelming likelihood that he will live his whole life amidst this close social group, he is likely to realize that he could suffer the most severe sanctions for offending the sense of propriety of his neighbours and kin. Hence there is relatively little deviation from community norms of conduct.

The modern society's way of life, with which readers will be far more familiar, is of course quite different. The variety of social roles available is very much greater, and the way people find their way into them involves a far greater element of personal choice compared to the folk community. Both men and women may choose from a far greater number of jobs; one may choose to some extent where one works and with whom; one may choose whether or not to marry and whom. People are highly mobile: they move from job to job, from countryside to town and from town to town, from low status to high and from high to low. Tradition counts far less in modern society than in folk society, but it never comes close to disappearing. However, the extent to which people's actions are influenced by calculations of efficiency and calculations of personal profit, rather than just tradition, is relatively very great.

Apart from one's close family and friends, one makes contact with many more people in modern society: but the relationships are very limited and impersonal. This applies, for example, to one's dealings with bus conductors, shop assistants, postmen, and government officials. Very often these people are part of a large, bureaucratic organization in which their official rank and duties matter more than their personal characteristics. People's lives become segmented; part of their time is spent in different places with different associates, behaving in different ways. They typically shift segments and rôles within the same day – to take the simplest example, waking up and eating breakfast with one's family, travelling to work with a group of regular companions, working with another group of people and going to a club meeting with yet another group before returning home at night. Since one's associates in the different segments of one's life are not likely to know each other, one is free to behave in one segment or situation in ways that one enjoys, and which those associates approve or tolerate, but of which others might disapprove.

The dichotomy between folk and modern societies not only distinguishes between (say) a South Sea island community and modern Britain, or between a 14th-century English village and its modern successor enmeshed in modern mass society by means of road, rail, telephone, radio and television. Within modern Britain too we can identify various folk-like communities: isolated rural settlements such as those of the Hebrides; enclaves within urban areas of immigrants from rural backgrounds; and – numerically the most important – certain working-class districts of industrial cities which have had a stable population, such as Bethnal Green.[2] In modern societies there remain areas of life where the principles of folk society still operate and are not likely to disappear.

The contrast I have drawn between these two types of social systems, though over-simplified, is drawn without (I hope) indulging any preference for one or the other. Many earlier writers on this subject, though, have been quite partisan. Some (who might loosely be called the 'noble savage' school) have regretted the passing of folk societies with the close integration of the individual into his society, the colourful rites of the seasons shared by all, the co-operation of kin and neighbours in livelihood and leisure. They have emphasized the so-called 'anomie' of modern society, where deviant conduct is rife (crime, suicide, drug addiction, mental illness), self-interest increases boundlessly, and the common good is neglected, eased only by the compulsive consumption of goods, services, amusements, status objects and 'kicks' of all kinds.

Other writers have taken the opposite side in this issue. They have emphasized that urban and relatively modern societies have produced most of the music, art, literature and virtually all of the science that we enjoy. They have also emphasized that individual freedom of conscience, the liberty made possible by the rule of law, and the entire possibility of individual self-realization can only exist in a modern type of society.

This dichotomy between folk and modern societies involves, as already acknowledged, a large measure of exaggeration for the purpose of clarifying or highlighting various features. Many real-life societies will not, therefore, fit one of the two models in all or most respects. This does not mean that the models are invalid. They do not purport to be accurate descriptions of actual societies but rather an analytical device to sharpen our insight into the workings of real-life societies that are far more complex – so much more complex, indeed, that it is very difficult to see how they operate without the aid of such simplifying devices.

The typical folk society has a more coherent and clear-cut set of norms than the typical modern society. Although the norms of one folk society differ from the norms of another, in each society the adult members understand perfectly well how they are supposed to behave in given situations: for example, how husbands and wives are supposed to behave towards each other. Moreover, all members of the society uphold the same norms. In modern society it is different. Within the same society different groups of people subscribe to different sets of norms. For example, in some families the husband is considered to be obliged to give help with the housework, in others it is considered the wife's sole responsibility. More generally, it might be said that some families uphold a 'traditional' concept of conjugal relationships while others uphold a 'modern' version. Only on a few very general matters could one find society-wide agreement, for example that husbands should not beat wives, that parents should care for their children, that married couples should be faithful to each other. Thus what seems at first to be a lack of norms or standards in modern society is rather a lack of *common* standards. People in the same society are conforming to one of several different sets of norms. Sociologists speak of different 'sub-cultures' existing within modern society, each one having a set of norms, standards and symbols by which part of the population lives. In the next section we discuss the way in which such distinct sub-cultures are associated with different social classes. If one takes the trouble to ascertain what the different sets of norms are, then, it can be seen that the members of a modern society pattern their behaviour with reference to the norms of their sub-culture.

When all this is said and done, though, it probably remains true that the average inhabitant of a folk society conforms more closely to the norms of his society than the average inhabitant of modern society conforms to the norms of his sub-culture. Why should this be so? Two complementary reasons can be suggested.

One is that the crust of custom and habit, sanctified by tradition and mythology, that exists in folk society crumbles away with the transition to modern society. While it is there, it tends to restrict people's awareness of other modes of conduct. Of course, even in folk society, people can always perceive at least two possible courses of action in any given situation: one being what is laid down as the right and proper thing to do and the other being the selfish or otherwise improper response to the situation. But in folk society, where virtually the only behaviour one sees is that which conforms to the societal norms, those norms come to exercise a powerful mystique. In modern society this mystique is broken. One sees a variety of normative standards being upheld and followed in one's own society and many more beyond its borders, across which information travels with an ease unknown in folk society. Hence it becomes not uncom-

one may be "Be yourself"
or "To thine ownself (be true)"

non in modern society to hear it said that, since there are such
flagrant contradictions between normative systems, none of
them have any real validity and one can do as one pleases. It is
this feeling that there are no authoritative standards, I suggest,
which accounts in part for the lower level of conformity in
modern society.

The second reason lies in the fact that the social controls or
constraints that operate so powerfully in folk society to prevent
deviance from norms do not operate so well in modern society.
We have already suggested what the nature of these controls is,
and will now consider them a little further in the light of our
own concept of moral education. According to this concept,
conformity or 'good conduct' is not enough. The morally educated person, as defined, is able to give a reason for his actions if
challenged. That reason should be a 'rational' one, in that it
must be conceived in the form of a general imperative which
takes some account of the interests and feelings of other people.[3]
In terms of this definition, I suggest that the basic character of
folk society is such as to load the dice very heavily against the
possibility of morally educated behaviour. Even in modern
society this kind of rationality is rare, but the conditions that
make it possible exist more commonly than they do in folk
society.

What are the features of folk society which (I am suggesting)
tend to restrict very severely the chances that people will behave
in a morally educated fashion? One feature is the narrow range
of possible courses of action perceived by the typical member of
folk society. It is generally true that the norms of folk societies,
differing in so many ways, resemble each other in discouraging
contact with the members of other groups. This results in a
provincialism or narrowness of outlook being typical among
members of folk society. A sharp distinction is made between
'our group' and all other groups, us and them, they being bar-
barians whose way of life is alien and disgusting. There can be
no question of the customs of other groups being possible patterns for the members of folk society to consider following,
except under special conditions where one culture dominates or
sets the pattern for another.

Hence the scope for rational choice is very restricted: generally it lies just between conforming or not conforming to the dominant norms. Further, the habit of exercising such choice has little chance to develop. In modern societies, by contrast, one may be in frequent contact and have intimate relationships with persons who belong to culturally different groups: persons of different religions, political persuasions, social classes, or people originating in culturally different regions. Cultural variety or pluralism is part of the everyday experience of life in modern society. Hence the average member is aware (more or less) of a wider range of possible courses of conduct or normative alternatives. This does not guarantee that he will choose among them rationally, of course, but without real alternatives he cannot choose at all. The point here is that life in modern society presents a variety of alternative courses, whereas folk society severely restricts them.

Another feature is the very high price of non-conformity in folk society. It is not possible for an individual to deviate from the official norms of his society without suffering penalties so severe that all men of independent conscience are forced to choose between compromising their principles and facing death, exile, penury or universal vilification. This applies almost as strongly to an isolated mining town as it does to a remote and primitive island community. Consider the severe sanctions that would face any miner who turned up for work during a strike; he would be shunned absolutely by all other miners and their families, i.e. all other members of the community, and barred from re-employment as well if the miners had a strong union.[4] Non-conformity is less costly in modern society for several reasons. An individual's social life is segmented. This means that he may defy official norms (say) in his private life while his work-mates and employers are unaware of this. Or, if aware, they may take the view (peculiar to modern society) that it does not concern them. Consequently he would not suffer their disapprobation. Conversely, his occupation might involve him in violating certain people's concept of honesty; but so long as he was not caught and publicly exposed in the courts, he could keep the reputation of an upright person among his neighbours and family. Modern society is socially and culturally pluralistic: Protestants and Catholics, conservatives and socialists, high-brows and low-

brows, vegetarians and others are all accepted members. Hence
it is relatively easy for someone to change his group membership,
renounce the group whose norms he dislikes and take up membership in another group whose norms are more congenial.
Then, again, one can always disappear into the anonymity of
the big city, and escape from the social sanctions of gossiping
neighbours and nagging relatives.

In these two different kinds of societies the members tend to
develop two characteristically different types of mentality.
Modern society develops and requires in its members a mentality with wide-ranging interests and imagination. Modern man
takes a much wider interest in the activities of government than
does folk man, who regards it as a force like the wind, to be respected but not questioned. Modern man informs himself and
holds opinions. He pictures himself in another man's position
imagining how things might look from that perspective and how
he would do the job differently. Folk man is not imaginatively
mobile like this, playing at other men's roles. On the contrary,
folk man's outlook is very narrow. Reporting on a survey conducted in the Middle East, Daniel Lerner shows how those who
were more deeply involved in the modern facets of their society
had more definite ideas on a range of questions put to them than
did those who were more involved in the traditional or folk
society.[5] Respondents were asked such questions as 'If you were
made editor of a newspaper, what kind of a paper would you
run?' or 'How do you think people who go to the movies differ
from those who don't?' The 'traditionals' or respondents with a
folk-society outlook, were quite unable to think themselves into
the situations and so could not answer. Merely to put them down
as 'don't know' does not convey the gulf separating them from
respondents with the mass-society outlook who had so much
more imagination and capacity for empathy, which are key components of the morally educated person.

The relevance of this very brief description to moral education can be brought out still more clearly if we consider the *range
of concepts and questions available* to members of the two types of
society. For example, the word '*agathos*' in Homer (often translated as 'good') describes those qualities which a nobleman of
that time must possess in order to fulfil his rôle properly – it is

roughly equivalent to 'kingly, courageous and cunning'. To ask the question 'Is he *agathos*?' was to ask a *factual* question. It was difficult, if not impossible, for anyone to ask 'But is it *agathos* [good] for noblemen to be kingly, courageous and cunning?' For in order to ask this question at all, in the way that we could ask it today, there has to be a word like our 'good' which is not tied down to fulfilling a particular function in a particular way. But '*agathos*' was tied down to just that: 'in Homer, "*agathos*, but not kingly, courageous or clever" would not even be a morally eccentric form of judgement, but as it stands simply an unintelligible contradiction'.[6]

Important changes in Greek society (war, colonization, trade, and the increased awareness of other cultures and values brought by these) resulted in a general loosening-up of rôles and functions that had been regarded as fixed, and hence in uncertainty about the use of such concepts as '*agathos*'. Thus in fifth-century Athens, as the activities of Socrates and the sophists show, it became possible to use concepts like '*agathos*', '*arete*' and '*dikaiosyne*' ('good', 'virtue', 'justice') in free-floating ways that had hitherto been impossible. One could ask what was really '*agathos*', what true '*dikaiosyne*' was, what was the '*arete*' of a human being as such (rather than of a nobleman or a king). In the Homeric world the possibility of asking such philosophical questions, or of entertaining *different concepts* of goodness, moral virtue, etc., would have been extremely remote. Comparing the Greece of Homer with that of the fifth century, then, we see a society changing from a condition quite close to our model of folk society to a condition several degrees closer to the mass-society model.

This type of social change, with a corresponding change in the flexibility of moral concepts, can be paralleled by many other instances.[7] The importance of it for moral education is overwhelming. For truly moral thinking – that is, forming moral views in an autonomous way, for the right sort of reasons (see pp. 117–18) – cannot get off the ground without the availability of these flexible concepts and of alternative answers to moral questions which this flexibility permits. The change is analogous to that between the 'heteronomous' and 'autonomous' stages in the moral thinking of children, which have already been described (pp. 256–71). Briefly, so long as a person is conceptually restricted to answers like 'Because that's the rule', 'That's what a good nobleman" means', or 'Your duty just *is* that' – so long as he regards morality as something *given* – then it is to this extent impossible for him to exercise a fully moral choice, namely that it is impossible for him to exercise choice about what his moral principles shall be.

Of course such a person can exercise choice in areas that *we* might regard as open to moral questioning, even though he does not. A Homeric nobleman or a medieval baron has more power and scope than (say) a modern factory-worker or a private in a twentieth-century army. *We* might say that he has 'more opportunities for moral choice': thus we might criticize Agamemnon for 'unwarranted aggression' against Troy, or Odysseus for 'piracy on the high seas'. But in the society we are criticizing, these activities were not defined as either moral or immoral: they were part of what kings and ship-captains did. In much the same way, we may wonder how past societies tolerated for so long these phenomena to which we refer as 'slavery' or 'the subjection of women'. To us, alternative views are possible: we face these phenomena as moral issues. But to most members of past societies, the phenomena seemed part of the 'natural order': women were just naturally inferior, and some people were just natural slaves. We may blame these people (if we are interested in attributing blame) for lack of awareness, or for not treating other people as equals, or for not questioning what they took to be the natural order. But to do this is, in effect, to say that there were large areas in which they simply did not think morally at all, and to add that they ought to have done.

Our general point here, then, is simply that these conceptual limitations (which preclude autonomous moral choice in whatever areas they operate in a society) do in fact correlate with, or perhaps are caused by, certain sociological factors. Thus we have suggested the importance, in the folk society, of such factors as the strength of family groups, of tradition, of religious sanction, of ignorance of other cultures and values, and so forth. It would in principle be possible to conduct studies to test the hypothesis that members of these societies are conceptually limited in the present sense. Such studies would be chiefly a matter of discovering

how individuals in that society thought about morality – a
analysis of their literature and language might be our mos
obvious method here. We should then be able to see whethe
the conceptually limited societies were also characterized by th
social features mentioned above (strong family feeling, lack o
communication with other groups, etc.): that is, that they wer
'folk societies'. Any such detailed verification would, of cours
demand much more rigorous definitions and an immense amou
of detailed analysis of particular societies. Suffice it to say for th
present that these concepts are useful tools with which to begin
consideration of the development of autonomous morality o
moral education, and may lead to promising hypotheses.

Our particular interest in autonomy need not blind us to th
virtues that may be characteristic of the folk society; but we mu
be clear about exactly what it is we may find praiseworthy her
and how far this relates to moral education. The standard com
parison between Sparta and Athens in classical Greece is
good illustration.[8] What we admire about the Spartans is the
devotion to duty, their conscientious obedience to the norm
of their society, their self-control: in a word, the general *eunom*
('law and order') which prevailed in the Spartan state. What w
dislike is their failure to think intelligently about their norm
their total ignorance of and lack of consideration for the i
terests of non-Spartans, and their inability to maintain any sel
control or moral sense outside their own community.[9]

When we talk of the 'moral virtue' of the Spartans, then,
call some Spartan a 'good man', we shall be thinking primarily o
his conformity to Spartan norms. But consider how he will star
in relation to our moral components.[10] *Within his society*,
may consistently treat other Spartans as equals, and hence sco
highly on PHIL: he may have an adequate insight into the
feelings (EMP): he may show great self-control (KRAT): and h
may have sufficient factual knowledge at his disposal to make th
right moral judgments (GIG). But his score on DIK and PHRO
even within Sparta, will be low: for he will regard his principl
as given, and not to be reasoned about. Moreover, *outside h*
society his scores on the other components are likely to be lo
also.

Such a person may count as a 'good man', but only within h

own – or his own society's – terms of reference. The use of 'good' here approaches the functional use of the Homeric 'agathos' mentioned above; and it is insufficient for the concept of the morally educated man. There are plenty of people whose thought and behaviour may be adequate within a particular group, but who earn only moderate praise from us because of their lack of any genuinely autonomous and universal morality. (Thus a teenager may behave very 'morally' towards other members of his gang, but show little real moral sense outside it.) An adequate score on any of the moral components would, of course, have to relate to the subject's thought and behaviour towards human beings *in general*, and not merely to the particular group with which he identifies himself; and as we have seen, this criterion is not an imposition on our part – it is rather that the logic of morality itself (as opposed to the logic of group-*mores*) involves autonomy and universalized judgements.[11] Hence it is misleading to say, as we may be tempted to, that because the Spartans were 'good at their morality' they were (in the full sense) 'good men' or 'morally educated'. For what they had was not an autonomous and universal morality, but rather a set of strongly-enforced *mores* which were not intended to operate outside Sparta.

Ancient Sparta is of course not the only case, and may not even be a typical case, of the folk society; but on the basis of this illustration we may now see more clearly the points which may be made in favour of the folk-society member. In general, what impresses us is his ability to *play his social rôle adequately*: and we may certainly represent this as an ability to keep those particular contracts which he is expected to keep in his society.[12] This is, indeed, impressive, and we have seen earlier (see Part I, pp. 119–20) how the notion of keeping contracts is central to the concept of morality. But what we have here is, as it were, the germ or undeveloped prototype of morality: the same kind of prototype as we find in young children, and often described by anthropologists as 'custom' or 'tribal' morality. This may represent, indeed, a developmental stage which is necessary to acquire a fully autonomous morality: but it is no more than that.

On behalf of the folk-society member, therefore, we may make three points:

1. We may wish to praise his sense of duty and ability to live up to his own principles. He may, indeed, score highly on KRAT outside his own society as well as within it; and it would be possible (though in our view unwise) to lay particular stress on this as against the other components.[13]

2. We may wish to make the point (already made in connection with the Homeric society) that it is not the folk-society member's *fault* that he lacks an autonomous morality. This again betokens a particular concern with the assignment of praise and blame, and a desire to give due weight to the importance of 'moral effort'. Due weight must indeed be given; but it must be remembered that, in assessing how far a person is morally educated, we are not *only* concerned with this particular aspect of his personality.[14]

3. It does not of course follow, from the fact that there is more *possibility* of autonomous moral behaviour in a pluralistic mass society, that everybody will necessarily take proper advantage of that possibility. The behaviour of the Athenians, as contrasted with their Spartan contemporaries, shows that whilst they may have had more opportunity to acquire most of the components (PHIL, EMP, DIK, PHRON and GIG), they had not always in fact acquired them: or, when they had, that their self-control (KRAT) was not always good enough to enable them to transmute these other components into virtuous action.[15]

If we extrapolate the two extreme cases from this illustration, we may no doubt say that there is little to choose between a totally conditioned conformity on the one hand and a totally amoral selfishness on the other. But whatever the difficulties which impede the member of the pluralistic mass society from taking advantage of the possibility of autonomy, at least the possibility is there: and it would be surprising if some members at least did not appropriate it. Nor must it be forgotten that, however much respect and admiration we may have for the folk society and its members, it is a hard and inescapable fact that the great majority of us have to live in a very different kind of society. And this modern society of ours, while it is more difficult for the individual to cope with, does offer the possibility of really rational, autonomous life in the sense specified in Part I

Some of the points made above, then, may act as a salutary reminder of the importance of that *eunomia* which may be characteristic of some folk societies. But equally we must never forget that such *eunomia* must be made to subserve the purposes of a genuinely autonomous morality.[16] To forget this would be to fall into the error of Plato,[17] who appears to have been so impressed with the misuse made by the Athenians of their autonomy that he recommends a society more like that of Sparta. The dangers of this line of thought are too well known to need comment here.[18]

The distinction between folk and modern society, though a useful tool of analysis, will only take us just so far. It makes clear the point that folk societies have certain built-in obstacles to morally educated conduct, but it ignores some very important distinctions among non-folk societies. On the one hand we have the *pluralistic* modern society, that is, one with a fairly high degree of free enterprise in economic affairs and democratic political institutions. On the other hand we have the *totalitarian* modern society. There the production and distribution of goods and services is centrally controlled by the machinery of a one-party political system, which also maintains a very wide-ranging control on all the activities of its members. 'Whatever is not forbidden is compulsory'. In fact, modern technology, especially in communications, makes it possible for totalitarianism to be quite effective, where earlier despotism permitted more freedom merely through its administrative inefficiency. Clearly in such a society also the possibility of morally educated behaviour in our sense tends to be precluded.

The only kind of society where morally educated behaviour may be more than a rare and heroic act is the pluralistic modern society. Yet even within this kind of society it is not an everyday affair for the average individual. Irrational habit[19] is a very large component in everyone's life and so, too, is expediency. Actions based on either of these principles will not qualify as 'morally educated' actions, which the actor must be able to justify by reference to some non-authoritarian reason. Within pluralistic modern societies there remain various factors tending to make it hard for people to behave morally in this sense.

One such factor has been suggested by David Riesman in his

discussion of 'other-directedness'.[20] This is a character pattern which he sees emerging among the American upper-middle class, and typified by the person who feels driven at all times to conform to the expectations of his associates; not just out of expediency, but because he feels that group standards and norms are generally right, and because he feels unhappy and insecure when he is the odd one out. Riesman suggests that this character type is becoming increasingly common because it represents an effective response to a characteristic problem of modern society, namely the absence of a feeling of involvement with one's fellows in a community of common destiny. One response to this felt lack of an all-embracing folk-type community involvement has therefore been to invest extra sentiment in a variety of small groups in which one spends part of one's life: one's family, as always, but also one's work-mates, one's neighbours and other groups such as, in the case of the young, a teenage clique. While one is actually in the company of one of these groups, their norms of behaviour acquire a tremendous influence, over-riding any private notions the individual may have had about right and wrong conduct, even to the point of eliminating all thought of them.

Riesman suggests that it is especially the upper-middle class, whose highly mobile career-patterns tend to require quite frequent changes of residence, work-place and hence acquaintances, that has developed (at least in the U.S.A.) the other-directed way of life, because they have suffered more than other segments of society from the de-communalization process just outlined. Children growing up in this social class are actually trained implicitly to be other-directed by their other-directed parents, claims Riesman. These parents emphasize to their children the importance of getting on well with their peers, which implies learning to conform to peer-group norms and coming to *need* to conform to them.[21]

We have outlined some broad features of the kind of society in which we ourselves live, the environment we have to cope with. If there is any one feature which stands out as pre-eminent, it is that the possibility of *individual choice* exists to a relatively high degree. Perhaps it is true that the degree of such choice or freedom has diminished under the encroachment of increasing government control and the need for licences or permits to do many things that one could formerly do at will. But it may be argued that this contraction of freedom is felt only by a privileged minority, while the net effect of this kind of regulation has been to increase freedom for the average person. If one person is prevented from installing a smoky furnace in his house or factory, *his* freedom is restricted but the freedom of many more people to enjoy the clean air is preserved. Even if one does not accept this argument about trends in the aggregate amount of individual freedom, I think at least it must be accepted that someone growing up in modern Britain has much more scope for individual choice in his life than a citizen of a Communist 'people's democracy', more than a medieval villein, more than a New Guinean, and more than a Hebridean Islander.

What use do people make of this wide scope for individual choice? In particular how much use do they make of their scope for *moral* choice with respect to other people? We are not concerned here with intellectual choice, or how well-informed they are – except insofar as it is necessary to be well-informed about some things in order to act morally. Nor are we concerned here with aesthetic choice: what kinds of things one cultivates a taste for and what kind of a taste one develops. Those who are concerned with education in the round are, of course, concerned with all three aspects of individual growth.

The concept of moral behaviour used here requires that a very full use should be made of the opportunities for choice in order that an individual should qualify for high scores on his moral conduct. This does not mean that he should necessarily opt for some of the more exotic or bizarre forms of conduct, but that he should be able to *consider* a range of possible courses of action, and should be strong-willed enough actually to opt for them if they recommend themselves.

People react in different ways, of course, when faced with choices. Some will find deep satisfaction in being able to express their individuality in their moral behaviour (as well as in their intellectual and aesthetic choices); in choosing whom they want as friends, in moulding their friendships and other social relationships in some sort of accordance with their own ideals about how they should live. Other people will not even see the possibility of such choices. Perhaps they have never seen the different models of human relations that exist around them: or, if they have seen, have not considered them but only the ones prevailing in the narrow, folk-like social enclave in which they grew up. Or perhaps they are other-directed conformists to the norms of their peer groups. Or perhaps their emotional needs are so strong and ungoverned that they can only conceive of the kind of social relationship which gratifies their insistent (perhaps neurotic) needs; for example, one in which they can dominate others or one in which they can find the security of being dominated.

A third kind of person sees the choices that can be made. Indeed he sees them as choices that *must* be made, since he lacks the single-minded, ready-made answers of the two previous types. However, he lacks confidence in his ability to choose wisely: sometimes, but not necessarily, because he actually lacks the ability to choose wisely. This type of person may be the most anxious and unhappy of the three types outlined here. One might hypothesize that he is the kind of person who succumbs most readily to the various pathologies of mass society, such as heavy drinking, depression, compulsive and conspicuous consuming; or (in certain circumstances) to the appeal of authoritarian movements, whether political or religious, which give the 'complete answer' to life's problems, together with comradeship and a strong leader in whom to put one's faith and hopes. Here we touch on a subject far too big and important to be taken up here, namely the social bases of 'irrationality' in modern society.

This is the challenge of moral education from our present point of view: to prepare children for life in modern society so that they will see the variety of choices open to them, and be able to choose and act according to acceptable criteria. Clearly personality factors are important here. Different people in the same situation will act differently: some will see more choices existing than others will; some will choose, others avoid making choices; some will live up to their choices, others fall down. These personality differences can, in theory, be traced back to causal factors lying in either the hereditary nature of the individual, or in his upbringing and experiences, or in the two of them working together. Some of these factors have been considered, from the psychological standpoint, in Part II (A). In the following section

I shall try to suggest some ways in which the social experiences of the young with their parents, peers, teachers and others may be important in affecting their moral development.

B. 'YOUTH CULTURE'

A general feature of 'modern' societies is the gap that appears between adults and the young: they have different ideas and attitudes: and, in particular, their attitudes towards the other age-group tend to become more stereotyped and more prejudiced. The amount of time which the young spend with their parents is much greater in folk than in modern societies, where the young are gathered together in schools for a large part of the day over many years. There they are segregated from the bulk of the adult world (including their parents), and are exposed to the concentrated influence of their age-equals. Intermediate between these two extreme types we find the apprentice system, where a parent transfers control over his child to another adult *in loco parentis*. Even this relatively slight break from the tight parent-child relationship of folk society represented a significant beginning of the growth of the gap between the generations, as witnessed by the riotous conduct of medieval apprentices on public holidays. But our main concern here is with the present, and with the relevance of modern youth culture to an understanding of the behaviour of young people and of what affects it.

A 'youth culture' or 'teenage culture' seems to have emerged in Britain and elsewhere, as it had already done in the U.S.A. and as it is likely to do in other pluralistic modern societies. The details of youth culture or teenage culture vary from place to place and from time to time (especially the latter), but certain broad features remain similar. The most outstanding features are its distinctive aesthetic styles. Whatever the current teenage fashion may be in dress and adornment, music and dancing, slang and other mannerisms, usually it will contrast quite clearly with the fashion accepted by most adult members of the same society. Indeed this may well be the real function which youth culture serves for its adherents, to assert their independence from adult dominance and authority. By dressing and adorning themselves in styles not shared by their parents and perhaps abhorred by them, they show that they do not need parental approval. There are two different attitudes that young people may show in their choice of styles: one is to strive for real individuality in dress and manner, the other is to express solidarity with fellow teenagers by wearing what serves as their uniform. In any event, both involve the repudiation of parental and adult standards.

If this were just an aesthetic assertiveness, the significance of youth culture would not be nearly as great as I believe it actually is in Britain today. The significance of the aesthetic revolt in progress here is that, in its more extreme forms, it indicates a general attitude of revolt that is reflected in other areas of behaviour too. In other words, teenage culture involves some norms of conduct which are significantly different from those accepted in adult society – specifically in middle-class adult society. In particular it seems that many young people's norms of sexual conduct are quite different from those urged by their parents and elders – whether or not they are different from the actual behaviour of those adults in their own young days. Also I shall offer some evidence to suggest that the norm of deferred gratification[22] is rejected in contemporary British youth culture.

In line with this interpretation of youth culture I would suggest that it is more or less beyond the control of adults (including those who make a living from it). It represents a crystallization in some form of the needs and desires of teenagers. The 'needs' referred to here are, of course, the ones *they* feel rather than their 'real' needs as perceived by adults – psychiatrically qualified or otherwise. This is why it represents a threat to the efforts of adults to train their children to behave in the way they (the adults) think proper and to hold the values and standards that they (the adults) think good.[23]

We may picture the teenager, then, as being placed between the rival appeals of two patterned cultures or ways of life – the youth culture and the 'official', middle-class, adult culture represented by the school and, for some, by their parents too. The youth culture has arisen relatively recently; and its existence may be supposed to affect both the likelihood of young people behaving in given ways, and the likelihood of their exercising a degree of rational choice whatever their behaviour.

Below the age of fifteen the British youth is forced by law to attend school. There he finds that teachers and others have constructed a complex set of rules and unstated expectations for him to conform to, with rewards and punishments of very limited kinds to back them up. These schools only work really successfully to the extent that their pupils are committed to their role as pupil; to the extent that they *care* about doing well and being well thought of by their teachers.

Out of all the expectations attached to the 'pupil' role two seem especially significant. One is that his indulgence in various things that give instant pleasure should be restricted in favour of other things that are less agreeable at present but supposedly rewarded in the future: less T.V., less comics, less play and more homework (deferred gratification). The other expectation is that he should accept a subordinate status compared to all adults and specifically to all teachers at school.

Of course, there have always been pupils who would not accept these expectations. What has happened in the last few years, I suggest, is not just that the number of such pupils has increased but that a new 'contra-role' has emerged. This is the role of 'teenager' which is, roughly, an inversion of the official 'pupil' role. In place of the officially-expected deferred gratification it puts an emphasis on spontaneous gratification or hedonism. Similarly it repudiates the idea of youth being subordinate to all adults and asserts, in effect, that teenagers are 'grown up' in the sense that they are equal in status to adults though different in kind. What I am suggesting is that, on any given social level, the amount of support a schoolboy can get from his fellows for rejecting the values that the school is trying to put over is now greater than ever. In conflict with the school is a rival view of life which is held fairly self-consciously, though not very explicitly, by a fair number of pupils in common. This is the British equivalent of what various American sociologists have called 'youth culture'. Perhaps because it is so new, it seems that the teenage movement in Britain has a quality of buoyancy, assertiveness and collective self-awareness that is not found among American teenagers. They have already arrived, while ours are still experiencing the thrills of emancipation.

It follows from this way of looking at the problem that all the discussion about differences and conflict between mods and rockers is far less relevant than the differences between teen-agers who are highly committed to the role of teenager (wheth-er as mod or rocker) and those who are not, especially the ones who are highly committed to the role of pupil.

These notions are admittedly speculative, but they lead to more down-to-earth ideas and hypotheses that can be tested against empirical data. We are led to the idea that youngsters at school can be characterized by the degree of their commitment to the official role of pupil; that they can likewise be character-ized by the degree of their commitment to the role of teenager; that the strength of these two will be inversely related; that both will be related (in opposite directions) to being an under- or over-achiever;[24] that both will likewise be related to their con-duct at school; and that teenage-commitment scores tell us more about the academic achievement and conduct of boys at school than knowing whether they consider themselves mods, rockers, or neither.

In a recent survey of 540 fourth-year boys in four London schools,[25] I tried to measure the degree of commitment to the pupil role on the basis of answers to the question: 'Which of these would you most like to be?':

one of the school's best scholars;

one of the school's best sportsmen or athletes;

one of the school's best prefects;

one of the school's most popular pupils;

none of these appeals to me.

Respondents were allowed three choices in order of preference. I took it that a first choice for 'best scholar' represented the highest level of commitment to the 'pupil role', a second choice the next highest, a third choice the third level, and no choice for 'best scholar' the lowest level of pupil commitment.

The degree of commitment to the role of teenager was mea-sured by more devious means, since it did not seem susceptible to the same direct approach. On the basis of observation and interviews it seemed that certain behavioural indicators could be used for this purpose. One section of the questionnaire, there-fore, presented a list of activities that seemed to be involved in 'making the teen scene' for respondents to mark the ones that applied to them. This list included: regular listening to pop music radio stations, wearing teenage fashions, being keen on dancing, and hanging around coffee bars. These items correspond to the hedonistic aspect of the teenager role. Other questions asked about smoking and going out with girls. These two items appeared to be important for their symbolic connotations of being 'grown up'. The three component indicators of teenage commitment ('making the teen scene', dating and smoking) are quite well intercorrelated and highly significant; therefore they are combined together to give a more powerful measure of the degree of teenage commitment.

We can make two checks on the validity of this measure, and at the same time, get some insight into the psychological quality of teenage commitment, as follows: Firstly, it is possible to correlate this measure with attitude to school. One might predict that high teenage commitment would go along with unfavourable attitudes to school. This is indeed so. Secondly, we can correlate teenage commitment with an attitude-scale measuring belief in deferred gratification. I have already hypothesized in the initial discussion of teenage commitment that it involves a tendency to reject the school's heavy emphasis on deferred gratification. In fact, these two measures are inversely related, as was hypothesized.

Now we may test the principal hypotheses listed earlier. High commitment to the pupil role tends to go with being an over-achiever (relative to one's I.Q.) and *vice versa*. It also tends to go with having a good conduct rating from one's form-teacher or housemaster. Being highly committed to the *teenager* role tends to go with being an under-achiever (relative to I.Q.). It also tends quite strongly to go with having a bad conduct record. Parenthetically we may note that only one of the three indicators of the teenage commitment used here (self-reported smoking rate) is, by itself, significantly related to both academic achievement and conduct.

In this survey subjects were also asked whether they identified themselves as mods, rockers or neither. On first glance it seems that rockers are more likely than mods to be under-achievers and to have poor conduct ratings, while 'neithers' are least likely to qualify as either. When we break down the figures in full detail, though, it appears that the rockers only come out with such bad conduct because, on the whole, they have higher teenage-commitment than the mods – at least in this sample. The figures on under- and over-achievement are much more confused and hard to interpret.

I would conclude from this analysis that one can predict more about boys' behaviour in school (achievement and conduct) from knowing their degree of teenage commitment than we could from knowing whether they call themselves mods, rockers or neither: that is, assuming that we were limited to one piece of information. It seems that much discussion of the teenage issue has been side-tracked by the more obvious and exciting differences between mods and rockers, consequently missing the point that a fundamental shift in the relations between generations is in progress.

Of course, it is hard to know what is cause and what is effect in this interesting pattern of relationships. Pupils who are strongly committed to the teenage role tend to be under-achievers and have poor conduct ratings. But which came first? For some it may be that fortuitious flirtation with the teenager role led to lower achievement and poorer conduct in school, as the influence of new associates and self-fulfilling prophecies by teachers began to operate. For some, initial low achievement may lead to increasing teenage-identification as a means of restoring damaged self-esteem. For most, I suggest, there is some common factor or set of factors that leads to *both* teenage commitment and the other behaviours. For some of them this is home background. (In the same study it was found that sons of manual workers were more likely to have high teenage commitment, more likely to be under-achievers and more likely to have poor conduct ratings than sons of non-manual workers.)

However, when we look at pupils who are deviating from the behaviour that is modal for their home background (over-achievers or good conduct pupils from manual homes, under-achievers or bad conduct pupils from non-manual homes), we see that their deviance tends to be reflected in their level of teenage commitment. Middle-class pupils with bad conduct tend to have high teenage commitment (atypical for their social class) and working-class pupils with good conduct tend to have low teenage commitment (atypical for their social class). We cannot go into the reasons why some young people have conspicuously more ambition, self-control or other personal attributes than other young people from apparently similar backgrounds. It may be that we over-looked an important part of 'background' which is not similar. The point here is that these differences show up in other ways; notably in the level of teenage commitment. It seems, therefore, that a young person's adjustment to the choice between the roles of 'pupil' and 'teenager' looms rather large for him in the general process of shaping his life and making himself into the kind of person he will be.

It is not too hard to suggest how youth culture may influence the behaviour of young people or, at least, how it may give us a better insight into their behaviour. However, it is considerably harder to suggest what relationships there might be between youth culture and the moral quality of behaviour in terms of our criteria of moral education. Here are some notes towards a first attempt:

First, we must note that the problem can be approached in two ways, and be quite sure which we are using at any given time. We may compare two societies, one with and one without a youth culture. This includes the comparison of the 'same' society before and after the emergence of a youth culture. We may, alternatively, make comparisons, *within* a society that has a youth culture, between those young people who are keenly involved in it and those who are not. Here I shall make several points with respect to the first kind of comparison. (Note that it is not possible to make logical inferences from a point concerning an inter-society comparison to a within-society comparison – unless a considerable amount of background knowledge could be assumed, which it cannot here.)

In some circumstances, youth culture changes nothing – morally speaking. If an unreflecting conformity to parental norms is replaced by an equally unreflecting conformity to the norms of the youth culture as mediated by peer group associates, actual behaviour may be totally different, but is not necessarily more or less 'morally educated'.

In societies without well-developed youth culture the forms of youthful rebellion probably are or were more varied, I suggest, since youth culture offers a blue-print for rebellion, mild or strong. The hypothesis of diminishing variety would seem to suggest falling moral standards. But the opposite could also be argued. Given a clearly-developed youth culture, the potential rebel can more easily see what he is getting into before he moves. So it is possible that the actual incidence of symbolic rebellion might have increased (that is, the numbers who wear the clothing and hair-styles of defiance), while simultaneously the level of teenagers' awareness and rationality in choice also increased. Thus today's teenagers could be acting more morally (in our terms) than those of an earlier generation.

From the parents' point of view it may be less painful to accept the unwanted behaviour of one's children when it can be seen as part of a vast movement by a whole generation rather than as a personal reproach and affront to particular parents. Those with rebellious children can commiserate with each other about the rotten state of the world, society and the younger generation, without necessarily feeling that they have uniquely botched the raising of their children. If this leads to fewer parents acting hysterically at the first signs of independence from their children and to fewer parents giving up all attempt to communicate with them, it might be somewhat easier for the children to grow up morally. The hypothesis is that, if parents are calmer and more intelligent in dealing with their teenage children, the latter will not need to spend so much effort and energy in fighting unnecessary battles with their parents. Hence they have the opportunity to concentrate more on tackling the problems of growing up rationally, perhaps incidentally developing some of the qualities of character that are involved in being morally educated.

To test these hypotheses will need either international comparisons or comparisons between different communities in the same nation, where one has a well-developed youth culture and the other has not. Within any society having a youth culture, too, it will be of much interest to establish the relationship between standards of moral behaviour and involvement in teenage culture. Are young people who are highly involved more or less likely to score highly on moral development tests compared to those who are less involved? There is no reason to assume one hypothesis rather than another, for the relationship is likely to be an extremely complex one, contingent on various other factors.

C. SOME FUNCTIONS OF YOUTH CULTURE IN MASS SOCIETY

Youth culture, scourged by many an adult Jeremiah, is not only an important key to the behaviour of the young but also a key to the functioning of society. It seems that urban-mass society gives rise to youth culture because it makes the process of growing up so much harder.[26] Compared to most folk societies it takes longer to reach adulthood; one has to spend many years in school, for there is much more to be learned – academic success being related to the kind of life one has as an adult, though not a condition for gaining adult status *per se*; it involves wrenching oneself from the affective and relatively comfortable relations of the family to play competitive roles by impersonal standards, not only in adult life but also in preparation for it in school.

At the same time as the young are put under these strains and are vaguely looking for some kind of relief, two other features of pluralistic mass society provide other necessary factors. The young are herded together into schools for long periods, where their mutual influence on each other is greatly increased. And businessmen, seeking to make money, are brandishing various kinds of distractions before them – pop records, teen magazines, 'kinky gear', hair-styling, dances, coffee-bars and all the other things with which they exploit the teenage market. So it happens that fads and fashions sweep through the teenage population very rapidly, play an important part in their lives and symbolize barriers that exist between themselves and adults.

One may feel that their taste is deplorable; but it is *their* taste. It is ludicrous to suppose that pop music and teenage fashions are foisted on the reluctant young by diabolically clever businessmen. The really clever and successful ones have been those most in touch with the real desires of teenagers. The despair and pique of some educationalists, clergy, youth leaders and other adults at their lack of success in getting across to the young have led them into grotesque misinterpretations such as this. The fact that pop music and other facets of youth culture have swept across national boundaries to the extent that they have, arousing spontaneous enthusiasm even in countries where the government has specifically tried to ban them, suggests that the desire for them is quite genuine.[27]

Given the restiveness of youth growing up in mass society, we may consider a possible alternative to the kind of youth culture we know. In a dramatic form, this would be for the government to conscript all youth at an early age into a compulsory, part-time youth movement, so that their emotional discharge can be channelled towards collective symbols of the whole society. Well-known historical examples of this practice include the Hitler Youth and the Young Communist League. Is it conceivable that some such movement could operate in a liberal society? Let us assume that they would not be led to do anything obviously undesirable, such as beating up members of minority groups. Assume also that those who control the movement are exceptionally liberal and dedicated to the principles of true moral education. Hence they refuse to let it be used to inculcate excessive or unthinking loyalty to the state, and they concentrate instead on programmes that contribute to the moral education of the youth, that increase insight into the feelings of others, concern for those feelings, the ability to make decisions for valid reasons and the ability to carry them out.

This may seem an attractive suggestion: but – apart from its dependence on a body of 'moral educators' of proved merit, which we are unlikely to be able to establish for some time – it could be argued that a youth movement so conceived could not achieve anything that could not in principle be achieved, without the danger of totalitarianism, in a remodelled school system. Totalitarian youth movements have been so successful (in terms of their founders' intentions) because they permitted the expression or discharge of youthful emotion towards symbols that had been made meaningful to them (flags, banners, uniforms, parades, leaders). There was a degree of harmony between the needs or desires of the mass of members and the intentions of the political leaders, which would probably not exist in a low-temperature youth movement dedicated to moral education. If there is no emotional release through the official activities of the youth movement, members will tend to seek this elsewhere;

and the official organizers will lose control of them. The organizational basis may be partly retained for illicit goals: thus youth-movement squads or patrols might defy their adult leaders and turn to unofficial thuggery. Or the organization may virtually break up, as members get swept into mob activities, such as attacking foreign embassies. Again, the members may quietly withdraw their loyalty from the movement, and immerse themselves in pop culture, grudgingly making their minimum effort for the movement. One way and another, the compulsory youth movement offers no simple solution.

Youth culture, I am arguing, operates in our kind of society as a balm for troubled teenagers. Significantly, it seems that youth culture in Britain is mainly the culture of the non-mobile, working-class youth – not exclusively, but at least in that they are the ones with the deepest involvement: and they are also the majority. (Remember that data were reported in the last section showing a correlation between high teenage-commitment and under-achievement.) Youth culture is the new opium of the teenage masses. What they want to forget is not any material hardship but the boredom and failure of school-days, the frustrations of being a sub-adult with one's life restricted by umsympathetic and 'square' adults, and the boredom and dullness of adult life lying ahead.[28]

Youth culture also serves the upwardly mobile and hard-striving youths, especially those working for exams either full-time or part-time, who need straight-forward relaxation from hard work and worry. But the functions which youth culture fulfils for these young people is different in kind, if not also in importance, from the functions it performs for the majority of teenagers.

In modern Britain it seems that some of the visible factors that used to differentiate social classes are disappearing. Some things that used to be exclusive to the middle classes, such as good clothing, dining out, cars and foreign travel, are becoming more widely enjoyed; other things that were (supposedly) exclusive to the working-class are being avidly adopted by the middle-class, such as television, beer-drinking and a less rigid formality about what counts as 'good manners'. Among teenagers of all social classes, youth culture has helped to reduce barriers, at the same time as it has increased the barriers between adults and youth – even within the same social class. This is what some writers mean when they claim – somewhat extravagantly, perhaps – that the most important social barriers are no longer those of class but those of age.

Some problems

A crucial element in moral education is always likely to be a social relationship between adult and youth. At present this is one of the greatest obstacles to more effective moral education. The rise of mass society undermined the folk pattern of adult-youth relationships, where son worked alongside father and learned by example how to be a man and a bread-winner. The relationship between apprentice and master formerly followed the same pattern, as did that of daughter and mother. It should not be assumed that the young necessarily liked that arrangement: but there was no alternative open in folk society, and it worked. That there was some chafing at the bit may be surmised from records of apprentices' riots in medieval towns. But even without police or similar agents of law enforcement, the fabric of society was not seriously threatened.

Mass society has extended the range of possible choices open to the young: one can be a 'swot' or a 'skiver', a 'square', a 'with it' teenager or a beatnik, a believer, agnostic or atheist, upwardly mobile or down – to mention only the more obvious. This increased choice goes along with the fact that the young are no longer destined to follow in their parents' footsteps. That implies that the parents' control over children is drastically reduced. Fathers no longer have control over the sons' economic future, unless the son chooses to enter the family business.[29]

Thus a most powerful sanction for conforming to parental wishes is lost. Much attenuated, this sanction passes into the hands of teachers and school heads, who can affect a pupil's future through their testimonials. But this sanction is a very pale shadow of the power of the folk-society father: for pupils know that, though they may antagonize teachers by failing to conform to norms of good conduct, they are entitled to the crucial certificates so long as they learn the necessary material and show it in exams. The teacher's power is even less than this suggests, indeed, because a large proportion (perhaps a majority) of pupils are not actively interested even in these certificates.

The teacher-pupil relationship comes into existence in mass society: but, as presently found, its contribution to moral education seems less than it might be. This is not so much a reflection on the efforts of individuals as a sign that the relationship is inappropriately structured. We shall see[30] some possible modifications of the relationship that might increase its effectiveness. Effective or not, it is significant that the teacher-pupil relationship comes into existence in urban-mass society as part of an emerging pattern of social life. Other social roles, besides that of the teacher, have also appeared, such as the youth leader or scoutmaster, devised by people who wished to draw the young into relationships in which adults might influence or morally educate them (according to their lights). At present it is impossible to tell how effective they are, since properly-controlled research has not been done.[31]

The effectiveness of *existing* youth clubs and organizations on the moral development of their young members is one thing, but the *potential* national contribution of an expanded youth service is another. If they do any good, it may be that serious official support for them, hitherto lacking, could significantly raise the general level of moral education. The Albemarle Report[32] showed only 700 full-time youth leaders in England and Wales, and that public expenditure was only £2¾m. per year or 16s. *per capita* of population between 15 and 20 years. Perhaps it is not very surprising that only 30% of youth are attracted to all youth services, despite the exertion of much voluntary work.

The problem is not just one of money and staff, but also of the right approach. A basic dilemma exists over how far a youth worker should go in making concessions to the reluctant ones. Should he stick by certain rules, such as hours of opening, required dress, membership dues and duties, or should he get them in at any cost? If he sets rigid standards he will not reach many young people; if he is very flexible he may get them in but never have any morally educational effect on them. Is the ideal to be flexible enough to get them to join, and then, when they have developed a degree of commitment or loyalty to the club, gradually to demand more from them? We await answers to these and other questions.

Some organizations, concerned about the 'unattached' or 'unclubbed' teenagers, have trained youth leaders to go and *seek out* these young people. After they have been club members for a while, some of the formerly 'unattached' young people are trained as leaders themselves who, under supervision, start new groups of the unattached. The most dramatic kind of youth work, though, must surely be that of the New York City street-gang workers, who attach themselves to an existing gang that is causing enough trouble to need a full-time watchman. This role of 'street gang worker' is now well-known in lower-class neighbourhoods, and gang members are said to be proud of the official recognition implied in being assigned a gang worker. They know what he is there for, what he wants and what he can do for them. He can speak for them to the police and get them out of small-time trouble. In return he may be able to get them to accept certain basic rules, such as a ban on drugs and weapons.

These examples are isolated ones. On the whole, mass society is very lacking in effective relationships between youths and adults. This means that those young people who do not get on with their parents often have no alternative models or sources of support, and it means that young people in general are unnecessarily limited in their choice of adult models. Mature moral development requires that the individual should have a greater degree of choice than merely between a total acceptance of, or reaction against, his parents.

Those who are responsible for planning and policy making in mass society have also been highly deficient in devising and providing facilities for the young – very simple things that could contribute indirectly to their moral education, or at least would take some of the sting out of the violent forms of teenage rebellion. We enter here on a vast topic, but two points are worth a brief mention:

1. One feature of life in mass society, as we noted earlier, is that a large proportion of social relations are impersonal and give no scope for the expression of emotional feelings. So even if modern life were no more frustrating than old-time folk society, though it probably is, there would be a problem of un-

discharged emotions (including aggression). How to deal with such aggression at school and elsewhere is a major problem, complicated by the possibility that much vandalism and brutality may not be just the result of aggression, but specifically of aggression directed against established authority.[33]

2. It might be useful to provide some form of residence (as is done in certain primitive societies) as an alternative to their homes, which are often far from satisfactory. These would not be conceived as 'institutions', still less as Borstals, but as a normal feature of teenage life. There they could live under the eye of some friendly but responsible adult, if they so desired. For those still at school, this would be an alternative to making boarding facilities more readily available.

This possibility reminds us, of course, both of the Y.M.C.A.-Y.W.C.A. movement, of the college hall of residence and of various other arrangements: but we might wish to avoid some of the imposed *mores* of many such institutions. Such a scheme might be an effective way of bridging the gulf between adults and teenagers insofar as this cannot effectively be done in official educational institutions. Of course, we need to know much more about teenagers and their problems before being able to specify more exactly what kind of residence is needed. But the existence of youth culture, and our understanding of its function for teenagers in a mass society, may at least start us thinking along the right lines.[34]

Notes to Chapter 7

1. For a more extensive discussion see J. Bensman and B. Rosenberg, *Mass, Class and Bureaucracy*, (Englewood Cliffs, N.J., Prentice-Hall).

2. Michael Young and Peter Wilmott, *Family and Kinship in East London* (Penguin Books).

3. See Part I, pp. 75–80.

4. Of course, there are many substantial differences between the social structure of a primitive island community and that of an isolated mining town existing as an enclave within modern society. I am arguing, however, that the differences are less significant than the similarities for the purposes of this discussion.

5. Daniel Lerner, *The Passing of Traditional Society* (Glencoe, Ill.: Free Press), Chapter 2.

6. A. C. MacIntyre, *A Short History of Ethics* (Macmillan, New York), p. 6. See also the whole of that chapter, from which this example is borrowed.

7. cf. A. C. MacIntyre, *op. cit.*, pp. 93–4, on the concept of duty. And no doubt this kind of change applies to more than moral concepts. Thus the possibility of the Bishop of Woolwich arguing for the kind of God we meet in his *Honest to God* depends on a social and conceptual background very different from that of (say) Christians in the Middle Ages, to whom his God would be unrecognizable. In particular it depends on the ability to make some sort of distinction between scientific explanation and religious belief, so that God is no longer a super-being with magical powers. Thus it becomes possible to argue, as Tillich does, that what may have looked like religious belief in past societies was in fact not religious belief at all (whatever that is), but just myth, superstition, or bad science. See A. C. MacIntyre's 'Is Understanding Religion Compatible with Believing?' in *Faith and the Philosopher*, (ed.) J. Hick (Macmillan's).

More precisely, it is only when we begin to make distinctions of this kind that we can identify separate areas of belief at all. Thus in many folk-societies what we separate under the different titles of 'custom', 'law', 'religion', 'morality', 'tradition' and 'convention', were not separable in practice. In this book we have defined 'morality' and the 'morally educated person' by making distinctions that many past societies simply did not make, and (with their limited conceptual apparatus) could not have made. The distinctions are none the less real ones: and the definition is not an arbitrary twentieth-century imposition – any more than it is arbitrary to say that medieval alchemists were not really doing science. Our understanding of what morality and science are is clearer than theirs. (See also pp. 117–18.)

8. See Thucydides' *Peloponnesian War*, translated by Rex Warner, (Penguin Books), pp. 51–2 and 118–19, and J. B. Bury's *History of Greece* (Macmillan's), pp. 395 and 326 (1931 edition).

9. See Thucydides, *ibid.*, p. 66 and Bury's *History of Greece*, pp. 130–6, 514–16 and 560–1.

10. See pp. 192–5.

11. See p. 77.

12. It is chiefly this, perhaps, which impresses those writers of the 'noble savage' school, who look with especial favour on those societies (separated from our own by time, by distance, or by the fact that they are merely the author's own invention) in which justice flourished, debts were punctually repaid, truth was on everyone's lips, and the basic decencies of family and social life were preserved.

13. There is a tradition, which may be roughly associated with Kant and the Protestant movement, to emphasize that aspect of morality which we described under such titles as 'sense of duty', 'moral effort', 'obeying one's conscience', and 'will-power'. This must certainly be given its due weight, as it is in the KRAT-component; but morality is not uniquely concerned with it.

14. That religious picture which presents God as adjusting rewards and punishments in the after-life solely with regard to the moral efforts of individuals (and not with regard to their ignorance, false beliefs, lack of awareness, or failure to identify with other people) makes a useful point: but it is not the only point worth making about morality. Again (in our terms) KRAT is important; but so are the other components.

15. See, e.g., Thucydides, *ibid.*, pp. 134–5 and 358–66, or Bury's *History of Greece*, pp. 415–16 and 427–8.

16. See Part I, Chapter 3, pp. 126–38.

17. See *Republic*, Book VIII.

18. See K. R. Popper's *The Open Society and its Enemies* (Routledge).

19. See Part I, pp. 133–6.

20. David Riesman *et al.*, *The Lonely Crowd* (Garden City, N.Y.: Doubleday).

21. The individual whose actions are dictated by the standards and tastes of his current group is not 'morally educated', regardless of whether the group in question has norms as 'good' as a troop of Rover scouts or as 'bad' as a gang of vicious thugs.

22. See pp. 334–5.

23. See Erik H. Erikson (ed.): *The Challenge of Youth* (Garden City, N.Y.: Doubleday).

24. An 'under-achiever' is one whose level of academic achievement is *below* what might be expected on the basis of his I.Q.; an 'over-achiever' is one whose achievement is *above* what might be expected from his I.Q.

25. Barry Sugarman, 'Involvement in Youth Culture, Academic Achievement and Conformity in School', *Brit. Journal of Sociology* XVIII (June 1967).

26. James S. Coleman, *The Adolescent Society* (New York: Free Press).

27. Peter Laurie, *Teenage Revolution* (Anthony Blond).

28. Alas for Marx, alienation has produced not revolution but pop music.

29. The main exception to this is that parents may remove a child from school once he is over the minimum leaving age, and spoil his chances of entering a chosen career.

30. See pp. 380–84.

31. The problems involved are basically similar to those raised in our discussion of different types of school: see pp. 371–3.

32. *The Youth Service in England and Wales* (H.M.S.O.).

33. One could think of simple (perhaps over-simple) ways of determining when either kind of aggression operated, and which might also help to diminish or institutionalize it: (i) competition of adolescents against adults at a fairly basic physical level, e.g. in such activities as boxing, wrestling, football, etc.; (ii) setting aside derelict sites where disused cars and other such objects could be smashed up ('aggression playgrounds'); (iii) shooting-galleries where caricatures or effigies of authority-figures were set up so that bullets, bricks, rotten eggs and so on could be projected at them (Japanese employers are reported to do this for the benefit of their staff). I offer these three possibilities merely for the sake of example.

34. Thus regulations or petitions from residents which force coffee bars to close early and turn the teenagers out on the street seem to be asking for trouble. If the pub is the working man's club, the coffee bar is the teenager's, dingy and unattractive though it may look. They want a place of their own to pass the time and meet friends. This shows up also in their greater patronage of the cinema compared to adults and their lesser patronage of T.V. It would be most interesting to test the hypothesis that juvenile crime rates were correlated with the lack of facilities for the young. Until that research is done, though, it seems an eminently plausible view.

CHAPTER 8

HOME AND SCHOOL

A. SOCIAL CLASS AND HOME BACKGROUND

EVERY teacher and every other person who deals with children or young people appreciates the relevance of home background to understanding their behaviour. This is clearest in the extreme cases: the young trouble-maker whose parents send him to school looking scruffy and with holes in his shoes, whose father is often out of work and whose mother cannot cope; the well-behaved and responsible child who is sent to school looking neat and clean by parents who take a close interest in what he does at school, save their money carefully and keep their lace curtains clean. Most readers could probably elaborate the characteristics of these extreme examples in considerable detail. The aim of this section lies in another direction, namely to show how the concept of home background may be refined and made more useful, so that it can be used to account for much less extreme differences in behaviour.

Sociologists are at present revising their notions of social class and stratification, but the basic ideas remain.[1] We may take any population of people and classify them according to the occupation of the male head of each one's family. Then we may classify these occupations according to their income, prestige and power. If we ignore those occupations with large discrepancies between one of their three ratings and the others, we can then group the remainder into a small number of strata or social classes. Thus we might group together bank managers, senior business executives, doctors and lawyers along with their families into one social class, foremen, clerks, salesmen and technicians along with their families into another, plumbers, carpenters and brick-layers with their families into another and unskilled workers with their families into another.

Given some such stratification-procedure, sociologists have shown that each social class tends to have a different way of life, and different customs and standards – even in modern society, where class differences are much less than formerly existed. Of course there is overlap and lack of clarity about boundaries between these sub-cultures, but it can be maintained that those who grow up in one social class rather than another learn a subtle complex of assumptions, ideas, tastes and norms, which they share with those who grew up in the same social class but not with those who grew up in a different one. Class-equals tend to have the same ideas about many things, such as what does and does not constitute good table manners, correct dress, the right way to speak to adults, a proper bed-time for children, which things take priority over doing homework and which do not, and so forth. Those of another social class or home background are likely to have different ideas about these things.[2]

It is easy to document social class differences in overt behaviour or personal experiences. Many examples could be given. Those who grow up in families with high social status are more likely to go to church, to college, or abroad compared with those in low-status families; they are less likely to die in infancy, have an I.Q. below average, or be seriously injured on the road. They are more likely to drink pink gin and play polo, less likely to eat fish and chips or play hop-scotch.

We may also look at the behaviour of members of different social classes from the point of view of how far it conforms to or deviates from communal norms. Members of lower-status families are convicted of crimes in general more often than those of higher status. This fact is no doubt due in part to the greater severity of law enforcement against the lower-status members of society, but not necessarily entirely due to that. For separate types of crime the correlations with social class vary greatly, so that we may have considerably more confidence in saying that crimes of violence are committed more often by persons of low status than high status, whereas for fraud it is the reverse. Alcoholism is more common at low-status levels. Premarital sexual experience (or the admission of this) is similarly correlated with low social status.

So long as we divide the population into just two status levels or social classes, it would be true to say that the higher class conforms more strictly to the communal standards of conduct than the lower one does. When we divide it into four or more classes, though, the picture changes. It is not the upper class but the middle class which conforms most highly. Thus the upper class has higher rates of alcoholism, divorce and sexual deviance than the middle class does. They are also more eccentric in various matters of taste and style, such as in clothing.

It is important to remember, though, that conformity to social norms or standards is not synonymous with morality. According to our definition, conduct cannot be considered moral without some consideration of the intentions and reasons of the individual in question. This means that, in analysing the sub-cultures of the different social classes, we must pay special attention to the manner in which the characteristically different life-experiences of different social classes result in their members developing different views of life, with different images of the world or assumptions about how it operates, and different values or norms about how one should behave.

In the state of present knowledge it is only possible to suggest the outlines of the subject. We shall have to simplify the problem by using a breakdown into just two classes: a higher-status level in which the middle class is put together with the (much smaller) upper class, and a lower-status level; the two corresponding very roughly to a division between manual and non-manual workers. In some respects this analysis may not do justice to the facts, but we do not yet know enough to justify a more complex analysis. At some future time it will be necessary to pay separate attention to the upper class, the upper- and lower-middle classes, and the upper and lower working classes. Also it will be necessary to compare those with stable social positions to others who are moving into positions different from those in which they grew up. Here we shall deal with two broad social classes, each composed of people who grew up in families of similar status, and look at some of the most generalized factors that permeate the typical attitude to life found among the members of each class.

The sub-culture of the higher-status level[3] involves a wider knowledge about a wider range of subjects than that of the lower-status level. It is not just that the higher-status person has more highbrow interests and perhaps does *The Times* crossword. It is also that the higher-status person knows more about the matters that actually affect the whole population, such as the working of the educational system as it affects their children, taxation, birth control, and politics; partly because they tend to read more magazines, the more 'serious' or informative newspapers, and listen to more of the informative radio and T.V. programmes. Higher-status persons also express more interest in politics than those of lower status, and more interest and concern over their children's school careers. They are less often 'Don't knows' than those of lower status.[4]

As well as being better informed, the higher status person is more prepared to appraise the sources of his information and prevent himself from being cheated either financially or intellectually. He is far more likely than the lower status individual to be a subscriber to *Which?*. He is also more sophisticated in his understanding of cause and effect in the world around him, and in his insight into the motivations of people.

Those who grow up in the higher-status level start to acquire skills in the use of language and the more complex forms of conceptual thought even before they begin school, while the children of lower status families usually do so to a much lesser degree. With this handicap the latter perform more poorly in school than their peers from higher-status homes, especially on tests set in verbal form. This theory is put forward by Bernstein,[5] who argues that the handicap consists not in the smaller vocabulary of the lower status child but rather in the way he combines his words into sentences. Again, it is not just that his grammar is poor but more that he is restricted to short, descriptive, stereotyped and often incomplete sentences. He is unable to express meanings of any complexity or subtlety, to indicate how one event depends on others, results from others, precipitates others; or to convey intentions, motives or feelings (other than the most obvious). He cannot express these shades of meaning, and in his social milieu he does not hear them expressed by others. They exist for him only in the world of school, in the world of books and those mass media that he selectively ignores. In effect, they do not exist for him. To those who come from the lower-status sub-culture, meanings expressed in this more subtle and complex language of subordinate clauses and qualifiers are alien and incomprehensible. If this is so, it implies that the experience of life is profoundly different in the two sub-cultures.

Those who live in the sub-culture of the lower-status group, given their less adequate intellectual comprehension of the world around them, tend to find the world extremely confusing, uncertain and with little patterning or regularity. Not only does it seem beyond the grasp of such a person's mind at the present, but he cannot see the possibility of reducing some part of this complexity to order, or of understanding how it works. Far from being a predictable affair, the environment is constantly throwing unexpected threats in his face. This is true for the physical as well as the social world, but the latter is more relevant to our present concern. In the experience of lower-status people, there is probably more impulsive behaviour, certainly in the behaviour of parents to their children. On top of this, behaviour that is actually quite patterned and predictable does not seem so to them, because of their generally poor level of comprehension. Hence one of the differences between higher- and lower-status sub-cultures lies in the degree of orderliness and *patterning* which the world seems to them to possess.

Higher-status people do not just contemplate the patterns of nature, however: they believe that one can and should influence them. Man can master his environment; he can control events for his own benefit. He can dam rivers, make fortresses, cultivate crops, manufacture products, raise loans, write to his M.P., or organize pressure-groups. And to do so is laudable. Among lower-status people, daunted by the mysteries of nature and society, and lacking confidence in the possibility of achievement, a more fatalistic outlook prevails. Max Weber[6] and others have held that the value of activism emerged on a socially significant scale only with the Protestant Reformation, and has been transmitted from one generation to the next among the middle classes.

In the sub-culture of the lower-status level there is seemingly less concern with the possible long-term consequences of their present actions than one finds among higher-status people. Those of lower status live more for the present; the future is not very important to them. Even insofar as they are aware of future consequences, they are not as likely as those of higher status to let this affect their present behaviour. In the higher-status background it is taken for granted that a good future requires some sacrifice now, and that this deferment of gratification is both prudent and meritorious.[7] Children from higher-ranking homes learn to ration out their sweets rather than eating them all at once, save their pocket money, refrain from being rude to people they do not like or from expressing other socially unacceptable feelings such as anger, boredom or impatience; and they give up valuable time, that could be spent watching T.V. or reading comics, to do homework. It is not any specific behaviour pattern that is significant, but the general characteristic of taking into account the *future* consequences of present actions and letting them influence what one does now.

Particularly at the age of adolescence and early adulthood (before marriage), there is a contrast between the perspectives embodied in the sub-cultures of higher and very low status-groups. In the very low group there is considerable tolerance for the young if they want to abandon school work and have a good time now; since there is a generally held assumption among these people that adult life is destined to be a hard struggle, so they might as well enjoy themselves while they can. 'You're only young once'. They do not see any future pay-off for sacrifices made in youth. To them, unlike the higher group, the future is fixed and cannot be changed so far as they can see.

There is a significant congruence between the general emphasis on future orientation found in the higher-status group and the career pattern which these young people expect to follow. Whereas the manual worker reaches full earning capacity more or less quickly (depending on his level of skill), and then remains on a plateau, the white-collar worker proceeds more gradually, but may continue to increase his earning power throughout his working life. The rate at which it increases varies and is affected by the way he acts. He can speed it up by studying for extra qualifications, or by demonstrating to his boss an attitude of outstanding dedication, or by just working harder. Knowing this is likely to reinforce quite strongly the belief in future-orientation or deferred gratification among those in middle-class careers.

We have now examined several themes that differentiate

between the basic outlook on life characterizing those who occupy higher and lower status-levels. Those considered were: knowledge and comprehension of the surrounding world, verbal and conceptual sophistication, assumptions about the patterning and controllability of the environment, and the values of activism versus fatalism and future versus present orientation. Now we turn to consider what grounds we have for supposing that these sub-cultural differences might be preconditions affecting moral educability.

One of the criteria for acting rationally in the field of morality is that the individual must have an effective grasp on what is happening in the real world and take account of it. Hence he needs to assume that the world operates in a regular and patterned way, and that it is in principle predictable and subject to control. He must by definition *intend* to do the action for which we are evaluating him. Thus he cannot be a fatalist, but must believe that he has some part in determining events. He must also feel an obligation to use such power over events as he may possess. Just as the morally educated person cannot be a fatalist, nor can he be a creature of impulse. The consequences of his actions necessarily lie in the future, so that unless he thinks of the future and is concerned about the future consequences of his actions we cannot regard him as intending them. If he does not intend them because he does not consider them, then he cannot be counted as acting rationally at that time.[8]

Let us now turn to consider how the class-related differences in outlook on life which we have discussed may result from differences between social classes in the patterns of family life. Specifically we shall examine various aspects of the parent-child relationship as it differs between higher and lower-status families.

The higher-status parent explains why the punishment is being given, in terms of rules or categories of approved and disapproved behaviour. 'You must not do that *kind* of thing' (e.g. damage other people's property, or hurt people's feelings, or disobey your parents.) It is not the *actual kinds* of behaviour forbidden or enjoined which are significant here, but rather that general rules of conduct are being taught. This means that the child can handle new social situations outside the family more effectively than the typical lower-class child. The latter may learn to do or not to do many *specific* things that his parents want, such as not putting his elbows on the table, not interrupting his parents when they are talking, or removing his toys from the living room floor. It seems, however, that the child in the lower-status family does not learn his expected behaviour through *rules*, in the sense of agreements among people to behave in certain ways. He clears away his toys because Dad gets upset if he leaves them there, not because there is a rule about tidiness which members of his family recognize.

The child from a higher-status family, brought up to organize his behaviour in the family in terms of rules, probably adjusts more readily to new social situations outside the family. The rules are different, but he is more highly sensitized to their existence. This applies not only to the school, where the rules are many (though only partly formalized), but also to the informal social relationships among pupils. The higher-status parent's attempt to bring up his child to understand certain abstract rules of good conduct both presupposes, and tends to develop, in the child a relatively sophisticated intellect and language-power. It involves learning to generalize, think in abstract terms and discriminate between situations on the basis of abstract criteria. In this way it contributes to both linguistic and conceptual skills.

For a child to have a high level of linguistic facility implies that at least one of his parents (or perhaps a substitute parent such as a grandparent) has spent a good deal of time talking to him, and has treated him as a 'person' in the sense of someone whose questions and ideas, though naive, are to be taken seriously. Indeed this kind of child-centredness (or intellectual indulgence of the child) seems to be an important element of the higher-status background in its own right. It may well be that this is the real factor underlying the often-remarked association between size of family and parents' social status, or size of family and child's academic success. Thus working-class children who passed the eleven-plus were found in more than one study to have fewer brothers and sisters than those who did not pass. Not only are parents who successfully restrict the size of their families likely to have more characteristics of the higher-status sub-culture, but they also have the time and inclination to give a lot of attention to their children.

In the higher-status family, parents treat their children less impulsively: and this helps them to grow up as less impulsive individuals. The child is not spontaneously clouted for doing something annoying and/or forbidden, though he or she may well be physically punished. The difference between higher- and lower-status families seems to lie less in the frequency of physical punishment than in the choice of situations in which to apply it, and the atmosphere in which it is applied. The higher-status parent does not punish just because the child has made a mess or a noise or some other kind of nuisance; he or she punishes because the child has done something which, if permitted to develop, would lead to an undesired behaviour pattern.[10]

The factor of parental consistency is worth special mention. It is essential to the higher-status type of parent-child relationship, because we have postulated that this involves training the child to follow *rules* of conduct. Rules necessarily imply consistency. Parental (rule-governed) consistency is a necessary condition for the child to learn similar behaviour. Deferred gratification cannot be seen to pay, and will not be learned, unless the future reward can be confidently expected. Parental inconsistency from one time to another, sometimes rewarding and sometimes not, prevents the development of a future-orientation.

Higher-status parents set higher standards for their children, or at least they expect things of them at earlier ages than other parents.[11] Moreover, they carefully grade the standards of achievement that they set their children, so that they are high enough to stretch them but not so high as to induce despair. In this way these children get their motivation to try hard at a wide wide range of 'problems' or 'challenges' (not necessarily competitive ones), such as those presented in the classroom, which leave other children cold and uninterested. Higher-status parents are also less authoritarian than lower ones, and permit their children more say in decision-making. The father and mother also share power between themselves, instead of there being one dominant partner, as is usual among the lower-status families. This factor of the distribution of power within the family seems to have a significant effect on the way in which children develop. In one study, Strodtbeck[12] was able to show that, in families with an authoritarian father who dominated both wife and son, the latter grew up with little faith in his ability to master the environment and change things so as to improve his life.

To summarize, I have suggested that among the features differentiating the parent-child relationship in the high status family from that in the low status family are the following: the relationship between parents and children is consistent in the standards of conduct which are defined in terms of general rules; it is child-centred in that much time is spent on the care of the child and in 'taking him seriously'; it is non-impulsive in the sense of rewarding and punishing not on impulse but only after considering the likely effect on the child's character development; it involves standards of conduct and performance that get progressively higher, but not arbitrary demands for instant obedience by an all-powerful parent.

Of course, this has been a highly selective and abbreviated account of social class differences in how the world is perceived and responded to. The efforts of previous writers and researchers to throw light on this question, to which I am very heavily indebted, have been directed in the main to accounting for social class differences in academic performance, conformity to social norms, or general adjustment to school. I have selectively adapted their conclusions so as to throw some light on the possibility of class differences in moral educability. As a hypothesis I am suggesting that certain values and assumptions are preconditions for high standards of moral conduct, and that certain features of the parent-child relationship are preconditions for the development of these values and assumptions. I shall not here consider the question of where the preconditions of academic performance, conformity and moral conduct diverge one from the other. This is a task for another occasion.

Discussions of child-rearing behaviour which are mainly concerned with differences in conformity usually emphasize one feature of the parent-child relationship, which is fundamental to it but not to our present concern with moral education. This feature concerns the degree to which the child learns to experience feelings of guilt as part of a system of internal controls on behaviour (or 'conscience'). Given regular attention and affection from his parents (whether the biological progenitors or surrogates), the child apparently comes to internalize the norms and values of the same-sex parent. He (or she) wishes to be like him (or her) and to live up to his (or her) expectations. Because parents dominate the environment of the infant to such a great extent, the way they treat it must be of paramount importance to it. If they are loving, they inadvertently cultivate the infant's need for love (somewhat like a narcotic addiction). If they then withhold or temper their love when the child does things they dislike, that child is likely to be rather anxious to do what is wanted from it. Margaret Mead has described the American middle-class family in these kinds of terms,[13] and I suggest that something like this is involved in other societies. The balance is an especially delicate one, and might break down on at least four counts: over-indulgence (love without standards), lack of affection, over-severe standards, or inconsistency of standards. If successfully applied, though, this training produces a person who conforms to social norms even when no one is watching. It may be possible to argue that internalization is a precondition for moral education. I am not sure what the grounds would be. In any event we must avoid the elementary mistake of thinking that the development of conscience is sufficient for moral education.[14]

It seems then that moral educability (like so many other desired things) is correlated with social status. But moral educa*bility* (which represents a potentiality) is not necessarily the same as being morally educa*ted* (representing an achievement). How closely the latter reflects the former depends upon the structure of the educational institutions that complement the work of the family. If the schools discriminate in favour of pupils from high-status homes, or even if they treat all strictly equally, those with the initial advantage of high-status homes will become the most morally educated. If, however, the schools compensate for these initial inequalities by discriminating in favour of those from lower-status homes, then there might be little or no correlation between home background and moral education. It will be fairly clear that this is not the situation that exists.

The area of family and home background which we have discussed in this section is one that has commanded a relatively large amount of attention and research. Yet clearly we are still dealing to a large extent in inference and speculation. Mainly this is due to the fact that our definition of moral education is a novel one; hence previous research is only indirectly relevant. We know, for instance, that social status (especially as measured by length of education) is correlated with people's willingness to permit free speech for others who have non-conventional political opinions (such as Communism or atheism).[15] This attitude is closely related to the moral education component PHIL (concern with the feelings and interests of others). But this is just a fragment of a large picture.

Only research can tell how much of this hypothetical picture is correct. When we have acceptable measures for the components of moral education (EMP, PHIL, etc.)[16] we shall be able to see which of them correlate with the assumptions and values we have discussed, and which with the various aspects of the parent-child relationship. For in the present context these are the factors that really matter, rather than other differences of social class which crystallize people into the patterns of their distinctive sub-cultures.

B. THE SCHOOL

Although 'the school' can be treated as a separate topic, it is important to remember the close connexion between school and home background; and we may emphasize this point by first considering one possible interrelation, of a rather depressing kind. As we have already seen, children from different kinds of families come to school with advantages or handicaps relative to each other – certainly in their capacity for academic work and probably also in their ability to make the social adjustments expected of them. The trend of academic performance has been plotted in the primary school by J. W. B. Douglas.[17] He shows that not only do middle-class pupils score more highly on average than working-class pupils at the age of eight, but that the gap widens between the ages of eight and eleven. I would hypothesize that a similar process occurs with various aspects of adjustment to school, such as liking it, accepting it, or conforming to the rules. Here too, one might guess, children from higher-status homes tend to increase their lead over the others.

What are the dynamics at work here? I am suggesting that the process resembles the well-known vicious circle. The child from a less advantaged home initially tends to do less well at school work than his peers, and also tends to find more difficulty in understanding and accepting the way in which teacher wants him to behave. The experience of getting answers wrong while others get them right is humiliating. So too is the experience of being rebuked more often than others for doing things that teacher considers anti-social: for not playing 'nicely' or for not respecting the rules of the school – the written and especially the unwritten ones.

This kind of child develops a self-concept that first reflects and then reinforces his relative failure to meet standards of academic work and conduct. 'I'm not a very clever bloke', he thinks (perhaps subconsciously), and stops expecting to do well. Then he stops trying. If he is assigned to a low stream in the school, as it quite probable, his poor self-image will seem to be amply confirmed.

The fact that he comes to school less well-trained socially than many of his class-mates is likely to be noticed by his teacher, who may well decide that, in order to help keep discipline, this pupil and others like him should be kept on a stricter rein than the 'more reliable' ones. If some of the class are allowed out of the classroom or out of teacher's view to carry out some project or exercise, or if some of them are allowed to use some new and exciting but potentially messy materials (say, for painting or model-making), our friend will quite likely be excluded from the privileged group, because he is a greater risk. He is more likely to get lost, break something, spill something, or play the fool – so the teacher thinks (probably correctly). These restrictions hurt him more than they would hurt others precisely because he is less well trained to sit still, be quiet, or suffer boredom without rebelling. Even if they did not hurt him intrinsically, the fact that he (and some others) are not allowed as much freedom as some pupils is galling as an act of discrimination.

The poor victim becomes alienated from school. It represents humiliation in several dimensions. Repeated failure leads to demoralization, which leads to defeatism and reduced effort, leading to worse failure. At some such point a basic personality factor enters in to determine whether he becomes an apathetic, listless zombie or an aggressive, hostile trouble-maker. Once he is set on either course, the tendency is for it to go progressively further. This seems to be more true of the aggressive course, since this kind of pupil attracts exemplary punishment, which accentuates his hostility and may lead him into ever more and increasingly extreme rebellion.[18] The ultimate impasse is reached when pupil and teacher lock horns in a struggle which each feels very deeply that he must win in order to maintain his self-respect. Either way, apathy or rebellion represent a virtual write-off for any prospect of morally educated behaviour.

1. The School's Functions and Pupils' Adjustment

The dynamics of interaction between pupil and teacher within the school are conditioned by the relationship between the school and the larger society. That is, the teacher's behaviour towards the pupil and the expectations imposed on the pupils are influenced by the pressures bearing upon the school. What are some of these? What functions does education actually perform for society? In discussing this question and hoping to throw some light on processes within the school, we take up the rôle of detached observer (like the man from Mars) and try to see what social consequences follow from what is done in schools, whether or not anyone intended it so.

The cynical man from Mars might say that the function of the school is mainly custodial. It is, he might say, a mass child-minding service that makes it possible for mothers to go out to work, play bingo, give charity coffee mornings, or whatever they do. If he were very cynical, our Martian might say that the average school is a sort of low-security Borstal for keeping the young off the streets for half the day. After all, he could cite the fact that delinquency rates are highest when schools are closed: in summer evenings, at week-ends and during holidays.[19]

The most hallowed traditional function of the school has been to pass on to the young knowledge and skills that are presumed to be important. The 'three Rs' of earlier days are still the basis of this part of the school's work, though educators have tried to broaden it very substantially. Reading they try to teach in a foreign language as well as in the child's native one; writing now means composition as well as penmanship; arithmetic makes a place for geometry, algebra and other things too, soon for the 'new maths' perhaps. But this is only the beginning. History is more than study of kings and their battles; geography more than the learning of rivers and capital cities. Economics has found a place in some school curricula, and more exotic subjects besides.

The cynical Martian might say, at this point, that nothing has really changed except the syllabuses of exams. Education remains a system that prepares pupils for exams, just as athletes have to be prepared for a contest or cows for a dairy show. In recent years, however, the material prescribed has (apparently) become more interesting. Our Martian might retort that the way in which this new material is actually taught reduces its interest-value almost to the level of the old-fashioned rote-learning. This is not so much a matter of incompetent teaching but (he might say) of teaching methods that are exam-orientated, rather than subject-orientated or pupil-orientated.

Another function which the school might perform is the teaching of general *skills*, rather than just facts. Reading clearly includes both categories. Insofar as one learns the sounds of different letters and the meaning of different words, one is learning new information. But insofar as one uses reading to acquire new knowledge, it is more like a skill in the present sense. Newer educational theory has tended to emphasize the importance of this kind of general intellectual skill (literacy and now numeracy), rather than just learning assorted bits of information. Modern society changes so rapidly, especially in its technological features, that whatever one might learn in school may be obsolete by the time one is an adult. 'Education only starts when you leave school'. Successful adjustment to living in this kind of society requires the ability and readiness to continue learning throughout one's life. The person who cannot do this, whether at the level of *New Scientist* or *Reader's Digest*, or even the *Daily Mirror*, will be a bewildered and alienated citizen – probably an unhappy one too. On the whole, the odds are against his being a success in his occupation either. Finally, in terms of the criteria of moral education, such a person is likely to feel insecure and anxious (especially when faced with decisions to make), and hence to depend more than most on habit and impulse, as well as on manipulation by others.

If one accepts this point, then it follows that educators need to be able to inculcate a favourable attitude to learning new things. It ought not to be so very hard. After all, curiosity is one of the most general features of young children – until it is crushed out of them by parents and teachers because it is so very inconvenient.[20] Some educators have indeed taken this point and introduced 'research projects' into the classroom, in which pupils find out things for themselves by going to standard reference sources or other library books, or by going outside the school and interviewing people, or by their own observation. The intention here is to make learning more enjoyable by letting pupils study things that interest them and by letting them do it in ways that they can enjoy. Very much more research is needed to find out how well this approach actually works: what difference it makes to the amount eventually learned, to attitudes towards schools and towards learning.

Of course it is not just a matter of being able to absorb new ideas but to select and exercise discrimination: to tell the reliable report from the untrustworthy and to make allowance for the bias and slant in messages from tainted sources. These critical abilities can be cultivated in school. Some teachers are coming to feel that it is as important to examine in class their pupils' favourite T.V. programmes, their favourite newspapers and magazines, and the advertising to which they are exposed, as to discuss the motivation of Jane Austen's characters or the imagery of Shakespeare's verse.

A third function the school performs for society more or less effectively is to extend the *social* skills of the child. This is most clearly seen in the nursery or primary school, where the child has usually had little experience in interacting with others of his or her age and even less with grown-ups outside his family. This is a profoundly important function, and deserves emphasi because it is much less obvious to most people than the functions already mentioned. Imagine a well-educated parent who is also a good teacher, and who has plenty of spare time. Would it be good for such a parent to educate his or her own children at home instead of sending them to school? Despite its obvious attractions, my answer to this question is 'Definitely not'. In explaining the reason for this view I shall outline the theory of the school's function in making possible the transition from a life bounded by the family and its intimate, personal relationships to a life of participation in the many other facets of mass society in which other kinds of relationships (notably impersonal ones) are found.[21]

In the family the child learns how to form relationships of a close and affectionate kind. This is true in both folk and mass societies. Now in folk societies virtually all one's dealings with other members of the society are close and affectionate. People know each other as individuals: they know a lot about each other. Thus in folk society one treats people outside the family more or less as one has learned as a child to treat family members. (Of course there are exceptions; some people must be avoided because they stand in prohibited degrees of kinship or are lower in caste, others must be treated with great deference because of their higher rank, but this does not affect the main point here.) In modern society, however, many of the relationships people have with each other are limited and impersonal. Relationships with shop keepers, bus conductors, the T.V. repairer or the clerk in the tax office are fundamentally unlike family relationships. The two parties have very limited interests in each other, defined by the business they wish to transact. All that matters is that each does what is required by their limited relationship; for example, the passenger should pay the correct money and state his destination, the bus conductor should issue the ticket and provide any information the passenger requests concerning his journey and the bus service. If one of them dislikes the other's style of dress it makes no difference. If the passenger requests information about the price of turnips in the supermarket, the conductor is not required to give it. If either of them asks the other how many children he has there is no obligation to answer. He may choose to answer, but asking the question goes beyond the bounds of this kind of relationship, and if the asker tries to insist on getting an answer we would assume that he was drunk or an imbecile.

When children first go to school they are usually scared of the teacher. After that wears off they try to treat teacher much like mother. Now teacher, even in the primary school, does not want to be mother to thirty children; she cannot, for quite practical reasons, and anyway she is not supposed to be. After a while the child probably comes to accept this new kind of relationship. Teacher is warm and affectionate but (unlike mother) only up to a point. Moving up from the infants' to the junior school, teacher gets a little more distant, progressively more concerned with learning tables and spelling, progressively less interested in what little Brian or Louise did at the week-end. Then with the move to secondary school the transition to a relatively limited, impersonal relationship between specialist subject teacher and pupil is completed. Perhaps the move would be accomplished more easily if it were less abrupt than it usually is, but that is another matter.

Many pupils find it quite hard to adjust to the progressive depersonalization of their relationship to teachers. I would suggest that the adjustment is especially hard for those from a lower-status family background, and that this is a significant element in school difficulties of these children. Just as this adjustment to certain relatively limited and impersonal social relationships seems to be necessary for success in school, so too, I suggest, it is necessary for occupational success in mass society. This set of social skills would not be learnt by the child who was educated at home by his parents.

The school also makes a significant contribution to developing the pupil's social skills in getting along with his peers. In school he is thrown together with many of them. With some he may have casual relations, friendly or unfriendly, with others he may have close friendship or bitter hostility. On the other hand he may have virtually no relationships with any of his peers. This kind of pupil may be extremely studious and regarded by teachers as a model pupil, but the prognosis for his future happiness is not good, unless he finds a career in which the recluse is accepted as normal.

One kind of clique or peer group that is found in most schools is worthy of mention. This is the group of boys who have been friends since they were very young, usually live near each other and meet outside school as well as inside. It appears that they are typically low achievers, low also in relation to their I.Q.s, early leavers and generally antagonistic to school. They often have very close relationships among themselves, spending much time together and insisting on a very exacting loyalty to and from each other. With this there often goes some hostility towards pupils outside their group, not to mention teachers. I suggest that it would be wrong to think of these pupils as 'sociable'. On the contrary, I believe that they are very lacking in the facility for making new friendships on any level, and that this is why they have stuck so closely together for so long. Somewhere between these extremes of the reclusive isolates and the tight, cliquish gangs lie the majority of the pupils.

The implications of these different degrees of involvement with one's peers for moral behaviour are intriguing but largely untested. Research is needed here. Meanwhile one may hypothesize that members of the kind of clique described are likely to be extreme conformists to clique-sanctioned ideas of right and wrong. On that basis their morality would be rated low. The isolates are most free from peer-group pressure, but are likely to be slavishly conformist to norms set by their parents or teachers. Moreover, they are likely to lack sympathetic insight into the thoughts and feelings of others. On the whole, one might guess that the most autonomous and rational moral behaviour would be found among those who were members of some fairly loose-knit peer group, on the grounds that they have some sense of security from membership and participation (which the isolates probably lack) without the total commitment or imprisonment of the others in their group. This speculation must not be taken as truth, but provides some interesting and suggestive hypotheses that should be tested by research.

Another function which the school performs for society is to mediate between youth and the labour market. It may provide information about different occupations and guidance about the individual's suitability. It can influence both his general level of ambition and his specific career choice. It plays a crucial part in the process of competition for scarce jobs by preparing pupils for the crucial exams, and also by evaluating their work and character in testimonials.

Recently the trend has been for many more pupils to be entered for external exams, and for pupils to have impressed upon them very emphatically how closely their occupational prospects are related to their academic success. There is a point of further sociological interest here. As more occupations are specifying that entrants must have a minimum number of examination passes, this implies that selection for jobs is put on a more objective basis than personal recommendation or interview alone. It also implies that there is more incentive for pupils to make an effort at school. The point about the increasing proportion of non-grammar school pupils being entered for external exams is not just that 'they have a goal to work for', but that school has probably come to have a more obvious relevance to their later lives. The exams would not mean so very much unless employers were interested in them.

The introduction of external exams in secondary modern and comprehensive schools may have other consequences that are unanticipated. While it may increase the motivation and commitment of those pupils who are being entered, it may make the remainder feel even more alienated from the school than before. Since the criteria of success in examinations are so clear, there is a huge temptation for teachers and heads to enter pupils who are not really clever enough, to enter pupils for too many subjects and sacrifice depth or breadth of study (or the more enjoyable aspects of it), to over-emphasize the passing of exams relative to other goals of the school. This temptation is apt to be especially strong in schools where the head feels under pressure to justify his school and/or himself. It is so much easier to demonstrate success in C.S.E., G.C.E. or university admissions than success in teaching a real appreciation of some subject, an ability to get on with other people, or a respect and consideration for their views. Hence the less tangible and less measurable aspects of the school's work tend to get pushed aside in favour of the measurable.[22]

One possible result of the present situation would be quite ironical. Suppose that educators should become more concerned with goals of moral education and seek to do more about it in their schools. Suppose too that they do not wish to jeopardize their exam records, because of parental pressure, concern with pupils' careers, or some other reason. This would mean that the innovations concerned with moral education will tend to be directed at the non-examinees in the school, those in the lower streams. Fine, one might think. After all, they are generally in greater need of any kind of extra assistance. Moreover, modern thinking about moral education more often than not implies brightening up school work from the pupils' point of view: and this again is exactly what the non-examinees, even more than the other pupils, seem to need. Yet the ironical point is that these reforms, inspired by a greater concern with moral education and the whole pupil, are likely to be *perceived* as having been devised for the special benefit of the dullards; hence a stigma will be attached to them and may rob them of their potentially beneficial effect. This need not happen if these innovations are applied equally to pupils on all ability levels, however.

Now let us try to refocus this general analysis of the school's functions on to their implications for moral education:

1. Failure to master basic intellectual skills involves progressive failure in school work and exams. More significantly, it implies a low competence in analysing and comprehending the novel situations that a person will inevitably meet in later life. Without a minimum ability to understand or conceptualize problem-situations, a person is unlikely to act morally, and more likely to act impulsively or according to some unquestioned traditional maxim.

2. Failure to adjust to the demands of limited, impersonal, 'non-affective' social rôles also implies an inability to handle many social situations of a kind endemic in modern society. Not being able to manage the rôle according to official (or institutionalized) rules, such a person cannot choose whether to play it one way or the other because he does not have that much control over the situation.

3. Academic failure or getting low marks in school, if we may in imagination separate it from the learning of basic intellectual skills, tends to lower the pupil's self-esteem and to create

anxieties and a feeling of insecurity. This state of mind, I would suggest, makes it exceptionally difficult for a person to have self-insight, concern for the interests and feelings of others and the ability to live up to any self-chosen moral standards. In other words, he scores low for many components of moral behaviour.

4. Failure to get along with one's peers deprives a person of an important defence against these same anxieties and feelings of insecurity.

To the extent that different ways of running a school make success in these different spheres easier or harder, they affect the chances of their pupils being morally educated or not. In the next section I shall discuss some hypotheses that try to specify what aspects of school organization are crucial in this way, and what research on this problem is needed.

2. Variations in School Structure

In the last section we looked at the dynamics going on within the school involving teacher-pupil interaction, the reactions of pupils to their success or failure in different aspects of school life and, thirdly, the balance or interaction between these different aspects or functions of the school. The emphasis there was on the basic elements of similarity underlying differences in schools, teachers, communities, homes and pupils. The purpose of this section is to seize upon some of the differences between schools of different kinds, and consider how they might affect the process of moral education.

Schools may be run in different ways, and clearly this may make a lot of difference to the effect which the pupil's years in school have upon his character. To give a fairly obvious example, one would think that five years in a Jesuit boarding school would have a different effect from the same time spent in a run-of-the-mill secondary modern school. But the effect which a school actually has may not be the effect intended by those who run the school. For example, it seems that while the official intention of Borstal and other correctional institutions is to make its inmates more law-abiding, the actual effect of attending such places is often quite different – to enlarge the inmate's criminal skills and the range of his professional underworld contacts through mixing with these hand-picked law-breakers. Much research is needed to find out what different effects (if any) different kinds of schools have on the pupils who are exposed to them.

To reduce the problem to its very simplest terms: Mr and Mrs A. have a child: they want him to be morally well-educated: they are permitted a certain amount of choice in which school their child shall attend. Is he more likely or less likely to turn out morally well-educated if he goes to a boarding school or a day school, a coeducational or a single-sex school, a large one or a small one, a comprehensive or a selective one, one where the teaching is academic in the traditional sense or one where it is 'progressive' or 'pupil-oriented', one with a stern head or a kindly head? – and so forth.

Unfortunately the state of our knowledge at present does not permit us to give Mr and Mrs A any confident advice, except that they should beware of *any* advice. 'X is a very good school' usually turns out to mean either 'Pupils from school X get very good G.C.E. results' or 'School X gets pupils from "very good homes"' or 'School X is very old'. The point of this section is to emphasize how seriously research is needed in this area and to suggest some starting points.

I. SOME PROBLEMS OF METHODOLOGY

When researchers get down to conducting the kind of studies that are needed, we shall not discover overnight what is the perfect kind of school for moral education (or for any other objective). Rather we shall discover whether (say) single-sex or co-educational schools work better, whether streamed or un-streamed schools work better, whether pupil-oriented teachers or subject-oriented teachers are more effective, and so forth. Of course the school that is good for one kind of pupil may not be good for another kind. Also, the school that is good for one thing may not be good for another. One type of school, that develops (say) more tolerance than another type of school, may be less effective in developing some other component of the morally educated character. This is a further problem for empirical research. Similarly, it *may* turn out that greater success in moral education can only be obtained by accepting lower levels of academic work. There is actually no reason to suppose this is so,[23] but if it were then policy-makers would have to choose between them. I have alluded to the influence of the school on the pupil's character as if this were an easy thing to establish, at least in principle. Actually it is not at all easy, even in principle. A number of assumptions and qualifications have to be made, if we are to talk of the influence of the school itself on the growth, or stunting, of its pupils.

In effect we are trying to do what the experimental scientist does when he compares the effect of two different drugs on two groups of patients with the same illness. Unfortunately, for this kind of research we cannot usually assign pupils to school A or B, or to teacher A or B, as the medical researcher assigns patients to drug A or B. As a result these comparisons usually contain an element of doubt as to how well the subjects were matched. For example, suppose that tolerance of other people's views is an essential part of being morally educated, and that we have an acceptable means of measuring people's tolerance. We might compare the tolerance-scores of pupils at a comprehensive school with the scores of grammar school pupils of the same age. But this could be grossly misleading. It would be interesting to know if scores were higher at one school than another, but this would not mean that the school itself had influenced pupils' level of tolerance. Suppose that grammar-school pupils were more tolerant than those at comprehensive schools. Two other explanations could account for this. Grammar school pupils have higher I.Q. scores (true) and more intelligent people may always tend to be more tolerant regardless of school influence (conjectural). Also, grammar-school pupils tend to come from higher quality homes (true), and pupils from such homes tend to be more tolerant regardless of school influence (conjectural).

If we can hold I.Q. and home background constant, however, we remove these difficulties. Suppose we can find pupils at comprehensive schools who match another group of grammar-school pupils in at least age, sex, home background and I.Q. (while the schools are also matched in some basic respects such as staffing ratio, staff quality, and facilities), and then show that there were significant differences in average scores.[24] From this one may draw *some support* – though not positive proof – for the hypothesis that because these pupils went to one kind of school rather than the other their attitudes are affected, i.e. they are more tolerant or less. The weak point still remaining is that pupils are not randomly allocated to one type of school rather than the other; hence those who are more prejudiced might tend to have congregated in one school in preference to the other. This could be avoided if any area were arbitrarily divided in half and, before families had a chance to move, only comprehensive schools were provided in one half and only selective schools in the other. Not often will such an opportunity exist.

The same logic applies to any other kind of comparison. For instance, instead of comparing comprehensive and selective schools we could compare single-sex and co-educational schools, or streamed and unstreamed schools. Thus we could compare the effectiveness of different techniques of teaching. Pupils taught by one type of teacher in various schools could be compared with other pupils of similar age, sex, I.Q. and home backgrounds who were taught by another type of teacher in the same schools.

Although the difficulties of this kind of research are probably even greater than research into family background, it does have one great attraction. Knowing what we do about home background, its connexion with success in school and probably with moral education too, it is still hard to know what we might do about it. Suppose these theories about home background were much more solidly based than they are and suppose everyone agreed that this kind of home was desirable. What could be done to change the behaviour of parents towards their children? Probably not much, although pre-school play centres might have an important contribution to make. If, however, one way of running schools could be shown to get different kinds of results from another way and if everyone agreed that these results were preferable, then something could be done about it. By legislation or other means schools could be changed over to the demonstrably more effective mode of running.

II. SOME POSSIBLY IMPORTANT SCHOOL FACTORS

(a) *Size* (*number of pupils*). One might expect pupils to identify more strongly with the school as a community when it was small rather than large. This is to imply that they have a keener concern for the collective welfare, and that each would feel that his part in the whole was a more significant one. To this extent the proportion of rebels, withdrawers and other misfits should be smaller. On the other hand, the small folk-society kind of school may evoke its own kind of rebellion – that of the pupil who does not see a way to fit into the narrow range of activities open. From this point of view, the large school which offers a large variety of curricular subjects, sports and extra-curricular activities, has the advantage. The small school is more like the family from which they have come and so presumably easier for the pupils to adjust to, while the large school is more like the mass society in which the pupils will eventually have to live. Presumably smallness is at a much greater premium for the primary school than the secondary school, but just *how* much we cannot yet tell. Research should be directed at two distinct questions: firstly, whether the large or small school makes a deeper mark on its pupils; and, secondly, what kind of mark it makes – whether it is conformity to a specific pattern or a capacity for autonomous decision.

So far there is little research on the importance of size. The most relevant study concerns the effect of school size on pupils' participation in extra-curricular activities and on the satisfaction they derive from it. The data come from older pupils in one large and four small high schools in the U.S. mid-west.[25] The authors show that although the large school provided more numerous and more varied activities than the small school, there was no difference between schools in the average number of activities per pupil: and the average small-school pupil actually took part in a greater variety of activities. Moreover, small-school pupils were more likely to hold positions of responsibility in their extra-curricular clubs. Because of this, the researchers show, the small-school pupils derived from their activities more satisfaction on six separate counts which they assessed, although large-school pupils derived more satisfaction on three other counts connected with vicarious enjoyment. Large-school pupils who held responsible positions in the clubs, though, tended to report satisfactions more like those of small-school pupils and less like those of their other large-school peers.

(b) *Comprehensive or Separate*. There has been fierce debate over the merits and demerits of the comprehensive school in Britain. A substantial part of this debate, though, has not been concerned with the supposed effects of comprehensive compared to separate education, but with doctrinal questions such as whether it is right or wrong *in principle* to separate children into different schools. This does not concern us here. Another substantial part of the debate has been over the results of the two systems in terms of the utilization or wastage of talent. Again, this does not concern us directly. We are concerned only with the effect of comprehensive or separate education on the moral development of pupils.

By a 'comprehensive' school system I mean one that accepts pupils from the entire spectrum of ability and achievement (except for the handicapped and E.S.N.). It may or may not be a neighbourhood school; it may be larger or smaller than separate or selective schools; it may have better or poorer buildings; and so forth. We are not concerned with any of these factors but exclusively with the breadth of intake. What difference does this make?

The advocates of the comprehensive school claim that the presence of pupils from 'better homes' raises standards of work and conduct above the general secondary modern level – not just the standards of what is actually done but also the perceived standards of what seems to be expected by both teachers and other pupils, which subtly influence the level of pupils' strivings. This is a self-sustaining process – a virtuous (rather than vicious) circle. On the other hand, say the opponents of comprehensive schools, exposing the pupils from 'good homes' to those from 'bad homes' has the reverse effect – namely lowering standards. Who is right, then? Is the influence of the good element or the bad element stronger?

As for G.C.E. results, Pedley has shown that fully comprehensive schools in this country get somewhat better G.C.E. results than do the aggregate of all maintained schools.[26] Concerning attitude and behaviour at school, we have some data on comprehensive and secondary modern school pupils from the

Newsom Report.[27] Comprehensive pupils truanted less than secondary modern ones, were far more co-operative over school uniform, belonged to more school societies (boys only) but were considered less co-operative about discipline by their heads. The last finding, depending as it does on a non-objective rating, may be misleading. It could be, for example, that comprehensive heads set higher standards than secondary modern heads, since they have the example of more first-class pupils before them and hence may have been over-severe in rating their pupils.

Miller[28] compared the values and social attitudes of pupils with matched I.Q.s from three grammar schools and three secondary moderns with other pupils of similar ability in three comprehensive schools. He found that high-ability comprehensive pupils had a higher regard for practical subjects than did grammar school pupils, and that low-ability comprehensive pupils had a higher regard for academic subjects than did secondary modern pupils. This he calls 'narrowing the cultural gap'. He found that the amount of agreement between high- and low-ability comprehensive pupils on the social standing of various occupations was higher than that between grammar school pupils (who upgraded white collar jobs) and secondary modern pupils (who upgraded manual jobs). This he calls 'a tendency to greater social unity'. He found, thirdly, that the quality of leisure interests (proportion of 'active' relative to 'passive' ones) among average- and low-ability pupils was higher in the comprehensive schools than in the secondary moderns, while among high-ability pupils the comprehensive average was as high as the grammar school. This he calls 'raising the cultural level'.

The weakness of this study is reported by the author himself, who admits that his comprehensive schools were on the whole newer and characterized by greater enthusiasm among their staff than the segregated schools. On these grounds we are forced to discount the 'raising the cultural level' finding. Making allowance for the unfair advantages of the comprehensive schools, perhaps this finding should be taken as another example of 'narrowing the cultural gap'. In other words, perhaps the comprehensive school raises the quality of leisure interests relative to the secondary modern and lowers them relative to the grammar school.

Finally, there are two studies on non-academic aspects of pupil behaviour that tend on the whole to reject claims for the advantages of the comprehensive school. Currie[29] surveyed 1,400 girls and boys, concluding:

The comprehensive school pupils did not indicate superior attitudes to school, nor to the value of continued schooling. A noted feature of the evidence produced is the general tendency for the modern school groups to possess better attitudes, when compared with the comprehensive groups and to possess at least equally good attitudes to those of the grammar school groups.[30]

Even allowing for Currie's dubious sampling procedures (he chose his schools on the advice of a friendly and 'knowledgeable' headmaster and his pupils were selected by their own headmasters), his findings reinforce the doubts already expressed over the defects of Miller's study.

On the other hand, tending to support the pro-comprehensive position, Currie reports that:

By comparison with other secondary schools, the comprehensive school pupils exhibit far less emotional upsets and tensions, less discouragement with school progress and report stronger feelings of satisfaction and success with their school work.[31]

A more confident assertion that there are no significant differences between the different types of schools comes from a study by Futcher.[32] He studied 770 boys and girls of 14 to 15 years of age in London schools using covariance analysis to control for the effect of I.Q. on attitudes. His conclusion is:

Attitude to school, confidence and social behaviour are positively correlated. All the schools appear to be quite successful, and in general equally so, in fostering these traits. Where differences were significant, it appeared that the Comprehensive School was advantageous to lower modern stream boys, but not to upper modern stream or 'grammar' boys. This was noticeable in the tests of attitude to school and social behaviour . . . Contrary to expectation, it was rarely found that comprehensive schools closed the gap in attitude scores between 'grammar' and 'modern' pupils. In several instances, the gap was even widened.

The advocates of the comprehensive school claim that the opportunity to work and/or play with pupils who are very different from oneself is morally educative in itself or, at least, potentially so. To what extent pupils of different kinds actually do work and play together depends on how the comprehensive school is run. Certainly it cannot just be assumed that they will mix. Previous research suggests that in schools that are streamed, whether they are comprehensive or not, birds of a feather really do flock together rather than mixing with others.[33] If the different types could be got to mix, however, some of the prejudices that generally exist between people of different backgrounds, interests and abilities might be reduced. To that extent they will be more morally educated. On the other hand, if pupils of different kinds are just thrown together in the same school with no special care taken to encourage and facilitate mixing, the opposite could happen. Pupils from the more privileged homes might rise to the top streams, collect all the prizes, and take over the leading positions both as prefects and leaders in extra-curricular affairs. Along with an absence of inter-mixing, this kind of situation could increase prejudice and intolerance on both sides.

(c) *Streaming*. This refers to the grouping of pupils who are presumed to have different levels of ability into separate classes or forms. The main objectives of this arrangement, as stated, are to improve academic learning, but there may also be effects on moral development. Both the issue about streaming and that between comprehensive and separate schools have a basic element in common: they both have to do with how far dissimilar kinds of pupils are brought together or separated in schools. Separate streamed schools clearly separate the different kinds most thoroughly, and unstreamed comprehensives the least. Streaming within the comprehensive may introduce a very high level of separation too. Thus the difference between education in comprehensive and separate schools depends on whether there is streaming within them or not. It could be that the unstreamed comprehensives produce better morally educated pupils than the streamed separate schools, but that streamed comprehensives have relatively little advantage over the separate schools – or even none at all. This is, of course, mere conjecture aimed solely at clarifying the questions to be answered by research.

There have been many studies designed to assess the effect of streaming on academic learning, but the results have been contradictory and confusing. The only point established with some consistency is that teachers on the whole prefer teaching streamed classes and believe that streaming improves attainment. A study by Daniels[34] in Britain, where the great majority of primary schools are streamed,[35] found that children in unstreamed primary schools drew ahead of others with similar I.Q.s who were in streamed schools. However, the two most impressive studies (one concerning primary schools in the U.S.A.[36] and the other concerning secondary schools in Sweden[37]) both concluded that streaming or ability grouping had no clear-cut effect on academic attainment, either positive or negative.

Some writers have considered the effect of streaming on pupils' self-esteem or morale. While it has been possible to show that morale is poorer in lower than in higher streams,[38] it has not been shown that low achievers are happier in unstreamed schools than in the low streams of a streamed school. It is still an open question.

Problems of prime concern in this area would seem to include the following: How does the pattern of interaction between pupils of different abilities, interests and backgrounds vary with different degrees of streaming? To what extent do other arrangements (such as a strong house system) within the school that is streamed boost the interaction level? Is there any relationship between the amount of such interaction and the amount of prejudice or tolerance among pupils?

(d) *Houses or other Sub-Units within the School*. It is widely assumed that houses make an important contribution to the process of moral education. If we consider the grounds on which this assumption might be based, we find some interesting points of convergence with some of our previous factors. Since the house usually cuts across ability levels as well as age levels there is the possibility of social mixing and development of tolerance (if these two are related, as we hypothesize). Since the house is smaller than the whole school it is presumably easier to identify with, like the small school. Then again, the rôle of housemaster usually requires him to be concerned with 'the whole pupil' rather than just his academic work in certain subjects. Thus the relationship to the housemaster may be another factor of importance: the fact of having another guide, philosopher and friend aside from subject-teachers, form-teacher and head.

The house may account for more or less of the pupils' energies and loyalties. The more it does, the stronger I would expect its effect on pupils to be. This need not be a good moral effect, for the close, folk-like community of the house may as easily inculcate values of bullying and sadism as those of tolerance and brotherliness.

It may be instructive to compare the British institution of the house with the American fraternity or sorority, which also functions within the secondary school and is a more immediate focus of activities, loyalty and intra-school competition. Unlike the house this is a selective and voluntary association. One is not automatically assigned to membership but rather competes for it. Not all who wish for membership can have it, and some will have to settle for membership in a fraternity that is generally agreed to be not the best. Houses, on the other hand, can more easily maintain the belief among their members that theirs is the best house. Lastly, it is necessary to note that the selection-criteria and values of the fraternity-sorority system are generally 'social' in the snobbish sense. This is a reflection and result of the fact that they are not controlled by the teachers (except very minimally), but are run by the senior pupils and former members.

(e) *Teaching Methods*. We can assert with some confidence that here we have one of the most important factors of all. A study of U.S. primary schools already cited[39] concluded that in accounting for differences between pupils in their academic attainment the differences between teachers counted for more than even the differences in pupils' I.Q.

One line of theory and research has examined the effect of the teachers' degree of authoritarianism on the pupils' development. Over twenty years ago Anderson and others[40] showed how a dominating infant teacher who curbed the pupils' spontaneous ideas to a relatively great extent produced more rebellious and aggressive behaviour among her pupils than a less dominating teacher. Unfortunately this study was confined to only two teachers and their classes. A more recent study by Flanders,[41] involving thirty-two teachers, classified them according to the degree of pupil-participation which they permitted or encouraged. He found that in classes with more pupil participation there was more successful academic learning, and fewer discipline problems: and pupils' attitudes were more constructive and independent. This was true for both maths and English classes. Flanders emphasizes that the teachers who encouraged more pupil participation did not do so indiscriminately. At some stages of a learning project they exerted decisive leadership, and at others they concentrated on eliciting and organizing pupils' ideas. The outstanding feature of these successful teachers was perhaps their flexibility in varying their rôle-playing according to the situation.

The factor of authoritarianism or dominance in teaching falls readily into a larger picture, in which several factors coalesce to produce two teacher-types contrasted in several ways at the same time. With a certain amount of caricature, we may distinguish these two types of teacher: the traditional, academic, 'subject-oriented' teacher and the progressive, 'pupil-oriented' teacher. These two types represent the extremes. Although most of the profession will fall well in between them, the descriptions of the extremes should help us to recognize smaller differences among the mass.

The subject-oriented teacher believes in the paramount educational value of his subject or 'discipline', and so places very great importance on following and covering a syllabus. (This is independent of any need to pass external exams, however.) Therefore, he tends to deprecate digressions or discussions, and likes the flow of talk to be very one-sided – from *his* side. After all, he does know more than his pupils. He believes in being rather formal and distant in his relationships with pupils, confining them in any case to the lesson-situation. This kind of teacher does not feel he needs to know about the backgrounds and interests of his pupils and, in any case, does not feel he has to make much effort to relate his lessons to the things they understand and care about. He does not expect pupils to appreciate the value of the rigorous intellectual discipline that he has to offer, or to submit willingly to the arduous training

required. Hence he accepts that a good deal of coercion ma
be necessary in education.

The contrasted 'pupil-oriented' teacher wants above all t
get pupils involved in their work. So he is pleased to pursue
spontaneous discussion that some pupil initiates even if it is
from some points of view, a digression. This kind of teache
believes in being quite informal and friendly with his pupil
outside lessons, and he is interested in their personal growth i
the widest possible way.

Whether teachers can be classified in this way remains to b
seen. Whether the various characteristics hang together in th
way I have suggested also remains to be seen. Above all, i
remains to be seen whether the pupil-oriented teacher, who i
actually concerned with the moral education of his pupil
actually tends to produce more morally educated pupils o
not.[42]

Some readers may wish to protest at any attempt to dissec
the teaching process in this kind of superficial analytic way. T
make the attempt is certainly not to deny that teaching is a
exceedingly subtle process. Indeed one can only hope to teas
out of it the most limited kind of evidence as to what it is like.[43]
But those who suppose that the behaviour of the teacher in th
classroom is too complex and elusive to be analysed have in fac
been proven wrong by the ingenuity of some researchers. O
course they are very far indeed from being able to trace the result
of different kinds of teaching; but they have been able to pin dow
some of the patterns and variables in teachers' behaviour.

For example, a large American research project reported b
Ryans[44] involved trained observers watching teachers in th
classroom and rating their behaviour on eighteen separat
variables, such as the extent to which they were fair or partial
kindly or harsh, confident or uncertain, stimulating or dull. O
statistical analysis it was found that these eighteen variables fe
into three clusters, which means that teachers who were rate
highly on one tended to have high ratings on other variables i
the same cluster. The three clusters were warmth or friendliness
being systematic or businesslike, and imaginativeness. Whe
relationships among the three clusters were examined, there wer
significant and provocative differences between primary an

secondary school teachers. Among primary school teachers all three clusters were highly intercorrelated. That is, those who were warm and friendly were also likely to be businesslike and also likely to be imaginative. Among secondary school teachers, however, the three clusters were much more nearly independent of each other, especially the friendly and businesslike ones. That is, secondary school teachers who are friendly are neither more nor less likely to be rated as businesslike than those who are aloof. Conversely, knowing that a secondary school teacher is rated as businesslike does not enable one to say whether or not he is friendly or aloof.

One possible inference from this would be that the rôle of the primary school teacher is more consensual or generally agreed upon. Primary school teachers are either good or not so good; all are aiming at the same standards of performance – friendly, imaginative and businesslike. Secondary school teachers may be aiming at different standards, though, since there are different concepts as to how their rôle should be played, perhaps subsumable under the 'traditional *versus* progressive' dichotomy already discussed. Thus the traditional concept of the teacher might be businesslike, aloof and either imaginative or 'routine'; and the progressive concept might be businesslike, friendly and imaginative.

Of course the analysis of teaching methods cannot ignore the kind of pupils being taught. The kind of teacher who is successful with middle-class and ambitious pupils may not be successful with unambitious, working-class pupils. Research will have to take account of this point: and if it not only upholds the general idea, but can specify what kind of teacher works best with what kind of pupil, then a certain amount of re-assigning of teachers could boost the effectiveness of our schools quite easily. At least this is easier than retraining programmes.

The social interaction of teacher and pupil is bound to be affected by the attitudes and expectations which each of them holds with respect to the other.[45] About this we know very little as yet. We suspect, of course, that pupils from different backgrounds have a different image of the teacher and a different set of attitudes towards him or her. One suggestion is that they differ not just in how favourably they look upon teachers, but rather

in the conditions on which they are prepared to adopt a favourable attitude. Thus it may be that working-class pupils have just
as favourable an attitude as middle-class pupils to a teacher whom
they regard as competent and conscientious, perhaps even more
so. When they consider he is not, however, the working-class
pupils withdraw their favourable attitude. Unlike the middle-
class pupils, it seems, they have not been trained to accept the
authority of people on the basis of their position or office
alone.[46]

  If this hypothesis could be shown to be correct it would, in a
sense, only advance our understanding as far as the next question: that is, on what sort of basis do pupils of different kinds of
backgrounds evaluate the performance of their teachers? What
do they expect from them? Various unsystematic impressions
and fragments of data suggest that failure to adjust to school
(mainly among lower-status families) is much more common at
the secondary level than it is in the primary school. This could
be due in part to the age of the child. Also, I suggest, it is due
to the change in the teacher-pupil relationship between primary
and secondary school. The change from the friendly, intimate
pupil-oriented teacher of the primary school to the relatively
aloof, impersonal, subject-oriented teacher of the secondary
school is much harder for the pupil from a working-class background than it is for the middle-class pupil. The latter has had a
better training for dealing with relationships that are governed
by impersonal rules rather than by the wishes of the individuals.
He has also had better training in the ability to organize his life
into different departments and keep them separate. Both the
impersonality and the segmentation of rôles in the secondary
school are, I suggest, two of its features which are especially hard
for the working-class pupil to cope with.

  Similarly, the attitudes and expectations of the teacher towards the pupil need investigating; and the most fruitful approach is possibly to look for differences related to the social
background of the teachers. According to the social class of their
parents, they could be either upwardly or downwardly mobile
or they could be stationary. In Britain quite few teachers come
from upper- or upper-middle-class homes,[47] qualifying as
downwardly mobile. About a third of the men and rather less of

he women come from manual-working-class homes, so qualify-
ng as upwardly mobile. The remainder come from 'intermediate
homes'. According to their exact position within the teaching
profession and their fathers' exact position within the intermediate category, they could be stationary, or upwardly or downwardly mobile.

The teacher who has been upwardly mobile, presumably
by reason of strong ambition, plenty of deferred gratification and
hard work, may find it extremely hard to deal sympathetically
with pupils who are not ambitious and hard-working. The
teacher who has voluntarily been either stationary or downwardly mobile, not because of failure to succeed in another
profession but because of some positive draw to teaching, may
be more successful because he can accept the validity of values
besides those of ambition and achievement better than his
colleague can. At present this is speculative; although Himmelweit has shown that teachers who had been most sharply
upwardly mobile had the most authoritarian attitudes, and were
more likely to feel that 'the wrong type of child' was allowed into
he grammar school.[48]

f) *Curriculum.* It seems reasonable to suppose that the subjects
that pupils study in school make some difference to their moral
education. By this I do not mean that some subjects are inherently
more morally educative than others – I think this may be argued
either way. Rather I refer to the view that it does one more good
to study or do things one wants to study or do rather than things
one does not want to. Of course, pupils cannot be left to decide
for themselves whether to learn to read or not or whether to
learn basic arithmetic – though I think every possible effort
should be made to make it as enjoyable as possible for them.
Beyond these really basic intellectual skills, though, I would
hypothesize that a relatively wide element of choice by pupils,
in what they will study and how, will lead to their being better
educated morally and even academically too.

If we wish to make a real effort to arouse interest and involvement, however, we have to do much more than just produce text
books with colour-pictures entitled: *Fun with Ancient History.*
We have to admit many more subjects and activities to the school

curriculum. Indeed I would think that there are few things from which some educational value may not be prised by the ingenious teacher; producing plays, mending broken toys, making new ones, learning to play the mouth organ, visiting places of interest and writing reports, producing a magazine, dismantling an engine and putting it together, conducting an opinion survey, camping, and so on.

Of course they can do things like this in extra-curricular clubs or youth groups. The point is that only those pupils who are already relatively well-educated morally (or on their way to being) take part in these groups voluntarily. What this suggestion involves, in effect, is bringing the groups or clubs into the normal school day, so that those who most need these activities will get them. The implicit assumption is that they will benefit more from these things than they do from the more conventional lessons.[49]

(g) *Studying Separately or in Small Groups*. The word 'classroom' automatically conjures up for most people a picture of many pupils sitting at separate desks, all pointed towards a teacher who sits or stands at the front and devotes considerable efforts to preventing pupils from communicating directly with each other. There is, however, another kind of classroom – one where pupils do at least some of their work in groups. What are the advantages and disadvantages of the two systems? Once more the situation is that we do not know. All we can do is to summarize the arguments on the two sides.

The traditional view is that pupils will 'mess about' if allowed to work together and will learn less than if they worked alone. On the other hand, it can be argued that working together makes the work less tedious, and so more is done and the pupils learn more. It is sometimes claimed, by those who argue this, that individuals who fool around will be brought to task by their peers. Whether that is true we do not know, but even if it is not the teacher can still perform this function. The assumption made here is that group working elicits more enthusiasm and motivation from pupils than individual working because each individual's efforts are then a contribution to a group goal, and if successful are rewarded by the favourable attitudes of his peers.[50] (If the group has had some choice in what it is working on, one would expect it to generate more motivation still. This is a separate point, however, and was briefly discussed above – under 'Curriculum'.) It may also be hypothesized that group working helps to develop some basic social skills, such as perceptiveness of the expectations of others, the ability to fulfil them (and the ability to evade them gracefully); and that it fosters the development of a secure self-image, relatively free from anxiety. Both hypothesized results of group working would appear to be necessary conditions for good moral education.

The danger here, from the standpoint of moral education, is that group working might make pupils very other-directed: that is, extra-sensitive to the expectations of their peers, but no more able to withstand them. One way to prevent the working groups from becoming too oppressive would be to make sure that the same pupils did not work together for too many different subjects. More important, though, is probably the rôle of the teacher. If he or she intervenes firmly on behalf of deviant pupils, it might be possible to establish the principle of tolerance on the one side and standing up for what you think right on the other.

The working group could also function as a discussion group with guidance from the teacher, evaluating the performance and behaviour of members. This might work as a means of releasing tensions both inter-personal and intra-psychic and clearing the ground for higher standards of moral behaviour. Or, again, it might work oppressively, to force all members into conformity with the ideas of the controlling element. The rôle played by the teacher could, once more, be crucial in determining which way the discussion group developed. If it developed in an undesirable way, of course, it could be dissolved quite easily.

The last three factors discussed here (curriculum, teaching methods and group/individual working) are likely to be closely related in practice – so closely that my insistence on considering them separately may seem artificial to some readers. Some of these inter-relationships are as follows: The expanded curriculum implies teachers who are sufficiently pupil-oriented to be able to build the bridge between pupils' interests and the educational aims of the school. The pupil-oriented teacher will want to employ such a curriculum, since it seems necessary to develop the pupils' character in the broadest way, and will also favour some use of group working for the same reason.

The expanded curriculum can only be operated effectively by pupil-oriented teachers. No subject-oriented teacher would be flexible or broad enough to cope with the range of subjects and activities. Nor would he have the understanding of pupil-culture necessary to build bridges from it to the official culture of educationalists. Whereas the pupil-oriented teacher would welcome curriculum-broadening as offering more potential involvement for many pupils, the subject-oriented teacher would oppose it as a betrayal of traditional academic standards to those of the pop culture and audience ratings. The group method, requiring more subtle forms of supervision by the teacher, seems to call for the pupil-oriented one: and it is this kind of teacher who is more likely to favour group methods, because of their greater potential for arousing pupil involvement and aiding his personal growth in ways not known to the traditional individualistic approach.

(h) *Boarding or Day School* and (i) *Single-sex or Coeducational*. These two pairs of differences have been much discussed, and various views and hypotheses put forward (often in a way betokening great strength of feeling or prejudice). It has been variously suggested that boarding schools develop consideration for others and a sense of responsibility: that they generate homosexuality: that they form a tightly-integrated community which suits adolescents : that they are 'unnatural' and 'artificial': that their proper function is to educate children whose home background is disastrous: that they are needed to produce an élite of future leaders.[51] (I omit arguments based on grounds of politics or justice, rather than on educational considerations.) Similarly it has been argued that coeducational schools exercise a civilizing influence on their pupils: that they make life more difficult or embarrassing for growing adolescents: that they are essential for 'sex education': that they offer a more 'natural' background for education: that they are more 'unnatural' and 'artificial' than single-sex schools.[52]

The reader must excuse us from any discussion of these points here, for two reasons. First, it is not at all clear what exactly is *meant* by the categories 'boarding' and 'co-educational'. Much that is said and written about boarding schools seems in reality to be about independent schools of high status: some of these are not wholly or primarily boarding schools at all (e.g. St Paul's and Westminster), though they may share many of the characteristics of boarding schools. Is the criterion of a boarding school simply that the pupils sleep on the premises? Or that they take their meals there? Or that they spend most of their time there in the evening? These and other factors may be important for moral education. Again, 'coeducational' might cover a range extending from the school which permits certain minimal relationships with the opposite sex on rare occasions, to the school where boys and girls live together in the fullest possible sense. Boarding coeducational schools are plainly very different from day coeducational schools. The categories are so blurred, and overlap so much, that it is hard to say anything both helpful and unambiguous.

Secondly, and more importantly, practically no serious research has yet been published in either field,[53] although various pictures have been painted, in very different colours, of boarding and coeducational schools. The only piece of completed research which may be worth mentioning here has shown the existence of *some* differences between single-sex and coeducational schools. The difference in question has nothing to do with moral education. It concerns the average number of 'O' level passes in the G.C.E., in which single-sex schools tend to do better than mixed schools (except, curiously, in the case of middle-class girls).[54] This has no direct interest, except insofar as it suggests that it is not entirely ludicrous to think that the sex composition of schools might affect the influence they have on their pupils.

Working towards some understanding of how schools of different kinds function, I think this is the way we must proceed: We begin by comparing schools and establishing some of the points on which they differ. From this we work towards identifying some of the organizational features which are essential to their functioning. Then, looking at the way these features vary from school to school, we try to assess how the variations affect the working of the school. Lastly we attempt to grasp the way in which the various organizational features of the school interrelate in the actual life of the school.

In the discussion of this section we have stopped short of the last task – and of course this is very unsatisfactory. We are rather in the position of the student watch-maker who has taken his first few clocks to pieces but cannot put them together again. True, he is not much use to someone with a broken clock: but he does *know* more about clocks than the man in the street. Obviously he cannot be satisfied with such a restricted understanding of clocks, and we cannot be satisfied with our present understanding of schools. However, at the time of writing it does not seem to me that a reasonable essay can be made in this direction. Clearly, though, that will be our next and most urgent priority. I am only concerned that the reader should not think that the kind of static and 'mechanistic' analysis presented here represents in any way our notion of what the sociology of the school is about.

This section has only dealt with some of the more obvious factors of school organization. Some readers will feel that I have ignored the most important factors for moral education which are traditionally supposed to be the 'atmosphere' of the school and the charismatic qualities of the headmaster or other teachers. The 'atmospheric' factor I have not included, partly because it seems to pose especially severe problems of definition and measurement, and partly because I think it may be regarded as a product of the kind of organizational factors discussed above. If so, it is not only easier but more fruitful to deal with the latter directly.

There is a further reason for my disinclination to take these traditional 'explanations' very seriously in this context. Suppose it is true that a dynamic headmaster is extremely important for successful moral education. What can be done? Can every chief education officer pull a dozen dynamic headmasters out of central stores and put one in each of his schools? No, because the quality is a rare one – perhaps trainable but not manufacturable. If however, it could be shown that streaming or non-streaming gave better results (on some agreed criterion), then almost every school in the country could implement the finding and benefit from it. If we discovered that one kind of teacher rather than another got better results, the implications would be a little more complex. Colleges of Education, Departments and Institutes of Education could reorient their selection procedures and teacher-training courses accordingly and offer retraining programmes. But, since teaching depends upon basic personality factors as well as training, changes could not be so quickly implemented as in the former (streaming) example. The question 'Who shall retrain the retrainers?' is not as serious as it might appear, since there are teachers and teacher-trainers espousing different views of the teacher's rôle. It is a matter of handing over control to those whose views will have been supported by research.

Postscript

There is a certain similarity between moral education and launching rockets. To get the rocket launched on course, each of the rocket's stages must be ignited at the right time: and to get a person on the way to being morally educated it seems that he or she must have certain kinds of experiences at certain stages of life.[55] Thus in the first months of life a secure and affectionate relationship with a mother is necessary. At later stages the child needs a father who is affectionate but sets definite standards, good relationships with playmates of the same age, and teachers and other adults who command his respect. When we know more about the human developmental process we may be able to isolate the critical periods for each of these and other experiences. Even at present, though, we can be fairly confident that if an infant is severely deprived of a mother's (or mother substitute's) affectionate care, he or she will not easily be morally educable, however much care is lavished on him or her later. (This is like failure of the rocket's first stage. If and when the second stage fires the rocket will have already crashed to the ground.) But success at the first stage does not guarantee eventual success. That comes only if subsequent stages are performed appropriately and within the time limits. Thus children from homes that meet the minimum standards may go to inadequate schools, and so fail to become morally educated. Or their schools may be satisfactory, but after leaving school they may be deprived of necessary facilities for recreation and further development. Thus there are several stages at which the process of moral education or development may break down.

To elaborate this point (at the cost of violating the rocket analogy), it may be hypothesized that the less adequate is any given stage of a person's moral education, the greater are his chances of failing at a later stage. Put differently, this means that in order to attain a given level of moral education those who have had relatively poor experiences at the earlier stage will need relatively superior chances at the later stage. If this is desired it seems to be necessary for public agencies to intervene in some ways to ensure that this happens. Otherwise what most often seems to happen is that children from the most disadvantaged homes go to the most over-crowded schools with the least qualified teachers, while those who go to the 'best' schools with the most favourable pupil-teacher ratios are generally those from the most privileged homes.[56]

If policy-makers wish to improve the level of moral education, therefore, the earliest phases of the child's experience should have first priority. They may be tackled through parent education; one can try to persuade parents to treat their children differently; one can try to make it easier for them to do so by training them in family planning, for example; one can supplement the family by providing nurseries and play-centres for the very young, and by providing better primary schools (with smaller classes, for instance).

It may be that the impact one can make on the family situation is quite limited. But in the school and the provision of youth facilities there seems to be a great deal that could be done. Some of the relevant factors have been mentioned in what has been written above, and in Part III we shall consider some practical suggestions.

B.N.S.

Notes to Chapter 8

1. See for example Kurt B. Mayer, *Class and Society* (New York: Random House).

2. Joseph A. Kahl, *The American Class Structure* (New York: Holt, Rinehart and Winston).

3. The following section draws quite heavily on J. Klein, *Samples From English Cultures* (Routledge and Kegan Paul).

4. B. Barber quoted in B. Berelson and G. A. Steiner (eds.), *Human Behavior* (New York: Harcourt, Brace and World) p. 486.

5. B. Bernstein, *A Socio-linguistic Approach to Social Learning*, in J. Gould (ed.), *Penguin Survey of the Social Sciences* (Penguin Books).

6. Max Weber, *The Protestant Ethic and the Spirit of Capitalism* (New York: Scribner).

7. Louis Schneider and S. Lysgaard, 'The Deferred Gratification Pattern', *American Sociological Review*, XVIII (April 1953), pp. 142–9.

8. Someone may do something, intending A to follow it but because of his bad judgement B may follow instead. How we classify such behaviour in moral terms is a tricky point – and in any case one for the philosopher not the social scientist.

9. See for example H. T. Himmelweit, 'Social Status and Secondary Education since the 1944 Act', in D. W. Glass (ed.), *Social Mobility in Britain* (Routledge and Kegan Paul).

10. M. L. Kohn, 'Social Class and the Exercise of Parental Authority', *American Sociol. Review*, XXIV (1959), pp. 352–66.

11. Marian Winterbottom, 'The Relationship of Need Achievement to Learning Experiences in Independence and Mastery', in J. W. Atkinson (ed.) *Motives in Fantasy, Action and Society* (Princeton, N.J.: Van Nostrand).

12. Fred L. Strodtbeck, 'Family Integration, Values and Achievement', in A. H. Halsey, J. Floud and C. A. Anderson (eds.), *Education, Economy and Society* (New York: Free Press).

13. Margaret Mead, *The American Character* (Penguin Books).

14. See also Part II (A), pp. 100–101.

15. Survey data from many different countries supporting this point is reported in S. M. Lipset, *Political Man* (Garden City, N.Y. Doubleday), Chapter 4 ('Working Class Authoritarianism').

16. See Part I, pp. 192–5.

17. J. W. B. Douglas, *The Home and the School* (MacGibbon and Kee), p. 46.

18. John Webb, 'The Sociology of a School', in *British Journal of Sociology*, XIII (1962), p. 264.

19. A. M. Carr-Saunders, H. Mannheim and E. C. Rhodes, *Young Offenders* (C.U.P.), Chapter 5.

20. H. A. Presser *et al.*, 'Social Conditions for Successful Learning', in Oeser (ed.), *Teacher, Pupil and Task* (Tavistock).

21. Talcott Parsons, 'The School Class as a Social System', in A H. Halsey *et al.* (eds.), *Education, Economy and Society* (New York Free Press).

22. When we can produce satisfactory measures of the morally educated person, then heads can stand up on speech day and announce that 'although school X got more G.C.E. passes *per capita* than we did, their pupils are much less morally educated than ours' – if they really want to

23. I should suspect the reverse.

24. Better still, we should measure pupils on the variables that interest us before entry and after some time in the school, and compare the amount of change.

25. Roger G. Barker and Paul N. Gump, *Big School, Small School* (Stanford University Press).

26. 'Comprehensive Pupils do best in Exams' (*The Observer*, January 17th, 1964: report of a survey by Robin Pedley).

27. Central Advisory Council for Education (England), *Half our Future* (H.M.S.O.), pp. 232–3.

28. T. W. G. Miller, *Values in the Comprehensive School* (Oliver and Boyd).

29. Keith Currie, 'A Study of the English Comprehensive School System with Particular Reference to the Educational, Social and Cultural Effects of the Single-Sex and Co-Ed Type of School' (unpub Ph.D. thesis, University of London, 1962).

30. *ibid.*, p. 258.

31. *ibid.*, p. 386.

32. W. G. A. Futcher, 'A Comparative Study of Attitudes and Personality Traits of Children in Certain Comprehensive, Grammar and Modern Schools in London' (unpub. M.A. thesis, University of London, 1960).

33. Sugarman, 'Teenage Boys at School' (unpub. Ph.D. thesis Princeton, 1966).

34. J. C. Daniels, 'The Effects of Streaming in the Primary School' *British Journal of Ed. Psych.*, XXXI, pp. 119–27.

35. Brian Jackson, *Streaming: an Education System in Miniature* (Routledge).

36. Miriam L. Goldberg *et al.*, *The Effects of Ability Grouping* (Columbia Univ. Press).

37. Nils-Eric Svenson, *Ability Grouping and Scholastic Achievement* (Stockholm: Almqvist and Wiksell).

38. Francis Chetcuti, 'A Study of the Morale of A and C Stream Pupils in Secondary Schools' (unpub. M.A. thesis, University of London, 1960).

39. Goldberg *et al.*, *op. cit.*

40. H. H. Anderson, in R. G. Barker *et al.* (eds,), *Child Behaviour and Development* (New York: McGraw Hill), pp. 439–84.

41. Ned A. Flanders, 'Some Relationships Among Teacher Influence, Pupil Attitudes, and Achievement', in B. J. Biddle and W. J. Ellena (eds.), *Contemporary Research on Teacher Effectiveness* (New York: Holt, Rinehart and Winston).

42. One hypothesis, often neglected by liberals and progressives, is that the *vagueness* of 'progressive' teaching and curricula fails to provide a sufficiently clear framework for the child and hence increases his insecurity: whereas old-fashioned disciplines and subjects – and marked examinations – at least avoid this error. (See Part I, pp. 133–6 and Part III, pp. 406–9). There is still, in many countries, a fashionable belief in the merits of being 'child-centred', 'pupil-oriented', etc., no doubt as a continued reaction against an excessive formalism or authoritarianism that used to be all-pervading and may still be in need of criticism. But in some educational circles (notably in the U.S.A.) the tide of fashion has begun to turn, and one hears a good deal more about the importance of 'discipline', 'authority', 'intellectual bite', and so forth. Until more serious research has been done, however, these fashions are more interesting as indicators of the psychological attitudes of their adherents than as guides for future educational planning.

43. The situation is in principle the same with all scientific endeavours which amount, in effect, to dipping flimsy fishing nets into the vast, swirling and fast-moving waters of Nature. One does not assume that the lifeless bits of evidence dredged up for close inspection show one what the real Nature in action looks like. We stand on the banks and study the stream as it rushes by, formulating theories that try to account for some small feature of its behaviour. Then, considering the extremely limited kinds of evidence we are able to scoop up in our fishing nets, we work out what catches would tend to confirm a particular theory and which would lead us to reject it. For example, the theory that black fish and white fish always avoid each other would have to be rejected if one small fishing net brought up several black and several white fish together. The fact that the fish were dead when examined would not necessarily lead us to conclude that all such fish in the river were dead, since we know that removing them from the water

kills them. Corresponding to the fishing nets are all the techniques devised for scientific observation: the telescopes, microscopes, seismographs, and carbon tests as well as the questionnaires and observation-schedules with which we attempt to study the behaviour of people.

44. David G. Ryans, *Characteristics of Teachers* (Washington, D.C.: American Council on Education).

45. For an excellent discussion of this and other points see Willard Waller *The Sociology of Teaching* (New York: Wiley).

46. D. F. Swift, 'Educational Psychology, Sociology and the Environment', *Brit. Journal of Sociology*, XVI, (December 1965), pp. 345–8.

47. Jean Floud and W. Scott, 'Recruitment to Teaching in England and Wales', in A. H. Halsey *et al.* (eds.), *op. cit.*

48. Hilde T. Himmelweit, 'Socio-Economic Background and Personality', *Internat. Soc. Sc. Journal*, VII (1955), pp. 29–35.

49. It must be reiterated very emphatically that this view is put forward as a hypothesis and nothing more. Some teachers find it convincing; others do not, but the necessary research has not yet been done.

50. O. A. Oeser (ed.), *Teacher, Pupil and Task* (Tavistock).

51. For some of these views see John Wilson's *Public Schools and Private Practice* (Allen and Unwin).

52. See John Wilson, *Logic and Sexual Morality* (bibliography), pp. 139–40.

53. Dr Royston Lambert's work in the boarding-school field is as yet incomplete: but see his contribution in Graham Kalton's *The Public Schools* (Longmans).

54. J. W. B. Douglas and J. Ross, 'The Effect of Sex of School on Academic Results for Sex and Class Categories' (*Where*, May, 1966).

55. Readers with a more traditional disposition may prefer the analogy of a steeplechase to that of the rocket. Either will do just as well.

56. This could only be justified by some theory advocating a leadership-providing élite in the moral sphere. But if anyone holds such a theory, it is nowhere coherently stated or put into practice. See Part I, pp. 100–101.

Part III

WHAT CAN WE DO ABOUT MORAL EDUCATION?

CHAPTER 9

PRACTICAL POSSIBILITIES

IT is an integral part of the job of any operational research project like our own to act as a sort of entrepreneur between the academic disciplines and the world of action (what some people call 'the real world'). The two more strictly 'academic' tasks of (a) establishing a proper conceptual framework, and (b) getting some 'solid' or 'hard' empirical results, do not exhaust our obligations. We have to find out what can, in practice, be *done* with some chance of success. This is implied by the word 'operational'.

The obvious difficulty with this is that we cannot make recommendations until we know what to recommend; and this might be thought a good reason for saying no more here. There are, however, a number of considerations which fall (so to speak) between theory and practice, and the importance of which may help to justify this part of the book. One of the more obvious is that, in the area of moral education, which is still largely uncharted and which nevertheless urgently demands some kind of action, much of the work must inevitably proceed by trial and error. On this point our attitude is tolerably unambiguous. It seems most desirable that teachers and others should try out various practical possibilities in moral education, as indeed they are doing already – in as intelligent and well-informed a way as possible, of course, and with proper regard to the dangers inherent in new methods: but certainly without undue hesitation. This is why it is worth writing briefly about practical possibilities.

One of the things that may inhibit the process of trial and error is the curious view (if it is a consciously held view at all) that inaction is somehow safer, or more respectable, or less open to attack on moral grounds, than action: that sins of omission are less important than sins of commission: that, if we do not know what to do, we ought to do nothing. There is a lot to be said for this principle if one is dealing with some delicately-balanced ecological situation. 'Letting Nature do her work', if you are ill, may very likely be better than taking something that may be beneficial but will more probably upset the situation still further. But moral education is not a 'natural' process in this sense: and one is tempted to suppose that what lies behind inaction is the feeling that if you do something and things go wrong, it's your fault, whereas if you do nothing and they go wrong, it isn't. This is certainly not true in any simple sense.

It is easy to overemphasize the breakdown in authority, the uncertainty about morality, and the more concrete phenomena of crime, delinquency, etc., that worry us: and if our concept of moral education were that criticized in Chapter 1 – roughly, that so long as people behaved themselves they could count as 'morally educated' – then we might well conclude that things were not too bad, and be hesitant about initiating changes. But the somewhat more sophisticated and demanding concept that we have outlined suggests that a very great deal is wrong. There is a sense, indeed, in which our criteria make demands more like those of the religious believer, who claims that we are all unprofitable servants however hard we try, than like those of the policeman, who is quite happy provided no actual crimes are committed. Once we bring in the idea of inadequacy at the moral skills, as opposed to the idea of simply not breaking the law or causing overt trouble in other ways, we set our sights not only differently, but much higher.

Where should Moral Education be done?[1]

To make a vague plea for some kind of initiative and experimentation is inevitably to raise the general question 'In what institutions may moral education best be carried on?' Plainly it is not possible to answer this question until we know far more than we do about the empirical facts: and it will never be possible to give it a single answer, since one would want to say different things about different kinds of institutions and different kinds of children. But the question is relevant, not only to any immediate practical possibilities, but to the way in which we should direct our research (for instance, it would be silly to conduct enquiries into the possible moral education of adults in evening classes, if in fact such education can only be effective for children at school or in the family). We have, therefore, to take some sort of stance in the face of the question, even if we cannot answer it properly.

I raise the question primarily because people do, in fact, adopt all sorts of stances towards it which seem muddled or doctrinaire. Some say 'Everything important happens in the home', or 'All the damage is done in the first five years'. Others say 'It's not the business of us parents, what do we send our kids to school for, after all?', or 'The churches ought to take care of all that'. Those in charge of various institutions say things like 'Moral education isn't our job, we're here to teach academic disciplines' or 'to train teachers' or 'to get the children to pass their exams' or 'to produce more technologists'. Of course none of these statements is absurd: but they are very often the product of some kind of conceptual confusion, which is worth a brief examination.

Some of the confusion is caused by a falsely monolithic picture of 'the' right institution to engage in moral education, 'the' critical or formative periods in a person's upbringing, etc. As we have seen, the skills and abilities which define a morally educated person are very various, and it is extremely unlikely that any one age (such as the first five years) or any one arena (such as the family) is all-important. Moreover, even if it were true that all or most of the key critical or formative periods fell within a certain age-group and were determined by a certain institution, we should not be too quick to write off the potential importance of other ages and institutions. For instance, suppose the essential foundations of most moral attributes were laid in the family during the child's first five years: it would not follow that schools had necessarily only a small part to play. We must distinguish between how much influence schools *do* have and how much they *could* have; and the notion of a 'critical period' is partly dependent on what educational or therapeutic techniques are available or could be invented. Consider, for instance, three possibilities:

(a) The nursery school might be able to do a lot for the child in his early years, so that to say simply 'It's the family's job' would be misleading.

(b) Primary and secondary schools might be able to do a great deal by way of *recouping* the errors or misfortunes of family upbringing.

(c) Primary and secondary schools might be able to have *the same sort* of influence that families have, given new arrangements and improved techniques in moral education.

Further confusion is caused by talking about 'the' purpose of an institution – school, university, training college or whatever – as if institutions were allotted purposes by some kind of natural law or divine fiat; whereas in fact we can change institutions and use them for whatever purposes we choose. There is a tendency for authorities to use 'the' purposes of their institutions as alibis: moral education is very difficult, and one is tempted to get out of having to do it if one possibly can – unless one confidently believes in some ready-made authoritarian way of doing it which is easily applicable. Even making all allowances, one can hardly see how this sort of evasion can fail to be both self-stultifying and morally questionable. Self-stultifying, because the avowed aims of such institutions may very well not be adequately fulfilled unless they pay proper attention to the moral and psychological needs of their students: and morally questionable, since any institution which (under whatever terms) has young people in its care can hardly avoid some moral responsibility for their well-being.[2]

The field for both practice and research in moral education is, therefore, wide open. This follows, indeed, from the non-authoritarian and non-partisan concept of moral education that we have put forward: for it is fairly obvious that a liberal concept of this kind is not uniquely applicable to a single type of institution. Indeed, it is perhaps partly because moral education has usually been conceived in partisan or authoritarian terms that it has been (and still is) commonly regarded as the preserve of a particular set of people – the elders, the priests, the parents, the housemasters, etc. Hence, although there are a great many questions to be asked about the particular responsibilities of particular people, and although there are obvious dangers in people becoming over-zealous or fanatical about moral education (in a way which would certainly distort the liberal interpretations we have offered), none of us should be unduly hasty in making general disclaimers of responsibility.

The terms of reference of our own particular research are such that it will be chiefly geared to what might be done in schools and other such formal educational institutions. This is still extremely vague, since this last phrase could include anything from a nursery school to a university: but until we are clearer about what particular institutions might in fact successfully do, we cannot tie ourselves down more precisely. The reasons for concentrating on schools are purely practical. All children have to go to school: and however inefficient schools may be in some directions, they are at least organized institutions with which communication is possible, and which may be induced to take the problem seriously. (Even if it were true that 'everything important is done in the home', it might still be more efficient to tackle the problem via the schools, rather than try to reach all the parents in some direct way.)

Naturally this does not mean that an operational research project of this nature can disregard extra-institutional factors: indeed, what can in practice be done successfully in schools may be largely determined by those factors. But it is not within our competence to undertake the important but endless general task of why people behave and think morally as they do. We must rather rely, at least to some extent, upon the findings of other workers in this field. Our intention is rather to approach the problem from another angle. To put it roughly, we should say something like 'A morally educated person should display certain characteristics: a lot of people lack some or all of these characteristics: given the psychological and sociological backgrounds, what sorts of things can schools and other institutions do which will generate these characteristics?' We would hope that these things would be tried out in schools, that we should be able to test their efficacy, and hence that we should eventually be able to make specific recommendations. Of course this is to cut a very long story far too short: but it may help to show the extent to which we shall be dependent upon the cooperation and good-will of teachers and other educators as well as of other research workers.

A. SUGGESTIONS FOR THE SCHOOL[3]

There is therefore, I think, a case for mentioning here a few practical possibilities in moral education: but this will be more misleading than helpful, unless we are absolutely clear what sort of case it is. Certainly it is *not* that we are in a position to advocate or recommend any of these possibilities: even those that are now practised in schools and elsewhere have not in general been validated by any very serious empirical research. Nor do we regard ourselves as having some magical intuition or insight about effective methods of moral education. There is no safe way towards finding out the right methods except by hard work.

Rather the case is this: Many people are now beginning to think about moral education (whether under this title or another). Courses and conferences are held on the subject, and not a few teachers are trying out various methods of their own. There are also many who, whilst disclaiming any particular overt interest in moral education, nevertheless do a great deal which comes under this heading. All these people have some concept of moral education; and the methods they adopt will flow, whether consciously or unconsciously, from the sort of concept they have. Now in this book we have put forward a concept which may be new to many: and this concept naturally suggests certain *kinds* of possibilities rather than certain other kinds. It is, then, chiefly for the sake of illustration that these possibilities are worth mentioning. The way in which they could be realized in practice, and their actual efficacy when so realized, are another matter.

 Thus certain very general methods of moral education can be virtually deduced, as it were, from the concept of moral education itself. If moral education implies the ability to have reasons for acting, and to consider other people's interests, etc. it is almost a logical necessity that to develop these abilities we have to educate the child within a social group, in which he learns to talk, to relate to other people in corporate activities, and so on (as opposed, say, to leaving him on a desert island away from the wicked corruption of the world). From this there is a strong presumption, to say the least, that teaching the child to express himself orally and encouraging him to take part in rule-governed group activities are necessary methods of moral education: and from this one might reasonably be inclined to go on to the more specific opinion that, from the point of view of moral education, it would be better if more time were spent on teaching children to describe, explain and argue and less time on getting them to copy things down from the blackboard.

It may not be too misleading, therefore, to extract from our own account of moral education (particularly from the factors in Part II), and from other relevant literature, those general ideas which seem to be particularly important, and in terms of which one might reasonably start thinking about practical methods. They may be briefly listed as follows:

1. The pupil's need for a secure framework in terms of a group-identity.
2. His need for a personal identity in terms of feeling confident, successful, useful, and wanted, particularly in the case of underprivileged children.
3. The importance of close personal contact with adults.
4. His ability to develop moral concepts, and to communicate linguistically.
5. The relevance of rule-governed activities and contracts.
6. The importance of parent-figures and of a firm and clearly-defined authority.
7. The need to channel or institutionalize aggression.
8. The merits of cooperation as against competition.
9. The need to enable the pupil to objectify his own feelings.
10. The importance of getting the pupil to participate, and to make the educational situation 'come alive'.

I must stress that this in no way represents a summary of *all* the most important general ideas: it may well be, for instance, that the personality of the teacher is more significant than any of these rather vague notions. But we are confining our list of possibilities to those methods that might, in practice, and without any very dramatic social or educational changes, be actually used in schools and similar institutions. It would be possible to list other methods or arrangements for schools involving a good deal of long-term planning and reorganization, or to suggest general social changes of a quite different kind, but this is beyond our present scope. What might be done if one could play around at will with school buildings, have as many (and as good) teachers and as much money as one wanted, reorganize the welfare services, and arrange for social and political changes on a large scale, is not here considered. However, this need not perhaps depress us unduly. Insofar as such large-scale changes may be under consideration, they will have to be considered on the basis of what kind of education we want to provide. Such matters as buildings, finance and so forth should be services relating to the actual needs of children, not merely gestures betokening a vague desire for 'education', 'more scientists', 'greater literacy' and so forth.[4] In general one is not impressed by the extent to which large-scale measures are fitted to a proper understanding of children. In other words, it is only by starting from a consideration of what might be done with the children themselves, by existing teachers in existing institutions, that we shall gain a clear idea about what large-scale changes might need to be made.

How these possibilities should be categorized is a difficult matter. Particular categorizations or taxonomies must depend on particular purposes. I would ask the reader to bear in mind the distinctions drawn in Chapter 3 (pp. 138–41), which are for the sake of conceptual clarity only: but particular research designs in the future may require other quite different categories, and it is important to be flexible as well as clear. For our present purposes I have used two categories which are purely *ad hoc* and for convenience. They are necessarily imprecise, and one could have many jolly arguments about what to put under what heading: but I hope they will serve their purpose. They are the categories of *context* and *content*. Both relate to things that might be done, not only by those in charge of institutions – headmasters, principals, wardens, etc. – but also by individual teachers, youth leaders, faculty members and other educators: but they require some comments in their own right.

Context and Content

It is reasonable to suppose that, certainly in moral education and probably in education as a whole, the context in which some activity or form of learning occurs has been unduly neglected, and the content of the learning overemphasized. It is true that progressive educationalists, such as Dewey and others, have stressed the importance of 'child-centred' education, project methods, the play-way and so forth – though these ideas have not, in general, penetrated beyond the primary schools: but it is not clear that they have always done so for the right reasons. If you start by thinking: 'Now, children must learn certain subjects – mathematics, English, history and so forth – so how can we get them to learn these most efficiently?' you may end up with various opinions. You may think that a good old authoritarian method of beating Latin into boys works very well: or you may think that a 'Have fun with your Latin' system pays off better. But in either case you are thinking in terms of efficiency in a *subject*, in terms of a *curriculum*. But there is some reason to suppose that this is not what is required for moral education. It we are concerned with the child's ability to think about his actions, relate to other people and so forth, we shall more naturally consider the *context of communication* in which we put him, rather than what subjects we want him to learn. Thus (to take what may be a misleading example), it may not matter whether the child is learning English or history or mathematics, but it may matter a lot whether the teacher has a certain kind of personality, whether the child is taught to compete with his fellows or cooperate with them, whether the context gives him a chance to know the teacher and talk to him honestly, and so on.

The importance of stressing the content, on the other hand, lies in the need to avoid a hopeless mush and muddle in which the child learns nothing at all. Any context in which we place the child must have a purpose: and the purpose must be to develop some skill, knowledge or ability (whether cognitive or not) which will make the child more morally educated. The context must have point, and the child's performance in the context noted, assessed and improved. We need to establish as clear a set of criteria as possible for each context, so that we – and the child also – know what we are supposed to be doing, can try to do it well, and can observe as clearly as possible when we succeed and when we fail. Of course this is hard, and perhaps in the case of some contexts virtually impossible, to measure precisely. Nor do I suggest that all useful contexts must involve some puritan-ethic notion of effort or striving – a psychotherapeutic group, for instance, would not do so. But we must at least stress the notion of content sufficiently to enable us to answer the general question 'What are we trying to do here?' in as concrete terms as possible.

This is essential if we are to avoid an extension of the fashionable muddle mentioned above. Many people, understandably fed up with a solid curricular diet of Latin, French, mathematics and so forth, and laudably anxious to improve the children as people rather than just as potential examinees, remain dominated by the notion of a 'subject' or a 'curriculum'. Consequently they throw some subjects, like Latin grammar (which is at least intelligible if perhaps not very morally educative) out of the window, and admit a host of non-subjects with names like 'learning to live', 'human relations', 'citizenship', 'environmental studies', and so forth. They then try to structure the curriculum round these pseudo-subjects, under some such general title as 'response to life' or 'man and his environment'. There is nothing wrong with these phrases, so long as we know exactly what disciplines they are supposed to contain, and what counts as practising them successfully. But there is a strong possibility that this sort of programme may lose us the force and clarity of the old subjects, without gaining anything substantial for moral education.

This is partly because the notions (imprecise as they are) of context and content may become muddled up with the notion of an educational *aim*. What happens is this: we feel strongly that we want to achieve a certain result – to produce children who are 'mature', 'good citizens', 'cultured' or whatever. We may then simply translate these aims into 'subjects', which we call 'citizenship' or 'culture'. What we have omitted to do is to *break down* our aim or objective into its real components. Thus 'culture' isn't the name of a single pursuit which can be taught successfully between 10 and 11 every morning: to want 'cultured' people is to want people who have been initiated into a number of specific activities, each with their own standards – people who have read certain books, appreciate certain music, and so on. Until we break down our aims in this way we fail to face the two questions (a) 'What standards is the child supposed to meet in learning this?' (content), and (b) 'In what contexts can he best learn to meet them?' (context). Unless we are clear about these questions, we may produce nothing but a general muddle.[5]

Some of the possibilities which follow could not be described as educational processes (see pp. 138–41), but aim rather at establishing the preconditions necessary for such processes to be effective. But where the possibilities can be strictly called educational, we must (in view of what we have said above) try to get as clear as we can about the content before asking questions about the context. For unless we know what are the standards relevant to the educational process in question – what the child is supposed to be *learning* – we are not likely to be clear about what context will best enable him to meet those standards. It is, no doubt, reasonable to guess that a context of, say, close communication between pupil and teacher, or a friendly as opposed to a sarcastic or hostile atmosphere, will be effective for many different types of content. But it is still extremely important, for the reasons given above, that we should cash out our educational aims in terms of content first (as far as this is possible), and assess context in relation to these, rather than *vice versa*.

Since the possibilities that follow, as we have said, are extremely general, and intended primarily as an illustration of the concept of moral education as we have outlined it, we hope that teachers and other educators will not be inhibited from following their own ideas in the meanwhile. We hope however that they will be able to follow them more satisfactorily if they bear in mind what we have written so far: and perhaps some of the possibilities that follow may at least arouse their interest. Some may regard them as fantastic: to others they may seem boringly obvious. Others again, in my view more reasonably, may think them interesting but too vague, rightly maintaining that in such matters almost everything depends on exactly how, and by whom, any of the possibilities should be put into practice with specific groups of children. All we can do here is to suggest a few general lines of approach.

Some practical suggestions

(I) CONTEXT

(i) Making sure that the concept of moral education is properly understood, and that the task of moral education is responsibly undertaken.[6]

(ii) Making whatever basic arrangements are necessary to bring the pupils into communication with the educators.[7]

(iii) Making sure that the 'ground rules' of the institution are
(a) based on the right *sort* of criteria (even if there is uncertainty about the facts), and
(b) firmly enforced.[8]

(iv) Making the rules, and the point of the rules, as clear as possible to the pupils.[9]

(v) Giving the pupils some degree of self-government, and establishing close communication in rule-making and rule-following.[10]

(vi) Decentralizing the institution to produce psychologically viable groups[11] (e.g. a house system): basing the groups on factors that genuinely unite (e.g., perhaps, eating together, entertaining other groups, and other group activities which are significant to the children), without producing an artificial or illiberal community.[12]

(vii) Providing outlets for aggression, both in the 'letting off steam' sense (e.g. enough violent open-air activities) and in the 'challenging authority' sense (e.g. matches against the staff), that are unsophisticated enough to fit even the most primitive pupils (some kind of controlled fighting game, snowballing, battles in the swimming-bath, etc.).

(viii) Providing contexts which will significantly occupy the institution as a whole (e.g. some construction enterprise, mass camping or exploring, dancing, singing, etc.).[13]

(ix) Arranging the criteria of success in the institution, insofar as some competition is inevitable (and perhaps desirable), so that everyone succeeds in something and acquires some prestige and self-confidence thereby.[14]

(x) Arranging that there is some one person (e.g. the headmaster) who acts as the ultimate authority (at least in a psychological sense, so far as the children are concerned); and who is actually on the premises, and visibly concerned with the day-to-day running of the school.[15]

(xi) Making the significant teaching unit a small group, with the same 'teacher' or adult group-leader, perhaps over a period of years, with whom the pupils can form a close personal relationship: and fitting 'specialist' or subject-teaching as far as possible into this framework.[16]

(xii) Compensating for the increased man-hours (necessitated by smaller groups) by giving the children more free time, by using mass communication (e.g. closed-circuit TV) for factual information, by providing other contexts in which large numbers can be handled together (e.g. large-scale games, gymnastics, etc.), and by making more use of older children to supervise and help the younger.[17]

(2) CONTENT

(i) Understanding of concepts and meaning: this (in an elementary form) involves the notion of 'philosophy' and is designed to produce awareness and mastery of different language uses.

(ii) Understanding of the general concepts, and of the basic facts, of psychology and the social sciences, perhaps particularly anthropology.[18]

(iii) Mastery of other facts relevant to the prevailing morality of the child's society: e.g. the law, the system of government, the economic system, the 'professional ethics' attaching to certain jobs, etc.

(iv) The use of other subjects, perhaps particularly history and literature, designed to increase awareness of other people in society, to reinforce and correlate with (ii) and (iii) above.

(v) Activities designed to objectify moral or psychological problems: e.g. mime, drama, 'acting out' various roles (the bully, the cheat, the practical joker, and so forth), controlled 'group therapy'[19] sessions in which family and other problems are discussed overtly, discussions of particular case-histories of other people (taken from books, films or elsewhere).

(vi) Using 'psychological documentary' films and tape-recordings, with subsequent discussion to objectify the pupil's own problems.

(vii) Teaching the child to talk clearly, describe, dispute and acquire other language-using skills.

(viii) Using music and the arts, as relevant to the way in which emotions are objectified.

(ix) 'Religious education' used as a method of obtaining insight[20] and a sane outlook on life as a whole.

(x) Various kinds of games, designed to clarify the concept of rule-following, the point, purpose and mutability of rules, the notion of *contracting for* certain rules, etc.

(xi) The use of 'games', in the sense of microcosmic controlled social situations, acted out for special purposes under specific rules (e.g. the children act out a 'democracy', a 'dictatorship', etc.): the teaching of particular concepts by means of these games (equality, honesty, duty, justice and so on).

(xii) Teaching related to practical living, e.g. on sex, marriage, infant care, driving cars, dress and cosmetics, the use of money, etc.[21]

(xiii) Opportunities to 'patronize' and feel needed, i.e. to be responsible for and of service to younger children, old people, the poor, the lonely, animals, etc.

(xiv) Use of practical 'order-and-command' contexts, to see the point of discipline relevant to particular situations (e.g. in sailing, mountaineering, building and other operations with highly specific goals).

The implications of this sort of approach for some other fields are tolerably obvious. Thus, it would suggest that the selection of teachers should be on the basis of personality-type rather than academic qualifications or social image: that they should be trained more in such fields as philosophy, psychology and the social sciences: that they should have some kind of personality-training in the form of group therapy, and in general be fitted to use the methods outlined in (1) and (2) above. Similarly, one might suggest also that the excessive *mobility* of teachers made it difficult for any effective or long-standing relationships to be formed with the children, and that there was a case for encouraging teachers to remain in one place for a tolerably long period (rather like housemasters at boarding schools having a longish tenure). There are other implications for the importance of parent-teacher relationships, the concept of teachers who are also social workers, the architecture and topographical arrangements and location of schools, and many other things.

A general question arises here about how far one can expect to formalize, or 'institutionalize', the desiderata which some of these suggestions aim to incorporate. For instance, we may talk about the importance of letting adolescents criticize their schools and teachers: we might hypothesize that, if they are not allowed to do this openly, they will tend to cause trouble in other ('worse') ways instead. So we might recommend, say, that criticisms of this kind should be allowed in school magazines. But now, suppose the teachers dutifully allow this, yet are psychologically unable to handle it: suppose they get very angry, break off communication with the adolescents who use the magazine in this way, and so on.[22] Have we really achieved anything?

No doubt it would be ideally desirable first to select and train teachers who are psychologically adequate to handle this and other such suggestions, and only then to implement them: otherwise we may get no more than an empty form, or an institution which does not do the job it is supposed to do. Sometimes one might even think that premature institutionalization may make matters worse (rather like introducing full democracy into a very backward society). But, on the other side, it is also possible that the acceptance of the institution by teachers means that teachers will be able to learn, from the existence of the institution, how to handle it and react appropriately to it. A good deal of research and trial-and-error is required here.

This point shows, however, the crucial importance of the first stage of moral education: namely, that teachers and others should understand the *general aims* which lie behind the suggestions. If they can understand and accept them, then there is some reason for hoping that they will at least try to handle them properly; and even if they fail, they will know that they have failed and that it is their fault (rather than blame someone else). What we require, therefore, is *intelligent acceptance* on the part of teachers and other educators. This is a very different matter from insisting on a new selection and training process for teachers, which might itself take a great many years to formalize: and in any case, much of the training would be directed towards producing the kind of intelligent acceptance I am talking about.

B. MORAL EDUCATION AND TEACHERS

To go further into this question, however, is unnecessary and might be misleading. It may be more useful to pick up one point[23] made earlier, in connexion with a possible reaction on the part of teachers to new possibilities. Those who have actually to *do* the work (as opposed to just writing about it) in schools and other educational institutions are likely to react to any new educational task as yet another demand on their time, money and energy. 'Oh, lord, now we'll have to do moral education as well as keeping the register and teaching arithmetic and taking games ...' (a school-mistress). This reaction is by no means confined to teachers: 'I suppose you think the Treasury will find money to pay for moral education as well as new school buildings, mumble, keep our priorities straight, mumble, mumble, too large classes, mumble ...' (a civil servant).

It is possible that we argue unconsciously as follows: 'Schools are institutions where teachers teach subjects to children. If you introduce another subject, like moral education, there will be less time for subjects now in the time-table. If you want to add it to the existing time-table, you will have to have more school-hours, which means more teachers and more schools, and perhaps even teachers specially trained to do it. All this will cost money, or be an additional burden on teachers'. This stems from a stereotyped picture of a school. To see how stereotyped it is, imagine a similar argument beginning 'Families are institutions where parents teach subjects to children ...' and ending '... an additional burden on parents'.

We have, I hope, by now a sufficiently clear picture of moral education to appreciate that this reaction is unnecessary. The arguments are as follows:

(a) Even if moral education were 'an additional burden', it is likely that doing it efficiently would save a vast quantity of time and money. Consider the amount we now have to spend because of vandalism and other forms of delinquency, Borstals, probation, illegitimacy and so forth.

(b) 'Moral education' might not involve 'an additional burden' but just a new way of organizing existing subjects, institutions and personal relationships; so that it would demand no more time and money.

(c) More interestingly, moral education might facilitate the educational task of teaching subjects, so that it would save time and money.[24]

Much more research needs to be done before saying anything very definite on this third point, but it is worth pursuing briefly.

Few people can fail to be struck by the enormous wastage in subject-teaching. To take one outstanding example amongst many, a boy who does five periods a week of Latin or French for two academic years with a view to taking 'O' Level has spent nearly 300 hours on the subject, not counting homework. For this number of hours the results are usually rather meagre. What is lacking? Something, one presumes, in the area of motivation: interest, incentive, cooperation, the relationship with the teacher, the boy's psychological attitude to work in general and books in particular – all these are plainly important. Time spent on improving these general factors may be time well spent. Many teachers know very well that if their pupils make some sort of positive transference to them – and this involves factors which have very little to do with time or money – they will make much more progress than could be achieved by hours of continued teaching over the desk-tops in a situation where teacher and pupil know little about each other and care less.

This point is of course a very old one, but it tends to be forgotten: or, perhaps, despaired of. When teachers and other officials have a hard time keeping their heads above water in the existing situation, any suggestion of change is likely to appear as an added burden. Nor does it sound very practical to raise still more general issues – whether moral education is not a more important matter than subject-teaching, or whether there is really any point at all in teaching many of the subjects that we do teach. Even if, as I have argued elsewhere,[25] much of the curriculum is a result of the inertia of tradition and a curious academic myth about 'scholarship' and 'mental discipline',[26] teachers are still paid to teach it. The G.C.E. and other examinations are still there: parents, headmasters and educational authorities still have certain expectations: and teachers have to work the system, however much they disapprove of it. In much the same way, it is not surprising that underprivileged factory workers are more concerned about shorter hours and better pay than any new or exciting concept of running factories. Further, just as the lack of communication and our inability to produce a mechanism for evolving contracts that are freely entered into, and firmly adhered to, has for many years made a hopeless patchwork of our economic system, so too the gulfs fixed between ordinary teachers, headmasters, local authorities, parents, government departments, departments of education and training colleges has produced a situation where the average teacher cannot be expected to do much more than cope adequately with his job, survive, and if possible make a bit more money.

In fact, it appears, at least on a cursory glance, as if teachers 'cope with their jobs' remarkably well: and not only in the academic field. We are still apt to forget, though several inquirers have pointed it out, the vast amount of work that is done in that area which may be variously described as 'moral education', 'the socialization of the child', 'learning to live', 'character training', etc. Much of it, perhaps, is done informally or even unconsciously – as the natural expression of the teacher's personality, in extra-curricular activities or just odd moments during school life, in the way they handle school meals or even the distribution of milk. Much is also done in the context of curricular lessons – perhaps particularly in the teaching of English, or religion, or history. So much is written about juvenile delinquency and other symptoms of the breakdown in authority that we lose sight of what has been and still is achieved on the credit side of the account.

Yet it remains true that teachers are under very heavy pressure; and not all this pressure takes simple forms, such as long hours, not enough pay, and too large classes. Much more important, from the point of view of moral education, are the status and rôle of the teacher. Two brief quotations from one of C. P. Snow's heroes make the point as well as any other. He soliloquizes:

In a sense, I myself have lived by my wits since I was eighteen; a fail ure in an examination, a bad start in research, a mistaken choice – *an I should have been a schoolmaster all my life*; and I shall be old before forget it.[27]

and again, when he is wondering what to do if he gives up pure
science:

Teaching? Not academic teaching, which is instructing people in
unimportant subjects by a method in which one does not believe. But
real teaching, getting into people, feeling with them. I might enjoy it –
but I should run into another catastrophe. For I was too dangerous a
heretic to be allowed power in the most conventional of human activities.[28]

In so far as this feeling is current today, it is at once not very
encouraging for the future of moral education, and a very strong
indication of the changes that need to be made in the status and
rôle of teachers. For the feeling implies the belief that teaching
in schools is a second-rate activity. Lip-service is paid in such
phrases as 'forming the minds of the young', 'having a vocation',
'spreading the light', and so forth, but it cuts no ice. Our society
does not genuinely believe in what Snow calls 'real teaching';
if it did, the teacher would have a higher status, and would be
given the freedom to play this rôle. My guess would be that the
lower financial rewards given to schoolteachers, as against other
professions (including teaching at a 'higher' – significant word!
– level), reflect, rather than engender, this belief. As one teacher
said: 'All the good teachers are getting out, and now that there's
all this higher education it's easier for them to get out. You can
do more of what you want that way – with the students as people
as well as with your subject.'

Of course schoolteaching is not a second-rate activity; but in
order to sustain this belief we have to evolve a new concept of
teaching and new criteria of a 'good teacher'. This can only
happen if we accept some such description as 'moral education'
as a central part of the teacher's rôle: if we succeed in clarifying
this description, hammering it into some kind of practical shape,
selecting teachers with this role in view, training them to carry
it out, and rewarding them accordingly. It is at this point that
our research work is, inevitably, connected with society as a
whole. For much depends, not on what research workers manage
to achieve, but on whether society is prepared simply to recognize what teachers are doing by way of 'moral education'
already, and what they could be helped to do more of in the
future, as central in the way I have described. This is, I think

crucial for teachers themselves: for it is only in this way that a body of men and women perhaps unusual for their intelligence and idealism can get the sort of recognition it deserves.

It is in this wide context that the teacher's role must be understood: and the notions of moral education and – what is intimately connected with it – of mental health give us some indication of where to look for our new standards. As one writer says,

Teaching is peculiar in that the very immaturity of the pupil demands of the teacher greater self-restraint, objectivity and self-knowledge than are demanded of any other professional person except perhaps the psychologist or psychotherapist.[29]

The vagueness of the concept of mental health, and the difficulties of measurement, should not deter us from the most vigorous attacks on this front. Not that teachers do not have many other important roles – the transmission of culture, the straightforward teaching of subjects, the superficial socialization of the child, and so forth: but there is a sense in which his rôle as a moral educator who must himself be morally educated his rôle as a *person*, one might almost say – is crucial.

The crisis in the teaching profession thus represents only one aspect in the general social crisis concerned with the need for new standards; but it is possible that the more general problems may best be tackled in the arena of education. Those many teachers who are dissatisfied with their prescribed rôles, and with the educational system in general, need to be given a clearer set of categories and visible signs by which their new rôle – which, in some language or other, many teachers are already expressing enthusiasm to adopt – may be clearly defined. This is a central task for educational research. How far existing teachers are capable of playing this rôle we do not know: and it would be quite improper of me either to pat the teaching profession on the back or to kick it on the behind. No doubt, as one publication says (in a rather silly and pretentious near-tautology), 'The number of teachers enjoying adequate mental health is undoubtedly limited':[30] but this is not much help. What we want to know is the answer to questions like 'What does "mental health" mean?', 'How do you measure it?',

How do you select teachers on this criterion?', 'How do you train them in "mental health"?', 'Should some teachers specialize in "mental health" or "moral education" and others specialize in teaching specific subjects?', and so forth. These questions await answers.

When we have such answers, it is not absurd to believe that the teacher's rôle, status and training will fall into line behind them. Once we are clear about our new standards, and have some effective way of measuring them and training people to achieve them, teachers may be able to take what I personally would regard as their rightful Platonic place as the proper leaders or guides of the rising generation, and hence of our future society. Those teachers, for instance, who in primary or secondary modern schools happen to be unusually expert in moral education will be properly acknowledged and rewarded, as are those in 'higher' education whose more obviously-testable academic expertise now brings them rewards and status. Instead of one or two simple-minded success-ladders, based on academic attainments, length of training, 'experience' and other criteria which may often be wholly irrelevant to a teacher's actual effectiveness, we may be able to define more clearly different rôles requiring different types of personality and different types of training.[31]

All this is very much in the future. But it is important to consider the problem from this point of view, if only because it is too easy merely to shout for 'more teachers', 'more training colleges', 'higher pay', and so forth. Teachers are not like machinists or skilled artisans: they are not even like dentists or doctors. They deal with whole people, not merely with certain specific aspects or needs of people. Not only in schools, but in universities also, there is a danger that we may treat education as if it were some form of mass production: as if the problems were merely economic or administrative. The teacher or professor, on this view, could easily be replaced by a teaching machine, a set of lecture notes, or closed-circuit television. Much can and should be done in education by such mechanical means: but it is instructive to consider what cannot, in principle, be done. For this brings out the teacher's real rôle. And if we lose sight of this rôle, or fail to devote as much attention, planning and research to it as we devote to other forms of education, then we shall end up with a very thin sense of 'education': and we shall find very few people possessed of any ability or idealism who want to go in for education in this sense.

Notes to Chapter 9

1. See also Part II (A), Chapter 6, and Part II (B), Chapter 8.

2. For instance, boys and girls of 17 may be under a fairly tight school discipline and be living at home: they may a few months later be pitchforked into a university where they are away from home, and under virtually no discipline at all – indeed they may not receive much personal attention of any kind from the staff. It is somebody's job to do something about this. Universities might just argue, I suppose, that it's not their job and that they need not have any policy about it at all. What they can't reasonably do is to *have* a deliberate but muddled policy which fails to meet the real situation.

3. See also Note B (pp. 448–58).

4. See pp. 18–19. Moral education is a classic case: there is not much point in spending money (whether frenetically or grudgingly) on buildings, replanning educational systems, extending the training of teachers and generally making overt moves which may display more enthusiasm than intelligence, unless and until we are reasonably clear about what moral education is and what sort of thing we want to happen to children in schools. And if we are not to be blown by the winds of politics or fashion, this is to some extent a matter for experts.

5. Of course these concepts require a much fuller treatment. See R. S. Peters, *Ethics and Education*, Part One (bibliography).

6. This is boringly obvious, but I suspect it is more than half the battle. For instance, there are some people in some institutions, e.g. housemasters, who are effectively saddled with responsibility for moral education, at least in some sense of the phrase. But elsewhere one has to search hard for such rôles. Searching, one can find and list chaplains, 'moral tutors', 'personal tutors', Deans of Students, Wardens of Halls, proctors, officially appointed psychotherapists and so forth: but the very variety of titles, some of which seem to be more ritualistic than functional, indicates a high degree of incoherence.

Of course there are unsolved problems here. Do we want special 'counsellors', or is it always better to use people who have rôles in the institution already? Who do pupils naturally talk to – their form masters, or their games masters or who? Who has the relevant image or prestige? And how far should all this be formally institutionalized at all, as opposed to leaving it to informal relationships (or to chance)?

7. This again is obvious and vague. But if you are going to morally educate children, then – to put it extremely – your initial approach may

have to be more like an anthropologist winning the confidence of a strange people than like a subject-teacher instilling a particular discipline or handing out information. In many institutions there is, to a greater or lesser extent, a kind of cold war between teachers and children: any serious communication is impossible, and moral education cannot get off the ground because the first step has not been made. What forms this first step should take is not easy to say; but perhaps they would amount to producing something like a family-type atmosphere – which is by no means incompatible with strictness. 'Ordinary' schools and institutions might borrow a great deal in this area from schools for the 'maladjusted', 'emotionally disturbed', and so forth.

8. See pp. 148–54.

9. See pp. 432–4.

10. It is boring and vague to keep talking about communication, but it has to be recognized that its importance crops up everywhere. The dimension of 'strictness–liberality' in rules may be much less important than other dimensions, such as 'consistent–inconsistent' or 'explained–unexplained'. For instance, one school insists on rather strict standards of dress for certain occasions. The justification given is that 'it's good for the children to make an effort and wear something different'. The motivation may be some partisan feeling, quasi-moral or quasi-aesthetic, like 'it looks awful if they don't wear proper suits' or 'jeans are unsuitable for formal dances'. Whether this justification is sound, or this motivation rational, may in fact not matter much: what may matter is whether the staff succeed in getting across to the pupils that they are out to enlarge their experience and help them in the interesting topic of what sort of clothes to wear, and that the rules are designed for that purpose. One may sometimes be tempted to the view that it doesn't matter much if a school has what are in fact unreasonable rules, so long as the staff are – and are seen to be – well-intentioned and sensible as opposed to moralistic or silly.

11. Features relevant to this group, and to the teaching-groups in (xi) below, might be:

(a) Using older pupils to help the younger, or brighter pupils the more backward, with their work.

(b) Using *milieux* other than the classroom; e.g. a camp, a boat, a bus, a skiing party.

(c) 'Staging' the group to suit its activities, e.g. by arrangement of the room, positioning of the pupils, etc.

(d) Uniting the group by primary means of communication, e.g. dancing, drinking, eating, playing games together.

(e) Mixing the group from time to time with members of a different social class, creed, colour, age, sex, etc.

(f) Basing the group on cooperative rather than competitive activities.

Taking this in conjunction with (xi) – and also with (ix) – we can see the kind of problems involved in deciding what sorts of groups we want where and for what purposes. The following points may be relevant:

(a) Particularly if the pupils are going to learn something which requires close personal communication (as opposed to, say, being told the facts of chemistry), the basic teaching unit mentioned in (xi) seems especially important. I should guess that any attempt to 'rethink the curriculum' or 'get away from the subject approach' would fail without a teaching context which produced much closer communication than is customary.

(b) How these groups would fit in with other possible groups (such as a house or a whole school, whether houses should be built up of teaching units or on some other basis, how big either type of group should be – all these are questions requiring further research. And they would of course have different answers for different kinds of pupils and purposes.

12. This points to an unsolved problem. There may be unifying factors – common hatred of the institution, fear of the authorities, excessive and artificially-induced competition with parallel institutions, etc. – which are not morally educative: and there may be harmless factors, which don't really unify, like making a house up out of all those whose names begin with letters A–M in the alphabet and awarding a house cup if the A–Ms get more O Levels than the N–Zs. Which factors genuinely and effectively unite is a question for the social psychologist.

13. The important points here are that the enterprise must (a) be simple enough for everybody, (b) involve everybody, (c) be exciting, (d) be sufficiently self-contained to maintain a coherent and interdependent group. Suppose you got a houseful of 80 boys to construct, with expert assistance, some simple but large Viking-type boat and row it up the Seine or somewhere. This is the sort of thing that might work very well, however naive it may sound.

14. This aims to achieve some sort of equality among the pupils. Some seem to maintain that this is inherently, or perhaps logically, impossible in any society (see, e.g., R. Dahrendorf's essay in *Philosophy, Politics and Society*, second series, ed. P. Laslett). I disagree (see my *Equality*, pp. 180 *et seq.*). But in any case those who control the criteria of success in institutions can do as much as they can in this direction.

15. This is only a guess, and there are those that talk of running schools as oligarchies rather than as supervised monarchies. A dyarchy of headmaster and headmistress may fit the psychological facts satis factorily in some circumstances. But I suspect that many liberal idea in this general area make insufficient allowance for the child's need fo a clearly visible authority and a firm framework. All this needs a lot o further research.

16. See note 11, p. 442.

17. The reaction of many teachers, by now almost automatic bu not unjustifiable, to many practical suggestions is to say 'What can yo do with such large classes?' Of course, this is a crying scandal, and o course a better teacher-pupil ratio would be an enormous help. On th other hand, we may be able to do a lot more than might be supposed, i we are prepared to reorganize drastically. If we start by saying: 'Right so we have to cope with x numbers of children, given y numbers o teachers: how can we do this best?', it is apparent that to organize th children's entire day into a number of set periods and classes is onl one of a number of possible answers; nor is it clear that this is the bes answer, either from the viewpoint of moral education or from mor strictly academic or examination-orientated viewpoints.

18. A part of the myth about 'subjects' tempts us to suppose *priori* that only certain subjects are suitable for children of certain age or ability: 'You can't teach them psychology when they're only fou teen'. 'Philosophy is hard enough for adults, how can you teach it t children?' What causes the trouble here is the idea that words lik 'philosophy' or 'psychology' are for some people irrevocably wedde to certain high-level studies: so that, if one suggested some activit suitable to a young age-group, the reply would be 'Oh well, I don't ca *that* psychology'. To which a brief answer is 'It doesn't matter wha you call it, but it is a useful thing to do; and it's as well to call "psychology" because the activity should have connexions with high level psychology which the teacher ought to bear in mind, and whic might help him to prevent the activity from becoming just a muddle

19. Of course there are all sorts of activities which may do mor harm than good. Much that goes on under such headings as 'grou dynamics', 'personal confrontation', etc., as well as specifically rel gious phenomena like certain forms of 'confession' or 'conversio may be of this sort. These one would hardly call 'therapy' because th effect (if not the intention) seems to be to indoctrinate or conditio not to improve insight and control. (This is the proper objection to certain type of religious evangelist, e.g. Billy Graham: not that wha happens is 'too emotional' – parts of psychoanalysis are very 'em tional' – but that he does nothing to increase rationality, and may i

deed diminish it.) But even when the intention is therapeutic, the effect may be pernicious if the situation is not properly handled, as in 'wild' psychoanalysis. So we have to be careful. See pp. 120–21, and Note B.

20. See H. Loukes, *New Ground in Christian Education* (S.C.M.).

21. The point of this would not be purely to make the content of education more 'real' or 'practical'. It is rather that signs of mental health or ill-health can be clearly pointed out in these areas. For instance, the purpose of teaching children about the use of money would not be solely or even chiefly to explain how little a pound will buy these days, or how you can get a mortgage: one would also want to show how and why people have very different attitudes to money, and how these are more or less rational. Similarly with dress, driving cars, sex and so forth. Thus it isn't so much that people don't know how to drive, in any simple sense: it's just that they sometimes drive, as we say, *like lunatics*. And 'sex education' isn't just a matter of telling the children *facts* (nor of laying down moral codes either): it's a matter of improving their awareness and self-control. See also Note B.

22. See also Chapter 8, pp. 380–85.

23. See p. 21.

24. See also Note B.

25. *Two Types of Teaching*, in R. Archambault's collection (bibliography).

26. That is, much of the curriculum *as taught*: of course a strong theoretical case can be made out for most of the usual subjects (e.g. as R. S. Peters has done in *Ethics and Education*, p. 157 *et seq.*, although I am not wholly convinced by it); but this says nothing about either what happens in practice, or – perhaps just as important – about the kind of reasons teachers themselves use as justifications and the way they present these reasons to pupils.

27. C. P. Snow's *The Search* (Macmillan), p. 150 (my italics).

28. *ibid.*, p. 278.

29. W. D. Wall, *Education and Mental Health* (U.N.E.S.C.O./ Harrap), p. 260.

30. *XVIth International Conference on Public Education, Proceedings and Recommendations*, p. 141.

31. See Chapter 8, pp. 380–85.

CHAPTER 10

KNOWLEDGE AND ACTION IN MORAL EDUCATION

IN this final chapter I want to take a quick look at some of the most important obstacles which might prevent (either now or in the future) our putting various methods of moral education into practice. The obstacles I have in mind are not material (such as lack of money) but conceptual or psychological, and it is because we can make an immediate effort to overcome them that they are worth mentioning. It has been part of the thesis of this book that the conceptual clarity, psychological posture and general approach of the moral educator are crucial to moral education: and without a proper groundwork of this kind any attempts to deal with the situation, however highly organized, are likely to be grotesquely unrealistic. I hope therefore that the reader will bear with me while we consider some factors of a more subjective nature.

Since this is only an introductory volume, it would be very natural for the reader to react to our remarks so far by saying 'That's all very well, but what have you *proved*?' or 'Jolly good, but what must we actually *do* in the classroom?', or 'O.K., but really we knew all this already'. The two general questions 'Have you advanced our knowledge in a particular discipline?' and 'Have you established beyond question the merit of some particular practical programme?' rightly represent the voice of conscience for any research worker, and one does not have to be doctrinaire to take them seriously. But there are certain fields of activity in which these questions may sometimes blind as much as illuminate: and moral education is one of these. They blind us, if and when we rely on a psychologically naive picture, painted only in black and white, according to which we are in a state either of ignorance or of knowledge: if we are ignorant, then we work and find out, and then we know, and then we simply put it into practice. The often-deplored gulf between academics and practical workers is largely due to the bewitchment of this picture.

The picture fails because it tacitly assimilates all cases of knowledge and action to cases of straightforward factual discovery followed by practice. Thus when the electricity fails, I find out where the fuse box is, learn how to mend a fuse, mend it, and then I switch on the light and it works. Here there is little room for half-knowledge, questions of methodology, problems concerned with my own motivation and personality, communication with other people, and the many other things which particularly bedevil those cases of knowledge and action that involve human relationships. In these cases, the fuse-mending model has at least to be supplemented – and sometimes replaced – by other models: and one talks more naturally of 'seeing things differently', 'learning a new method of approach', 'catching hold of a new skill' – even sometimes of a 'personal reorientation' or a 'conversion'. These vague phrases seem in place when one wants to describe, for instance, what happens when somebody comes to learn how to do philosophy, or is able to see children as products of their home environment rather than just as 'good' or 'bad', or recognizes that all the mad-sounding, psychoanalytic talk about unconscious desires is not just nonsense.[1]

Although this Unit is not, of course, in a position at present to translate any empirically-established findings into recommendations for practical action, this will face us in the future, and already faces all those many people who have the dual rôle of observers and actors: a duality affecting almost all those concerned with education. It is worth raising this point if only to make the problem a conscious one: it is important to realize that there are these two rôles, and that break-downs in the knowledge-action situation may occur in all sorts of different ways. It may be helpful briefly to categorize some of these ways along the following lines.

(1) Genuine ignorance and unreal doubt

The two categories here may be most quickly introduced by a rather depressing parable:

There was once a kindly missionary, who went to live in a remote island whose inhabitants had a Stone Age culture. Because they only had stone implements, they cut down trees very rarely, because it was such hard work. Hence they had few houses to live in, and few boats for fishing. Many of their children were destitute. The kindly missionary bought them some iron choppers, so that the children could have better houses to live in and more fish to eat. Within a year the islanders had chopped down almost all the trees in the island. Within two years the forest-land had become a swamp. Within three years it had become a malarial area. And within five years all the islanders had died of malaria, except for two married couples. The missionary died too.

The married couples had one child each: one a boy, the other a girl. At this point a well-meaning anthropologist came along. Soon the parents died, leaving the children to fend for themselves in a hard world. They tried to build a boat in order to catch fish. The anthropologist would not help them to build a boat, because he only knew about European boats, and he did not wish to introduce potentially dangerous European techniques and concepts into a society which he had not yet had time to study. So the children built a very bad boat, which sank and drowned them. The anthropologist, who was also in the boat (purely as an observer, of course), drowned too.

To generalize, it is easy to see that (a) there are of course cases of genuine ignorance, but (b) there are cases where we know, or ought to know, quite well what to do in a particular situation, but for one reason or another we don't do it. Now these reasons may be of various kinds. In this example, the anthropologist is bewitched by his rôle as an anthropologist – much as a teacher might say 'It's not my business if the boy takes drugs or bullies people, I just teach mathematics'. But there are other related kinds of bewitchment to which I wish to draw attention.

In one very similar type of case a person characteristically says 'Well, I suppose it is my business, but can I really be sure what to do? After all, I'm not a professional psychologist/sociologist/welfare worker/moral educator, so I'd better not interfere too much'. This often tends to happen under the influence of some highly sophisticated academic discipline which produces the appearance of profound scepticism. An intellectual *crise de foi* paralyses our common sense. (Thus people can be found to say that, after all, we don't really *know* that tables exist, that certain things are right and others things are wrong, and so forth.)[2] For example, we talk about the 'problem of old people';[3] and of course there are genuine intellectual problems here. But when it comes to action, we often make mistakes which arise not from ignorance or lack of adequate research, but from a failure to grasp firmly what we really know quite well. Thus, to plan and build expensive homes for old people in the remote country is silly, when what old people want is a bit of life and interest by mixing with the young. We know this, or if we don't we can easily find out by the simple process of asking them what they want. Briefly: there are things which we already know without having to do more research – though we must be very careful about deciding what things these are.

These are cases where we use the existence of professional expertises, or some similar excuse, to avoid taking a long, hard look at the people we are supposed to be serving. In contexts of practical education this happens very often. We have a number of institutional forms – schools, curricula, specially trained teachers, child welfare services and so forth – which frequently distract our attention from the pupils as *people*. In many such contexts, if we ask the simple question 'Do we know what this child needs?' the answer may be perfectly clear: and very often it may be an answer that we can put into practice without completely reorganizing the whole system. We know, for instance, that pupils require plenty of close personal contact with their teachers: that they need to talk about their family problems: that they want to know about sex: that they need to be able to feel successful in various school activities: that they need to understand adults and admire some of them: that boys need to express their aggression, and girls to feel that they can be attractive and acceptable as women, and so on. Even these pedestrian generalizations underrate the extent of our knowledge: for in dealing with particular children at particular times, educators who know the children can also often feel confident about knowing what the particular situation requires. We do not have to wait till all the research workers' cows have come home to be able to take some kind of action in these cases – so long as we do not forget that we know what we do know.

In other cases, very hard to distinguish either in practice or in theory from the above, the difficulty arises not because we fail to look realistically at what we know to be the needs of others, but because we fail to look realistically at ourselves. To balance the cases where parents and teachers think they know but do not, there are plenty of cases where they are doubtful or hesitant in an unreal way. Discussions and practical decisions about corporal punishment, discipline, when to be strict and when to be kind, whether to show patience or anger, etc. are only too plainly dogged by our own inability to recognize and deal with the feelings which we ourselves have in such situations. We lack the confidence to behave spontaneously towards our children – not because we are in genuine doubt about what is best to do, but because we are uncertain about what we feel and whether we should be feeling it.

From this arises a vast number of situations of the 'I don't know *what* to do about you, Johnny' or the 'Son, I think something's gone wrong with our parent-child relationship' type: unreal situations, because the fault lies in the psychological confusion of the teacher or parent. I hope to have shown, earlier in this book, that we can be clear and whole-hearted about our own views and feelings without having to buy some partisan view of morality, or some authoritarian metaphysic. Of course this is very difficult; but it is important to realize what sort of difficulty it is, rather than misrepresent it to ourselves as a difficulty soluble simply by more research, 'advances in psychology', or reading innumerable books on How to Bring Up Your Children. To be able to admit that there is something wrong with *us*, without at the same time representing this wrongness as a lack of moral virtue or an inability to accept a package-deal 'faith to live by', is to take a very useful and important step.

(2) Dishonesty and concealment

In the next category fall those situations where a certain group knows the facts (and may even know what ought to be done), but the general public does not know because the group will not communicate. Many situations of this kind are conceptually straightforward, and require little elucidation. Thus, most people who have taught in schools and similar institutions would agree that what actually happens there is very different from what is thought to happen by the general public: and that a significant part-cause of this is the desire of the authorities to cover up what they take to be disreputable. Of course it is easy to be shocked at this. Those who have held such positions of authority will appreciate the importance of some degree of professional secrecy if jobs are to be done properly at all, and those who have not should have sufficient imagination to do so. In particular, perhaps, one wants to avoid the situation in which the authority of the headmaster (or whoever) is invalidated in the eyes of the pupils as is likely to happen if his decisions are seen to be constantly questioned and inspected from outside.

There are, for instance, schools where the teachers walk in terror of being knifed or coshed. The school authorities know this, and no doubt the local education authorities know it also. But we are well acquainted to the point of boredom with the way in which any attempt to bring this out into the open is handled. Question: 'Is it true that ...?' Answer: 'No, no, much exaggerated; after all there are a few at any school ...'; or 'No comment: the matter is being looked into'. We do not hear 'Yes, it's terrible, X, Y and Z happen, however hard we try: have you any suggestions, can you help us?' This kind of dishonesty, which usually includes a laudable but rather literal-minded desire not to tell an actual lie, is not entirely, perhaps not even chiefly, the fault of the authorities. If parents and the general public would react less primitively to 'scandal', and devote more time to helping overworked teachers to do their jobs, there might be more honesty: as it is, the authorities are often scared off by the unhelpfulness of public reactions.

However, it is one thing to maintain secrecy and institutional solidarity in particular cases, and quite another to be silent or to convey a false impression about an institution's general policy, intentions or condition. It is quite possible to give an accurate account of the latter without turning the spotlight of scandal onto a particular pupil or teacher: and educational institutions themselves should, of course, welcome any intelligent investigation and criticism, especially if its ultimate purpose is to produce recommendations which will benefit the institution concerned. A good deal of what is called 'solidarity' or 'loyalty' is often a defensive posture adopted by authorities that wish to appear blameless: a posture that carries little conviction to the general public, and still less to the pupils in their charge.

Part of the trouble seems to be due to an extreme form of the view that one cannot be a member of an institution and yet criticize it in the world outside. This is essentially similar to the naive interpretations of 'integrity', 'loyalty' and 'practising what you preach', which we noticed earlier in reference to the moral education of children.[4] It is rather like saying that you can't honestly play a game unless you think that all the rules are sensible, or that you can't be a loyal member of society unless you think that all the laws are right. The result is to produce a state of affairs, in schools and other institutions, which conveys a sense of inertia and a feeling of dead weight: often combined with a certain uneasiness, characteristic of those who sometimes think that they may be sitting on the edge of a volcano but prefer to tell the outside world that it is a mountain just like any other, for the sake of public relations.

This kind of attitude often generates a more sophisticated kind of dishonesty, which is more difficult to criticize, because it is defended in depth. Such defences are usually erected *ad hoc*, and there is no end to them: there is not much point in offering any long-winded criticism, but perhaps an example may be helpful. In many (perhaps most) universities and similar institutions there is a lot of fuss and endless talk about student discipline, particularly in regard to sexual behaviour. Now whilst no doubt a lot of this fuss is due to irrationality on the part of the students, it might reasonably strike one as extraordinary that many institutions fail to spell out in any detail the rules which students are expected to keep. Students come to universities and other such institutions voluntarily, and to make it clear what they are contracting for if they come might seem no more than common sense. Vague phrases like 'decent behaviour', 'scandalous conduct', 'bringing the university into disrepute' and so forth testify to the apparent lack of any clear or coherent policy.

This incoherence may be due to a variety of reasons, of which we may list four:

(1) The authorities feel genuinely uncertain and muddled about what rules they ought to have:

(2) They feel certain about what rules to have, but uncertain about being able to justify them to the students or to the outside world:

(3) They feel certain about the rules and the justification, but do not want to spell them out in case this gets them into trouble with the students or with public opinion (the 'let sleeping dogs lie' or 'don't press the point' policy):

(4) They wish to retain the right to clamp down when they feel it necessary, without having to be bound by a rule-book.

Now, of these, (1) and (2) can be settled by further reflection – either on the lines suggested in this book, or on whatever theory the authorities may prefer. It is very difficult to believe that a university could not reach some majority agreement at least on the matter, or that it would not be able to produce a coherent statement. Reasons of type (3) and (4) no doubt carry more weight than students or other people without experience of administrative positions realize. But the point here is that a refusal to spell out rules which you are nevertheless going to enforce not only results in an intolerable impasse in communication, anxiety and hostility amongst those who are supposed to keep the rules, and a general atmosphere of distrust and uncertainty: it also confuses the authorities themselves – just as someone who consistently lies or suppresses the truth in public may easily become muddled in his own mind about what the truth actually is. Thus many authorities at sophisticated institutions will try to justify their apparent incoherence by some such arguments as (3) and (4) above: but the attempted justification would seem more plausible if the authorities were in fact as clear as they pretend to be. In practice these arguments function as rationalizations. The incoherence is real rather than apparent: and it is not the result of conceptual stupidity so much as of intellectual dishonesty or sheer laziness. They are dishonest about *their* own policy – not only about communicating that policy to others.

More often it is the reason for particular rules which remain obscure. An authority may ban long hair, 'bad language', skirts above the knee, and so forth. Because these things are immoral, or (in some quasi-moral sense) undesirable in themselves? Because they offend other people? Because they inhibit the development of the pupils? Because – a sophisticated form of defence – it is a good thing to have some absurd and (in themselves) unjustifiable rules which pupils can rebel against?[5] It might be more useful for authorities to examine their own motivation in these cases, rather than engage in lengthy but unreal disputes about the alleged justification, and, of course, to help their pupils to examine the pupils' motivation for wanting to break the rules or rebel against them. At least we could be told what sort of reason it is – if the authorities know.

Of course it is very easy to sit back and criticize; and I am not at all suggesting that educational authorities are any more dishonest than the rest of us. It is just that educational institutions are much more in the firing-line: particularly in this country, where there is a long-standing tradition (conceptually confused but nevertheless powerful) that institutions should be 'responsible for the morals' of their pupils. No doubt the sense of this phrase is wrongly conceived, and there are those who think that more educational institutions should be like (say) shorthand-typing schools – places where you just learn particular skills without any nonsense about morals or loyalty or public images. But to throw away the tradition would be to throw away the chance to do some proper moral education in an intelligent way, rather than in the confused authoritarian way to which these people rightly object. It is better for schools and universities to remain in the firing-line until they have learned how to stand up to fire.

(3) Lack of Communication

But it would be misleading to suggest that all our problems are due to a lack of factual knowledge, to unreal doubts, or to dishonesty. There are cases where we know what we want done, and are perfectly willing to say so, but where we lack the mechanisms to put our wants into effect. The case of deaths on the road is a classic example. Of course there are all sorts of economic and other problems about road transport: nevertheless most people (a) know perfectly well that bigger, faster and more private cars mean more deaths, (b) would prefer that such deaths didn't happen, even at the cost of some of us not having cars, or having to drive slower, less lethal cars (perhaps dodgems, or cars made of india-rubber). Yet nothing happens.

These are problems whose solution waits upon the creation and acceptance of some institutional form by means of which we can put our wants into effect. The difficulties are primarily those of communication and decision-making. In the case of moral education, I believe that a very large part of the practical problem is of this form. We do, indeed, lack both factual information and goodwill, and a sane approach. But we also lack the forms of communication which would enable us to *say* what we want done about it, and actually *get* it done. If we feel that we are not sure what we want done, we can at least recognize the kinds of skills that are required to achieve a rational view of such matters: we can select the people who are expert in those skills: and we can give them the necessary powers of action. We have a political machine which needs to be complex, because society is complex. But it does not have to be cumbersome. How cumbersome it is depends on how good the controls are: machines run away with us, not because they are big, but because we cannot get them to do what we want.

Yet even to say so much can be misleading in one important respect. For it may throw us back into a pseudo-professional approach, and suggest that all we have to do is to mark out some new area on the academic map, labelled 'communicational studies' or 'research on the integration of research'. And so of course we can; and, perhaps, should. But the temptation here is to be serious in the wrong way. For by so institutionalizing the problem, we are likely to build in many of the same difficulties and obstacles that trouble us already. In the academic world, just as much as in the world of diplomacy, business, politics or any other, there exist certain conventions, protocol, traditions, unwritten rules and stereotyped procedures: and in so far as these conventions themselves incorporate problems, we shall gain little by transferring them bodily to a higher level.

It would plainly be doctrinaire to maintain that all the conventions and stereotypes in any particular area were objectionable, or that they were all desirable, or that they were all harmless. As with ordinary social conventions, some are objectionable because they inhibit flexible communication: some are desirable because they make for clarity and act as a significant language: and some are harmless pieces of dead wood – often perhaps a nuisance, but often a kind of ritual enjoyable for its own sake. Whether any convention is desirable or objectionable is, no doubt, a matter of how it is used, how it functions in a particular system. Like language, conventions are of our own making: their existence, and our use of them, are the product of our own fears and desires: and there is ultimately no way of improving them without facing those fears and desires honestly. In one's bleaker moods one is sharply aware of the stringent limits which are inevitably placed on any impersonal or formalized attempt to solve problems relating to human beings: people will always find some way of turning the impersonal form to their own advantage. Since this is a necessary condition of human existence, it is futile merely to bemoan it. But only a fool would fail to note it.

This is why it is necessary to stress, in the field of moral education as in many others, the importance of those methods and skills which seem to offer some hope of our pulling ourselves up by our own bootstraps, so to speak: some hope of improving our own ability to communicate, as opposed to acting out our own deficiencies in what often amounts to a fantasy-world of conferences, committees, plans, reports and three-volume theses. This factor is one which we constantly tend to underestimate, because we have a vested interest in doing so. But any worker in the field of moral education who was not prepared to pay proper attention to a psychiatric or psychotherapeutic approach would either have a false picture of what his job required, or else would not be taking his job seriously: not because he has to be an expert in psychotherapy, but because his own psychological state is so closely interlocked with the nature of his work that he needs to attend to the one if he is to attend adequately to the other. Without this, we shall be unable to avoid those many situations, in public as well as private life, where something has, as it were, gone wrong from the beginning: where the thing is doomed from the start, not so much because we are stupid or malicious, but because we have unconsciously made up our minds and settled on our attitudes before we have begun.

Failure to take this properly into account involves generating new conventional myths, or supporting the continued existence of old ones. The result is an over-rigid set of categories which do not fit the case,[6] and which express themselves in a doctrinaire attachment to certain labels for their own sake: or rather, for the sake of the psychological security of those who commit this error. Regrettably but predictably, scholars and intellectuals seem no more free from this vice than anyone else. It is still common to hear questions asked in such conceptually naive terms as 'Is education a subject?', 'But is that really *philosophy*?', 'Does Professor X really have a *subject* to profess?', 'But aren't all psychologists *empirical* psychologists?', 'Is it an academic or a popular work?' and so forth. Such remarks often stem from a love-affair, or rather an infatuation, with certain words: a form of essentialism, based on the tacit view that a word must stand for one thing and one only. Sometimes this is backed up by a functionalist, almost a trades-unionist, attitude: 'philosophers' (because they are called such) must do one job only, 'sociologists' another (or perhaps they have a choice of several), 'scholars' or 'academics' have a specific set of standards which must be quite different from those of 'practical workers', and so forth.

Of course no sane person would subscribe to these beliefs when fully stated: but usually the damage is done by their being tacitly assumed. It is as if one were to take a monolithic view of a concept like 'marriage', and say that all couples whom we called 'married' had to have the same relationship with each other: whereas we know that different couples have very different marriages, and that no one form is ideal for all couples. As this example shows, we cannot of course conclude from this that it just does not *matter* whether a person is satisfying any standards or not. Anybody who fulfils any function – husband, wife, scholar, teacher, novelist or whatever – must make sure that, whatever he is doing, he is doing it well. Naturally an established tradition of doing something well can be a great help here. But equally it can be a hindrance, if it fails to allow for enough different things that are worth doing and can be done well. As with revising the curriculum,[7] we need to make more distinctions and to be much more precise and sophisticated about the very wide variety of standards that can be met. We have to examine, much more carefully and honestly, just what we are doing, what the point of it is, and what are the criteria of success. And it is just here that we are likely to be dishonest, lazy or over-hasty, because our identity is so bound up with what we are doing.

Because of these difficulties, I do not think that a great deal will be achieved unless the general public, as well as those in authority and those undertaking research, are filled with a sense of urgency, are prepared to demand that their wants be transmuted into action, and remain sufficiently vigilant to prevent the current of that action from becoming frozen into the institutionalized obsessional neuroses common to both the academic world and the world of governmental control. The institutionalized neuroses are the prices we pay for giving research workers, and governments, a long rope: God forbid that we should shorten it, but we need to give it an occasional tug to remind them that they are not just there for their own amusement. Not that they do not work hard: but hard work may be as autistic as any other activity. The duty of the general public to listen to the experts entails a corresponding right to demand that the experts at least try to say something which is relevant to human needs.

It is not surprising, but still somewhat disheartening, to observe that those people in academic, educational and political circles whom a naive person might have expected to take the lead in this matter do not in fact do so. A great many people still retain sufficient respect for the prestige of important or long-established institutions – the old universities, the famous public schools, the local and national centres of authority in education – to look to them for a lead. Yet in general, and with many outstanding exceptions, most of the impetus in this matter seems to come from below: that is, from new institutions whose prestige is still in the balance, or from institutions that are positively under-privileged. Compare, for instance, the interest to be found in schools for the delinquent or the maladjusted, in secondary modern schools, and in state education generally with that found in the established public boarding schools. Anyone who has observed, in the last few decades, the phenomenon of revolutionary change and radical re-thinking that has ocurred in the primary schools, but until very recently has left untouched the secondary schools – particularly those with social status or 'high academic standards' – will feel at home with this situation.

In view of the phenomena of war, delinquency, over-population and so forth the urgency of moral education hardly needs stressing: and unless we engender something approximating to a revolutionary spirit, and apply it to the liberal aims of thought, communication and action, events may well move too fast for us. Once upon a time there were Lunatics who lived on the moon. There was not much air, and so from earliest times it had been considered very immoral to breathe too much. But soon some Lunatics (particularly the younger ones) began to challenge this; and as their elders had by now forgotten exactly what air was, and could only claim rather feebly that God didn't approve of breathing, or anyway not much, the air began to be exhausted. Most people saw that something was wrong. Lots wrote to the papers deploring it; many suggested remedies, like only breathing through one nostril; some talked more sensibly of making more air by planting things and afforestation. This went on for a long time till the air was very short, and everyone got very excited indeed. The government tried a few things and set up Royal Commissions, but as it didn't know much about air, and actually didn't even know what ordinary Lunatics thought about air, this didn't do very much good. Some people had done a lot of good by planting things, but nobody paid much attention to them, since planting was considered a rather menial task; very few of the upper-class Lunatics even had a clear idea what it was. Some experts on air had written books on various aspects of air, but not many people read them; the members of the Lunatic government, who were always very busy, never did. Anyway, they were very hard to understand. So nothing much got done. There were lots of protest marches, and strikes, and demonstrations, and a spot of civil war: but this only exhausted the air all the quicker. After a bit it gave out, and they all died. That's why there isn't any air on the moon. (Or any Lunatics, either.)

J.B.W.

Notes to Chapter 10

1. The best exponent of this point is Professor John Wisdom. See his *Philosophy and Psychoanalysis* and his *Paradox and Discovery* (Blackwell).

2. See R. Bambrough, in the June (1964) issue of *Common Factor*.

3. 'If those that spend their time writing and reading articles *about* old people spent it on actually helping old people instead, there wouldn't be a problem' (an old person). No doubt false, but not silly.

4. See p. 167.

5. This leads to interesting difficulties. For if pupils ask 'Why should we obey those rules?', do we say 'For no reason: we really expect you and want you to break them sometimes'? This would be self-defeating. Or do we just say 'Aha, we're not telling'? But then how do you keep your real justification secret? After all, pupils can read: some of them even read books like this about the justification of rules. It seems to me safer to be honest.

6. See pp. 19–23.

7. See pp. 406–9.

TWO FEATURES IN THE PLANNING OF EDUCATIONAL RESEARCH

AT this particular point of time there is a good deal of talk and planning about research in the field of education, as well as a good deal of educational research that is actually being done. Although this subject is not central to this particular book, I append the following note on one particular aspect of it without much reluctance, for the following reasons.

'Moral education' is so vast a field that much of the necessary work will, of course, be done by other organizations than our own: and it must be properly planned. So far as I am aware, we are at present the only organization working on this particular subject under our own particular conditions: and since these conditions seem to me of great importance, I may perhaps speak of them without excessive apology. For although much has been written and spoken about the planning of research in general, the aspect of it about which I want to say something has received very little attention.

1. First, there appear to be two major gulfs, one of which is recognized, and the other of which seems not to be. The former is between the educational practitioners (teachers, youth workers, etc.) and research workers in the social sciences. Quite a lot is being done to bridge this gulf, and the public image of such disciplines as psychology and sociology is already a very strong one – strong enough, at least, to merit the inclusion in the Sunday colour supplements of articles labelled 'by a leading psychologist', and containing phrases like 'many sociologists have pointed out that . . .' or 'sociological research has proved . . .' Popular works on psychology and sociology sell like hot cakes, and it would be a very puritanical (or more probably, a very muddle-headed) social scientist who objected to such works on the grounds that they were more misleading than helpful. More seriously, perhaps, many efforts are made by various bodies, which we need not particularize here, to bring teachers and the

social scientists together by way of conferences, training, joint research and other methods. All this is not too bad.

The second gulf has two arms. It divides those whose business is with concepts and meaning (call them 'philosophers') both from the social scientists and from the practical educators. If this book has done nothing else, I hope it has indicated how dangerous this division can be in such a subject as moral education: and there is no reason to believe that it will not be dangerous for other topics of educational research also. Of course the gulf is not absolute. But the institutions (even at a university level) which can boast competent philosophers in the field of education are rare: and those that can boast a proper integration of those philosophers either with their counterparts in the social sciences, or with practising teachers, are rarer still. And outside such institutions, in less academic territory (that of the government and the civil service, for instance), this arm of the gulf is virtually unbridged.

To point to this gulf is not to be starry-eyed about the importance of philosophy in practical affairs, nor to voice the cry of a body of underprivileged, power-hungry philosophers who would like to set up as philosopher-kings *à la* Plato; indeed it may be thought that many philosophers are unduly hesitant about accepting even a part of the responsibility that Plato would thrust upon them.[1] It is simply to point out that if you start with a research title like 'moral education', 'comprehensive schooling', 'human relations in schools', 'student discipline and welfare', 'delinquency', or practically anything else, then a large part of the job is conceptual. Any coherent research in a field so vague as education requires, at the very least, a philosopher constantly at the elbow of other workers. Conceptual problems not only arise at the initial stages, but are apt to bedevil us throughout. The philosopher's remarks may often be tiresome, but often also salutary: in any case they are necessary.[2]

This situation exists partly because philosophy is still very widely thought of as a separate and mysterious activity, instead of as a useful tool which the research worker has to keep handy. The title 'Philosophy of Education' is still associated with the ͏angelike image of the philosopher,[3] instead of being accepted as a convenient heading under which to bring those philosophers who are interested in education into the arena of research. This despite a well-established and fruitful tradition of analytic philosophy in British, American and other universities, which would preclude any serious observer from writing modern philosophy off as 'a passing phase', 'fashionable', 'just playing with words' or 'nothing to do with real life'; and the more recent but very constructive work done by philosophers in the field of education itself.[4]

I do not know what can be done about this, other than by improving communication between philosophers and the general public: but if the point is not taken soon, a good deal of future research will suffer seriously thereby.[5]

2. But in the second place, what does it mean to 'bridge the gulf between' these three groups? A very naive person might argue: 'Well, philosophers and social scientists write their stuff down, and presumably people can read: also, philosophers and social scientists and teachers and others sit on the same committees, live in the same universities, and plan things together; so isn't the gulf bridged already?' The naivety of this is the failure to appreciate the conditions of communication necessary to get some proper research work done, and to get it into the heads of the people who can apply it. You could make a new subject out of this called 'the social psychology of interdisciplinary research', if you really wanted to: but one is tempted to say, in a rather pedestrian no-nonsense way, that what is really needed is a bit more common sense.

First, the ability and/or willingness of people to read books outside their own field is very small. This for many reasons. People in important jobs, like high-level administrators, don't have the time (nor perhaps the inclination). Other people aren't clever enough to understand the books. The books themselves are often written with a lack of clarity that confuses the reader, and often betokens the author's confusion as well. Some academics are scared of writing books that are easy to read, in case they are accused of over-simplifying.[6] Many people are strongly motivated against reading academic books in principle, perhaps associating them with the dullness of their own educational experiences. The books are often either hard to obtain, or else muddled up in public libraries with other quite dreadful or irrelevant books.[7] A good deal of the important stuff can only be found in obscure journals which are even harder to obtain, and whose elusiveness often drives people to read longer but more easily available books instead, in which they get hopelessly bogged down.

Further, there are important psychological reasons why people will respond to person-to-person talk, and not to the written word. The following is a common experience: You ensure that a group of people (not necessarily students) has read something: it might not even be a book, but just one or two sheets of paper. They say: 'Come and talk about this'. You go and talk, and although you say *nothing whatsoever* which was not much more clearly and succinctly expressed in the literature, they end up by saying 'Ah, *now* we understand what you're getting at'. This without elucidatory questions, or explanatory arguments, or anything except merely one's physical presence and vocalized syllables. Without this, it appears, the points made are not real to them. There may of course also be (conscious or unconscious) desires related, not to understanding the propositions, but to making sure that you are a reasonable *person* (or cautious, or enthusiastic, or charming, or whatever their conscious or unconscious criteria of acceptance may be); and, in general, irrelevant psychological factors of this kind play a far greater part in the acceptance of propositions than people like to imagine. This complicates the issue, but reinforces rather than weakens the general point I am making here.

Secondly, and more importantly, there is a singular blindness in our estimation of how close the integration of interdisciplinary research has to be, if it is to produce anything worth while. (That much educational research is inevitably interdisciplinary I hope I can by now take for granted.)[8] Interdisciplinary research should not mean just that an individual research worker in a particular discipline should be vaguely aware of other disciplines relevant to his subject: nor even that he should occasionally talk to those who practise the other disciplines and hold joint seminars with them: nor even that he should have an office or a study next door to them, in the same institution. It involves at least two things:

first, that a number of people of different disciplines should be formally presented with a common task; and second, that the conditions of communication should be properly set up.

The first of these is easy: the second hard. The factors chiefly relevant to the second seem to be:

(a) topographical and temporal – that their working and living conditions should make it easy for them to be in constant touch, and that they should have plenty of time to talk.

Informal communication is often as important as formal: and of the advantages which this particular Research Unit enjoys, not the least is that we are able to live on the spot.

(b) psychological – that the people concerned should not only be competent in their own disciplines, but capable of communicating them to their colleagues: avoiding both an intransigent dogmatism and the dreadful disease, which used to be attributed to discussions on the B.B.C., of everybody agreeing to differ in a chummy democratic way – with the result that no points are gained because no real confrontation ever takes place.

This takes an immense amount of time and hard work. It might be interesting, but somewhat too autobiographical, to describe how we have tried to handle these problems in this Unit; but at least, after over a year's work, I should want to maintain that, however badly we have handled them, this kind of set-up is virtually a pre-requisite for serious *interdisciplinary* research. I do not, of course, want to claim that other set-ups are a waste of time, or that the most excellent work may not be produced under quite other conditions, or that other research workers, in what I would take to be less suitable conditions, but with far more academic ability than we may possess, may not make our own efforts seem very puny. All I want to claim is that, if more attempts are made to do serious interdisciplinary work in the future – and my own view is that such attempts ought to be made – it would be very foolish not to bear these points in mind: and that the criteria for choosing the workers should not be confined to their academic abilities alone.

These points do not relate to other topics, such as (i) how best to communicate research findings to practical workers, (ii) the responsibility and general location of such research (how much should be done by universities, government-sponsored bodies, private enterprise, etc.), and (iii) more technical or academic problems about what areas specific teams should cover, what a sensible research programme would look like for a particular team, and so forth. These topics are already being adequately handled: or, if not adequately handled, at least intelligently discussed. But the above points seem to me to have a certain priority; for unless it is realized (or shown to be false) that inter-disciplinary research requires both the importation of conceptual skills, and the establishment of certain working conditions, anything that is planned is likely to go astray.

J.B.W.

Notes to Note A

1. *Republic* VII, 520.

2. See also Chapter 4, pp. 203–12.

3. Or, by those more sophisticated in philosophy (who should know better), with the name of a non-subject.

4. See particularly the work of R. S. Peters (bibliography).

5. Thus in Michael Young's interesting book *Innovation and Research in Education* (Routledge and Kegan Paul) philosophy is only mentioned in two tables (p. 141 and 143) listing actual and possible research fields, as a separate subject under the heading of 'Educational philosophy'. Nothing at all is said about the integration of philosophy with research in general. See G. H. Bantock, *Education and Values* (Faber), p. 153 *et seq.*

6. The idea of a book designed to satisfy pedagogic rather than scholastic criteria is hard to grasp properly, unless you happen to be a teacher. You have to ask and answer questions like 'Does it make people clearer?' rather than 'Is it right?': and the ultimate verification depends on what happens to the ordinary consumer/reader.

7. Under 'philosophy' in public libraries one may see A. J. Ayer's *Language, Truth and Logic* rubbing shoulders with Ada Astrologue's *Afterthoughts on the After Life.* (I need not say that the latter is a wholly imaginary volume.)

8. Doubters should ask themselves how many (logically different) skills or disciplines are needed to answer such questions as 'Do comprehensive schools break down class prejudice?', 'Ought religious education to be compulsory?', 'Does Latin train the mind?' and so on.

DIRECT METHODS IN
MORAL EDUCATION

EARLIER we listed the component skills or attributes[1] of the morally educated person, which should form the conceptual basis of moral education, and which could act as the ultimate tests of whether educational methods in this general field were successful. It was also pointed out[2] that it would take many years of research to identify those factors, in schools and elsewhere, which were relevant to and would improve the abilities and performances of children and adolescents in these basic attributes. But, as was also said,[3] this does not imply that schools should not try out various methods (as indeed they are already doing); and in Part III we listed a fair number of heterogeneous suggestions that might profitably be followed up.

The task of reducing these to a proper order is an immense one. But there is one category of teaching about which it may be worth while to say a little more, and which may profitably be compared with other categories and proposals. This is the category of what I shall call 'direct' methods: that is, educational endeavours designed to improve these skills in children by (so to speak) direct frontal attacks. Indirect methods cannot as yet be assessed: and consequently it is very much a matter of guesswork whether some of these methods are relevant *at all* to the moral skills.[4] On the other hand, we might reasonably be more certain that direct methods, if they work at all, work relevantly and to the right end.

The difference between direct and indirect methods is something like this:[5] Teaching children English literature, or having a course on 'the problem of old people', or creating a house- or tutor-system in the school, may indeed improve the above skills but they would do so only indirectly, and are not *obviously* geared to such improvement. It is possible that they may produce no improvement at all, or that only certain types of children are improved. On the other hand, a course specifically designed (say) to teach children what other people feel (EMP), or to help them to make up moral rules in particular situations (DIK), would (if it worked at all) be directly beneficial.

Therefore, whilst of course we can say nothing yet about the comparative efficacy of direct as against indirect methods in general, it seems that at this stage, i.e. before we have effective verification-methods, we ought to pay most attention to the direct methods. For we can have more confidence, at least, that these are rightly aimed, and of immediate relevance.

1. Present Practice and Proposals[6]

Most of these have firmly and rightly grasped the notion that teaching in this area should be 'real' to the children, i.e. that the materials and contexts of teaching should be directly related to the children's experience. This is obviously right, and 'directness' in this sense, which is different from the sense mentioned above, is plainly important. We need say no more here about a concept which is already so well understood.

The proposals mentioned are not specifically aimed at moral education, but more generally at such notions as teaching the child about 'the world we live in', 'ourselves and our environment', and so on. They are (for the most part) cast in the form of teaching the child *about the world*: that is (roughly) teaching him certain hard *external* facts, and giving him certain controlled experiences, so as to familiarize him with his environment in ways not normally covered by the curriculum.

What follows is in no sense a criticism of such proposals, and it should be stated at once:

(a) That they may be of great *indirect* advantage for moral education in general;

(b) More specifically they may substantially improve the GIG component (knowledge of hard facts, relevant to moral decisions);

(c) There are of course other educational objectives besides those of moral education (it might be thought a good thing in itself, for instance, for the child to know about industry, local government, the Press, affluence, etc.).

Granted this, however, it seems that proposals for 'direct' teaching of the moral skills (in our sense of 'direct') are remarkably few. In other words, there are not many proposals for teaching the child what we may call *internal* facts: or, more precisely, for trying directly to improve his PHIL, EMP, DIK, PHRON and KRAT.

To put the point another way, we can see that proposals of this kind offer only a partial (though no doubt very valuable) approach to particular topics. Thus topics we may generally describe as 'sex education',[7] 'the automobile', or 'choosing a career' are not sufficiently covered by merely factual teaching (e.g. about biology, the internal combustion engine, or salaries and pensions respectively). As well as the hard facts – and perhaps more important than the hard facts – the child needs to know about his and other people's feelings. Questions like 'How far do adolescents use sex as a means of proving themselves?', 'Why is it that people drive too fast and dislike being overtaken?', and 'What images of careers are young people influenced by?', are important (though even these questions, which are generalized, may be used as a defence against teaching the particular children about *their own* feelings).

It is again no criticism of these proposals to say that we may misuse them as a way of forgetting the real problems of the child and adolescent. To pick up an example just used, we know very well that choice of career (or, indeed, choice of marriage-partner) is not primarily a problem of lack of *information*. Of course this is part of the problem, and of course careers masters and others are doing a most important job in making such information available, arranging for children to visit institutions where they may want to work in the future, and so on. But the central problem lies in the adolescent gaining a clear idea of what he wants and what would suit him, rather than being able to find out how to *get* what he wants. It is the reasonableness of his self-image and his other images that is crucial: not so much the facts, but how he sees the facts. This point applies to the whole notion of 'being at home in his environment', which often (and rightly) lies behind many of these proposals; if the facts which we teach him about the environment are to do any good, we have to give him the right conceptual and emotional apparatus to approach the facts rightly. And it is plain enough that we cannot always, or even perhaps often, rely on children and adolescents having this apparatus already. It is in this sense that 'moral education' (in the sense we have given it) underlies, and may therefore either make possible or vitiate, existing proposals *even in terms of their own objectives*.

These remarks can, I think, be fairly applied to the large majority of proposals in this general area. But not to all. To give any adequate account of the aims and methods of other proposals would be an enormous task, not least because the proposers are so often unclear about them, or unable to express them clearly. What needs doing above all here is to establish a set of categories, a framework of objectives, within which such proposals can be located and against which they can be assessed. All we have tried to do is to give a reasonably clear account of *one* category (the category of moral education in the wide sense we give it), and of the means of assessing it. This category needs to be extracted from some of these other proposals which either border on or include it.

Thus even those authors who are (as of course many are) aware of the educational gap which the majority of proposals fail to fill[8] tend to be distracted by too many different aims. Some, for instance, are anxious to bring 'teenage culture' or 'pop culture' into the educational arena: others are impressed by the idea of community service – actually *helping* old people instead of just studying them: others again by the idea of improving the child's 'imagination' or 'aesthetic response'; and so on. The general desire for making the teaching 'real' to the child, and binding it closely to his actual experience, has not encouraged very much thought about the aims of such teaching. These are commonly expressed in vague phrases like 'learning to live', 'human relations', 'developing the imagination' and so on, which aren't much help.

When the category of moral education, as defined and assessed by our list of moral components, has been extracted from any of these proposals, there will still remain a large number of other aims which need to be clearly stated, and for which assessment-procedures need to be established. These aims can only be established by referring them to clearly-stated forms of knowledge or awareness; and good reasons will have to be given for the importance of encouraging these in schools. At the moment there seems to be a considerable gap between the work of philosophers[9] and other taxonomists on the one hand, and the vast volume of proposals either suggested or already practised. If this gap isn't filled, we may get a lot of proposals put on the mat which don't work: when we find this out we have to persuade teachers to junk them and try something else: and so on. (If I was a teacher I'd get pretty fed up with this.)

This isn't of course to say that new proposals shouldn't be tried until we have (a) a clear idea of the aims, and (b) an effective verification-procedure. But it is to say that research on these two latter is at least as urgent as the development of new proposals. The difficulty about such research is that this kind of taxonomy is very hard, and needs the closest possible liaison between competent philosophers who are studying the problem and those who are actually advancing or practising particular proposals. All this may already be generally appreciated, but needs constant emphasis.

About 'direct method' teaching of moral skills it ought to be said:

(a) That 'teaching' may not be an appropriate word to use here: we may rather want to talk of providing contexts of learning;

(b) The learning may be a learning of skills rather than facts;

(c) For *some* of the components, perhaps particularly KRAT, there may not be any appropriate direct methods of teaching at all.

Nevertheless, this is worth consideration; for it *may* be the case that the indirect methods proposed, which teach the child about external facts of society and his environment, cut virtually no ice at all in relation to moral education: that they leave his moral thought and action quite unchanged. Indeed this seems more than possible. Despite the element of guesswork that exists as regards the merits of any proposals, therefore, it seems that a frontal attack on the direct teaching of moral skills should be made. It would be very regrettable if, amid all the various new methods and courses that may be tried, none at all were of this kind.

2. The Teacher's Reaction

Many teachers would be in agreement with the points made above, and anxious to use any available or proposed methods. But they may also react against the idea of a direct attempt to teach the moral skills for one or both of two reasons:

(a) Because they may think that any 'course' of this sort would be intolerably vague and incoherent;

(b) Because they may think that it would be psychologically dangerous, causing emotional upsets in the children, and looking too much like some kind of amateur psychoanalysis.

In general the attitude of many people (not only teachers) is ambivalent: a part of them very much wants to make a direct attempt to teach and communicate in this way, but a part of them is frightened at the idea. A good deal of this fear may be unreal, but nevertheless the difficulties in (a) and (b) above are real ones.

The conceptual break-down of the moral components, however, enables these difficulties to be met. In order to avoid both the (very real) danger of vagueness and the (usually exaggerated) danger of 'wild' or amateur psychotherapy, we need to plan courses which aim specifically at improving one or the other moral skill, and are subject to strict intellectual control. The subject-matter of such courses (our own feelings, other people's feelings, etc.) can and must be treated just as objectively and coolly as any other subject-matter. We are not interested here either in 'making children have the right moral values' or in allowing them to let off emotional steam and upset themselves.

Besides getting clearer about just what sort of teaching is required, there is also a problem about the general framework of description under which this teaching should be proposed: in other words, a sales or communications problem. Those with greater experience than ourselves, e.g. the Schools Council, will be better able to judge this; but some points may be worth making here.

(i) There seem to be three general ways of starting off such teaching:

(a) As an extension of already existing school subjects (e.g. of English literature, history, etc.);

(b) As part of new or already existing *topics* (e.g. 'sex', 'the family', etc., where direct teaching of a moral skill could form one element in the study of the topic);

(c) As separate courses in their own right.

(ii) If we want to be sure that we actually do get this kind of direct teaching, and not something else, it seems that (b) and (c) are preferable: moreover, it is not easy to see how it can be fitted into existing subjects (except, perhaps, literature).

(iii) It may nevertheless be true that many teachers would take more willingly to (a) rather than to (b) or (c) – though I'd guess that (b) at least would be acceptable. But it may be that this reaction is partly due to the absence, hitherto, of any *clear* suggestion for types of teaching which aren't based on existing subjects, and that if clear suggestions were advanced teachers would accept them.

3. Possibilities for Direct Teaching

(i) EMP. Of all the moral skills, EMP lends itself most easily to the direct method. This is because there is an obvious subject-matter, namely 'what other people feel' and 'what I feel', with obvious questions ('In such-and-such a situation would Mary feel angry/depressed/frightened, etc.?', 'If you apologize for doing something wrong, what does the other person feel? What do you feel (a) before, (b) afterwards?' and so on). One way of looking at this is to say that learning EMP is learning the *meaning and correct application of feeling-concepts* (shame, anxiety, love infatuation, etc.); but it must not be supposed from this that what is needed is simply instruction in vocabulary. To apply these concepts correctly, i.e. to know/identify what he feels, the child needs to marry them up with actual or easily-imagined situations of real life. Honesty in admitting to one's own feelings and observation of other people's expressions, tone of voice gestures, etc., will be as important as linguistic ability.

The natural divisions in this teaching would be under the headings of various feeling-concepts, paying particular attention to those which are likely to cause difficulties to the pupils in question. Thus such notions as 'feeling inferior', 'wanting to prove oneself', 'resentment', different kinds of nervousness and so on might be particularly worthy of study. These concepts should, I think, be distinguished from moral concepts ('pride', 'loyalty', 'courage', etc.); though these might also repay study in reference to other moral components (perhaps DIK and PHRON). (One could envisage several books, consisting of passages from various authors which would make an immediate impact on the children, each book being devoted to a particular category of concepts: e.g. (1) FEELINGS, (2) VIRTUES AND VICES, (3) ATTITUDES/MOTIVES, etc. This needs a good deal more thought, and of course does not imply that books are particularly valuable as a teaching method for all children).

(ii) PHIL. The acceptance of others as equals can in principle be taught, by making clear to the child/adolescent what is meant by talking of other *people*: by showing, for instance, that this is not a matter of sex, class, colour, whether one has arms or tentacles, etc. but of whether one is dealing with a conscious and feeling creature. Again, this does not imply that the teaching should take the form of just *saying* this, or making philosophical points about it (though we need not be too hesitant in conducting straightforward and direct discussions with those children capable of it): it is rather a matter of presenting the children with particular situations, either real or imagined, from which they can generalize to reach the notion of human equality. Here again one would want to concentrate on areas of special difficulty, e.g. perhaps the tendency not to count old people, non-gang members, women, foreigners, etc. as equals. They would have to consider and be helped to objectify their own particular tendencies in hero-worship, feelings of superiority, and so forth.

(iii) DIK, PHRON AND KRAT. These again can be taught only in particular (real or imagined) situations, e.g. (to take an extreme case) in a controlled 'Lord of the Flies' situation.[10] It should be noted that the rational making of rules and decisions, and carrying them out (KRAT), is partly *dependent* on PHIL and EMP; so that what is taught here is, in a sense, more complex, and may depend on prior instruction related to PHIL and EMP. Here we need above all controlled contexts of action, where children and adolescents have to make, justify and stick to their rules. How far these contexts have to be real, and how far imagined, will depend on the pupils; but in both cases the important work consists in the *analysis* – criticism, explanation, assessment, etc. – of the choices made in the context, and the reasons offered.

4. Motivation

Will it be easy or difficult to give children and adolescents sufficient motivation for this kind of learning? Opinions here seem to vary very widely. There are those who think that it would be very hard to get them to take much interest in their own ways of moral thinking, awareness, feelings, etc. (as against taking an interest in 'external' topics): by contrast, there are those who are concerned lest they take too much interest, become 'too introspective', and forget about the importance of the external world. These views perhaps reflect the psychic states of their owners rather than any objective facts (see section 2 above).

Without further research it would be rash to do more than make guesses. But it seems highly probable (not to say truistic) that children and adolescents (a) are very much concerned with their own feelings, moral decisions, and relationships to other people, and (b) often find it difficult to communicate about them and improve them by some form of learning. (It is also a reasonable guess (c) that their concern in this area, partly because it is not catered for by any form of direct teaching, spills over into other areas and inhibits their ability to study 'external' topics with the appropriate energy and enthusiasm.)

The position seems to be, then, that there is indeed sufficient motivation, but that we have failed to provide forms of learning to cater for it: and also that, if we succeeded in providing these forms, the pupil's work and development in other areas (not related to moral education) would show a substantial improvement. No doubt everything turns on providing forms of learning that actually work; and this is a matter for further research, in which a great many factors will be relevant – the age, sex, class and other characteristics of the pupil, the type of teacher best fitted for such work, the kind of school organization and structure which will best minister to these forms of learning, and so on. But what we cannot say, I think, is that we ought not to try seriously to do this. The view that children and adolescents are 'not interested' is hardly tenable.

5. Some Parallel Cases

The general intention behind this form of teaching – roughly, to make a direct frontal assault on the moral education of children and adolescents – is nothing new. Apart from forms of communication institutionalized in the curriculum (notably religious instruction), there are innumerable contexts in which this is the overt or tacit aim. We may remind ourselves of specifically religious contexts – church services, morning assemblies, preparation for confirmation, and the use of the confessional: of 'serious talks' with housemasters and headmasters: of the whole apparatus of 'counselling' in schools: and of those services, still unfortunately regarded as auxiliary to education, of 'child welfare' and 'child care'. There are also examples less familiar to most readers, such as the Marxist 'self-criticism' groups, and the activities of other groups formed under the aegis of near-religions (e.g. Subud, Baha'i, etc.).

It is important to realize that no objection can be made to these in terms of what they are (in a very wide sense) *trying* to do. There is nothing wrong, or un-British, or sinister in trying to meet the problem directly. The objections are different: either (1) they are seeking to impose authoritarian values, or thrashing about in an attempt to find authoritarian values for themselves: or (2) they have rejected authoritarian values, but are quite unclear about what they should be trying to reach instead. This, however, can be remedied by a clearer understanding of the proper objectives of moral education, in terms of our set of moral skills.

What follows from this is that the *contexts* within which such groups work (or have worked in the past) may be of great importance to us, even if their *aims* were mistaken or muddled. I stress this because it is fatally easy for liberals and 'progressives' generally to throw away the context with the aim. Thus it may be that the old-fashioned moral aims of the independent boarding schools were mistaken: but the context of education which they used may be immensely valuable. Again, the religious confessional may provide a useful context (which has reappeared in the psychoanalytic situation), however much we may disagree with certain religious doctrines.

There is also a fatal tendency for this form of education to be hived off under some particular title (often an administrative title), such as 'counselling', 'mental health', or 'child care'. It is not that the title itself matters much (although words mislead us more than we sometimes suppose): it is rather that this kind of departmentalization may debar us from a proper investigation of contexts which do not obviously fit into currently-accepted departments. Only a full and thorough understanding of the aims of moral education will save us from being bewitched by what is fashionable or what is administratively convenient; and only then will research and development in this area become profitable.

*

Until specific courses on these lines are drawn up, tried out in schools, and properly assessed, the above will inevitably appear as no more than a vague hope. But, as so often in moral education, it is more than half the battle to see clearly, and to be able clearly to describe, what *sort* of thing is needed. It is not too difficult to see how further research, and the efforts of practical teachers with plenty of experience and imagination, could give it a more solid shape.

J.B.W.

Notes to Note B

1. pp. 192–4.

2. p. 404.

3. p. 403 *et seq.*

4. The reader may find it convenient to be reminded, very briefly, of the attributes in question, before reading further:

(i) PHIL – the ability to treat other people as equals.

(ii) EMP – awareness of one's own and other people's feelings, wants, and interests.

(iii) GIG – mastery of factual knowledge relevant to moral decisions and personal relationships.

(iv) DIK – the ability to formulate rules and make rational decisions relating to other people's interests.

(v) PHRON – the ability to formulate rules and make rational decisions relating to one's own interests.

(vi) KRAT – the ability to put these rules into practice.

5. See Chapter 3, pp. 138–41.

6. Some of these appear in the Nuffield Feasibility Study (in collaboration with the Schools Council), *Society and the Young School Leaver*, in *The Popular Arts* (Hall and Whannel), p. 402ff. and in many other documents. Much of what goes on, in many countries, under the heading of 'civics' or 'citizenship' also falls into this category. (See *Civics and European Education*, published by the Council for Cultural Cooperation, Strasbourg.)

7. See my *Logic and Sexual Morality* (Penguin Books), p. 95–124.

8. See, e.g., Hall and Whannel, *op. cit.*, p. 393.

9. E.g. R. S. Peters, *Ethics and Education*, Chapters II and V: Paul Hirst, 'Liberal Education and the Nature of Knowledge', in *Philosophical Analysis and Education* (ed. R. D. Archambault), and 'Educational Theory' in *The Study of Education* (ed. J. W. Tibble).

10. William Golding.

SHORT READING LIST

This list is intended for the ordinary reader more than for those who have some professional or expert knowledge of the various topics. We have been guided not only by the strictly academic merits of the books, but (to some extent) by how easily they can be digested and (to a lesser extent) how readily they can be obtained. (Thus our references are to the paper-back edition, where this is possible.)

What books such a reader will want to make use of depends on who the reader is, how much he knows already, what he wants to get out of them, and how much time he has to spare. It is more important to get a proper grasp of the crucial points, and not to waste time on books that are not central to the subject, than to be in possession of a 'reading list' that, in this case, would be indefinitely extensible. This list, then, gives only some brief indication of the most relevant books: from these the more diligent reader may easily glean a host of further references if he wishes.

FOR PART I

A. Elementary introductions to modern philosophy:
  John Wilson, *Thinking with Concepts* (C.U.P., 1963);
  G. J. Warnock, *English Philosophy since 1900* (O.U.P., 1958).

B. Specifically connected with moral education from the conceptual viewpoint, or with relevant areas in the philosophy of education:
  (ed.) Israel Scheffler, *Philosophy and Education* (Allyn & Bacon, 1966);
  R. S. Peters, *Ethics and Education* (Allen & Unwin, 1966);
  R. S. Peters, *Authority, Responsibility and Education* (Allen & Unwin, 1963);
  (ed.) T. H. B. Hollins, *Aims of Education* (Manchester University Press, 1964);
  (ed.) R. D. Archambault, *Philosophical Analysis and Education* (Routledge, 1965).

C. Some books on topics in moral philosophy which bear closely on moral education:
  Aristotle, *Nichomachean Ethics* (Penguin Books, 1953): translated by J. A. K. Thomson;
  R. M. Hare, *Freedom and Reason* (O.U.P., 1963);
  John Wilson, *Equality* (Hutchinson's, 1966);

(ed.) I. T. Ramsey, *Christian Ethics and Contemporary Philosophy* (S.C.M. Press, 1966): see particularly essays by R. W. Hepburn, Iris Murdoch, John Lemmon, and P. F. Strawson;

A. C. MacIntyre, *A Short History of Ethics* (Macmillan's, New York, 1966).

D. Some books relevant to the philosophical problems of research in social science, and other cognate topics:

Peter Winch, *The Idea of a Social Science* (Routledge, 1958);

R. S. Peters, *The Concept of Motivation* (Routledge, 1958);

Charles Taylor, *The Explanation of Behaviour* (Routledge, 1964);

A. C. MacIntyre, *The Unconscious* (Routledge, 1958);

(ed.) Peter Laslett and W. G. Runciman, *Philosophy, Politics and Society* (Second Series) (Blackwell's, 1962): see especially A. C. MacIntyre's essay.

FOR PART II (A)

A. Moral traits; generality and specificity of personality variables:

H. Hartshorne and M. A. May, *Studies in the nature of Character* (Macmillan, New York, 1929);

H. J. Eysenck, *Uses and Abuses of Psychology* (Penguin Books, 1953);

H. J. Eysenck, *Dimensions of Personality* (Routledge, 1947);

H. J. Eysenck, *Crime and Personality* (Routledge, 1964).

B. Conscience:

J. C. Flugel, *Man, Morals and Society* (Penguin Books, 1955);

S. Freud, *The Ego and the Id,* (various publishers, 1927);

S. Freud, *Two Short Accounts of Psychoanalysis* (Penguin Books, 1966);

G. Stephenson, *The Development of Conscience* (Routledge, 1966);

See also Section A above.

C. The development of concepts:

J. Piaget, *The Moral Judgement of the Child* (Routledge, 1932);

M. Brearley and E. Hitchfield, *A Teacher's Guide to reading Piaget* (Routledge, 1966);

N. Isaacs, *The Growth of Understanding in Young Children,* (Ward, Lock, 1961);

N. Isaacs, *Piaget: Some Answers to Teachers' Questions* (National Froebel Foundation, 1965).

Kohlberg, L., *The Development of Children's Orientations Toward a Moral Order*

I. Sequence in the Development of Moral Thought, Vita Humana, 6 (1963).
II. Social Experience, Social Conduct and the Development of Moral Thought, Vita Humana, 9 (1963).

D. The growth of behaviour controls:

J. Bowlby, *Child Care and the Growth of Love* (Penguin Books, 1953);

W.H.O., *Deprivation of Maternal Care: A Reassessment of its Effects* (W.H.O., 1962);

A. Freud, *The Ego and the Mechanisms of Defence* (Hogarth Press, 1954);

F. Redl and D. Wineman, *The Aggressive Child* (Glencoe Free Press, 1957).

E. Child development:

C. W. Valentine, *The Normal Child* (Penguin Books, 1956);

P. H. Mussen, J. J. Conger, J. Kagan, *Child Development and Personality* (Harper & Row, New York, second ed., 1963);

P. H. Mussen, J. J. Conger, J. Kagan, *Readings in Child Development and Personality* (Harper & Row, New York, 1965).

F. Studies based on animal psychology:

L. Broadhurst, *The Science of Animal Behaviour* (Penguin Books, 1966);

K. Lorenz, *On Aggression* (Methuen, 1966);

N. Tinbergen, *The Study of Instinct* (Clarendon Press, 1955).

FOR PART II (B)

A. Folk and Mass Society:

J. Bensman and B. Rosenberg, *Mass, Class and Bureaucracy* (Englewood Cliffs, N. J.: Prentice-Hall, 1963);

Michael Young and Peter Willmott, *Family and Kinship in East London* (Penguin Books, 1963);

David Riesman *et al.*, *The Lonely Crowd* (Garden City, N.Y.: Doubleday, 1953);

Ronald Frankenberg, *Communities in Britain* (Penguin Books, 1966).

B. Youth in modern society:

(ed.) Erik H. Erikson, *The Challenge of Youth* (Garden City, N.Y.: Doubleday, 1965);

Peter Laurie, *Teenage Revolution* (London: Anthony Blond, 1965);

(ed.) T. Raison, *Youth in New Society* (London: Hart-Davis, 1966).

C. Social class and home background:

Josephine Klein, *Samples from English Cultures* (Routledge & Kegan Paul, 1965);

John and Elizabeth Newson, *Patterns of Infant Care in an Urban Community* (Penguin Books, 1965);

Richard Hoggart, *The Uses of Literacy* (Penguin Books, 1958).

D. The school:

Willard Waller, *The Sociology of Teaching* (New York: John Whiley, 1932);

J. W. B. Douglas, *The Home and the School* (London: MacGibbon & Kee, 1964);

(ed) O. A. Oeser, *Teacher, Pupil and Task* (London: Tavistock, 1962).

E. A general source-book, with much material relevant to several of the above areas and more besides:

(eds.) A. H. Halsey, J. Floud and C. A. Anderson, *Education, Economy and Society* (Collier-Macmillan, 1965).

FOR PART III

Some general works connected with moral education:

(ed.) W. R. Niblett, *Moral Education in a Changing Society* (Faber, 1963);

G. H. Bantock, *Education and Values* (Faber, 1965);

John Wilson, *Logic and Sexual Morality* (Penguin Books, 1965).

The reader who is interested in current aims, methods and experiments in teaching may glean most information from the relevant educational journals (e.g. *The Times Educational Supplement, New Education, The New Era, Comparative Education, Teachers World*, etc.).

An excellent source-book for the study of education in general is J. W. Tibble's collection *The Study of Education* (Routledge & Kegan Paul, 1966).

Also by John Wilson

LOGIC AND SEXUAL MORALITY

A highly unexpected approach by a philosopher – via fact, logic, and science – to the problems of morals and sexual behaviour in society.

'He puts the problems of sexual morality in their proper context, the general moral attitudes of the age ... Mr Wilson writes perceptively about sex and education, about sex and the law, and about the problems of individuals. He exposes the fallacies of both authoritarianism and liberalism with clarity and intelligence' – *Guardian*

'Quite a number of the opinions expressed will disturb, affront or infuriate some readers. Much of this book is challenging; little of it is dull' – *Teacher*